# THE NEW HANDBOOK OF STAGE LIGHTING GRAPHICS

## WILLIAM B. WARFEL

**Drama Book Publishers**

New York

Library of Congress Cataloging-in-Publication Data


Warfel, William B.
       The new handbook of stage lighting graphics / William B. Warfel.
          p.     cm.
       ISBN 0-89676-112-6
       1. Stage lighting--Planning.    2. Stage lighting--Drawings.
       3. Electric lighting.    I. Title
       PN2091.E4W34   1990
       792' .025--dc20                                     89-2356
                                                              CIP


Printed in the United States of America

# Table of Contents

# INTRODUCTION

## Purpose

This book is intended to provide students of stage lighting design with some guidance in the effective and economical use of graphics. While this guidance is not intended to dictate standards, the book does describe and adhere to certain standards adopted by the United States Institute for Theatre Technology (USITT) for the drafted light plot, and it presents commonly-used techniques from the professional theatre in the United States. Nevertheless, the book's primary purpose is to introduce the student to graphic techniques which are widely adaptable. Equipped with such good graphic tools, the lighting designer may then concentrate on the visual aspects of design, confident that he or she will be able to communicate all essential information to others.

This book is also intended to assist the teacher of lighting design. Many stage lighting courses tend to concentrate on such non-design subjects as lamps, spotlights, electricity and graphics. The result is that design, the expressive application of light to a text and production concept, is frequently crowded into a few short classes simply because the "hardware" aspects of stage lighting are so varied and complex. It is the author's hope that this book will assist the teacher in reducing the amount of class time spent on teaching graphics, thereby freeing more time for concentration on the actual design. It is also hoped that the students' graphic skills will develop to the point that their intentions will be clear to anyone reading the design documents. Thus, less valuable critique time will need to be devoted to the students' graphics and more can be dedicated to matters of design.

## The Organization of the Book

The process of creating and executing a lighting design can be divided into three phases: 1) concept, 2) technical and 3) realization. Graphics, in the form of lists, diagrams, visualizations, calculations, and drafting are vital to the lighting designer's art and craft in all three phases. This book is organized from beginning to end to follow

1

those three phases in the same sequence which a designer will follow while creating a design.

During the concept phase, the designer will need to use plot breakdowns, color keys, magic sheets and preliminary, or "concept," hook-up lists. These are all tools that help to organize the designer's ideas and to retain information in an orderly and easily read fashion. They might best be described as graphic techniques which help the designer to think. They are the subject of the first chapter.

Predictably, the technical phase involves far more graphics than either of the other two phases. In the concept phase, the graphics are for the designer's own use, and they amount to a sort of shorthand notation. However, in the technical phase, the actual instruments are chosen, and the plot, section, instrument schedule, hook-up, color cut lists, shop order, and focus charts are created, mostly for the use of other people. These documents must be complete, accurate, and, above all, readable. Chapters 2 through 5 deal with the graphic techniques useful in the technical phase.

During realization, the phase that includes rehearsals and performances, the paper-work reverts to being more for the designer's own use than for use by the rest of the production staff. During earlier rehearsals, the designer will assemble cue information on magic sheets and in cue lists. While cues are being set, the designer will need a cheat sheet to make calling for dimmers easy, and an assistant designer will need to record all cue levels and timings on a tracking sheet. Chapter 6 will describe these lists and discuss their use.

## The Computer in Stage Lighting Graphics

Computers are machines that are well suited to relieving the stage lighting designer of much of the drudgery of calculation and paperwork. Many home-written programs or software adaptations dealing with stage lighting graphics are already in existence, and several commercially available programs have arrived on the market. No doubt the time will come when most of the processes described in this book will be able to be linked together and handled on a computer. This could mean that the plot and all paperwork might be generated from some system of notations that describe the appearance of the stage as the designer has conceived it. As these words are written, such a program has not appeared.

In the following chapters, there will be discussions concerning those areas of lighting design to which the computer has been applied; and those applications will be described. Since most high school and college students in the United States are now computer literate, the language used to describe these applications will be written using a certain number of simple computer terms. Those not computer literate may skip the paragraphs dealing with computer applications, and still be able to gain mastery of all necessary stage lighting graphic techniques.

2

# CHAPTER ONE:
# GRAPHICS IN THE CONCEPT PHASE

## The Plot Breakdown

A plot breakdown is a step-by-step analysis of the action in a play, musical or opera. It is usually prepared in a graphic form in such a way as to list the important happenings in the play together with the lighting conditions required on the stage at that time. Writing a plot breakdown can serve both as excellent preparation for the first meeting with a director and as a basis for the cue structure for a production.

The plot breakdown should not be confused with the analytical essay. In an analytical essay, the student designer explains a point of view concerning the dramatic content of a play and discusses the lighting concept which grows out of that content. The plot breakdown is a detailed listing of the actual events that take place in the play. The selection of which events are important enough to the lighting design to be included in the plot breakdown will naturally be influenced by the designer's point of view.

For example, in the prologue of Sophocles' *Antigone*, the heroine reveals that she will bury her brother whose body lies outside the gates of Thebes, even though King Creon has forbidden it. This defiant act might best be carried out under cover of darkness. Then, in the parados, the chorus speaks of the rising sun and likens it to the rise of a new era, revolt and attack. One concept might call for a literal approach, accepting the idea that Antigone performed the burial rite before daybreak and that the chorus is speaking about a real sunrise. Such a concept might use a predawn to dawn to full daylight sequence for the lighting. The chorus' words about sunrise would be listed in the plot breakdown.

However, in a less literal approach to the play, the fact of the chorus' entrance would still be important, but the fact that the chorus speaks about the sunrise might not be. The joy at the end of a war, joy still not clouded by news of Antigone's disobedience, might be a more important fact to mention in the plot breakdown.

Two examples of plot breakdowns are shown on the following pages: one for a dramatic production and one for a musical. The nature of the play being produced will have an effect on the choice of column headings. Columns which will probably always be used are "Page" (in the script which the production will use, if possible), "Act/Scene", "Action", "Development" and "Notes". Beyond these, the designer may want to customize the breakdown to reflect the things that are important for a given production. If a rough cue list is being developed, a "Cue" column might be helpful. If an analysis of dramatic scenes reveals a clear pattern of beats within the scene, then a "Beat" heading might follow the "Act/Scene" column. In multi-scene productions, such as most of the plays of Shakespeare, columns for "Locale" and "Time of Day" will be very helpful.

It is important to distinguish between the two headings "Action" and "Development". In brief, "Action" is what the actors do, and "Development" refers to how these actions move the play.

In our example of the prologue of Sophocles' *Antigone*, the "Action" column will describe how the sisters meet, how they discuss Creon's decree, how Antigone expresses her determination to bury her brother, and how the women part in anger. The "Development" column will describe such things as the exposition of the preceding events, the establishment of the different characters of the two sisters, and how Antigone's determination to defy Creon's decree sets in motion the chain of events to follow.

It is important not to clutter a plot breakdown with columns which you won't use. A one-set play certainly does not need a column for "Locale", while the "Time of Day" is simply not applicable to some plays. The plot breakdown should be set up according to the needs of the production and to the designer's priorities.

Since each plot breakdown will be different, and since it will usually be used only once and set aside, it is a waste of the designer's time to develop some all-purpose form and have it copied. Also, designers soon discover that plot breakdowns are most useful if their columns are drawn wide enough to allow sufficient space for writing; and for that reason, some designers tape two pieces of yellow legal paper together side by side, or use some other extra-wide paper. A word processor with fifteen-inch-wide paper for the computer printout might be helpful; unfortunately the numerous columns in a plot breakdown make the line wrap-around feature, which cannot be disabled in most word processing programs, a problem. Therefore, while it is possible to set up a computer to type out plot breakdowns, it will probably waste time. The best method is to draw some columns and to use a pencil in jotting down the necessary information, even though the examples which follow are typed for clarity.

Plot Breakdown for BLOOMER GIRL

| PAGE | ACT/ SCENE | TIME OF DAY | LOCATION | ACTION OR MUSIC | DEVELOPMENT | NOTES |
|---|---|---|---|---|---|---|
| 1-1-1 | --- | --- | --- | Overture | | Follow spot on Conductor |
| 1-1-1 | I/1 | Afternoon | Applegate's conservatory | Women are waiting, playing piano, sewing, talking. | Exposition: all married, Daddy chose the men. | Sunlight through windows |
| 1-1-2 | I/1 | same | same | Ensemble: "When the Boys Home" – girls & mother. | | |
| 1-1-3 | I/1 | same | same | End song – Daisy enters. | We see Daisy as typical presumptuous servant. | |
| 1-1-4 | I/1 | same | same | Horatio enters. | We meet Pater Familias, everyone attends to him. | |
| 1-1-5 | I/1 | same | same | Evelina enters. | Ingenue, only one of the girls who thinks for herself. Only one not married. | |
| 1/1/7 | I/1 | same | same | Dolly Bloomer is discussed "The Lily" mentioned. | Feminism emerges as central conflict. | Sun wanes |
| 1-1-9 | I/1 | Late day | same | The Boys enter, reprise "When the Boys...". | Domestic picture complete. | Sunset starts |
| 1-1-10 | I/1 | same | same | End song – Horatio says he has picked husband for Evelina. | Horatio/Evelina conflict set – Evelina seen as independant thinker. | Sunset fades |
| 1-1-11 | I/1 | Evening | same | Dolly enters – general aghast reactions except Evelina. | Central character revealed, she is in bloomers. | Sunset gone |
| 1-1-12 | I/1 | same | same | Exerunt except Horatio, Dolly and Evelina. Dolly & Evelina plot to smuggle escaped slave. | Clear that the girls are to be shielded from Dolly. Underground RR element is revealed. | |
| 1-1-15 | I/1 | same | same | Dolly exits through window. | See Dolly all full of surprises. | |
| 1-1-16 | I/1 | Night | same | Jeff enters – mistaken identity business | Obvious this is the love interest. | Moonlight through windows |

*Fig. 1-1: A Plot Breakdown for a Musical*

5

Plot Breakdown for THE SEA GULL

| PAGE | ACT | TIME OF DAY | ACTION | DEVELOPMENT | NOTES |
|---|---|---|---|---|---|
| 350 | I | Early evening | Masha and Medvedenko enter. | See Masha as a somber, quiet person, Medv. as fussy, self-pitying man. | Dusk, just before moonrise but still light. Perhaps a lavender feeling? |
| 351 | I | same | Medv. describes play, Nina & Treplev's love, Medv. love for Masha, her indifference toward him. | The first mis-placed love is revealed. | Evening is probably slowly deepening. |
| 351 | I | same | Sorin and Treplev enter, Treplev sends Masha & Medv. away. | We learn about these two, Treplev idealist, possessive about his play, does not care for Masha. | |
| 352 | I | same | Treplev & Sorin discuss Madame Arkadina and the Theatre. | We sense Treplev's complex relationship with his mother, and his idealist's zeal for a "New Theatre". | |
| 353 | I | same | Nina enters, out of breath, in hurry to do the play and go. | We meet Nina: romantic, breathless, beautiful. | |
| 356 | I | same | Sorin exits to gather audience. | Sets up Nina/Treplev scene. | Building toward moonrise. |
| 356 | I | same | Nina and Treplev talk of their relationship. | Obvious Treplev loves Nina but Nina loves coming to the house because of who else is there. | Isolate an area for them as part of pre-moonrise look. |
| 357 | I | same | Dorn and Polina enter. | We meet two more characters and another one-sided love. | Moon is now up behind stage. |
| 358 | I | same | Crowd enters, incl. Arkadina, Shemraev talking. | Building toward first big conflict. | |
| 359 | I | same | The play begins amid some banter and joking. | We sense it will not go well because not taken seriously. | Full glory of moon over the lake is revealed. |
| 360 | I | same | "Will-Of-The-Wisps" appear. | Audience gets restless, talks. | Cue with smoke? or fabric? |
| 361 | I | same | Red eyes appear. | | Practical, we see Yakov light something. |
| 361 | I | same | Treplev stops play, rushes away. | Climax of act. We see extent of Treplev temperament, of Arkadina's selfishness. | |

*Fig. 1-2: A Plot Breakdown for a Drama*

## Color Keys

A color key is a simple diagram which indicates the colors a designer intends to use in a design, together with the directions ("angles") from which those colors will be used. Primarily, the purpose of the color key is to assist the designer in keeping track of color and angle choices. Secondarily, the color key is useful when an instructor critiques a student's lighting design, since the key describes the elements of the design in the most elementary way.

The color key is not necessarily drawn on a ground plan, though it may be. Often, a simple cross is used to indicate a typical location on the stage, and arrows are drawn to show the colors and directions to be used. Each arrow is labeled with the name or number of a color and with an indication of the mounting position which will be used to achieve the desired angle. To make the arrows more specific, other notations are sometimes included, such as "shin buster", "head high", "sunset", or "leaf gobos".

In a complex production, separate color keys might be drawn for each different situation: for example, for each act or for each set change. It is wise to draw a composite of the important information from all of the color keys after the individual keys have been completed in order to make certain that the mounting positions are not over-loaded and that the design is not complex to the point of being out of control.

As an example of the use of color keys, the following diagrams have been prepared for a hypothetical production of Chekhov's *The Sea Gull*. Since Acts I and II are exterior, a backdrop has been included.

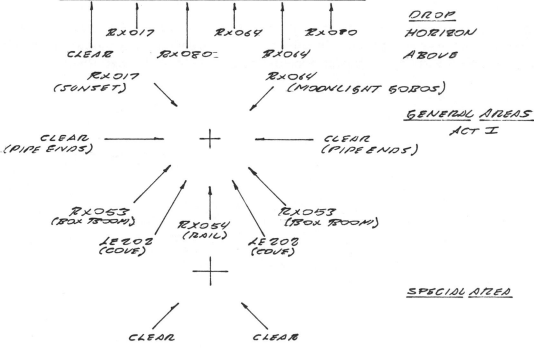

*Fig. 1-3: A Color Key for Act I of Chekhov's* The Sea Gull

Act I also has a special area around the stage for the play-within-a-play, and that is shown in a separate key. Many of the colors which appear in the Act I keys are also found in later acts, while some are for this act only.

Act II is also exterior, but in a different location. Since the act is set at a different time of day than Act I, some colors change. The color and angle choices for the backdrop were for the whole production, so they have not been re-drawn.

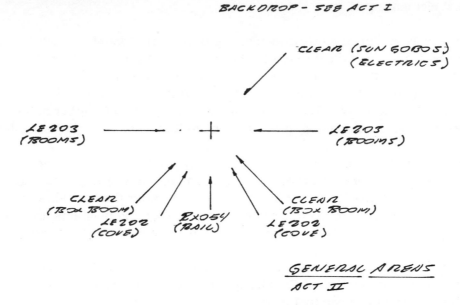

*Fig. 1-4: A Color Key for Act II of* The Sea Gull

Acts III and IV are played in two different interior settings. Since both interiors are box sets, the keys become quite simple. The Act III set has tall windows stage right, and the lighting designer has decided to bring sunlight in through them.

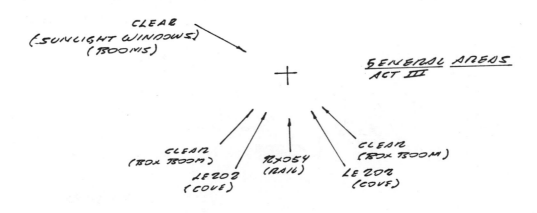

*Fig. 1-5: A Color Key for Act III of* The Sea Gull

In Act IV, there is a French door stage right, outside of which Nina appears for her final scene with Treplev. The lighting outside that French door is shown on a separate key.

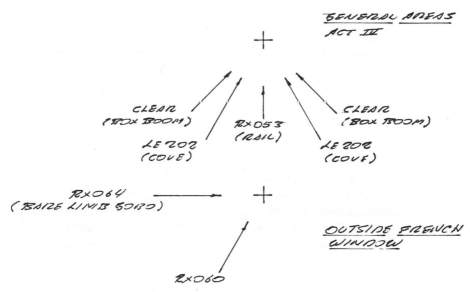

*Fig. 1-6: A Color Key for Act IV of* The Sea Gull

The composite color key for this production of *The Sea Gull* gathers all of the important information for the general area lighting into one diagram. In the composite key, the special areas in Act I and Act IV are omitted, as is the backdrop.

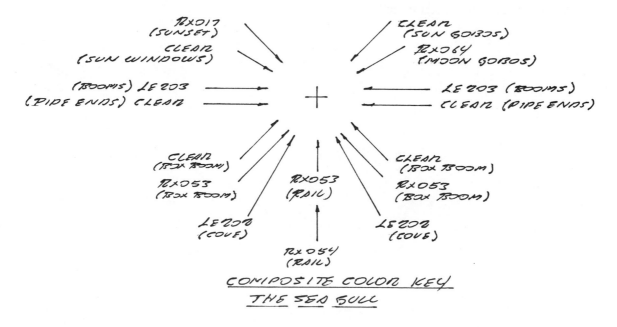

*Fig. 1-7: The Composite Color Key for a production of Chekhov's* The Sea Gull

## Magic Sheets

The term "Magic Sheet" has been in use for many years, and its origins are unclear. At one time, the term was used to describe the piece of paper which the designer used at the desk during technical rehearsals to help remember dimmer numbers. Later, the use of the term expanded to include many different forms of paperwork. In this book, the term will be used in what has now become its most common application: a sheet on which two or more small ground plans of the production are copied. The original magic sheet described above is now most often referred to as a "cheat sheet".

Making a magic sheet has become quite simple since the introduction of the electrostatic copier. Usually, the lighting designer will draw a very small (1/16" = 1'-0" or even smaller) and very simple ground plan of the production. Three copies of this plan are taped to a sheet of legal sized paper, and then the designer makes as many copies of the composite as are needed. Legal sized paper is convenient since more plans will fit on it than on letter sized paper, but it is up to the designer to choose which paper size is most convenient. In this example, note that the plans are mounted to one side of the sheet to allow room for writing. A left-handed designer made the example.

Usually, the magic sheet ground plan is so simple that it is possible to draw a composite of all plans for a multi-set production. All examples which follow are done this way. In some very complex productions, two or more plans may be needed, but usually it makes more sense to show only the barest essentials of the stage in the ground plan, and then to fill in specific setting details as needed.

There are several ways in which lighting designers make use of magic sheets. The most common are described next.

THE SEA GULL

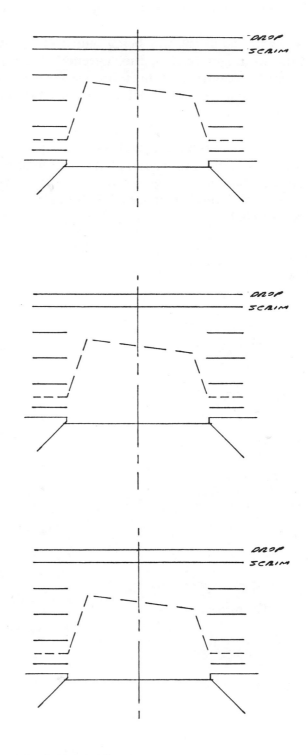

*Fig. 1-8: A Blank Magic Sheet*

## System Magic Sheets

The term "system" refers to a group of lights used together for a particular purpose in a production. In the color keys, each arrow represents a system, i.e. a group of lights having the same gel and being aimed at the stage from roughly the same direction. Thus, we might refer to the "Lavender Box Boom System" or the "Clear Side Light System". System magic sheets are used to help the designer to remember what systems are to be provided and which mounting positions will be used to achieve the required direction for each color.

The designer uses one magic sheet ground plan for each arrow in the color key, and then uses a few additional ground plans to record information about special lights, effects, or projections which may not appear on the color key but which should be accounted for. As an example, Figures 1-9 through 1-16 show several system magic sheets for *The Sea Gull.*

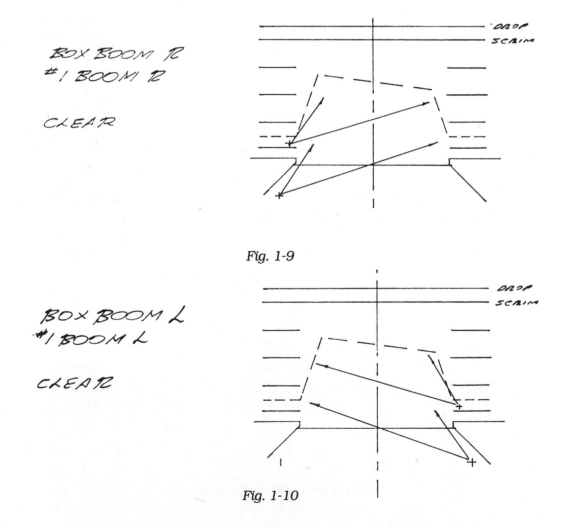

*Fig. 1-9*

*Fig. 1-10*

LEFT BOOMS
#1, #2, #3

LE 203

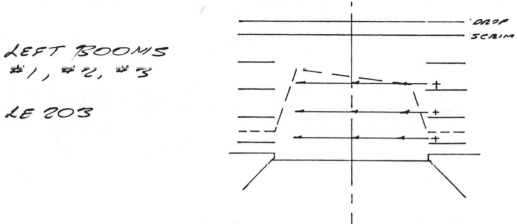

Fig. 1-11

RIGHT BOOMS
#1, #2, #3

LE 203

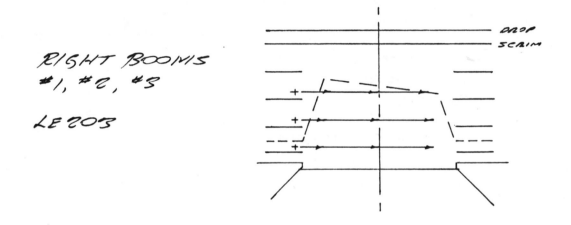

Fig. 1-12

#6, #7 PIPES
RX064
LEAF 50305 (MOON.)

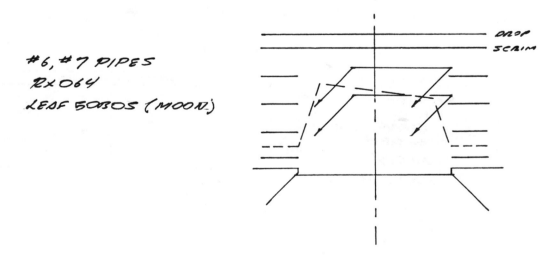

Fig. 1-13

#4, #6, #7 PIPES
CLEAR
LEAF BOBOS (SUN)

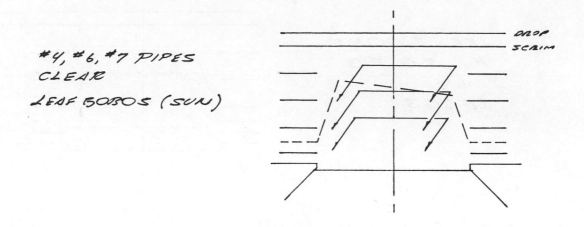

Fig. 1-14

RIGHT BOOM #2
RX 060
#3 PIPE
RX 064
WITH BARE LIMB GOBO

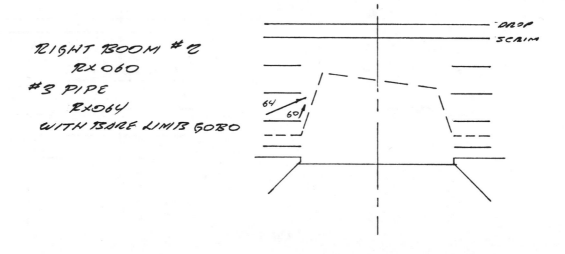

Fig. 1-15

#8 PIPE
CLEAR
RX 080
RX 064
DROP STRIPS

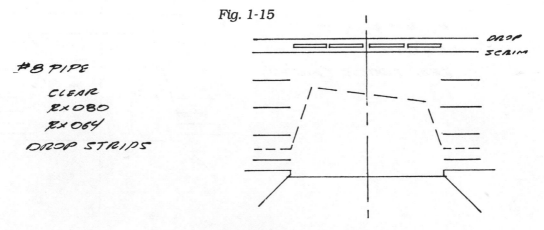

Fig. 1-16

## Equipment Magic Sheets

On system magic sheets we use arrows to show the direction of a system of lights and the area which that system is expected to cover. Equipment magic sheets take the process one step further, by not only recording mounting position, color and general focus, but also showing the specific instrument type and quantity. Since the choice of instruments is made as part of the technical phase, the preparation of these equipment magic sheets is usually not part of the concept phase.

In equipment magic sheets, each instrument is represented by an arrow which originates at the mounting position and terminates in the general area toward which the instrument will be focused. Labels are used to identify the instrument type, size and wattage. The examples which follow are taken from the system magic sheet samples.

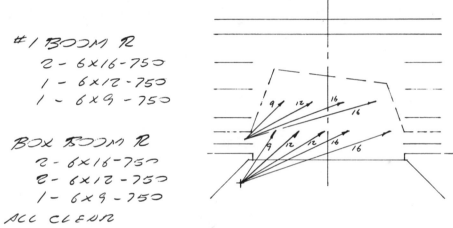

Fig. 1-17

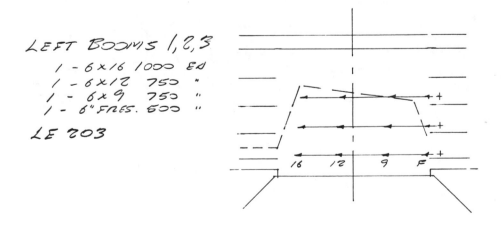

Fig. 1-18

#3 PIPE

   1 - 6X12T - 750
   Rx064, BARE
   LIMB GOBO

RIGHT BOOM #2

   1 - 6x9 - 750
   Rx060

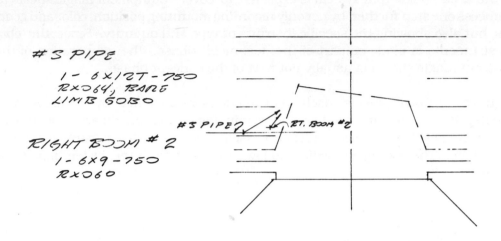

*Fig. 1-19*

#4, 6, 7 PIPES

   16 6X12T - 750

   LEAF GOBOS
   CLEAR

   SUN AND LEAVES

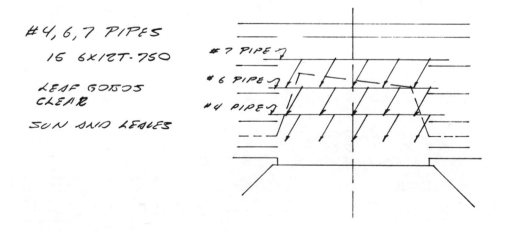

*Fig. 1-20*

## Magic Sheet Cue Lists

Blank magic sheets are very convenient for note-taking in rehearsals. By making notes about blocking, timing, furniture placement and so forth, the lighting designer can begin to develop a cue list. By using magic sheets for the cue list, a great deal of information about the requirements for the cue can be noted quickly. The following three examples are again from the hypothetical production of *The Sea Gull*.

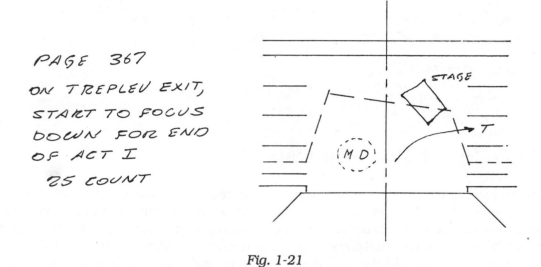

PAGE 367

ON TREPLEU EXIT,
START TO FOCUS
DOWN FOR END
OF ACT I
25 COUNT

*Fig. 1-21*

PAGE 369

OPENING OF ACT II
LEAF GOBOS
GROUP DISCOVERED
DOWN RIGHT
HOT DAY

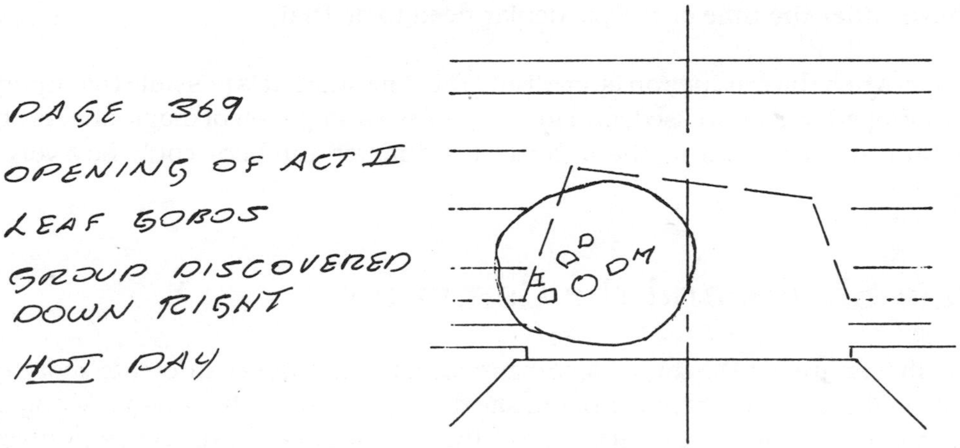

*Fig. 1-22*

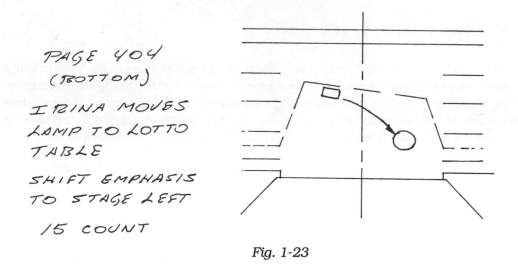

PAGE 404
(BOTTOM)

IRINA MOVES
LAMP TO LOTTO
TABLE

SHIFT EMPHASIS
TO STAGE LEFT

15 COUNT

*Fig. 1-23*

## Magic Sheet Hook-up Lists

Finally, magic sheets have been used as an elaborate form of hook-up list. Each ground plan represents a dimmer or a consecutive group of dimmers, and the information usually shown in the hook-up list in written form is presented graphically. It is quite simple to add dimmer numbers to the equipment magic sheets, once those dimmer numbers are known; but they will not be in numerical order, unless the equipment magic sheets were done in the order of the dimmer assignments in the first place. Since the equipment magic sheets will probably be done in the same order as the system magic sheets, and since those were quite possibly drawn before dimmers were assigned, the equipment magic sheets will probably not have been done in the order of the dimmers. This means that for the magic sheets to serve as a hook-up list, they will have to be re-drawn for that purpose. It is not likely that many lighting designers will have either the time or the particular need to do that.

However, when the production is small and the time short, it is possible that many steps will be skipped or compressed, and in such a case a single set of magic sheets showing everything and arranged in the order of the dimmer numbers, could be a very useful document.

## Magic Sheets and the Computer

Magic sheets are not the sort of documents which computers can create more quickly than people can. Aside from the blank sheets themselves, which can be copied easily by electrostatic reproduction (Xerox®), there is nothing routine or repetitive about them. Magic sheets simply record the results of the lighting designer's thinking, and thus will not be any easier to do on a computer than by hand or on a typewriter.

In one respect, though, the computer can be of assistance. If the lighting designer has access to a computer aided drafting ("CAD") system which can be used to draw the plot, it can also help make the basic magic sheet. It will be necessary to enter the essential information about the theatre and the production ground plans into the computer in order to draw the final plot. If the theatre and ground plan are combined into a single drawing file, and this drawing is plotted at a reduced scale (most plotters accept scale information at the time the plot is initiated), then the time required to make the reduced-scale drawing is saved. It is probably not worth the cost to buy a CAD system just to draw light plots, let alone to create magic sheets; but if one is available and the lighting designer can become proficient on it, then it will certainly be helpful to make double use of the information. This basic magic sheet ground plan was made with a CAD system. It is from a production of *Tartuffe* at the Yale Repertory Theatre. Notice that the two examples are drawn at different scales, and that the overhead grid is omitted from the smaller plot for clarity.

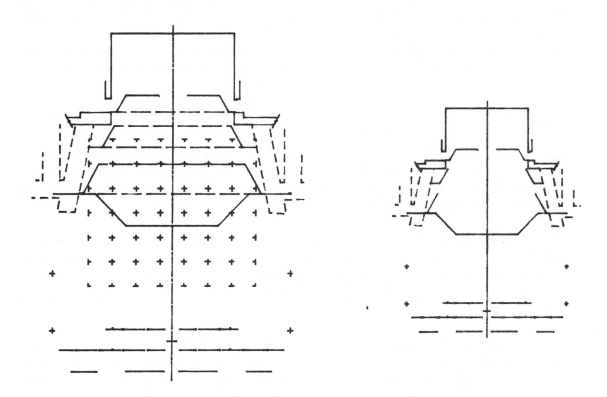

*Fig. 1-24: Magic sheet ground plans drawn with a CAD program*

## The Preliminary Hook-up List

Although it might seem premature, after the design has progressed through the system magic sheet stage, it is time to start considering how the lighting for a production will be controlled. This is not, strictly speaking, a graphic procedure; but since lists and schedules are very much a part of the subject of this book, we will take the time to examine the preliminary hook-up list now.

First, it is important to make a distinction between the two terms "dimmer" and "channel". Since the advent of lighting systems which provide a dimmer for each stage lighting outlet, control systems have been provided which allow the designer to group several dimmers together into a group for ease of manipulation. Such a dimmer group will be controlled by one of the control channels that the control board provides. Modern control boards usually provide a large number of control channels, numbered starting at "1", to each of which one or more dimmers may be assigned.

The preparation of a preliminary hook-up list does not require a list of the available dimming equipment or even knowledge of how many channels a certain board is capable of controlling. Later, there will be time enough to relate the design to the realities of a particular dimming system; first it is important to decide in the abstract how many control channels are needed to make a certain design work on the stage.

To make preliminary hook-up decisions, the designer must consider each system of lights by itself in order to determine how many control channels will be required to make each system best serve the production. If a system is simply intended to put a general color wash across the whole stage, then it may only need one or two control channels to be effective. Dividing that system into a dimmer for each light would be wasteful and, perhaps more important, a large number of control channels would be awkward to work with in rehearsal.

On the other hand, a system of lights from the cove and first electric, which provides visibility for the actors from the front, may need to have each instrument controlled separately in order to allow the greatest possible flexibility when composing the stage picture. The preliminary hook-up list helps the designer to arrive at and record these control decisions.

Because the decisions to be recorded on the preliminary hook-up list are made quite early in the design process, the list does not need to be too complex. In contrast to the multi-columned final hook-up list that will be prepared later, only two columns are really required: one for the channel number and one for a verbal description of which lights are to be controlled. Fig. 1-25 shows a portion of a preliminary hook-up list for the production of *The Sea Gull.*

The example in Fig. 1-25 was done quite simply on a legal pad with a few ruled lines. That is as much of a special form as is required for the preliminary hook-up list. There is not much detail about the individual instruments, since they may not even be chosen at the time the list is prepared. First, the list shows that the designer feels that the balcony rail system will need to be controlled in three groups, no matter how many instruments are eventually used for it. The next group of channels shows that ten control channels will be needed for the front light system. Next, we can see that the designer has set aside twenty-one channels for the three side light ideas, provided three channels for the leaf gobo backlights, one for the sunset effect, one for the moonlight, and so on.

| | | | |
|---|---|---|---|
| SEA GULL PRELIMINARY HOOK-UP | | | |
| 1 | BALCONY RAIL | 34 | |
| 2 | | 35 | |
| 3 | | 36 | CLEAR PIPE ENDS |
| 4 | | 37 | |
| 5 | | 38 | |
| 6 | | 39 | |
| 7 | | 40 | |
| 8 | STRAW FRONT | 41 | |
| 9 | | 42 | |
| 10 | | 43 | WARM SIDES |
| 11 | | 44 | |
| 12 | | 45 | |
| 13 | | 46 | |
| 14 | | 47 | SUNLIGHT LEAF |
| 15 | | 48 | GOBO BACKS |
| 16 | | 49 | SUNSET GLOW |
| 17 | | 50 | MOONLIGHT GOBOS |
| 18 | | 51 | BLUE WASH |
| 19 | | 52 | PRACTICALS ACT III |
| 20 | CLEAR BOX BOOM | 53 | PRACTICALS ACT IV |
| 21 | | 54 | STAGE ACT I |
| 22 | | 55 | FRENCH DOOR II |
| 23 | | 56 | BACKINGS, III & IV |
| 24 | | 57 | STOVE ACT IV |
| 25 | | 58 | |
| 26 | | 59 | SCRIM |
| 27 | | 60 | |
| 28 | | 61 | |
| 29 | COLOR CORR. | 62 | BOUNCE, TOP |
| 30 | SIDES | 63 | |
| 31 | | 64 | |
| 32 | | 65 | BOUNCE, FOOT |
| 33 | | 66 | |

*Fig. 1-25: A simple preliminary hook-up list for Chekhov's* The Sea Gull

It is possible to be slightly more detailed in the preliminary hook-up list by suggesting some degree of focus or direction in addition to the channel assignment. This may be helpful since listing the additional information provides a means of checking to be sure that enough control will be available within each system. Not only does the example following show that three channels are assigned to the balcony rail, it also shows that the designer wants to have separate control over the stage left, center and stage right areas.

Note that the following example has a slightly more drafted look than the first example, but that is not necessary. A ruled piece of legal sized paper would have done just as well.

THE SEA GULL -- PRELIMINARY HOOK-UP

| | | | | |
|---|---|---|---|---|
| 1 | LAVENDER RAIL SL | | 34 | DS PIPE ENDS ← |
| 2 | " " C | | 35 | " " " → |
| 3 | " " SR | | 36 | MS " " ← |
| 4 | STRAW FRONT DL | | 37 | " " " → |
| 5 | " " DLC | | 38 | US " " ← |
| 6 | " " DC | | 39 | " " " → |
| 7 | " " DRC | | 40 | DS WARM SIDES ← |
| 8 | " " DR | | 41 | " " " → |
| 9 | " " UL | | 42 | MS " " ← |
| 10 | " " ULC | | 43 | " " " → |
| 11 | " " UC | | 44 | US " " ← |
| 12 | " " URC | | 45 | " " " → |
| 13 | " " UR | | 46 | DS LEAF GOBOS ✓ |
| 14 | CLR BOX BOOM DL ← | | 47 | MS " " ✓ |
| 15 | " " " " ↗ | | 48 | US " " ✓ |
| 16 | " " " DLC ← | | 49 | SUNSET GLOW |
| 17 | " " " " ↗ | | 50 | MOONLIGHT GOBOS |
| 18 | " " " DC ← | | 51 | BLUE WASH |
| 19 | " " " " ↗ | | 52 | PRACTICALS ACT III |
| 20 | " " " DRC ← | | 53 | " " IV |
| 21 | " " " " ↗ | | 54 | STAGE AREA ACT I |
| 22 | " " " DR ← | | 55 | FRENCH DOOR SPEC. |
| 23 | " " " " ↗ | | 56 | ACT III BACKINGS |
| 24 | " " " UP CTR ↗ | | 57 | " IV STOVE |
| 25 | BOX SIDES DS SHORT ← | | 58 | SCRIM CLR |
| 26 | " " " LONG → | | 59 | " BLUE |
| 27 | " " " SHORT → | | 60 | " STRAW |
| 28 | " " " LONG ← | | 61 | BOUNCE TOP CLR |
| 29 | " " MS ← | | 62 | " " DK. BLUE |
| 30 | " " " → | | 63 | " " LT. BLUE |
| 31 | " " US ← | | 64 | BOUNCE FOOT CLR |
| 32 | " " US SHORT → | | 65 | BOUNCE FOOT DK. BLUE |
| 33 | " " US LONG → | | 66 | BOUNCE FOOT LT. BLUE |

Fig. 1-26. A more detailed preliminary hook-up list for The Sea Gull

# CHAPTER TWO:
# DESIGNING SYSTEMS WITH GRAPHICS

## Introduction

Most stage lighting designers select their instruments without extensive calculations or layouts on the drafting board. Once a designer has had a certain amount of experience, instrument selection comes as second nature. There are, after all, only a certain number of instruments available; and once the scale of the theatre is understood, the choices are almost pre-determined. An experienced designer will often lay out side light by choosing a "far" instrument, a "center" instrument and a "near" instrument, from memory.

The younger designer is not so fortunate. The techniques described in this chapter have been devised in order to help an inexperienced designer make instrument choices that will provide the right level of light in the right places. These techniques will, in time, help the young designer learn his or her own rules of thumb.

Some knowledge which is not included in the scope of this book is required in order to use these techniques. An understanding of photometrics, the measurement of light, is essential. Appendix A provides certain definitions and a brief explanation of spotlight photometrics to help with this. The Inverse Square Law is very important in photometrics, and the designer will need to be comfortable with that simple formula (also found in Appendix A). A knowledge of the Pythagorean theorem for the solution of triangles is most helpful, though triangles may also be solved by laying them out on the drawing board and measuring the unknown side.

In addition to knowledge of photometrics and triangle solution, certain information about the instruments available to the designer will also be required. The beam angle, field angle and center intensity information for each lamp in each instrument that will be used in the design are essential. Most manufacturers publish this information or will supply it if contacted. A format for laying out this information in order to use it on a drawing board will be found later in this chapter.

An accurate knowledge of the brightness (transmission factor) of the color filters that will be used is required. Some manufacturers provide this information in their sample books, and the brightness of most gels sold in the United States is available in print. In the event that no such data is available, the designer may derive it using a flashlight, a gel sample book and a light meter which is calibrated in footcandles and corrected for the human eye response curve.

A pocket calculator which has square and square root functions will also be very helpful.

## The Instrument Performance Diagram

The most convenient format for photometric data is the instrument performance diagram shown in Fig. 2-1. The 6"x9" ellipsoidal reflector spotlight is shown in symbol form to the left. The distance from the lens is drawn to scale (usually 1/4" = 1'-0" or 1/2" = 1'-0") along the axis. The beam and field angles are shown diverging from the lens. Illuminance readings in footcandles are shown in line with the various lamps that are used in this instrument. Adjacent to the lamp information is the intensity, in candelas, of the light at the center of the beam when that particular lamp is used in the spotlight.

It is best to draw an instrument performance diagram on tracing paper, acetate or some other transparent material, since they are used by laying them on top of a drawing. If it is impossible to make a transparent diagram, then you must do your layout on tracing paper and use the diagram under it. Since you will use the instrument performance diagrams over and over again, it is best to draw them on a durable stock.

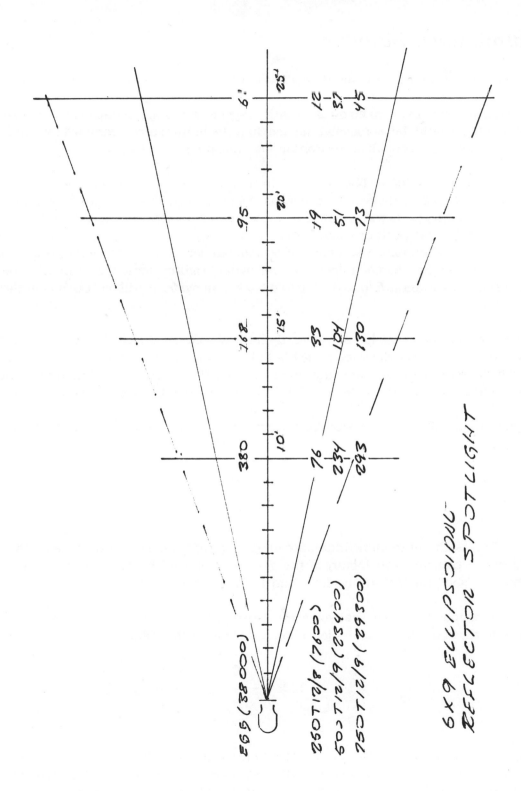

Fig. 2-1: A Typical Instrument Performance Diagram

## Illuminance Standards

Illuminance standards are simply the level of light, measured in footcandles, which the designer will attempt to achieve on stage from each instrument in a system. If a light meter were to be taken on stage after a system has been installed and focused, the reading would be somewhat higher than the illuminance standard because of the cumulative effect of all of the overlapping instruments.

The techniques which will be described in this chapter are based on the idea that light from frontal directions is most often used for visibility, and that light from the side, top and back directions will enhance pictorial interest by creating highlights. Systems of lights in frontal positions such as coves, balcony rails, and box booms will be designed to an illuminance standard of 50 footcandles. Since light from the highlight angles will not be visible unless it is somewhat brighter than that from the front, the illuminance standard for side, top and back light systems will be 100 footcandles.

If you are not using a gel in a system, then the system is simply designed for either 50 or 100 footcandles. However, if a gel is to be used, then the illuminance standard must be increased so that after the gel is placed in the light the resulting illuminance will be reduced to 50 or 100 footcandles, depending upon the angle of the system.

To adjust the illuminance standard to account for a gel, apply this formula:

$$S(2) = \frac{S(1)}{Y}$$

where $S(1)$ is the illuminance standard for the type of system being designed, $Y$ is the brightness (transmission factor) of the gel, and $S(2)$ is the adjusted illuminance standard. Note that $Y$ is always less than 1 since it is a percentage.

As an example, let us say that you want to use Roscolux 60 in a front light system. The brightness of that gel is .64 (or 64%). Applying the formula:

$$S(2) = \frac{50}{.64} = 78.13$$

you see that you will have to choose instruments which will give an illuminance of 78 footcandles at the true distance from the instrument to the area lighted. When the gel is added, the illuminance will drop to 50 footcandles.

## Computing The True Distance

The first step in any instrument selection process is to determine the true distance (called "throw" hereafter) from an instrument to the area on the stage to be lighted. The distance as measured on the plan is not accurate, since it does not take into account the height. The throw is computed by solving a simple right triangle whose two sides are the distance on the plan and the height of the instrument above the face plane. The hypotenuse will be the throw. (See Fig. 2-2)

The face plane is a plane 5'-6" above the stage floor, or above a platform, to which the dimensions for all lighting calculations are measured. It does not make sense to use the floor for the lighting calculations, because the actor's face is the most important object on the stage at most times. To be certain that the faces of the actors will be well lighted at all times, all design calculations are based on this face plane. The definition of the area on the stage which a system will light is dependent upon the set design. Usually a system will be designed to light a band across the stage. The width of this band is usually from wing to wing, unless some important scenic element or a platform interferes. The depth of this band is usually 10 - 12', but will be determined by the type of instrument which the designer chooses. In the beginning, only the width of the band is important. Figure 2-3 shows a typical band across the stage, with an arbitrary (for now) depth and center line to which dimensions will be taken. It is necessary to assign an arbitrary width to the band in order to establish some line for measurement. Ten feet is a good depth with which to start.

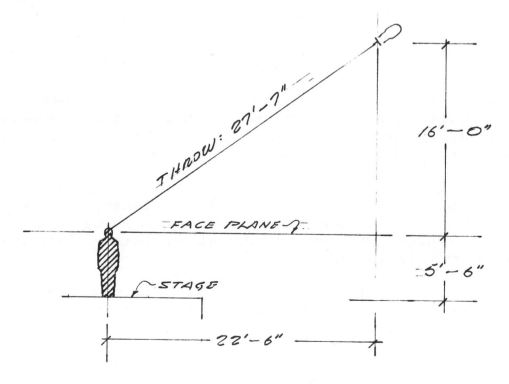

*Fig. 2-2: Calculation of a throw*

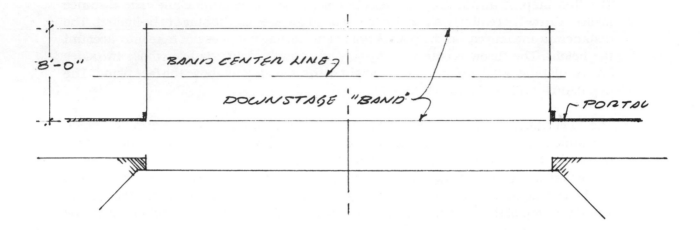

*Fig. 2-3: Illustration of a typical "band" across the stage to be lighted by a system*

## Designing Uniform Systems

A uniform system of lights is a system in which all of the lights are of the same wattage and type, and have the same parallel throw. In a uniform system, all of the lights will generally be mounted at equal spacings along a pipe or a rail. The steps required to lay out a uniform system are as follows:

1. Calculate the throw from the mounting position to the face plane and draw two parallel lines so that the distance between them is equal to the throw in the same scale as your instrument performance diagrams. Add a center line across the two lines, and indicate the width (limit to limit) of the band on one of the lines (see Fig. 2-4).

2. Choose an instrument which will produce at least the required illuminance standard at the distance of the throw, and draw its beam angle on the diagram. Note that in Fig. 2-5, the instrument was drawn at the center of the stage. This is a good place to start if you are designing a system which covers the whole stage, though you may choose any point across the band to start.

3. The distance between beam angle lines at the face plane line is the distance between instruments in the mounting position. Placing instruments at that spacing will allow the beam angle lines of adjacent instruments to touch. Since each beam angle line represents 50% of the illuminance at the axis of the beam, the two beam angles add up to 100%. The light from outside of the beam angle on one of the instruments helps to smooth out the field of the adjacent instrument (see Fig. 2-6).

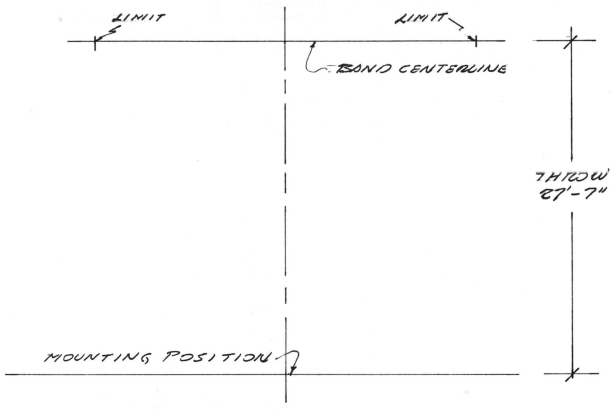

Fig. 2-4: *Basic layout for a uniform system*

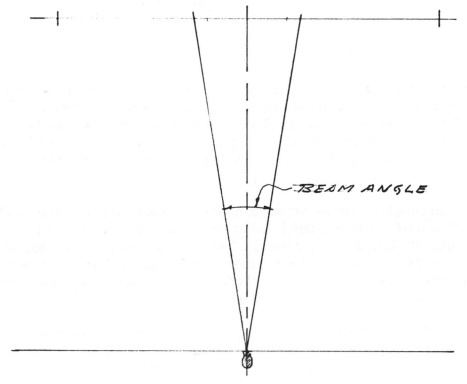

Fig. 2-5: *The first instrument in a uniform system*

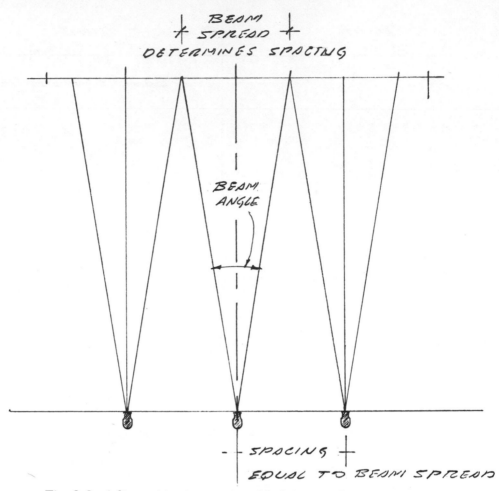

*Fig. 2-6: Adjacent instruments added in a uniform system*

4. If there is action at the sides of the stage as well as in the center, you will need to provide one instrument that has its center aimed just onstage of the wing. This may throw off the rhythm which you established by working outwards from the center. If this happens you will have to make adjustments by adding an extra instrument and allowing the beam angles to cross. Eliminating the center instrument to keep the quantity down is also an option (see Fig. 2-7).

It is an interesting fact that the two beam angle lines from a single instrument will add up to 100% even if the instrument is aimed at the band at an angle. In Fig. 2-8, the light at point "S" and the light at point "L", when added, will equal the light at point "C". This is easy enough to understand when you consider that the light at "L" is, by definition, half that at "LC", and that at "S" is half that at "SC". Point "SC" will be brighter than "C", and point "LC" will be less bright than "C".

The result of this interesting fact is that systems of lights which are focused at the stage at an angle, such as a 45° frontlight system from a cove, may be calculated by exactly the same procedure as for the straight system illustrated earlier.

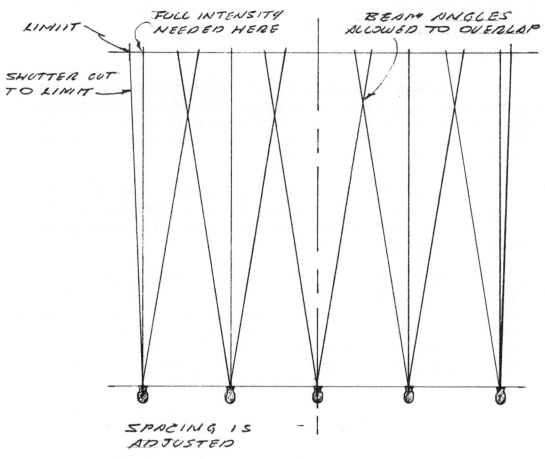

Fig. 2-7: *Uniform system adjusted to light the ends of the band*

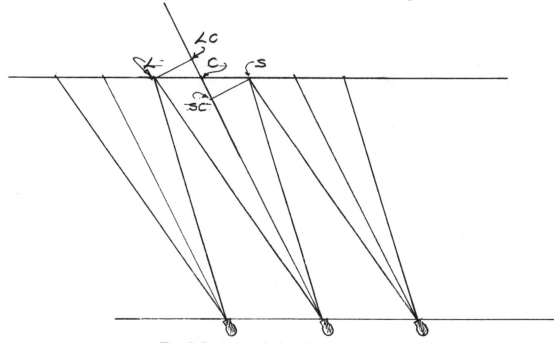

Fig. 2-8: *An angled uniform system*

## Locating The Next Band

Earlier, we saw that the depth of the band across the stage could not be predicted with great accuracy before the system was laid out, because the depth would depend upon the instrument chosen. Figure 2-9 is a section view which shows the downstage band which has just been designed in the example. In the drawing you can see that the beam angle of the instruments used in the downstage band crosses the face plane at a point which defines the band as being 10'-0" deep.

Now you can locate the next band upstage by touching the beam angle of the instrument which will repeat this particular system upstage to the beam angle of the downstage unit at the face plane. Some trial and error may be required, since you may not know what the upstage instrument is at first.

The fact is, however, you probably do know exactly where the mounting position for the upstage system is, since most productions tend to define possible mounting positions rather clearly. In proscenium productions, it is normal for the downstage front systems to be lighted from the cove or from box booms, and for these systems to be continued upstage from the first pipe or from a boom downstage. The designer rarely has the freedom to add mounting positions for front light at will.

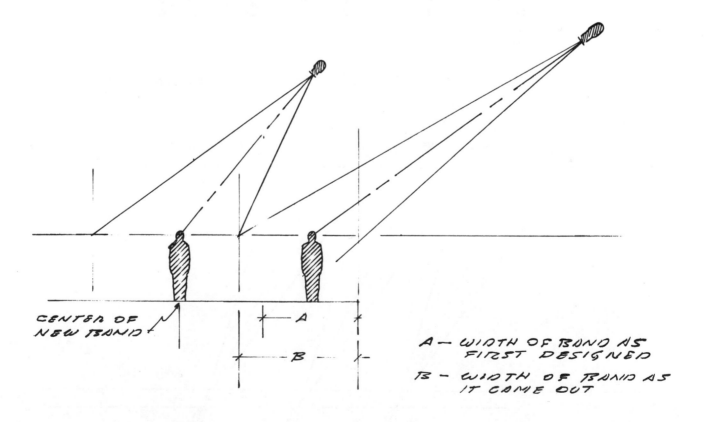

Fig. 2-9: Locating the next band

# Designing Non-Uniform Systems

Non-uniform systems are those which are made up of a variety of instruments chosen to give near-uniform illuminance from a clustered location. Examples of non-uniform systems are side lights mounted on a boom or at the end of a pipe batten, and box boom systems. The layout techniques for non-uniform systems are not as exact as those for uniform systems, but they will enable the designer to provide enough equipment so that the system can be focused with relative smoothness.

Non-uniform systems are usually laid out in an elevation view. For side light, when the mounting position is usually in a straight line relationship with the band being lighted, the procedure is quite simple. Once the boom location or the location of the end of the pipe are determined, the following steps are used:

1. Draw a front elevation of the stage, as shown in Fig. 2-10, showing the places farthest from, and closest to, the mounting location where actors will be working. Also show the face plane in this elevation. Make marks on the boom or on the pipe which indicate where instruments can be placed. For 6" ellipsoidals or Fresnels, and for PAR 64 holders, these marks should be placed 1'-6" apart on pipes and 1'-9" apart on booms.

2. Choose an instrument which will provide 100 fc (the illuminance standard for side light) at a point just onstage of the wing on the opposite side of the stage from the mounting position, and draw it in with its beam angles. This is shown as "1st" in Fig. 2-11.

3. Using the second mounting location (the next one down the boom or the next one offstage on the pipe), you must now select another instrument whose beam angle overlaps that of the first one, and that will give the required 100 fc where the axis of the beam crosses the face plane. This instrument is marked "2nd" on Fig. 2-11.

4. Now repeat the procedure, moving closer to the near side of the band (see "3rd" on Fig. 2-11).

5. When you reach the near side, you may have an area remainng which is so small that it does not make sense to add another instrument using the above procedure. In this case, you have two choices: (1) if there is very little action there (actors rarely stand at the side and face the wall), you can ignore it and assume that it can be filled when you focus, or, (2) you may select a small instrument simply to fill the gap, rather than trying to find some instrument which will suit the layout procedure. This is shown as "4th" on Fig. 2-11.

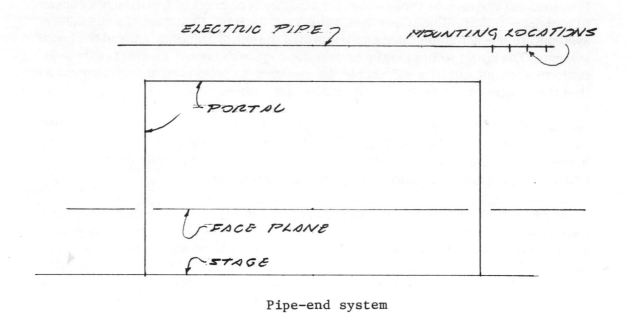

Pipe-end system

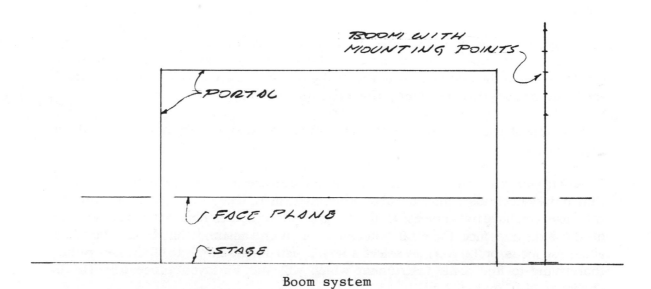

Boom system

*Fig. 2-10: Elevations prepared for side light layouts*

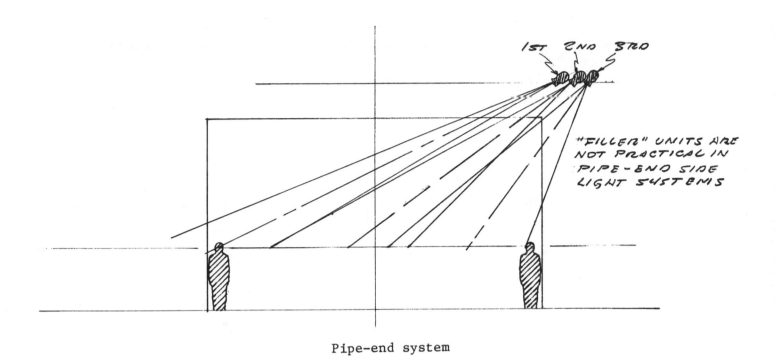

Pipe-end system

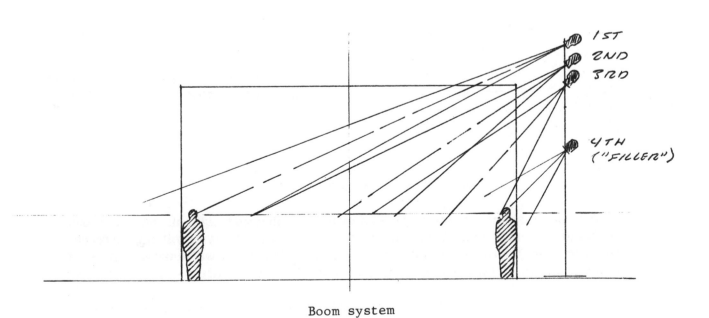

Boom system

*Fig. 2-11: Two side light systems*

The procedure to lay out box boom systems is somewhat more complex than for side lights, since the boom is not in line with the band on stage that is to be lighted. A special technique must be followed in order to compensate for this off-set relationship. Several things must be worked out before starting:

1. Obviously, you must determine the locations of the boom and the zone to be lighted in the plan. The band in this example is eight feet deep: an arbitrary choice just as it was in the case of uniform front light. (See Fig. 2-12)

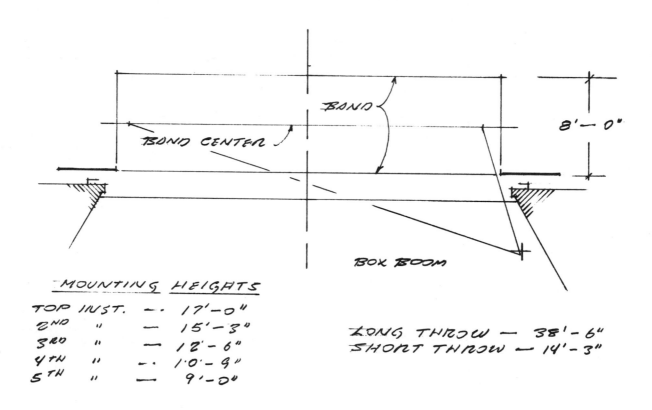

*Fig. 2-12: A box boom problem in plan view*

2. Now you must guess how many instruments you will need to light all the way across the band. You may guess too many or too few, in which case you will have to repeat the procedure; but this does not take a lot of time. Experience will make your guesses more accurate. (For this example it was assumed that 5 instruments would be needed.)

3. You must determine the heights on the boom at which instruments may be mounted. Assume one instrument will be mounted at the top, and deduct 1'-9" (or 2'-6" for 8" equipment) from the height for each instrument below that. The heights above the face plane of the instruments in the system are shown in Fig. 2-12.

4. Next, you must use the heights of the instruments and the distance in the plan to determine the throw from the highest instrument on the boom to the farthest end of the band, and from the lowest instrument to the nearest end that can be lighted from that position. These are also shown in Fig. 2-12.

5. Now you are ready to start your layout. On the plan in Fig. 2-12, there is a line from the farthest aiming point to the instrument location beside the boom. Extend this line beyond the boom until it equals the true throw in length. Do the same for the line representing the shortest throw (See Fig. 2-13).

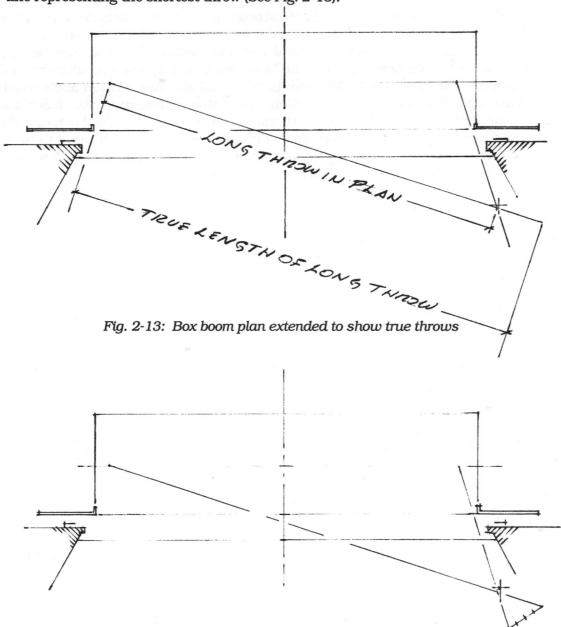

*Fig. 2-13: Box boom plan extended to show true throws*

*Fig. 2-14: The working position is drawn and the instrument locations marked*

6. Connect the ends of the two lines with a new line. This new line represents the boom for the purposes of calculation. The instrument symbols of the instrument performance sheets for the top and bottom instruments will be placed at the ends of this line, and you divide it in length according to how many instruments you guessed you would use. Since the example uses 5 instruments, the line is divided into 4 segments (See Fig. 2-14).

7. Now you proceed to lay out instruments very much as you would for a side light position except that you use this theoretical boom position as a basis for your layout, and you use 50 fc, the illuminance standard for frontal lighting. First, find an instrument which will give 50 fc (or more if a color is involved) at the farthest aiming point from the top position. Sketch in the beam angle of this unit and select the next instrument by finding one which delivers 50 fc and also has a beam angle which overlaps that of the first instrument. Continue in this manner until you reach the near side, and then decide whether an additional instrument is needed to fill out the system (See Fig. 2-15). Remember that this is simply a sketch used to make instrument decisions. When the plot is drafted, the instruments will be shown in a different format, not along an angled line.

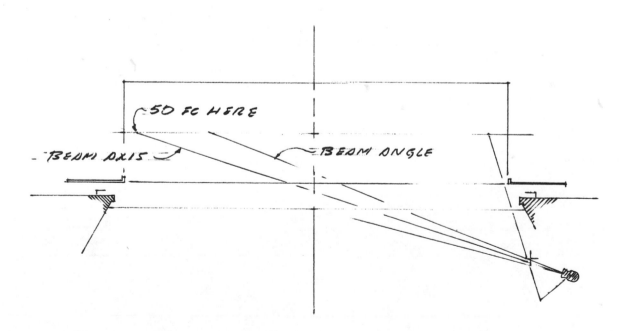

Fig. 2-15: The long throw instrument is chosen and laid out

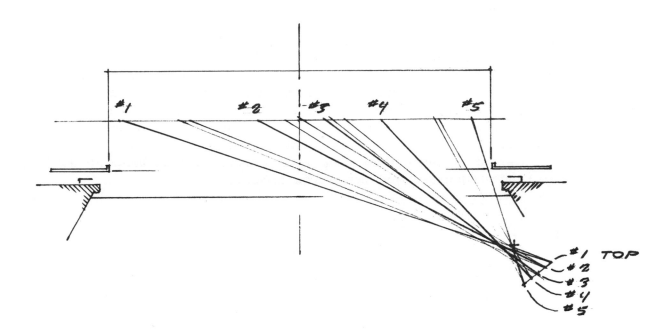

*Fig. 2-16: The box boom completed. Instrument spacing depends upon choice of spotlight for each throw*

These layout techniques certainly do not encompass all of the conditions a designer is liable to meet while laying out a production. However, the basic techniques are provided here, and simple ingenuity is all that is required to extend them to most conditions the designer will meet. The use of rough section drawings to determine if a light will strike the part of the stage it was planned for, or if it will, for example, pass through a certain window, will be discussed in Chapter 3.

## Designing Systems With A Computer

Certainly it is not beyond the capability of a computer to lay out these systems and draw them according to the designer's wishes. At the time of this writing, a program does exist containing photometric information for many instruments which will show performance for single, typical instruments at different distances and angles. Even though this program does not extend to multiple instrument installations, and does not make judgments as to which instrument should be used next in a non-uniform system, it has a number of useful features.

No doubt, there are programs in existence, privately written or even on the market, that search records and make the decisions required to assemble systems of lights. The reader may even be inspired to take the foregoing procedures and write his or her own program.

One word of caution is in order: do not spend time on exhaustive mathematics, carrying answers out to four decimal places. These procedures are on the level of rules of thumb, and do not represent great accuracy. Stage lighting instruments rarely emit light in the same distribution as claimed in the manufacturer's data. This does not mean the manufacturers misrepresent; it simply reflects the fact that there are many variables between lamps and instruments which can only be accounted for in averaged data. Also, because of the obvious necessity of keeping down the costs for any theatrical equipment, these stage lighting instruments and lamps are not finely tuned optical equipment and there will be variables.

# CHAPTER THREE:
# DRAFTING EQUIPMENT AND TECHNIQUES

## Introduction

Several aspects of drafting will be presented in this chapter: tools and materials; line strength, lettering, printing; and rough section applications. Conventions for light plot drafting will be the subject of the following chapter.

Since this book is written on the assumption that the person who is undertaking to draft a lighting design will either have, or be prepared to acquire, basic skill in drafting, only those aspects of drafting which are unique to lighting design will be discussed.

One general statement must precede any discussion of drafting technique for lighting designers: the importance of neatness cannot be overstated. This is not simply a sales device. If the plot is neat, clear and uncrowded, a critic will be able to follow the intent of the work, an electrician will be less likely to make errors, and the designer will be able to retrieve information from the plot with much greater ease. When neatly drawn and lettered, a light plot speaks highly for the designer and makes a fine addition to a portfolio. A plot that is composed well on paper is indicative of an ability to make well composed stage pictures.

## Tools and Materials

**PAPER:** Two basic types of drafting paper will be used in the design and presentation process. Much of the preliminary work on a plot, such as the design of systems described in Chapter 2, and many of the techniques described hereafter, are best done with tracing paper. Not to be confused with the clearer, more durable paper used for finished work, inexpensive tracing paper is sold in many forms. The most useful type is sold in rolls 12", 18" or 24" wide and 50 or more yards in length. It is usually yellow or beige in color. The 18" wide paper is convenient to use on a drawing board, but the 24" wide paper is also very useful for some section analysis work. Tracing paper is inexpensive enough to allow the designer to keep both widths on hand.

Because it is inexpensive, tracing paper may be used in quantity and discarded. It can be rolled over a ground plan, sketched upon, torn off and set aside while more paper is rolled over the plan and another idea is sketched. Prints can be made from tracing paper, though they are not as sharp as with clearer papers. Tracing paper is a thinking and testing medium, not a presentation product.

For the preparation of the final plot, the selection of a good drafting paper is very important. A high degree of translucency and resistance to erasure and to the abuse of day to day handling are important qualities in drafting papers; but these requirements should not lead the designer to selecting an expensive vellum or drafting film. A good rag content paper which takes well to pencil work and erasure is the best product. Light plots do not have to endure dozens of printings as architects' drawings may, and the chances are that the light plot original (as opposed to the prints made from it) will be put away as soon as the production is hung.

If a plot is being prepared for a touring production, or as a unit plot for a repertory theatre, a more exotic paper that can withstand a lot of handling may be in order. For most situations, however, a good quality drafting paper will be sufficient.

Unlike tracing paper, good drafting paper is rather expensive, and this may tempt the designer to buy a roll of narrow (24" or 30") paper. This is a mistake. Crowding too much material onto a small piece of paper tends to make a light plot unclear and messy, and should be avoided if at all possible. It is best to start with a piece of paper that is too large and to crop the margins before printing, so it is usually impractical to buy a roll of paper that is less than 36" wide. Unless they are working on a design for a very large stage, most designers prefer to draft their plots in 1/2" = 1'-0" scale in order to make them clear, readable, and accurate. The plot for even an average-sized stage will need to be drawn on a sheet which is no less than 36" wide by 42" long.

The need for generous paper proportions rules out the use of most preprinted drafting papers. The title block on such papers is rarely adaptable to stage lighting use and the borders printed onto the sheet are not erasable. Pre-cut sheets of drafting paper are available and may be used if the designer wants to buy and store them, but they can also be restricting unless they are large enough to handle the largest plot. The rolls of drafting paper are best because they can be stored with ease and because they allow a degree of flexibility in drawing size which cannot be duplicated by precut sheets.

**DRAWING BOARDS**: If one needs a large piece of paper to draw a plot properly, it follows that an even larger drawing board will be needed to hold it. To avoid undue cramping, a drawing board 48" wide by 36" from front to back is a minimum, and one 60" x 38" is even better. As is the case with any drafting board, a firm, very smooth surface is a must. Drawing boards may be covered with a variety of materials, some more durable than others, but the most satisfactory are the laminated flexible plastic materials made especially for drawing boards. Paper or illustration board, which is sometimes used to cover boards, not only wears out quickly, but also tends to retain marks and indentations from previous work, thereby interfering with new work.

**TOOLS:** The usual basic draftsman's tools are used in lighting design work. The set square (adjustable triangle) is most important, and is more apt to be used than a selection of 45° and 30° - 60° - 90° triangles, especially for section analysis procedures which are discussed later in this chapter. A good utility template, one that has a wide assortment of circles, triangles and squares, will be very helpful (see Appendix B).

The parallel rule is still the most useful basic drawing tool for lighting design. The need to establish lines that cross from a plan to a section, the need to draw long lines for drops, curtains or pipes, and the need to align booms on one side of the stage with booms on the other side all require a long, accurate parallel rule. Drafting machines, those devices that have two straight-edged rulers set 90° apart and that can be moved all over the board are intriguing devices; but their cost alone, not to mention their inconvenience, should discourage a lighting designer from considering them. The rulers on drafting machines are simply not long enough for many light plot drafting tasks.

The device which is unique to stage lighting design is, of course, the stage lighting instrument template. In the years since this book first appeared, such a wide assortment of these templates has been designed and marketed that it is now impractical to attempt to show them all in the text of this book. However, in Appendix B you will find a number of templates and related tools illustrated and discussed.

# Lines and Letters

**LINE STRENGTH:** In drafting, line strength varies according to the function of a line on the drawing. This is no less true of line weights used for light plots. It is possible on a light plot to identify at least six categories of lines which could conceivably be differentiated by line weight. However, to take the time to be that careful with precise weight and darkness of lines is usually not possible, or even necessary, in the theatre production time frame. The six categories, from darkest to lightest, are:

1. Instruments

2. Pipes and other mounting positions

3. Ground plans and/or parts of the theatre

4. Dimensions and call outs

5. Sight lines

6. Lettering guide lines.

With a pencil, it is not easy to draw six distinct line weights. If a plot is being generated on a computer CAD system, and a multi-pen plotter is available, then it is possible to have the plotter make the distinctions for you. A word of warning though: setting up the plot on the computer so that these separate line weights are properly and consistently entered will be time-consuming, and the designer will probably make several mistakes before a plot comes out right.

Even though the matter of line weight is not as vital as the list of six categories above might suggest, there are two cardinal rules to follow:

1. *NOTHING SHOULD BE MORE IMPORTANT ON THE PLOT THAN THE INSTRU-MENTS*

2. *ALL IMPORTANT INFORMATION MUST BE DARK ENOUGH TO PRINT.*

If these rules are followed, line weights on the plot will probably work out satisfactorily.

**LETTERING**: It is not uncommon to see a well-drawn lighting design rendered shabby and unprofessional looking through crude lettering. Again, although the quality of lettering has nothing to do with good or poor lighting unless it is so inadequate that the electricians cannot read it, sharp and attractive lettering can go a long way toward creating that all-important good first impression when one is selling one's work or meeting a crew for the first time.

This handbook cannot teach an inept draftsman to letter, nor will it attempt to do so. Textbooks on drafting techniques abound; and each contains certain rules, techniques and even tricks to help the student develop a good lettering style. Practice, obviously, is the key to success. Serious students of lettering are often made to do one hundred alphabets and number groups every week.

Here are a few suggestions concerning lettering on a light plot that are worth remembering:

1. Always use guide lines. The temptation to work free-hand in order to rush plot completion is to be resisted. Time gained is appearance lost, always.

2. Settle on one lettering size which will do for everything except the major parts of the title block and the instrument numbers, and always use that size. The uniformity will help the appearance of the plot, and the practice of that one size will help perfect your style. Lettering sizes can be divided into these categories:

a. The title of the play in the title block: up to 1/2" high is acceptable, if, and only if, the designer has the skill to make such large letters well.

b. The instrument numbers — those numbers inside the instrument symbol which identify the instrument in the position — may be as large as will comfortably fit inside the symbol and should be consistently sized throughout the plot.

c. All other notation should be of one size, which will vary from designer to designer, but which will average about 3/32" to 1/8" high.

3. Keep the orientation of your lettering to as few axes as possible. Most lettering should be horizontal — aligned with the bottom of the sheet — since that is the easiest orientation to read, and since guide lines for that orientation are easy to draw with the parallel rule. Depending upon the orientation of your instrument symbols on the sheet, you may need to do some lettering vertically, in which case it is best to choose one edge of the sheet, usually the one on the right, and align all vertical lettering with that. Some designers shift the alignment of vertical lettering according to the relationship of the notation to the centerline of the drawing. This is also acceptable provided the work is consistent throughout. The only acceptable departure from the horizontal/vertical alignments on a plot is in the case of a large group of instruments which are drawn at some different angle, in order to make the plot clear. In that case, the lettering may be at the same angle (see Chapter. 4).

Various mechanical and dry transfer lettering systems are now marketed to help designers and draftspersons dress up their work. Most of these are slow to use, unless you are very practiced; and most of them require a certain amount of skill in order to make the results really attractive. Some designers may find that their own hand is so hopeless that there is no way to make the plot readable except to resort to one of these techniques. In that case, it is suggested that you find one device and consistently practice with it. Some of these alternative systems are listed here in case the designer wants to investigate them:

1. The LeRoy Stylus: This device is a three-point writing stylus which has a lead or pen in one point, and pins in the others, one to ride in a fixed groove in the stencil rule, and the other to be guided through engraved letters in the rule. Rules of several styles and sizes are available. After each letter is drawn, the rule is moved along the straight edge until the next letter is in position.

The lettering thus achieved is passable in appearance at first attempt, but not really attractive until the user is quite practiced. The tools are costly, and the procedure is never as fast as hand lettering; but if one has decided to use a mechanical system, this one is very good.

2. Lettering Guides: These are simply templates which guide the pencil on the sheet. They are not expensive, and not sophisticated; they are also not as simple to use as their appearance might suggest. Letter spacing is not easy to master with these devices, but reasonable results can be expected in time.

3. Dry Transfer Lettering: Several manufacturers now sell this product in a bewildering array of sizes and styles, mostly intended to aid the graphic designer in

preparing work for the camera. Dry transfer lettering is applied by placing the desired letter, which is printed on a carrying sheet, over the intended location on the drawing and rubbing it. The letter is parted from the carrying sheet and sticks, by virtue of a waxy surface, to the drawing. The process is slow, letter spacing is a matter of some skill, erasure is by scraping with a knife point, and, contrary to good light plot graphics, the letters are always the darkest thing on the sheet.

4. The Kroy System: This is a system used in architecture to put large, very neat lettering on presentation drawings. Letters are typed, one at a time, on a transparent tape which is then peeled from a backing strip and stuck to the drawing. Again, time is a problem, and the resulting letters and numbers will be very dark. In printing, the edges of the tape sometimes show, reducing the impact of the letters. The initial investment for the typing machine will discourage most designers from trying this system.

# Printing

If a light plot cannot be reproduced full size by a blueprint machine or some other method, it is of no use. During the time that a production is being prepared, loaded out of the shop, loaded into the theatre and produced, several people will need copies of the light plot at the same time. The assistant lighting designer will need at least one copy, while the master electrician will need a good copy with which to work, as well as several copies to cut up to make "hanging cardboards" — pieces of the plot mounted on stiff cardboard — for the electricians' use. In most cases, this reproduction is by blue or black lines on white paper via the ammonia-developed technique.

The operation of the blueprint machine is quite simple. The original plot is placed against a piece of paper that has a light-sensitive surface, and the sandwich is passed through a machine which subjects the entire surface to intense ultra-violet light. The lines on the original cause shadows which prevent exposure of the treated surface under them. Then the print paper is bathed in ammonia fumes which cause the unexposed line shadows to turn dark blue or black, depending upon the print paper chosen.

It stands to reason that lines which are very light on the original will not make good shadows on the print paper, and thus will not make good copies. Many adjustments of exposure time and paper speed are possible; but the rule is still that the darker the original, the darker the print. Again, practice and experience will be the best guide.

Sometimes, the designer is not sure how many prints the electricians will need. In this case, it is desirable to give the master electrician a sepia print from which he or she may make blue prints. The sepia print is made in the same machine, using special paper which produces brown lines on a translucent paper; this print can then be used in the same manner as the original. However, since the drawing is now going through two stages of printing, the line work on the original must be even darker.

Graphic reproduction houses have available machines which resemble large electro-static (Xerox® type) copiers. These machines can make copies on bond paper and on translucent stock for blueprinting. They are also able to change the size of the print with respect to the original, so that a 1/2" scale drawing can be reduced to 1/4", for example.

## Section Analysis Techniques

When a symbol for a lighting unit is drawn on the final plot, it represents many decisions. The designer has studied the script, the setting, and the costumes and listened to the director's ideas. As a result of this preparation, the designer has conceived an on-stage effect which the light is intended to create, or at least to which it will contribute. The color, direction, relative intensity, and beam characteristics (such as sharp vs. soft, or plain vs. patterned) for the light have all been considered. Nevertheless, a number of very practical questions remain.

Where should the light be hung? What beam spread is going to be most useful? How many instruments will be needed? Can the effect be achieved from the second pipe, or should the third pipe be used? Can an instrument which is hung on the box boom get under the ceiling and still not spill on the back wall? Is there any position from which the backdrop at the end of the alley can be lighted without spilling on the black border above it? Questions such as these are best worked out in section analysis.

If you have been reading this book from the beginning, you have already encountered the rudiments of section analysis technique. In Chapter 2, the technique for laying out sidelight involved a front elevation of a sidelight position which was, in effect, a section taken along a line parallel with the footlights. In it the height, the on and offstage position, and the beam spread of the various lights chosen for a sidelight system were studied (see Fig. 2-11). When the technique for locating the next band of lighting was described in Chapter Two, section analysis was used to examine the blend between downstage and upstage lighting instruments (see Fig. 2-9). Section analysis is simply a technique for examining the relationship between a lighting instrument in a specific location and everything else on stage, with special attention given to the height of things. The remainder of this chapter will be devoted to some section analysis examples which are intended to help you understand the process step by step.

It is just as important for the lighting designer to have a section of the setting for a production as it is to have the ground plan. It is standard practice for a set designer to provide a centerline section, at least for half of the stage. If you need information for the side of the stage which the section does not show, you may have to construct it from the set designer's working drawings. If the production is being done according to normal practice, the information should be available in some form or other. The set designer will often use the section to show where lighting positions are available.

One of the most important uses of section analysis is to check these positions to see if they will work and to suggest adjustments if they are necessary.

Many section analyses can be carried out on tracing paper laid over the set designer's own section. This is true for any lights which are aimed directly up or down stage, or nearly so. In Figure 3-1, a section of a simple wing and border stage has been used to determine the trim of the electric pipes, keeping them out of sight lines. This is the most common use of section analysis. Obviously, the location of the most critical seat must be known before the section is drawn. In Figure 3-2, a section of the same wing and border stage is used to work out the backlight. This analysis would probably be done before the uniform system for the backlight is designed in plan as described in Chapter 2. Since it is critical to have coverage up and down stage, this analysis will help the designer to select which PAR and which axis of that PAR is best. Then, the uniform system layout will determine how many instruments are required. The designer must remember that it is critical to have backlight which lights the head of a person downstage but which is hung so that light does not get into the eyes of the audience in the first row.

It may be necessary to work back and forth several times between the section and various uniform system layouts — trying different pipe locations and different PAR lamps — before the final decision is made. This is why inexpensive tracing paper

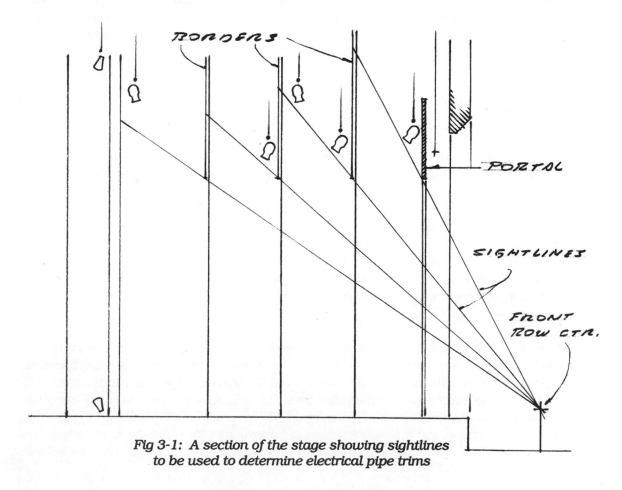

*Fig 3-1: A section of the stage showing sightlines*
*to be used to determine electrical pipe trims*

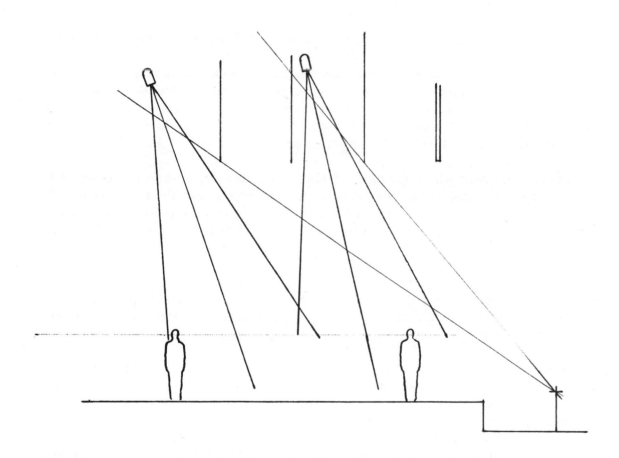

*Fig. 3-2: A section used to determine that backlight from
wide angle PAR units on two pipes will cover the stage*

should be used, so that it does not hurt to put it aside and draw another.

Note that the section analysis in Fig. 3-2 is not as complete as that in Fig. 3-1. It is not important to draw anything that is not involved in the decision you have to make.

Figure 3-3 shows plan and section views of a set for which the front light came from box boom positions only. In the action of the play, the actors were confined to the angled, raked platform, which is under a roof. The problem examined in the next two drawings

(Fig. 3-4 and 3-5) is how to light a person standing just inside the door with a light from the stage left box boom. Clearly, the most important factor is the height of the roof where the line from the boom to the actor crosses its downstage edge. This will help us to know how high the instrument can be mounted. To determine this, several steps are involved.

First, the plan is taped to the drawing board so that the parallel rule lies along the line from the location of the light on the boom to the center of the actor's position on stage. This line becomes a reference line for the section. For most problems, the reference line lies along the stage floor, and all vertical dimensions are taken from there. If there is some other surface which is more convenient for measuring — the auditorium floor or the surface of a deck, for instance — then the reference line may represent one of those surfaces. It is only important to be consistent (Fig. 3-4).

If your drawing board is large enough, you should be able to tape the section down with the plan in such a way as to align the floor in the section with the reference line in the plan (see Fig. 3-4). If not, you will have to transfer elevations by measurement, which is not a serious problem. Even with both sheets taped to the board, there will still be some measuring to do.

Next, a sheet of tracing paper is laid over the plan and section. As seen in Fig. 3-5, the new section along the reference line is developed by erecting perpendicular lines from the reference line in the plan for the position of the actor, the roof at point "A" (where the reference line crosses the downstage edge of the roof), and the boom.

The height of the actor is found in the section, and the actor is placed in the new section by drawing a line parallel with the reference line until it crosses the perpendicular line at the actor's position. A new figure is drawn there and is cross hatched in this example for clarity.

Next, the distance, "D", from the apron (in this case, the most convenient line to use) upstage to point "A" is measured and transferred to the section. In the section, a perpendicular is erected to the reference line at a distance equal to "D" from the apron; and where it crosses the section view of the roof, we have a height for point "A".

A line is drawn parallel to the reference line from the intersection of the new perpendicular and the roof until it crosses the perpendicular from point "A" in the plan. This new intersection is the location of the roof in the new section.

A line drawn from the head of the actor through this new intersection to the boom will guide you in the location of the light. Obviously, any light from that boom which is intended to light the actor must be mounted below that line.

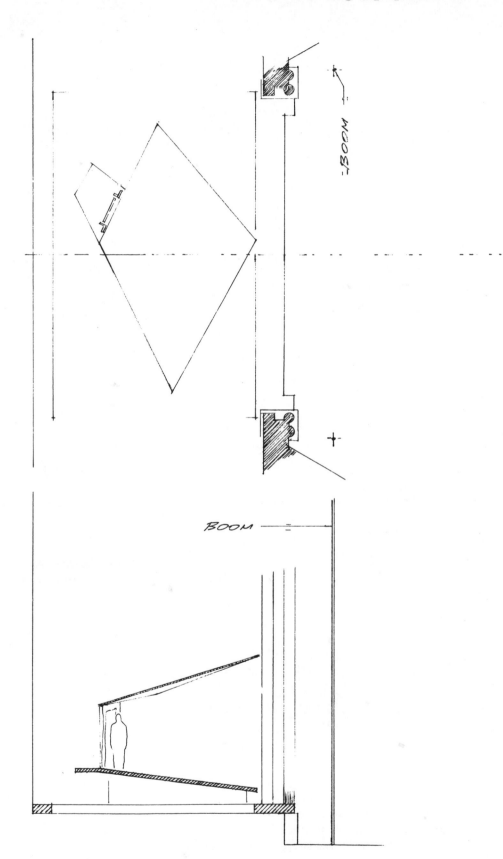

*Fig. 3-3: The plan and section of the Broadway production of Athol Fugard's Blood Knot. The boom stood outside the proscenium on the auditorium floor.*

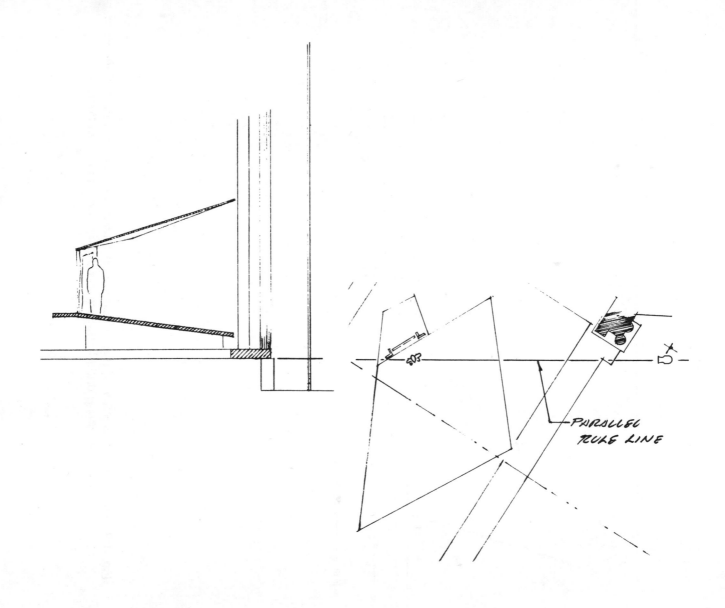

*Fig. 3-4: The plan is taped down so that the parallel rule runs between the actor's position and the light. Then the section is taped down with the stage floor on the same line*

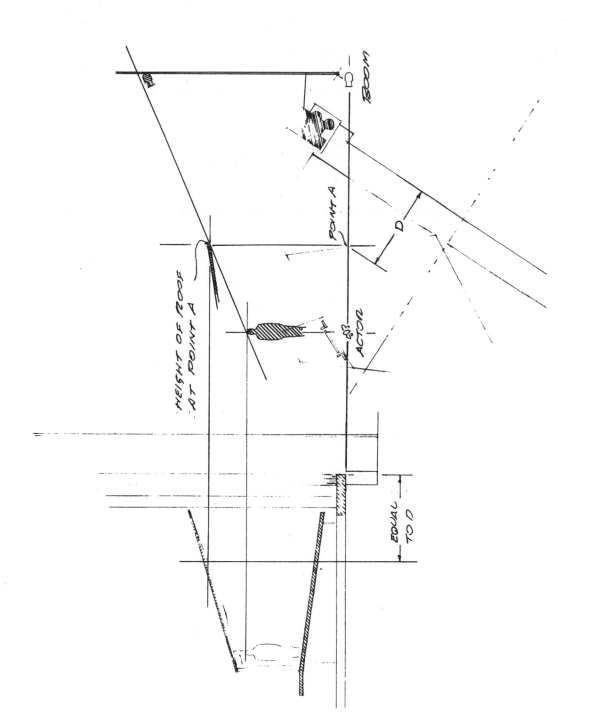

*Fig. 3-5: The section analysis is completed to determine the height of the roof at point A in order to discover how high on the boom a light may be placed to light the actor*

There are a great many situations in which section analysis is useful to work out problems such as this one. Some will be more complex, some less, but all may be approached through the use of a reference line section following the steps used in the example. The essential steps, then, are these:

1. Align the reference line with your parallel rule;

2. Erect perpendiculars to the reference line at each important location (in the case above, the actor, point "A", and the boom);

3. Determine the heights of the important elements (in the case above, the roof) by reference to the designer's section, through measurement or by alignment on the board;

4. Connect the important points with a line which will indicate where the light must be or where it cannot be.

Becoming familiar with the techniques of section analysis will take some practice. However, it will avoid many nightmares such as discovering, during a focus call, that the light will simply not reach the location you had planned for it, because the set is in the way.

# CHAPTER FOUR:
# LIGHT PLOT CONVENTIONS

## The Nature of a Light Plot

The light plot is a graphic device whose primary purpose is to show an electrician what equipment is needed, and in which locations, in order to realize the designer's goals for a production. The light plot also has two secondary purposes: to provide a record of which equipment was used after a production has been hung, and to provide a means for a student designer to present his or her ideas for the lighting of a production.

While opinions vary as to the value of the plot as a record (since other records exist by the time a production opens), and there is some question as to how effective the plot is as the only means to communicate a student's ideas, there is absolutely no question as to the plot's primary goal. Therefore, this book will concentrate on the plot as an electrician's working document, and will also note, where appropriate, ways in which the standards may vary when a class project, not a production, is the designer's purpose.

Since the plot is a guide to the installation of certain equipment in locations which are pre-determined by the designer, it stands to reason that clear definition of the various instruments and precise location information are paramount. Clarity is most important. For example, even the simplest plot may require decisions as to how to show two objects which, in plan, would occupy the same space. The decision must always be on the side of clarity.

## The Form of a Light Plot

The basic form of a light plot is quite simple. It is essentially a plan view of the stage, together with certain portions of the auditorium, showing lighting instruments in or close to their actual positions. The location of certain vertical lighting positions will be shown in the plan, while the position is actually detailed elsewhere. The plot is drawn from the point of view of an audience member, or, more precisely, the point of view of the designer during technical rehearsals. It is most convenient if it is one drawing, providing that the drawing is not too crowded to be clear. The plot may be broken into parts showing, for example, the electric pipes on one drawing, the booms on another and the equipment in front of the proscenium on a third.

## Scale and Scale Relationships

The most common scale for a light plot is 1/2" = 1"-0" in the United States (1:25 in countries on the metric standard). This is based on two considerations: 1. the set designer usually works in 1/2" scale for clarity, so the lighting designer receives the information in that scale; 2. on a crowded plot, smaller scales can become hard to read. Figure 4-1 shows the same information in two scales as a comparison. Plots in 1/4" = 1'-0" (1:50 metric) are not uncommon, especially when the theatre is so large that even a single position requires an unreasonably large sheet in 1/2" scale.

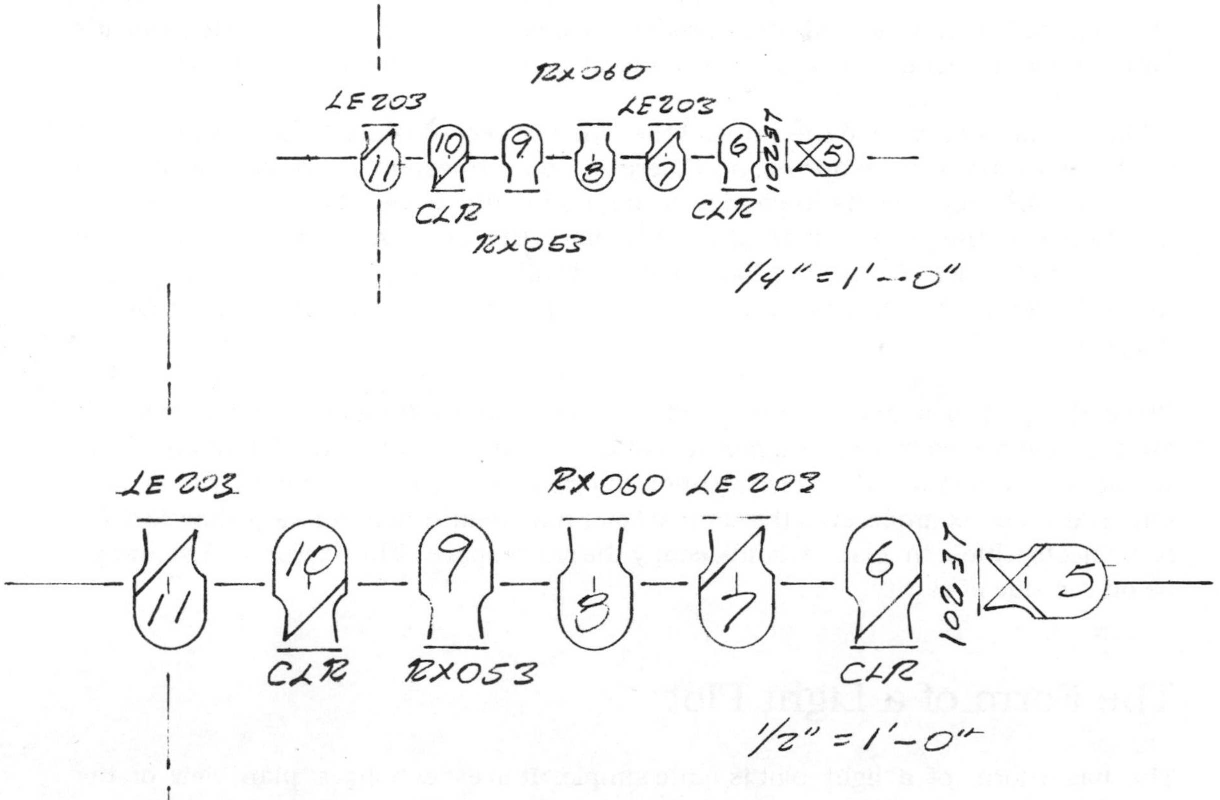

Fig. 4-1: A portion of an electrical pipe drawn in both 1/4" and 1/2" scale.
Note the crowded lettering in 1/4"

Not all portions of the light plot need to be in scale. In fact, since no lighting problems will be solved on the plot (that was done in section analysis) and since all positions are labeled as to identity and location, the only reason to maintain scale is to give a reasonable picture of the relationship between instruments within a single mounting position. Certainly an attempt to maintain scale in showing the location of the positions in front of the proscenium will result in a plot which has a great deal of empty paper at the bottom of the page, and a great deal of relatively crowded information at the top. Since there is usually no call to relocate the permanent positions in the house, they can be shown in a convenient arrangement which does, at least, maintain the relative position of each. (See Fig. 4-2).

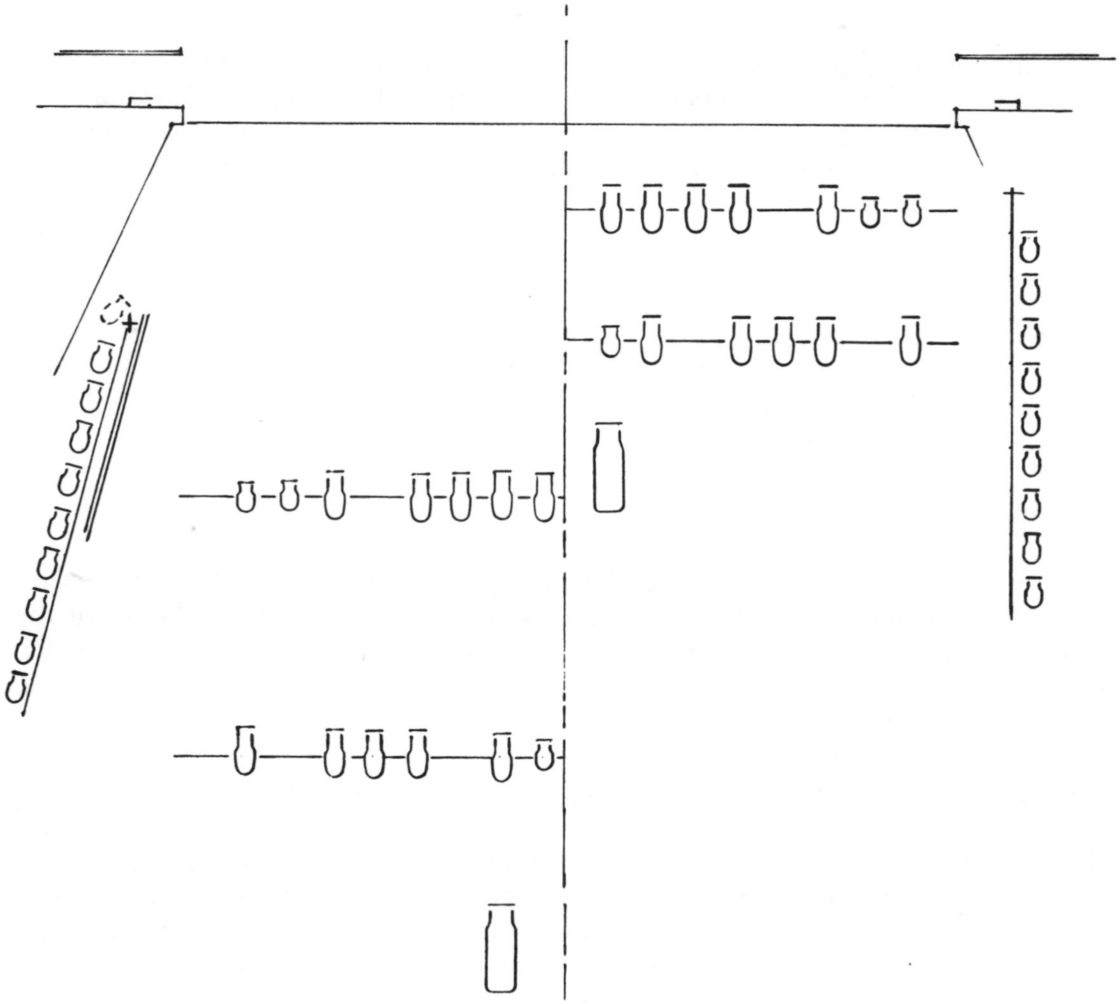

*Fig. 4-2: The auditorium mounting positions drawn in true locations (left) and condensed locations (right).*

On the part of the plot which shows instruments over the stage, it is better to maintain scale, since it is helpful to show how the electric pipes and booms relate to the setting. Electricians appreciate a plot which shows not only the pipes, booms, and ladders, but also shows the major parts of the ground plan in lighter lines underneath. This helps them to organize the load in and focus. In some cases, however, it may not be possible to maintain scale location for all positions, since some may be located on top of other positions. In such cases, one of the two positions may be shown out of its scale location (and be so noted), or all positions can be drawn evenly distributed on a sheet which does not show the plan. In every case, the name and location of each position should be clearly shown adjacent to the position (See Fig. 4-16).

# Getting Started

The lighting design is unique in the graphics of a production in that it must show a number of locations away from the stage — in the auditorium, over the audience's head, in a booth behind the seats — in order to establish mounting positions for all of the equipment required. Thus, the lighting designer must collect or prepare the following information to be ready to draft the plot:

1. The set designer's ground plan;

2. The set designer's section or sections;

3. A plan and section of the theatre or theatres in which the production will play;

4. The equipment magic sheets.

It will rarely be either useful or profitable to prepare a composite plan of the theatre and the production on a single sheet. Usually, the light plot is prepared using the set designer's plan as a guide, and making use of the theatre plans to prepare section analyses and to understand what positions are available and how much equipment will fit in them.

After this information is collected, the lighting designer must decide whether to do a preliminary, rough plot or whether to work directly on the final sheet. Time usually dictates that the preliminary be skipped. However, there is one disadvantage to this: at the outset, the plot may be located on the page in a position which later proves to be too close to one edge of the paper or another, so that awkward drafting compromises are needed to work around this problem. Starting with a very large piece of paper is one solution, if the designer has a board which is large enough; but the best solution is first to block out, in rough form, the positions, the instrument key, the title block and everything else on a piece of tracing paper, and then to use that to guide the final drafting.

There is one temptation which must be avoided at all costs: to trace with full line strength any part of the setting or architecture onto the plot before all of the other work is done. The set and architecture can be put in with very light lines as a guide, but should not be drawn full strength until all positions, notes, keys and title blocks are done. They can then be put in where appropriate and where they do not interfere with the essential information of the plot. This discipline will save a lot of erasure and time.

# Drawing Instruments

Instruments are, obviously, the most important detail on your plot. If you clearly distinguish the particular instruments from each other, you may well be rewarded with a relatively error-free hang. If your symbols are easily confused, then you will lose time in the focus while incorrect instruments are replaced. Most theatre schedules are prepared with a minimum of working time for lighting; therefore, such errors can damage your final product.

Any system of symbols that is clear and distinct, and that is described in a key on every sheet of the plot, will work as soon as the crew is familiar with it. Most symbol systems use the familiar instrument outlines available on stage lighting templates (see Appendix B), which are close to the correct size in scale since the shape goes a long way toward identifying the instrument intended. Systems that use invented symbols made from circles and squares do not offer these advantages.

The United States Institute for Theatre Technology (USITT) has adopted a standard set of symbol conventions which are shown on the following pages. The author has augmented the list with a few symbols which are marked with an asterisk (*). No single template exists which offers all of these symbols, but with a 1/2" and 1/4" plan template and a good utility template, most of the shapes can be created with ease. These symbols are drawn in 1/2" scale.

ELLIPSOIDAL REFLECTOR SPOTLIGHTS

Many of these units exist in two styles: older models using "T" lamps, and newer, axial mounted quartz lamp types. Both the standard (to the left) and axial quartz (to the right) types are shown.

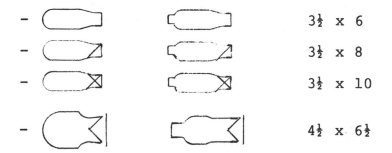

| | | |
|---|---|---|
| | | 3½ x 6 |
| | | 3½ x 8 |
| | | 3½ x 10 |
| | | 4½ x 6½ |

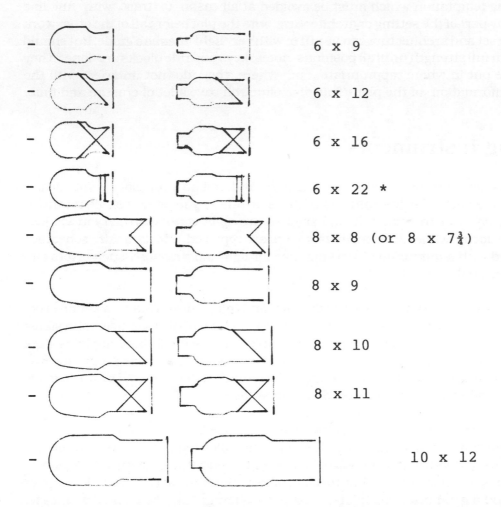

| | |
|---|---|
| | 6 x 9 |
| | 6 x 12 |
| | 6 x 16 |
| | 6 x 22 * |
| | 8 x 8 (or 8 x 7¾) |
| | 8 x 9 |
| | 8 x 10 |
| | 8 x 11 |
| | 10 x 12 |

Certain ellipsoidal reflector spotlights are built in a rectangular housing instead of the more traditional shape. Examples include the Colortran Mini-Ellipse™ family and the Strand Minuette™ line. These instruments are differentiated by field angle, not lens configuration, and the best way to show this is by writing the field angle into the symbol. This technique may be used with any instrument that is identified by field angle. These are simply examples of a large range.

| | |
|---|---|
| 40° | 40°, 4½" * |
| Z | Adjustable ("zoom") optics, 6" * |

The "Z" symbol may be used with any ellipsoidal that has adjustable optics.

Symbols for accessories or special provisions for ellipsoidal reflector spotlights are:

    Unit with iris

Unit with Pattern (or "gobo" or "template")

Unit with top hat, unit with half hat *

## FRESNEL LENS SPOTLIGHTS

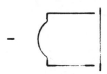    3"

6"

8"

12"

The barn door is the only important accessory for the Fresnel.

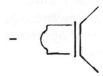    Two leaf barn door

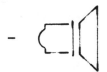    Four leaf barn door

PAR LAMP HOLDERS

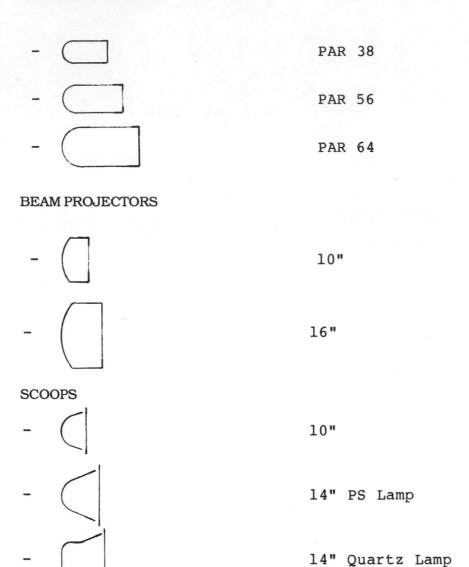

BEAM PROJECTORS

SCOOPS

STRIPLIGHTS

Striplight shapes do appear on some templates (one very good example is shown in Appendix B). While these may be useful, often the one or two on a conventional template do not scale the same as the striplights that will be used. The best approach is to draft the appropriate rectangle and to follow these conventions:

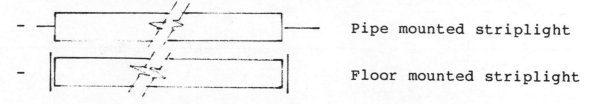

In plan, other drop lighting equipment such as Colortran Far Cyc™ or Ianero Iris™ will appear simply as rectangles. One template does show them in section, and this distinctive shape may be used in the plan, though the scale will be off:

  -  Far Cyc® *

  -  Iris® *

## PROJECTION EQUIPMENT

  -  Carousel

  -  Effects projector

## MISCELLANEOUS ITEMS

  -  Practical (chandelier, table lamp, fire)

  -  Followspot. This is a general symbol which may or may not work for you. Invent something.

## Instrument Notation

There is no clear standard as to the amount of information that should be put on and around the instrument symbol on the plot. The absolute essential information is not hard to define: a symbol that tells exactly, with the aid of the key, what size and type of instrument this is and what size lamp it should have. There must also be a number, large and clear, inside the symbol if possible, that relates to a schedule that lists all other information about the instrument. Nothing else is required.

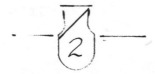

*Fig. 4-3*

To this basic symbol, several items may be added as the designer wishes or as the situation dictates. It is common practice to show the color filter, if any, that will be used.

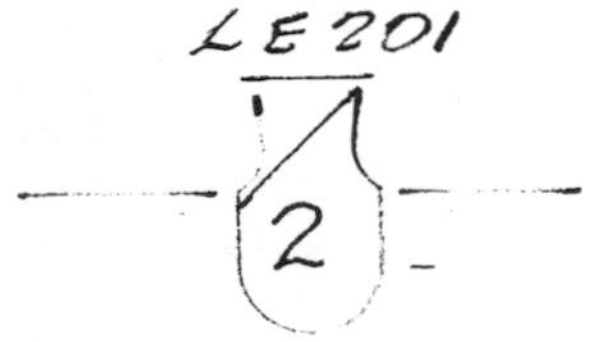

LE 201

2

*Fig. 4-4*

This allows the electricians to install the gel when the instrument is hung, thus saving a great deal of time in the focus.

It is sometimes useful to indicate the dimmer number adjacent to the symbol (see Fig. 4-5):

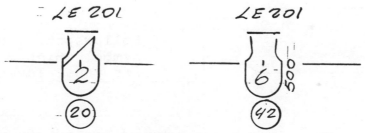

*Fig. 4-5*

If the lamp wattage in an instrument is different than that shown in the instrument key (see below), that wattage may be shown as above (Fig. 4-5). If a pattern is to be used, the template unit should be identified on the plot, and the pattern may be identified on the plot (see Fig. 4-6) or in the schedule or hook-up. Also, Some designers indicate the focus for a unit in some cryptic notation behind the instrument as an aid during focus:

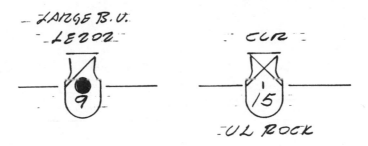

*Fig 4-6*

Some designers omit the focus from the drafted plot, and write it in just before the focus call to refresh their memories. It is also a good way to remind yourself of changes you must deal with.

If a light plot is being done for a class project (hereafter known as a "school plot"), more information may be included to make the student's wishes clear to the teacher. The USITT has provided a format for this which is as follows:

A --- Focus

B --- Instrument Number

C --- Circuit Number

D --- Dimmer Number

E --- Color

F --- Wattage (shown on each instrument)

*Fig. 4-7*

Clearly, a plot with this much on-sheet information will take a long time to draft. One advantage is that no schedule (See Chapter 5) is required, since all of the information is available on the plot. This makes critique easier for the teacher. However, having a proper schedule is a necessity when the plot is for production. Searching a piece of paper that may be the size of a small bedsheet for one bit of information will not speed things up.

Striplights require a special notation since they are essentially three or four (or even more) instruments in the same body. Two systems are in common use to deal with this: the letter system and the multiple number system. In these examples, the same three-color striplight is shown in each format:

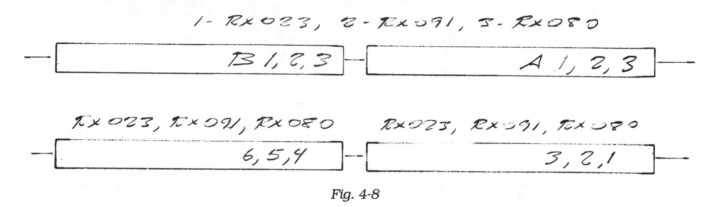

*Fig. 4-8*

The most important consideration with striplights is to identify each plugable entity with a distinct number so that it can be traced through the paperwork. Both systems accomplish that, though the letter system is more specific to the particular housing. The letter system also allows for easier color notation.

## Instrument Orientation

Two instrument orientation conventions are in common use: the aligned system and the aimed system. Both have their place.

The aligned system assumes that the plot is intended simply to get the right equipment installed, so it shows all units pointing in a uniform direction or directions. Focus is not indicated by the instrument direction, since focus does not concern the electrician as the equipment is being hung. The aligned system makes a very neat-looking plot, and it can be drafted quickly. Some aligned plots aim all units in one direction (usually upstage) but most will show them at 90° rotations depending upon general focus (frontlight, sidelight, backlight). The aligned system is the choice of almost all professional lighting designers.

The aimed system roughly indicates the focus direction of the instruments by showing them aimed toward the part of the stage they will light. While the direction will not be precise, the aimed system can be useful in school plots, again as an aid to the teacher. This system does require that the student concentrate on what each light is to do as it is drawn on the plot. It may also remind unexperienced crew members to leave enough slack in the wiring for focusing. Aimed light plots take longer to draft than aligned plots.

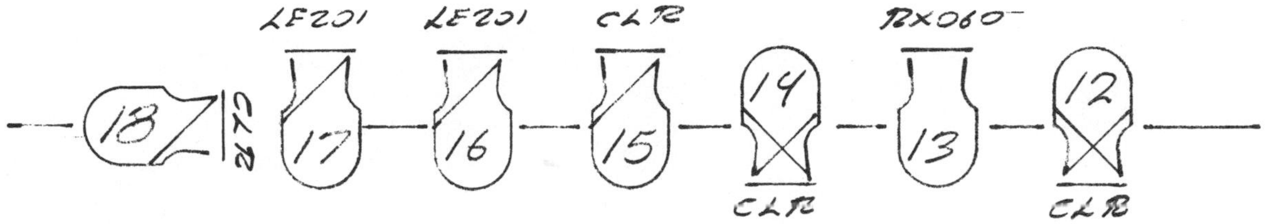

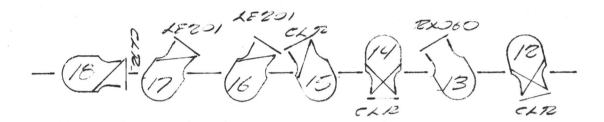

*Fig. 4-9: The Aligned System*

*Fig 4-10: The Aimed System*

# Instrument Numbering

The numbering of instruments on light plots follows a set of simple conventions. Two particular rules apply in all cases:

1.    The instruments in each position are numbered from 1 to n  in that position. Numbers never carry over from one position to the next. There will thus be a No. 1 Electric #7, a Box Boom Right #7, and a First Cove #7 all  on  the  same plot. An older convention of consecutive numbering of instruments  throughout the plot is now completely obsolete.

2.    The numbering is done logically according to where one might  stand  to  count  the instruments in a  given position. To  count  a  boom  which  has  two stacks of instruments on it, one  would logically stand on the stage  looking at the lenses and start at the top left unit,  count left to right, drop down a row, count left to  right again, and so on (See Fig. 4-11).  To count a pipe,  one would stand on stage, facing the auditorium, look  up  and count from stage left to stage right (see Fig. 4-12).

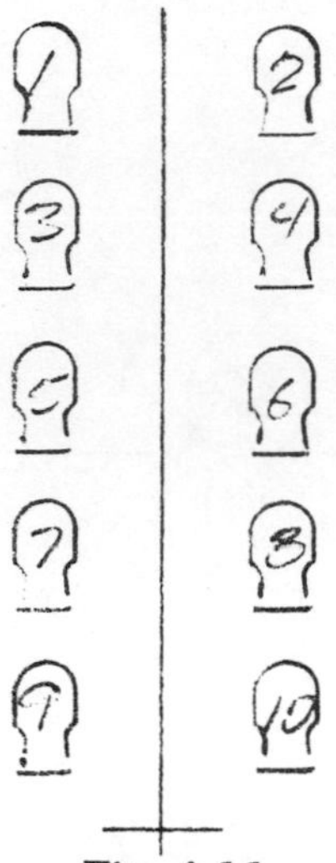

Fig. 4-12

Fig. 4-11

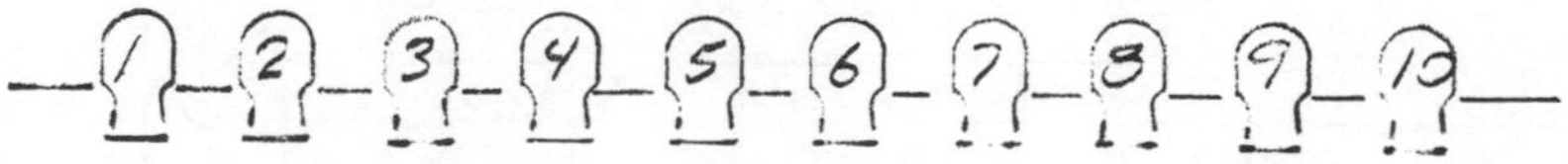

*Instrument numbering. Both views are from the stage looking toward the position*

Almost all numbering decisions can be made according to this logical procedure. Some less than clear situations can develop, however, when dealing with pipe grids and tensioned wire grids, neither of which are linear in nature. Pipe grids usually consist of two groups of pipes hanging at 90° to each other, so that the pipes running in one direction can be identified with numbers, and those running in the other direction can be labeled with letters. The decision as to the point of view to take when numbering pipe grid instruments may be arbitrary, or may relate to some specific location in the theatre such as the control booth or the closed side of a three-sided thrust. It is the designer's decision.

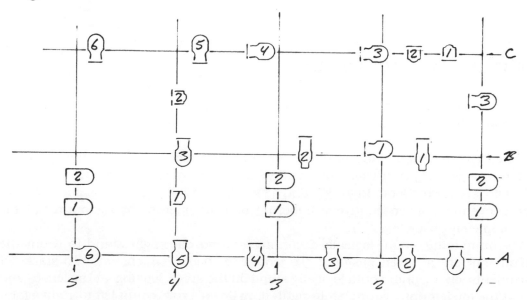

Fig. 4-13: *The corner of a pipe grid showing various instruments on east-west pipes (marked with letters) and north-south pipes (marked with numbers). Note that some confusion is possible at intersections.*

Tensioned wire grids are a different problem. The lights are mounted above the grid and shine through rectangular openings. There is no consistent mounting device such as a pipe. The numbering depends upon the only unambiguous factor; the opening through which the light shines. Each opening is given a unique name, usually based upon a column and row concept, as if the opening were a mounting position. The lights are then numbered clockwise around the opening.

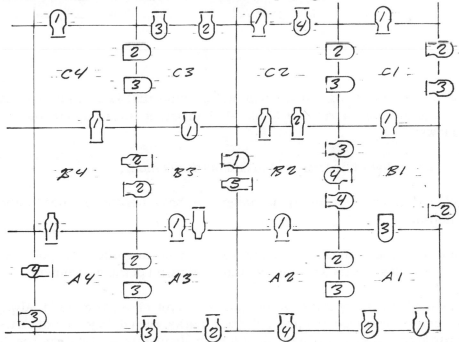

Fig. 4-14: A corner of a tensioned wire grid. Each opening in the grid becomes a mounting position, and those instruments which shine through the opening are numbered clockwise from the upper left. Note that adjacent instruments may have the same number or may seem to be in sequence while being part of different "mounting positions."

## Drawing Horizontal Positions

This section deals with techniques for showing lights on pipes, in coves, on balcony rails, and at the base of drops.

The spacing of spotlights on pipes is important, since crowding will make focus and maintenance difficult. The conventions are that 6" spotlights should be placed 18" on center, and 8" equipment should be hung 24" on center. Even though they are 8" in diameter, PAR 64 units may be placed 1' - 9" on center. The spacing of striplights depends upon the length of the unit, but when only striplights are mounted on the pipe, the space between units should be 6". The minimum spacing between adjacent electric pipes, or between electric pipes and nearby scenery is 9".

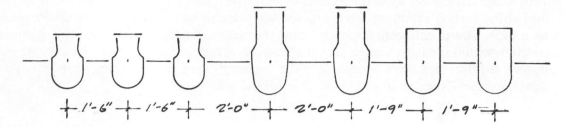

*Fig. 4-15*

The procedure for laying out a horizontal position that is symmetrical about the centerline of the stage and that will use all 6" instruments (a very common situation) is as follows:

1. Draw a very light line from end to end of the position.

2. Decide whether you want an instrument on the centerline. or one 9" either side of the centerline.

3. Make small, firm marks on the line 18" apart starting from the points chosen in step 2. These tick marks will guide you in locating all of the instruments.

4. Draw the instrument symbols and those notes you chose to include. Always locate the instruments centered on one of the tick marks, even if they are not all used. This will help to keep spaces available for additional instruments, and will give the electrician a quick way to mark off the pipe.

5. Between the instruments, draw in the pipe with a single, solid line so that it stops just short of the symbols.

6. If there is a long space between instruments, if they are sparsely hung, or if they are on uneven centers, use standard dimensioning techniques to locate them from the center line.

7. In a clear space near the position, make this note: "Instruments hung on 1' - 6" centers". One such note can serve for several positions if they are adjacent.

8. At the end of the position, make a note that identifies the position, or, if it is a temporary or movable position such as a rigging pipe, locates it.

9. If you are using 8" instruments, simply proceed the same way using 24" spaces, and for PAR 64's, 1' - 9".

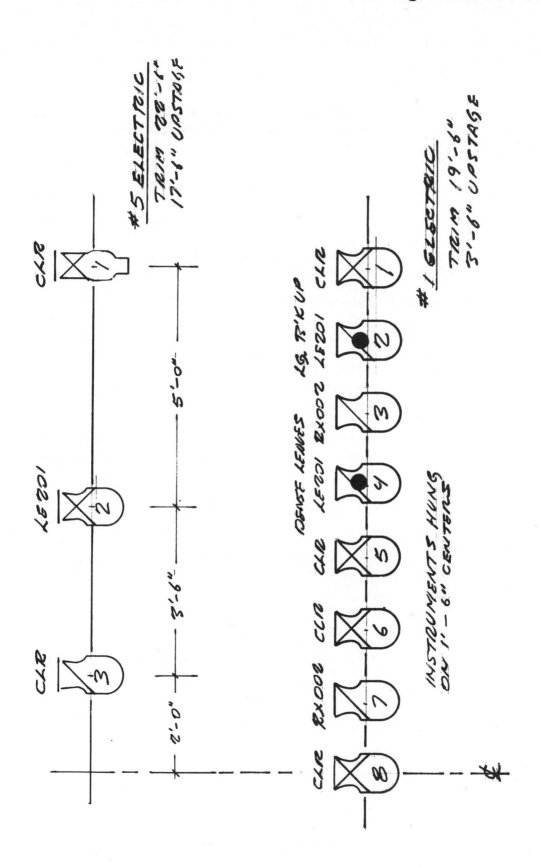

Fig. 4-16: Two horizontal positions showing different methods of dimensioning

Coves and balcony rails tend to have support members or other architectural details that affect where instruments can be mounted. These should be shown, and allowance should be made for them in the location of the instrument centers. In some theatres these obstructions may be so prominent that dimensioning is not required as long as the equipment is shown as it relates to these items. In this example, the numerous vertical pipes in the cove serve to locate the spotlights without tick marks.

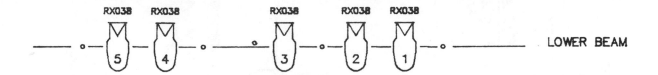

Fig. 4-17: A position with fixed "landmarks."

A position at the base of a drop is also horizontal, but it does not involve a pipe. In this case, the light guide line is drawn, but it simply serves to align the symbols. Unless a specific space is required between striplights (they are usually set 6" apart), instrument dimensioning is not required for systems that cross the centerline, though the location of the position (distance upstage of plaster) must be given.

Sometimes a pipe or other position is hung with instruments above and below. In this case, there are two choices available to the designer: 1. If there are almost as many instruments above as below, the position should be treated as two positions:

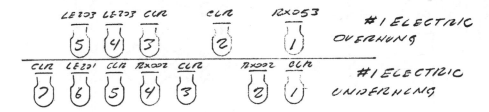

Fig. 4-18

2. When only one or two units are "overhung", this convention may be used.

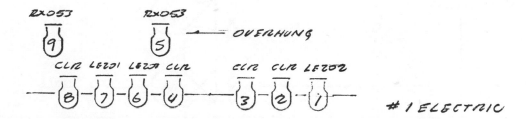

Fig. 4-19

If a pipe has a double set of side light units at the ends, the condition can be shown in this manner:

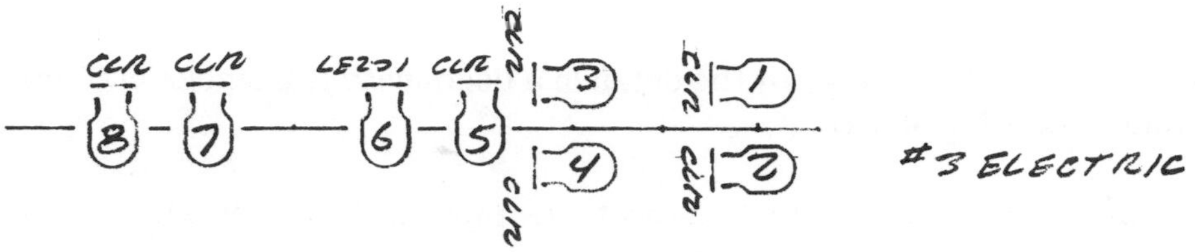

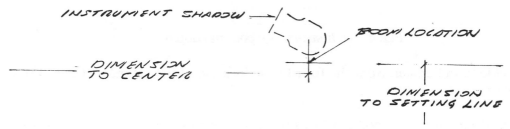

*Fig. 4-20*

If two or more positions will be superimposed upon each other in a true scale plan view, at least one will have to be drawn out of location. For a discussion of this, see "Scale and Scale Relationships" at the beginning of this chapter.

## Drawing Vertical Positions

Vertical positions can only be located, not detailed, in a plan view. For this reason, various devices have come to be used to provide a view which allows all equipment on a vertical position to be shown and explained. This will apply to booms, ladders, box booms, and auditorium side slots.

As with horizontal positions, spacing is critical. There is some latitude available in mounting sidelight booms with 6" equipment. 1' - 6" will work, but it is crowded and hard to focus. The minimum most designers allow is 1' - 9" center to center, with 2' - 0" being even better if there is room. 8" equipment is almost never used on booms and ladders, and only rarely on auditorium side slots. When it is used, it requires 2' 6" from unit to unit. PAR 64 units may be mounted 1' - 9" on center vertically.

The most common way to treat a vertical position on the plot is to indicate the location of the pipe with a cross and to locate that cross with respect to the center line and to plaster (or to some other set of references in a non-proscenium situation).

*Fig. 4-21: A boom base location*

After this cross is located, "shadows" — broken line outlines or shaded-in shapes of the instruments — are drawn beside it to establish the exact (or relative) location of the position. A label is provided to identify the position, and then a detail of the boom is drawn elsewhere on the plot or on another sheet, and related to the position with a similar label.

The procedure for laying out the detail of a boom with two stacks of 6" instruments is as follows (see Fig. 4-24):

1.  Draw a light vertical line to indicate the pipe, and mark it with small cross lines (tick marks) at the proper spacing

2.  Draw the instrument symbols using one of these two conventions: instruments pointing away, or instruments pointing down. The latter is the more common method but if there are top hats or half hats on the instruments, there will not be enough room for the color notation if correct scale is maintained.

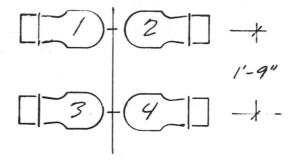

Fig. 4-22: Instruments pointing away

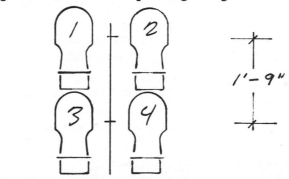

Fig. 4-23: Instruments pointing down

3.  Provide a dimension from the floor to the location of the sidearm of the lowest instrument.

4.  Somewhere near the detail, put this note: "Dimensions to sidearm, units 1'-9" on center". Obviously the center to center dimension could be different.

5.  Adjacent to the detail, put a label which identifies it, and which relates to the similar label at the correct location on the plan.

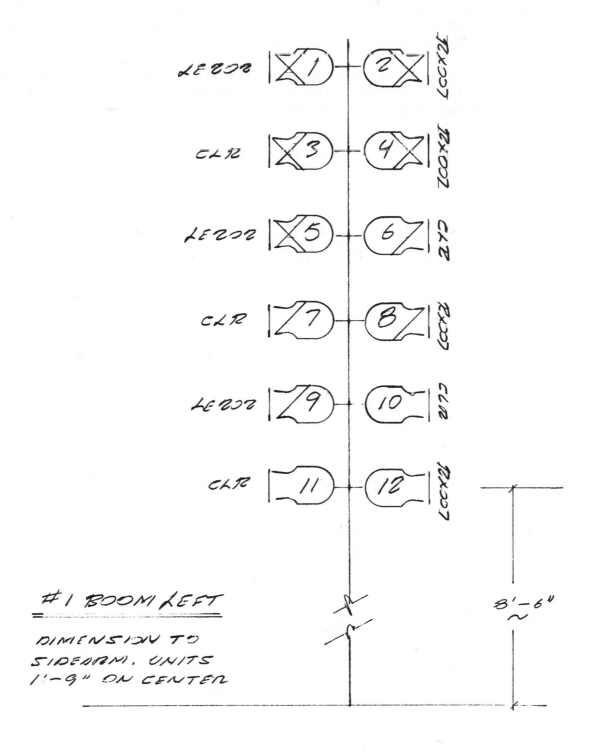

Fig. 4-24: A vertical position detail. Note that the color label may be done either way, depending upon space available. Note also the conventions used when a dimension (the height of the side arm in this case) is not drawn to scale.

There are two other ways of providing vertical position information, both of which might be called "adjacent details". One is the isometric method, and the other the fold-out method. They are both used to relate the position closely to the location on the plan, and they only work if there is enough room to use them. The isometric method is often used for box booms, usually because there is plenty of room on that part of the plot to use it (see Fig. 4-25). While not commonly used, the fold out method can help to explain complex vertical situations such as the one in Fig. 4-26.

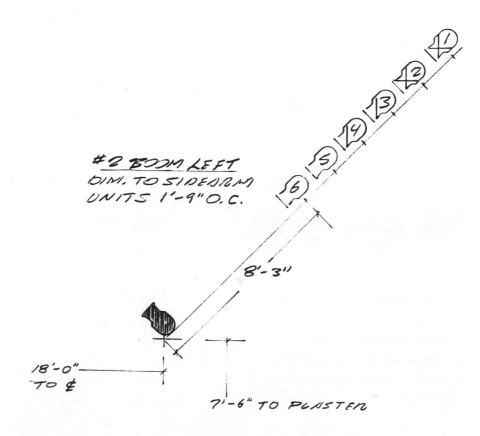

Fig. 4-25: A boom detailed by the isometric method.
Note the use of the shaded-in instrument shadow,
preferred by many because it is bold
and easy to spot on the sheet

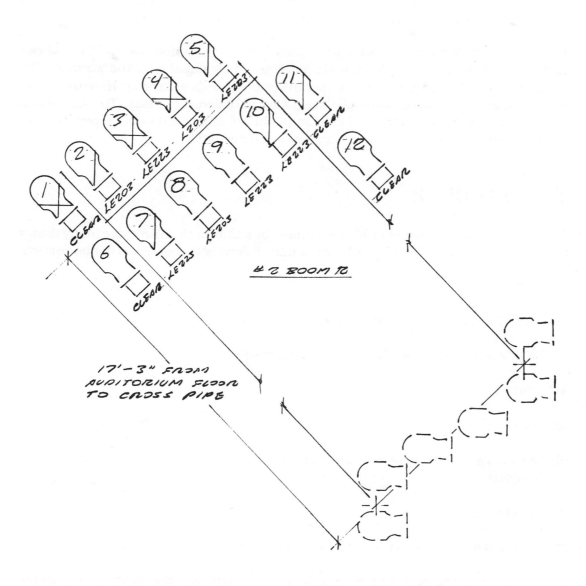

*Fig. 4-26: A vertical position detailed by the Fold-out Method. The position consists of two booms joined by a cross bar with instruments hung over and under the bar. This method differs from the Isometric method in that the "fold" is parallel with the face of the position.*

## The Instrument Key

Every sheet of every light plot should have an instrument key. This is the only way to be sure that the symbols will be interpreted correctly by the crew.

The key, or "legend" as it is sometimes called, is a very simple device that shows each symbol used on the plot and identifies the instrument type and wattage. The key also shows the meaning of any special symbols the designer may have used, and the meaning of such standard symbols as gobos, barn doors, or irises. The key is also the best place to show which pieces of information are to be found on a typical symbol and where. Examples of all of these are shown in Fig. 4-27.

## The Title Block

Every sheet of a light plot should be identified by a title block. There are many things which may be included in the title block, but the following items should not be omitted:

1) The Name of the play

2) "For ...(The producing organization)

3) The title of this sheet (if there are more than one)

4) "Lighting by ......"

5) "Scale: ...=..."

6) "Drawn by ..." (initials of draftsman if not the designer)

7) Date of issue

8) The number of this sheet (often a large number).

The date is important to understand. It is not the date that this particular drawing was completed; it is the date upon which the entire design, all sheets of the plot, all lists, orders and schedules are assembled into one package and issued. After that date, revisions are allowed, but they must be noted on or near the title block so someone looking at the drawing can check the date to find out if this print shows the most recent revisions.

Optional items which may be added to the title block include the names of the author, set designer, director, master electrician, the name of the theatre(s), and the dates of the production.

**LEGEND**

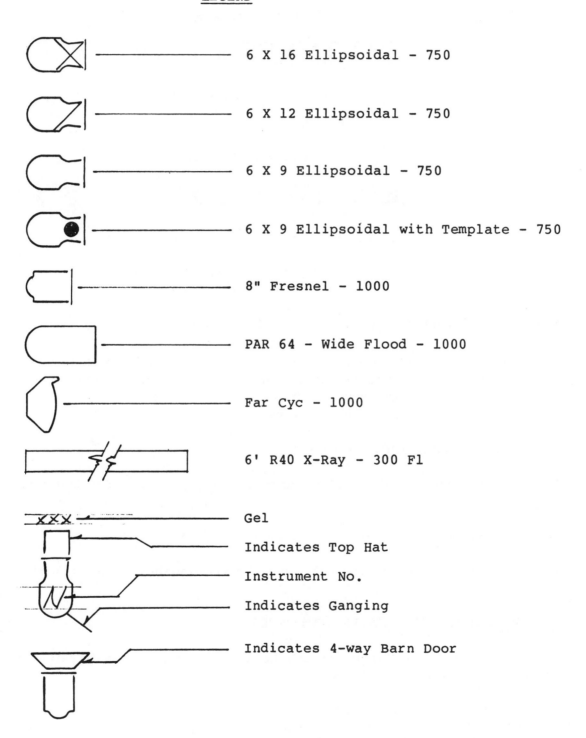

6 X 16 Ellipsoidal - 750

6 X 12 Ellipsoidal - 750

6 X 9 Ellipsoidal - 750

6 X 9 Ellipsoidal with Template - 750

8" Fresnel - 1000

PAR 64 - Wide Flood - 1000

Far Cyc - 1000

6' R40 X-Ray - 300 Fl

Gel

Indicates Top Hat

Instrument No.

Indicates Ganging

Indicates 4-way Barn Door

*Fig. 4-27: The Legend (Key) for a light plot. This would appear on every sheet.*

The title block is always placed at or very near the lower right hand corner of the sheet. This is where everyone will look for it.

YALE REPERTORY THEATRE

## TARTUFFE by MOLIERE

DIRECTED BY WALTON JONES

SET BY KEVIN RUPNIK

LIGHTING BY WILLIAM B. WARFEL

# LIGHT PLOT

SCALE: 1/4" = 1'—0"    DATE: 9/6/84

*Fig. 4-28: The title block for a light plot. This happens to have been drawn by a computer CAD system*

## Other On-Sheet Notes

It is certainly possible to have too many notes on a light plot, but that is a better failing than to have too few. Nothing should be left to instinct, to being worked out in the theatre, or to the electrician's discretion if it is a vital matter. If the practical should be wired through the deck, put a note on the plot to that effect:

"TABLE LAMP - WIRE THROUGH DECK".

If many instruments are to be hung eccentrically from a pipe, a note such as this may help:

"USE PIPE STIFFENERS TO SECURE AGAINST ROTATION".

If appearance is a factor, and you wish to make that clear to the crew, a note such as this is in order:

"PIPE IS IN VIEW, DRESS CABLE WITH CARE".

Anything that needs to be explained should be. The less guess work on the part of the electricians, the better your chance of having an error-free installation.

On-sheet notes should be drawn as close as possible to that part of the plot to which they refer. "Call Out" lines, single lines with arrow heads which point to the items referred to in the note, should always be used if possible, but should be of the proper weight (See Chapter 3 ).

# CHAPTER FIVE: LISTS AND SCHEDULES

## Conventional Lists

The plot almost never tells the crew, or the designer, everything they need to know about the instruments chosen for a production. Even when a good deal of information has been lettered beside every instrument symbol, as in a school plot, the information is neither in a convenient format, nor is it complete. It will always be necessary to prepare at least two lists. Depending upon the particular circumstances, it may be necessary to prepare as many as five. Collectively, these lists and schedules, as well as those described in the next chapter, are known as "the paperwork".

The paperwork that will be discussed in this chapter consists of the lists and schedules that the designer will prepare along with the plot. They are:

1) The Instrument Schedule

2) The Hook-up List

3) The Shop Order

4) The Focus Charts.

Each time an instrument is selected and drawn on the plot, it represents at least twelve decisions the designer has made. The information that results from these decisions has to be recorded in some manner that is convenient for the designer, the assistant designer, and the electrical crew to use. The lists and schedules are designed to make this as easy as possible. The information falls into four groups as listed here.

## Location Information

Each instrument in the production has a unique designation that is based on its location on the plot and that consists of a combination of the position name and the instrument number.

Position:    The mounting position where the instrument is located. "First Cove", "#3 Boom Left", and "Second Electric" are examples.

Number:   The instrument number which is unique to that instrument in the position. There may be a "First Cove #5", a "#3 Boom Left #5", and a "Second Electric #5".

# Descriptive Information

The physical facts concerning the instrument must be recorded. They consist of:

Type: The sort of instrument chosen, such as "Ellipsoidal", "Template Ellipsoidal", "Iris Ellipsoidal", "Fresnel", "Beam Projector" or "Striplight".

Size: A major dimension (or dimensions) that further identifies the instrument type. For ellipsoidals, this will consist of either lens information ("6 x 12") or beam spread data ("40°"). For PAR holders, the lamp diameter ("PAR64") is used. Fresnel lens spotlights are usually identified by lens diameter ("8").

Wattage: The power rating of the lamp chosen, as in "750" or "1K" (K = kilowatt).

# Electrical Information

Dimmer: Obviously, this is the dimmer to that the instrument will be plugged. It is almost always a simple, arabic numeral.

Circuit: The outlet and related wiring that will connect between the instrument and the dimmer. This is also usually a simple number, or it may contain some letters that designate a position.

Channel: In many control boards, dimmers may be patched to control channels in much the same manner as circuits are patched to dimmers in older systems. Thus, the control channel becomes a third entity to be selected and recorded.

# Functional Information

This is the information that relates to how the instrument will be used.

Focus: An indication of that area or object on the stage toward which this instrument will be directed. At the time the plot is prepared, this is usually a very general designation (details, if any, are given under "Notes") such as "USL" (up stage left) or "DC" (down center), "Long" or "Short", "Center Window" or "DL Rock".

Color: The color filter (if any) to be used. If no gel is to be used, "CLEAR" or "CLR" are entered. A blank entry indicates that a color choice is yet to be made.

Name: Some designers use descriptive names, based on function, to group and name the instruments in a system. Thus, they might note in a "Name" column on a schedule that a certain instrument is one of the "Cool Fronts" or "White Pipe Ends" or "Pink Box Booms". This simply provides another way to keep track of a large and complex layout. "Purpose" is a term sometimes used instead of "Name" in this context.

Notes: Any information that should be recorded about an instrument or its function and that is not listed elsewhere can be shown under this category. Items that might appear under "Notes" include accessories such as gobos and top hats, or a special mounting provision.

## Computers and Paperwork

In the earlier chapters of this book the computer has been mentioned as a possible tool for drafting and other tasks. The conclusion usually was that using a computer might be helpful, but not absolutely necessary. For the paperwork described in this chapter, a computer will be very helpful. To prepare the schedule, hook-up and focus charts, the designer (or some unlucky assistant) must write out by hand as many as twelve facts about each instrument in a particular order for each list or schedule. For a modest production of some 200 instruments, that is 2400 unique items to be written three times, or 7200 notations. It is possible to enter each item into a computer once, and then to allow the machine to re-order the information according to which list or schedule is needed. It is almost required to learn how to let a computer do this.

There are computer programs that have been written specifically for the stage lighting designer to use for the preparation of the paperwork, and there are some that combine plot drawing and paperwork preparation automatically. These are very convenient, but they may be beyond the means of a student, especially one who does not plan to continue in lighting design.

For such persons, simple database programs are a help. A little time is required to set up the database to sort and file in a convenient manner; but once that is done, the time saved is well worth the effort.

## The Schedule

The schedule will usually be the first list to be prepared after the plot is drawn since it is used to tell the electricians everything they can not learn from the plot (see Fig. 5-1). The schedule is organized according to the position, and the instruments are listed by number within each position. Thus the electricians can identify a symbol on the plot by position and number and look it up in the schedule.

All of the information in the four categories above should be worked into the schedule, but it is not practical to reserve a separate column for each. As you will note on the example page, several items have been combined. The position is listed only at the head of each section, the size, type, and accessories have been combined, and purpose and focus are joined. If the control system to be used had offered channel assignment (and the designer had decided to use it) an additional column would have appeared next to "Dim".

For the most part, the information remains grouped according to the categories described above. Location information appears first since the schedule is sorted according to it. Then the electrical information appears, followed by the descriptive and then functional information. The only exception in the example is color, which is moved to the last column by the particular program used to prepare it. Taste and personal preference often determine what information will go in which column.

## The Hook-up List

The same information recorded in the schedule must be repeated in the hook-up list, this time sorted according to the electrical information: dimmers, circuits, or channels. Where the schedule was prepared to lead one from a symbol on the plot to the instrument information, the hook-up list leads one from a dimmer, circuit, or channel number to the same information. This time the information is arranged so that the electrical data fills the first column, with the other information following.

By far the most common form for the hook-up is a listing by dimmers (see Fig. 5-2). Many theatres still have patch panels, and many others are wired with loose cable when the production is installed. In such theatres, only a dimmer hook-up will tell people, in an orderly fashion, which loads belong on which dimmers. In dimmer-per-circuit theatres, dimmer and circuit numbers are synonymous, and the dimmer hook-up is still the most useful list unless there is to be channel patching (see below).

In some theatres, it is helpful to have a circuit hook-up, mostly to use in trouble shooting or in replacing a patch cord that has inadvertently come out of a jack on the patch panel. Before computers, it was usually too time consuming to prepare a circuit hook-up, but since the machine will prepare it, the circuit hook-up has become more common. Since the electricians select the circuits as the production is installed, this hook-up cannot be prepared until later in the process (see Fig. 5-3).

```
==========                ====================                Page   1
SARCOPHAGUS               INSTRUMENT SCHEDULE                 06-04-1988
==========                ====================                8  :00pm
Yale Repertory Theatre
September, 1987
Lighting by William B. Warfel
===============================================================================
============
BALCONY RAIL
============
 Unit Dim    Cir   Type            Watts   Purpose/Focus          Color
 -------------------------------------------------------------------------------
   1    1    241   ALTMAN 12       1kw     WARM FRONTS/L          RX051
   2    2    242     "              "      WARM FRONTS/LC           "
   3    "    249     "              "      WARM FRONTS/RC           "
   4    3    251     "              "      WARM FRONTS/R            "
===============================================================================
==============
BOX BOOM LEFT
==============
 Unit Dim    Cir   Type            Watts   Purpose/Focus          Color
 -------------------------------------------------------------------------------
   1   17    15    6X16+TOP HAT    750w    WHITE BOX L/UR         LE202
   2   21    13    6X16A+TOP HAT    "      WHITE BOX L/LOW STAIR    "
   3   16    14    M'ZOOM 15-30    650w    WHITE BOX L/UL           "
   4    "    "       "              "      WHITE BOX L/UC           "
   5    "    11      "              "      WHITE BOXL/DR            "
   6   15    12    M;ZOOM 15-30     "      WHITE BOX L/DC           "
   7    "    6     M'ZOOM 25-50     "      WHITE BOX L/DLC          "
   8    "    "       "             750w    WHITE BOX L/DL           "
   9    1    7     6X9+TOP HAT      "      WARM FRONTS/DSL        RX051
                                           CORNER
===============================================================================
===============
BOX BOOM RIGHT
===============
 Unit Dim    Cir   Type            Watts   Purpose/Focus          Color
 -------------------------------------------------------------------------------
   1   22    59    M'ZOOM 15-30    650w    WHITE BOX R/DLC        LE202
   2    "    "       "              "      WHITE BOX R/ULC          "
   3    "    55      "              "      WHITE BOX R/DC           "
   4   23    56      "              "      WHITE BOX R/DRC          "
   5    "    54    M'ZOOM 25-50     "      WHITE BOX R/URC          "
   6    "    "       "              "      WHITE BOX R/DR           "
   7    3    60    6X9+TOP HAT     750w    WARM FRONTS/DSR        RX051
                                           CORNER
===============================================================================
==========
LOWER BEAM
==========
 Unit Dim    Cir   Type            Watts   Purpose/Focus          Color
 -------------------------------------------------------------------------------
   1    7    98    6X15A           750w    FRONT/L CORNER         RX062
   2    "    104     "              "      FRONT/DL                 "
   3    9    105     "              "      FRONT/DLC                "
   4    7    112     "              "      FRONT/UL                 "
```

*Fig. 5-1: A page from an Instrument Schedule. This one was generated
by Lightwright, a lighting paperwork computer program.*

```
==========                 ==============                    Page  1
SARCOPHAGUS                DIMMER HOOKUP                   06-04-1988
==========                 ==============                    8 :00pm
Yale Repertory Theatre
September, 1987
Lighting by William B. Warfel
===========================================================================
DIMMER INFORMATION:
    Dimmers 1 through 72 are 2.4 kw
    Non-dims 1 through 12 are 2.4 kw

DIMMERS
Dim   Position      Unit  Cir  Type         Watts  Purpose/Focus     Color
---------------------------------------------------------------------------
 1    BALCONY        1    241  ALTMAN 12     1kw    WARM FRONTS/L     RX051
      RAIL
      BOX BOOM       9     7   6X9+TOP HAT   750w   WARM                "
      LEFT                                          FRONTS/DSL
                                                    CORNER
Total Load: 1750 watts
---------------------------------------------------------------------------
 2    BALCONY        2    242  ALTMAN 12     1kw    WARM FRONTS/LC    RX051
      RAIL
       "             3    249    "            "     WARM FRONTS/RC      "
Total Load: 2 kw
---------------------------------------------------------------------------
 3    BALCONY        4    251  ALTMAN 12     1kw    WARM FRONTS/R     RX051
      RAIL
      BOX BOOM       7     60  6X9+TOP HAT   750w   WARM                "
      RIGHT                                         FRONTS/DSR
                                                    CORNER
Total Load: 1750 watts
---------------------------------------------------------------------------
 4    GRID BAY 4    32    163  6"FRES+TOP    500w   WARM              RX051
                               HAT                  FRONTS/BAL L
       "            42     "    "             "     WARM                "
                               HAT                  FRONTS/BAL LC
Total Load: 1 kw
---------------------------------------------------------------------------
 5    GRID BAY 2    63    182  6"FRES+TOP    500w   WARM              RX051
                               HAT                  FRONTS/BAL R
      GRID BAY 3    53    173    "            "     WARM                "
                               HAT                  FRONTS/BAL RC
Total Load: 1 kw
---------------------------------------------------------------------------
 6    GRID BAY 1    11    152  6"FRES+TOP    500w   WARM              RX051
                               HAT                  FRONTS/STAIRS
       "            12     "    "             "     WARM                "
                               HAT                  FRONTS/LANDING
Total Load: 1 kw
---------------------------------------------------------------------------
 7    LOWER BEAM     1     98● 6X15A         750w   FRONT/L CORNER    RX062
       "             2    104    "            "     FRONT/DL            "
       "             4    112    "            "     FRONT/UL            "
Total Load: 2250 watts
---------------------------------------------------------------------------
```

*Fig. 5-2:  Part of a Dimmer Hook-up generated by Lightwright.  Note
that the program totals the watts in each dimmer automatically.*

```
==========                  ===============                    Page  1
SARCOPHAGUS                 CIRCUIT HOOKUP                     06-04-1988
==========                  ===============                     8 :00pm
Yale Repertory Theatre
September, 1987
Lighting by William B. Warfel
=================================================================================
Cir# Dim  Position     Unit Type          Watts   Purpose/Focus      Color
---------------------------------------------------------------------------------
  1  38   GRID BAY 4    11  6X16+TOP HAT   750w    LEFT               LE203
                                                   SIDES/BAND 1 N
---------------------------------------------------------------------------------
  2  70   UNDER GRID     2  PRACTICAL      1kw     PRACTICALS         RX062
      "       "          3    "             "         "                "
---------------------------------------------------------------------------------
  4  39   GRID BAY 5    13  6X16+TOP HAT   750w    LEFT               LE203
                                                   SIDES/BAND 2 NC
---------------------------------------------------------------------------------
  6  15   BOX BOOM       7  M'ZOOM 25-50   650w    WHITE BOX L/DLC    LE202
          LEFT
      "       "          8    "            750w    WHITE BOX L/DL      "
---------------------------------------------------------------------------------
  7   1   BOX BOOM       9  6X9+TOP HAT    750w    WARM               RX051
          LEFT                                     FRONTS/DSL
                                                   CORNER
---------------------------------------------------------------------------------
  9  71   UNDER GRID     1  PRACTICAL      1kw     PRACTICALS         RX062
---------------------------------------------------------------------------------
 11  16   BOX BOOM       5  M'ZOOM 15-30   650w    WHITE BOXL/DR      LE202
          LEFT
---------------------------------------------------------------------------------
 12  15   BOX BOOM       6  M;ZOOM 15-30   650w    WHITE BOX L/DC     LE202
          LEFT
---------------------------------------------------------------------------------
 13  21   BOX BOOM       2  6X16A+TOP      750w    WHITE BOX          LE202
          LEFT              HAT                    L/LOW STAIR
---------------------------------------------------------------------------------
 14  16   BOX BOOM       3  M'ZOOM 15-30   650w    WHITE BOX L/UL     LE202
          LEFT
      "       "          4    "             "      WHITE BOX L/UC      "
---------------------------------------------------------------------------------
 15  17   BOX BOOM       1  6X16+TOP HAT   750w    WHITE BOX L/UR     LE202
          LEFT
---------------------------------------------------------------------------------
 16  43   CATWALK        4  6X9+TOP HAT    750w    LEFT               LE203
          LEFT                                     SIDES/BAND 4 N
---------------------------------------------------------------------------------
 18  41   CATWALK        7  6X12+TOP HAT   750w    LEFT               LE203
          LEFT                                     SIDES/BAND 3 N
---------------------------------------------------------------------------------
 19  20   CATWALK        8  6X9+TOP HAT    750w    WHITE BOX          LE202
          LEFT                                     L/BAL L
---------------------------------------------------------------------------------
 20  18   CATWALK        5  6X12+TOP HAT   750w    WHITE BOX          LE202
          LEFT                                     L/BAL C
---------------------------------------------------------------------------------
```

*Fig. 5-3: A portion of a Circuit Hook-up generated by Lightwright.*
*This list is useful only in theatres where circuits are patched to dimmers.*

The channel hook-up list is essential if the dimmers have been patched to control channels for ease of cue setting. In this case, the dimmer number becomes secondary, much as circuit numbers are in most theatres, and the channel hook-up becomes the hook-up list, the one most often used by the designer (see Fig. 5-4).

```
=========                ===============                     Page  1
LA BOHEME                CHANNEL HOOKUP                   06-04-1988
=========                ===============                       5 :19pm
Shubert Theatre                                       New Haven, CT
Yale Opera
Lighting By William B. Warfel
=========================================================================
DIMMER INFORMATION:
    Dimmers 1 through 224 are 2.4 kw

 Chn  Dim   Position      Unit  Type      Watts   Purpose/Focus    Color
 -----------------------------------------------------------------------
 (  1)  59   Box Boom       7    6X12      750w    Clr Box L 1 x    RX114
             2 L                                   11L
 -----------------------------------------------------------------------
 (  2)  58   Box Boom       6    6X12      750w    Clr Box L 4-6    RX114
             2 L                                   x 11L
 -----------------------------------------------------------------------
 (  3)  55   Box Boom       4    6X16      750w    Clr Box L 1 x    RX114
             2 L                                   CL
 -----------------------------------------------------------------------
 (  4)  56   Box Boom       3    6X16      750w    Clr Box L 4-6    RX114
             2 L                                   x 1R
 -----------------------------------------------------------------------
 (  5)  54   Box Boom       2    6X16      750w    Clr Box L 1 x    RX114
             2 L                                   12R
 -----------------------------------------------------------------------
 (  6)  53   Box Boom       1    6X16      750w    Clr Box L 4-6    RX114
             2 L                                   x 13R
 -----------------------------------------------------------------------
 (  7)  90   No. 1          2    6X12      750w    Clr Box L 12 x   RX114
             Electric                              8L
 -----------------------------------------------------------------------
 (  8)  90   No. 1          3    6X12      750w    Clr Box L 12 x   RX114
             Electric                              2L
 -----------------------------------------------------------------------
 (  9) 103   No. 1          4    6X12      750w    Clr Box L 12 x   RX114
             Electric                              2R
 -----------------------------------------------------------------------
 ( 10) 102   No. 1          6    6X12      750w    Clr Box L 12 x   RX114
             Electric                              8R
 -----------------------------------------------------------------------
 ( 11)  41   Box Boom       1    6X16      750w    Clr Box R 1 x    RX114
             2 R                                   12L
 -----------------------------------------------------------------------
 ( 12)  42   Box Boom       2    6X16      750w    Clr Box R 4-6    RX114
             2 R                                   x 13 L
 -----------------------------------------------------------------------
 ( 13)  43   Box Boom       3    6X16      750w    Clr Box R 4-6    RX114
             2 R                                   x 1L
 -----------------------------------------------------------------------
 ( 14)  37   Box Boom       4    6X16      750w    Clr Box R 1 x    RX114
             2 R                                   CL
 -----------------------------------------------------------------------
 ( 15)  39   Box Boom       5    6X12      750w    Clr Box R 4-6    RX114
             2 R                                   x 11R
```

*Fig. 5-4:  One page from a Channel Hook-up generated by Lightwright.*
*The program always displays channels in parentheses to set them
apart from other numerical sequences*

# The Shop Order

If a production is to be mounted in a theatre that has its own inventory of equipment available, a shop order is not usually required. However, if the equipment is to be rented from an outside shop, the designer is required to prepare a shop order. The format of the list will vary, but two basic forms predominate: the packing list format and the cumulative format.

## THE PACKING LIST FORMAT:

The packing list format is found most often in the professional theatre in New York City. This shop order format breaks down the list of equipment to be supplied according to mounting positions, since that is how it will be packed. Each position's equipment, hardware, accessories, cable, and color are packaged individually and marked accordingly, and the designer's list is used to check each item off as it goes into the road box. The traditional Broadway shop order listed everything required for each position, even the pipe, since the productions would make two or more stops before opening in New York, and different houses present different conditions. Today, such productions usually open with a long run of previews before the press is invited, and they play only one house. Thus, the house conditions are easier to deal with, and certain items (such as pipes when the theatre is already equipped with them) need not be listed (see Fig. 5-5).

Another recent development that has changed the make-up of the traditional Broadway shop order is the introduction of memory systems. Gone are the old "piano boards" with their restrictive loading and heaps of preset boards and plugging boxes. Today, the master electrician will often figure out the cable runs and the dimmer rack locations, removing those items from the designer's list. The following discussion and examples assume that the designer is listing the cable.

## ITEMS TO BE LISTED FOR EACH POSITION:

1.  BASIC HARDWARE. This includes the pipe, the boom or ladder. Examples:

    a.  1 pipe 45' long, or
    b.  1 boom 18' high with flange and top eye, or
    c.  1 ladder 3'0" wide by 6'-0" high with 5 rungs
           1'-6" o.c.

2.  LIGHTING INSTRUMENTS. These are broken down by types such as 6x22, 8" Fresnel, PAR 56 Striplights.

Examples:

> a.　12　6 x 16 - 750 W. ellipsoidal with lamp. c-
> clamp, color frame, or
>
> b.　16　6 x 12 - 750 W. ellipsoidal with lamp, side
> arm, color frame, top hat, or
>
> c.　1　1000 W. worklight with c-clamp.

3.　CABLE. If cable is to be ordered from this list, it should be planned to run from the board or dimmer rack location all the way to the instruments, with plenty of slack to be used to fly the pipes and to avoid obstructions along the way. The distinction between cable and jumpers used to be much clearer than it is today. In the days of piano boards and plugging boxes, cables ran from the board to the light or to a twofer. They had large stage plugs (connectors designed for use with plugging boxes) on the male end, and pin connectors on the female end. Jumpers had pin connectors on both ends, and were designed to go from a twofer to an instrument. The advent of three wire, grounded circuitry doomed the awkward stage plug, and the electronic dimmer racks now in common use are built with pin connector outlets. The distinction between cables and jumpers now seems to rest simply with length and function.

Cables are usually bundled in groups of eight, with outlets spaced so as to fall about where the instruments will hang. Only the longest and shortest cable need be named. For example:

> a.　8 cables 75/120'

Twofers and jumpers to go from the twofer to the other unit in a pair are called out with the cables.

> b.　8 cables 100/140' with twofers and 20' jumpers

When more than one bundle goes to a pipe, they are usually labeled according to length. The short bundle goes to the end of the pipe nearest the switchboard, while the long bundle goes to the far end.

4.　ACCESSORIES AND COLOR. Color may be listed toward the end of the position, or it may be shown in a separate list altogether. The essential hardware, aside from the instruments, also appears at the end of the position's list. Such hardware includes:

> a.　Pipe stiffeners: thin pipes with c-clamps which
> are used to prevent a pipe from rotating.
>
> b.　Scenery guards: hoops 18" or 24" in diameter clamped to the pipe and

used to prevent moving scenery from striking the lights. They are also helpful in getting a loaded pipe into position behind a portal.

c. Skirts: strips of heavy, fire-resistant fabric about 18" wide and ranging to 24' in length. They are used to keep hot lighting units away from direct contact with scenery, and thus to guard against fire. They are listed for any position near scenery. Horizontal skirts are used on pipes, and vertical skirts are used on booms.

5. "GARBAGE". Units mounted alone without specific mounting positions. These are listed as if each were a position. Example:

   a. USC Hallway
      1  10"  400  W  wizard with lamp, mounting flange, color frame.

6.   CONTROL. The control package, whatever its makeup, is listed   at   the   end. Different  rental  shops  have different sizes and capacities of dimmer racks, but the designer  must  state  what  is  needed  to realize the production.  Examples:

   a. 200 20 amp dimmers

   b. 60 50 amp dimmers

   c. Memory control board - 260 dimmers, 100 channels.

7.   EXTRAS.  Found  at the very end of the list are all of the  extra  items  which  do not fit elsewhere. This includes cross-over pipes, chandelier pipes, spare lamps and other accessories.

## THE  CUMULATIVE  FORMAT:

The cumulative format dispenses with the position-by-position breakdown, and simply lists all required equipment by types — instruments first, followed by accessories, cable, and control equipment (see Fig. 5-6). This format is used in most smaller shops which will not ship the equipment packed by positions. Most shop operators prefer a cumulative list to use in preparing their estimates, and the designer may be asked to prepare both.

```
                        BLOOD KNOT

                Lighting Equipment Shop Order

Designer: William B. Warfel                      Oct. 30, 1984
          89 Greenway Street                     Page:  1
          Hamden, CT 06517
          (203)288-8627
```

GENERAL ITEMS
_____

```
    House is equipped with pipes.

    Booms for this production are part of the set, and thus are not called
    out here.

    Box Booms are in place.
```

FAR BOX BOOM LEFT
_____

```
    11   6X22-1000 Ellipsoidal
     5   6x16-1000 Ellipsoidal
    16   Single Sidearms
    14   Circuits, 2 Twofers
    16   Color Frames
    14   Cuts Roscolux
         10 - #63
          2 - #54
          2 - #88
```

NEAR BOX BOOM LEFT
_____

```
    12   6X16-1000 Ellipsoidal
     5   6X12-1000 Ellipsoidal
     8   Double Sidearms
     1   Single Sidearm
    15   Circuits, 2 Twofers
    17   Color Frames
    15   Cuts Color
         10 Lee #223
          2 Roscolux #54
          2    "      #88
          1    "      64A
```

-------------------------------------------

CONTROL
_____

Front End: Strand Mini Light Palette

Dimmers: 100 2.4 KW (allows 8 spares)

*Fig. 5-5: Portions of a Packing List Shop Order*

```
==========                =================================          Page  1
SARCOPHAGUS               TOTALS OF ALL INSTRUMENT TYPES             06-04-1988
==========                =================================             10:15pm
Yale Repertory Theatre
September, 1987
Lighting by William B. Warfel
========================================================================

     7 - 10" BP   @ 750 watts

     2 - 14" SCOOP   @ 500 watts

     7 - 3" FRESNEL   @ 150 watts

     2 - 4.5X6.5  @ 500 watts

    16 - 6" FRESNEL   @ 500 watts

     6 - 6"FRES   @ 500 watts
     6 - TOP HAT for 6"FRES

    40 - 6X12  @ 750 watts
    20 - TOP HAT for 6X12

     9 - 6X15A  @ 750 watts

    17 - 6X16  @ 750 watts
    11 - TOP HAT for 6X16

    15 - 6X16A   @ 750 watts
     1 - TOP HAT for 6X16A

    18 - 6X9  @ 750 watts
     1 - SHARP B'UP for 6X9
    12 - TOP HAT for 6X9

     7 - ALTMAN 12  @ 1 kw

     2 - C'TRAN 30   @ 750 watts
     2 - TOP HAT for C;TRAN 30


     7 - M'ZOOM 15-30   @ 650 watts
```

*Fig. 5-6: Part of a Cumulative Shop Order. This one was generated by Lightwright*

## Focus Charts

The focus chart is a special form of the schedule which is intended to keep an accurate record of the focus of each instrument. The focus chart is prepared using information available from the other lists and is filled in, usually by an assistant lighting designer, during the focus call. The correctly executed focus chart will make it possible to restore the focus of any instrument which has slipped, has been bumped, or has otherwise lost focus during the production.

The focus chart should be made up ahead of time to show all of the information from the schedule that will be helpful during the focus call. The new information which will be entered on the chart will include:

1. Where the designer stood when the light was focused. This will be recorded in feet upstage of the plaster line, the apron, the setting line, or some other fixed location, and feet to the right or left of center. In an arena, some other coordinate system may be more convenient.

2. The shutter cuts of ellipsoidal reflector spotlights. These may be described in words according to landmarks on the stage ("to apron", "SL door frame", or "frame to window"), on a circle diagram, or on a small ground plan.

3. The condition of the lens focus of an ellipsoidal ("sharp" or "soft").

4. The degree of spread of a Fresnel lens spotlight ("full flood" or "1/3 flood").

5. The lamp orientation of a PAR ("up/down" or "cross stage").


One reason to put most, if not all, of the information from the schedule on the focus chart is to save time during the focus. The assistant will have the focus chart, and will be calling for the dimmers to be focused. The charts should be arranged in an order that agrees with the most sensible sequence for the focus, and thus can be used to call for the next dimmer each time. When questions such as: "What circuit is this on?", or "What gel does this take?" arise, the answers are right there.

There are many formats for focus charts. The most elaborate involves a large stack of magic sheets, with the focus information recorded on the small scale ground plans. These are very thorough, but quite time consuming to set up. Most focus charts do not include ground plans, but rather provide blanks to fill in with the requisite information. The two examples which follow are chosen to show both ideas.

```
========                ============================        Page  5
LA BOHEME               FOCUS CHART - No. 3 Electric        06-05-1988
=========               ============================             1 :23pm
Shubert Theatre                                             New Haven, CT
Yale Opera
Lighting By William B. Warfel
============================================================================
Unit                              FOCUS                    Type        Color
----------------------------------------------------------------------------
 1   Ch ( 84) Daytime Skylight               @             8"          LE203
                                  FILL SKYLIGHT            FRESNEL
         Dim 150                  --------- ---------      1kw
                   US             SR                       Sf . + . Hd
                   DS             SL                       Sp . +(.)Fl
                   TP             BT                       Axis:
----------------------------------------------------------------------------
 2   Ch ( 82) Night Skylight                 @             8"          LE161
                                  FILL SKYLIGHT            FRESNEL
         Dim 149                  --------- ---------      1kw
                   US             SR                       Sf . + . Hd
                   DS             SL                       Sp . +(.)Fl
                   TP             BT                       Axis:
----------------------------------------------------------------------------
 3   Ch ( 91) Moonlight Wash       14    @  UR             PAR64       LE201
                                                           MFL
         Dim 157                  --------- ---------      1kw
                   US             SR                       Sf . + . Hd
                   DS             SL                       Sp . + . Fl
                   TP             BT                       Axis: L - R
----------------------------------------------------------------------------
 4   Ch ( 88) Red Festival         15    @  6L             6X9 TEMP    RX041
                                                           750W
         Dim 160    ALL CUTS      --------- ---------      1kw
                      OPEN                                 
                   US             SR                       Sf . + .(Hd)
                   DS             SL                       Sp . + . Fl
                   TP             BT                       Axis:
----------------------------------------------------------------------------
 5   Ch ( 45) White Sides L 10 x 9L  10  @  9L            6X12        LE203
         Dim 147                  --------- ---------      750w
                   US OFF ACT II ARCH  SR                  Sf(.)+ . Hd
                   DS OPEN        SL                       Sp . + . Fl
                   TP TO BASE OF LAMP  BT OPEN             Axis:
----------------------------------------------------------------------------
 6   Ch ( 78) Lavender Wash ULC     9   @  7L             8"          RX082
                                                           FRESNEL
         Dim 146                  --------- ---------      1kw
                   US             SR LITES FACE            Sf . + . Hd
                   DS             SL OF WALL               Sp . +(.)Fl
                   TP             BT                       Axis:(.)
----------------------------------------------------------------------------
 7   Ch ( 45) White Sides 10 x C    10  @  4L             6X12        LE203
         Dim 147                  --------- ---------      750w
                   US OFF ACT II ARCH  SR                  Sf(.)+ . Hd
                   DS OPEN        SL                       Sp . + . Fl
                   TP TO LEG      BT OPEN                  Axis:
----------------------------------------------------------------------------
```

*Fig. 5-7: An example of the Focus Chart format generated by Lightwright. Note that six different shutter cut designations are given. "TP" (top) and "BT" (bottom) are lways used, while the choice of the others depends upon how the instrument is aimed.*

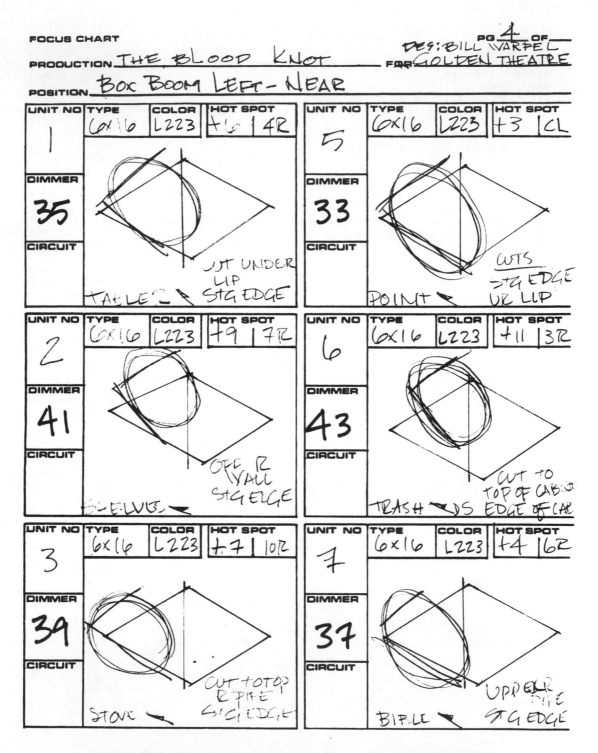

Fig. 5-8: *A hand-made focus chart. The set for the production consisted of only the trapezoidal platform shown. The production was wired as a dimmer-per-circuit, and so the "Circuit" space was not used.*

Filling in focus charts is a job for an experienced, cool-headed person. When the focus is moving quickly, or when two persons are focusing different parts of the stage at the same time, the demands on the assistant are intense. However, the benefits of an accurate, well done set of focus sheets are extensive. No touring production could operate without them. When one returns from dinner on the night of the first preview and finds that the carpenters have moved five units in order to put in some masking, all of the time and effort of preparing focus charts will seem worth while.

# CHAPTER SIX:
# THE REALIZATION PHASE

With the completion of the focus, the designer is ready to bring the lighting to life on the stage. The technical phase is, or should be, complete; drafting and lists have been prepared, revised, and updated. Now, in the realization phase, new forms of paperwork become important. Three classes of paperwork will be discussed and shown in this chapter:

      1) Cue Lists,

      2) Cheat Sheets,

      3) Tracking Sheets.

## CUE LISTS

Cue lists are very simple devices, and it is something of an exaggeration to include them as part of a discussion of graphics. However, certain graphic techniques do apply.

Figure 6-1 shows the first page of a set of cue notes taken in a late rehearsal (before moving to the theatre). The magic sheet form was convenient to use in order to indicate quickly where certain actions happen. This use of the magic sheet was also shown in Chapter 1. Aside from the convenient ground plan, this format offers no advantage over a list kept on a legal-size pad.

Note that the count, the duration of the cue in seconds, is recorded in the list as a number in a circle. As long as no other use is made of the circle device, the count is easy to spot on the page. Also, the page number in the script or, in this case, the score, is given. Naturally, the designer must be working with the same script as the stage manager, since placing the cues in the stage manager's book is one vital function of the Cue List.

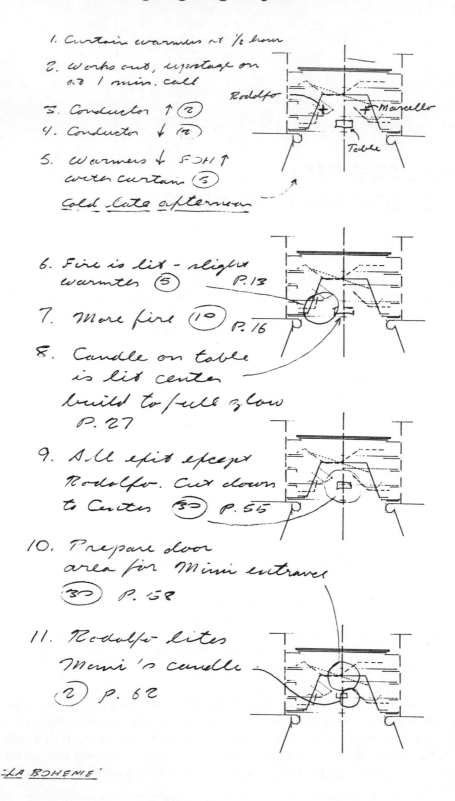

1. Curtain warmers at ½ hour.

2. Works out, upstage on  
   at 1 min. call

3. Conductor ↑ ②

4. Conductor ↓ ②

5. Warmers & FOH ↑  
   with curtain ⑤  
   <u>Cold late afternoon</u>

6. Fire is lit - slight  
   warmth ⑤        P. 13

7. More fire ⑩ P. 16

8. Candle on table  
   is lit center  
   build to full glow  
   P. 27

9. All exit except  
   Rodolfo. Cut down  
   to Center ㉚ P. 55

10. Prepare door  
    area for Mimi entrance  
    ㉚ P. 58

11. Rodolfo lites  
    Mimi's candle  
    ② p. 62

<u>'LA BOHEME'</u>

**Fig. 61-:** *A Cue List for the opening of Puccini's* La Boheme *made with Magic Sheets.*  
*Note that counts are encircled and the page number is given wherever possible.*

# THE CHEAT SHEET

One of the most important pieces of paper the designer will prepare is the cheat sheet. As explained in Chapter 1, this term refers to a piece of paper that the designer has on the desk during technical and dress rehearsals that provides a quick reference to all dimmers and their functions. The idea is that calling for the right dimmer to change the dimmer setting for a certain light or group of lights should be a matter of glancing at the cheat sheet and finding the dimmer number immediately.

The example shown in Figure 6-2 is simply one designer's format. The form of these cheat sheets varies from designer to designer. While it is possible to use several magic sheets to make up a cheat sheet, this is awkward since it is good to make the sheet as portable as possible; therefore, the fewer sheets of paper the better. Whatever the format, it should be remembered that the cheat sheet will be used in a dark auditorium on a poorly lighted desk. Simplicity and clarity are essential.

The example shown is drawn from the designer's point of view during rehearsal. Arrows obviously indicate direction of light. Where two numbers are shown on opposite sides of a slash line, it means that at that given point two lights in a system are focused, one from one side and one from the other. Obviously, the numbers are channel numbers if a dimmer-per-circuit system is in use, but they are dimmer numbers for a patching system.

# TRACKING SHEETS

Tracking sheets are used to keep a record of every dimmer reading in every cue. In the era of lighting control systems which not only store all cues in their memory, but also provide hard copies of the information from a printer, it may seem redundant to have a person sit in the darkened theatre and write down all of those numbers. In fact, many designers have taken the attitude that such effort is wasted, and have dispensed with tracking altogether.

However, many designers can provide proof of the continuing usefulness of tracking sheets. Usually the proof is in the form of horror stories which tell how the disc was erased with all of the cues, or how the machine crashed in the middle of the production and the evening was saved by the tracking sheets. These examples, spectacular as they might be, do not describe the only reasons for keeping tracking sheets.

Tracking sheets are most useful at the desk during rehearsals as a quick reference to previous or future dimmer readings. If, after working with several dimmers in a certain cue, the designer decides to restore the cue to the original settings, copying from the tracking sheet will probably be the only quick way to accomplish the restoration.

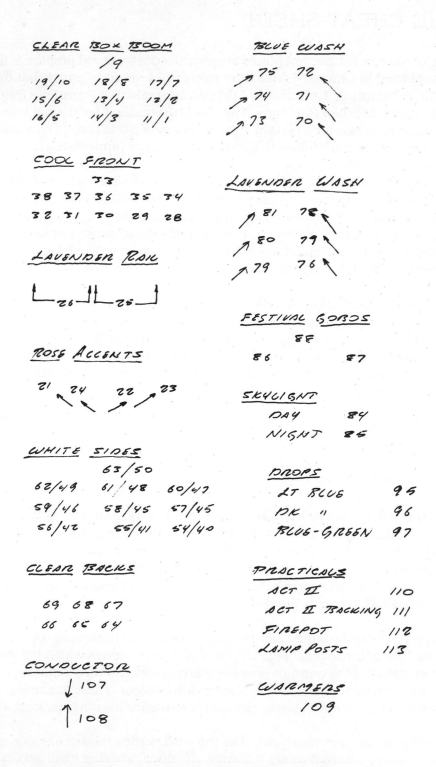

*Fig 6-2: A designer's Cheat Sheet showing all information required to call for specific dimmers during a rehearsal. It is drawn from the designer's point of view in the theatre.*

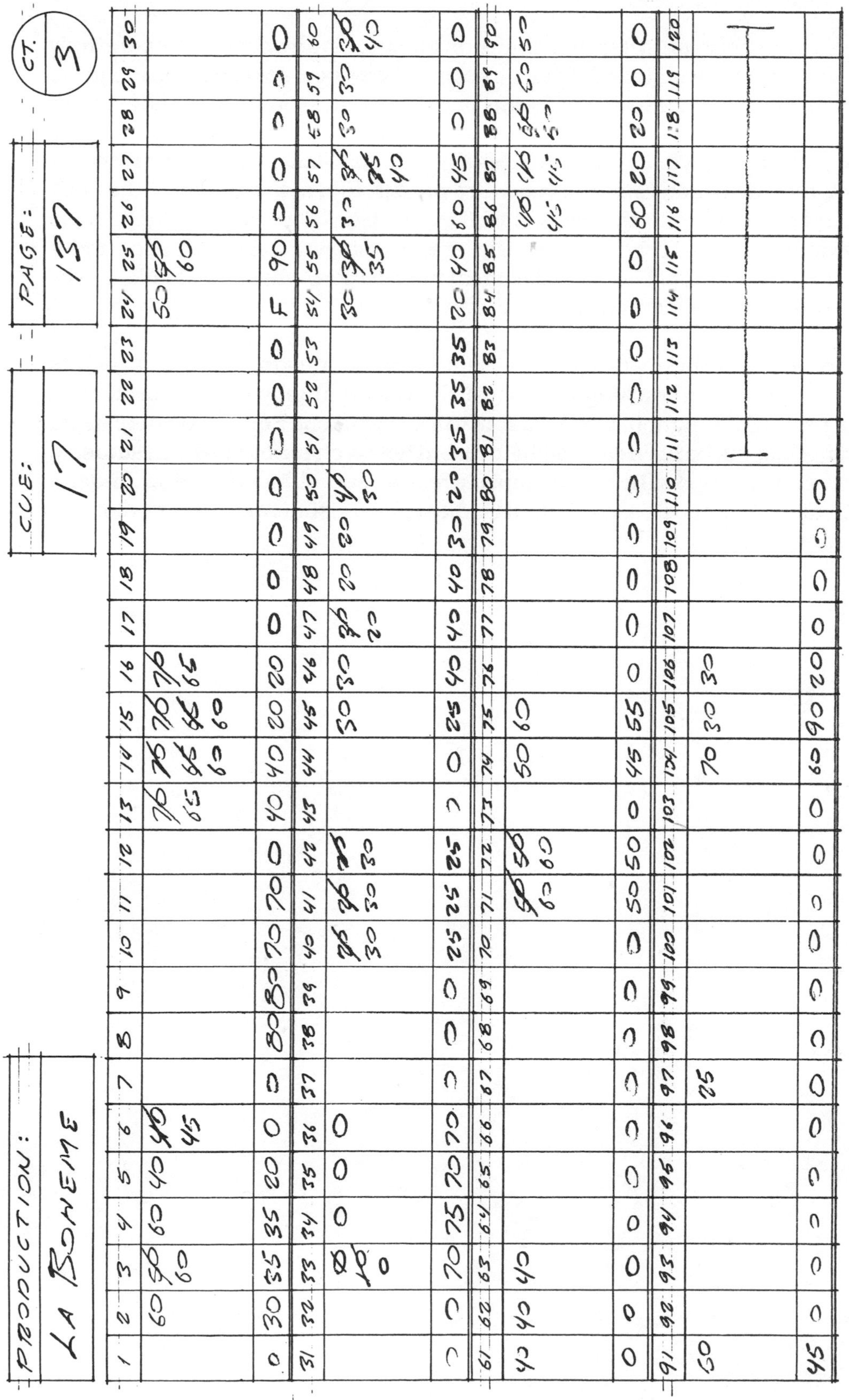

Fig. 6-3: A typical tracking sheet. Each sheet represents a cue with dimmer settings shown in the spaces under each channel number. Readings from the previous cue are shown in the small space at the bottom, while altered intensities are recorded in the long space above. To save time as different readings are tried, the old reading is crossed out rather than erased. The sheet can be cleaned up later. Note that channels 111 through 120 are not used in the production.

While almost all memory control systems can provide output to a printer, comparatively few theatres have printers installed. Thus, tracking sheets become the means to move a production to a new theatre with a different control system. Moreover, in the absence of a printer, tracking sheets are the only means to restore a production to the control system's memory in the event of a sequence of errors or machine failures which obliterate the recorded information. Even with a printer, the tracking sheet is the most useful record. It is kept up to the minute, while a printed record was probably made after the previous evening's rehearsal. In the example shown, the large space under each channel number is used to record current information, while the smaller space records the reading in the previous cue.

Opinions vary as to the best writing instrument to use on tracking sheets. Pencil is the only medium to use on tracking sheets which will eventually be kept clean of all but the most recent information, since erasure will be common. Some designers insist that a different color ink be used each night to record how a channel has been adjusted during the rehearsal process. In the example, when several numbers appear under a channel with all but one crossed out, it indicates adjustments that were made without erasure.

# APPENDIX A

## An Explanation of Photometrics

The definition of the term photometrics is found in the word itself: photo (light) metrics (measurement). Photometrics is that branch of illuminating engineering that deals with the measurement of light.

Only a few simple terms and formulas from this extensive discipline are required for the stage lighting designer. We really only need to know about the performance of spotlights, how to read the manufacturer's data for them and how to take into account the distance of the throw.

*A lamp will burn with a certain LUMINOUS INTENSITY (I), sometimes called CANDLEPOWER, which can be thought of as radiating in all directions uniformly.*

*This LUMINOUS INTENSITY can be measured along any line, and is expressed in CANDELAS (cd).*

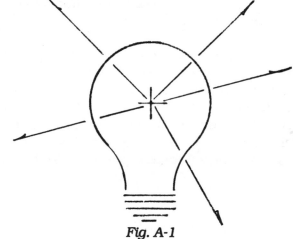

*Fig. A-1*

The candela is an international unit, used all over the world whether the local measurement is in the English or Metric system.

The candela only deals with intensity in a single direction, and does not get involved with the quantity of light. We need to understand the concept of quantity to go on, so it is best to think of the source of light as being located at the center of a sphere. The sphere shown here has a radius of 1 foot.

*If the area of this part of the surface of the sphere is 1 square foot, and if the light source at the center has a Luminous Intensity of 1 CANDELA (1 cd),then the quantity of light distributed over this 1 sq. ft. area is 1 LUMEN.*

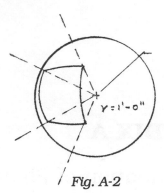

Fig. A-2

The lumen is the international standard of luminous flux (flux describes the continuous flowing of light from a source to a surface). If the source had a Candlepower of 10 cd, then there would be 10 lumens on the 1 sq. ft. surface.

If we took a common light meter and measured the light at any point within that 1 sq. ft. area, we would find that the illuminance (E) at that point is 1 footcandle (fc). Had the intensity of the source been 10 cd, the illuminance would have been 10 fc. Illuminance is best understood as an expression of lumens per square foot in the English system. In Metric terms, illuminance is expressed in LUX, and is equated to Lumens per square meter.

This is all understandable as long as the distance does not change. Lumens and footcandles have a direct relationship to candelas. But, if the distance is increased, the area over which our one lumen is distributed becomes larger, and so the illuminance goes down because there are fewer lumens per square foot. This is the basis of the Inverse Square Law. In our example of a source of 10 cd, if the radius of the sphere is doubled, the area becomes 4 sq. ft., the square of the radius. Instead of 10 we have 2.5 lumens per sq. ft., and an illuminance of 2.5 fc.

*If the distance d2 is two times the distance of d1, then the area of the large square is four times that of the small square.*

*Therefore, if the intensity of the source is 100 cd, and if d1 = 2 and d2 = 4, the illuminance at A = 100/4 = 25 fc, and the Illuminance at B = 100/16 = 6.25.*

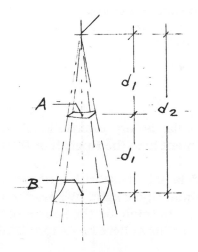

Fig. A-3

You can test the Inverse Square Law against the values shown in the Instrument Performance Diagram shown on page 25.

So, this formula reads:

$$\text{Illuminance} = \frac{\text{Lum. Intensity}}{\text{distance squared}} \quad \text{or} \quad E = \frac{I}{d2}$$

# APPENDIX B:
# INSTRUMENT TEMPLATES

It is difficult to imagine a stage lighting plot which has been hand-drawn without using a template to assist the designer in forming the instrument profiles. While it is conceivable that a plot could be prepared using circles, triangles, squares and rectangles to represent various instruments, it would probably not be very easy to read; and it certainly would not look like a stage lighting plot.

The template, that unique device which every designer needs to make the familiar shapes on the plot, is available from many sources and in a wide variety of shapes, scales, and sizes. However it was not always so.

One of the earliest templates was distributed free by New York-based Century Lighting, the company that survives today as the American division of Strand Lighting. Century used to give away a 1/2" scale template that showed various instruments in section, complete with the yoke (see Fig. B-1). This template is now regarded as a collector's item.

Lighting Associates, originally in Chicago but now located in Chester, Connecticut, makes a broad selection of templates. The mainstay of their line is the Theatrical Lighting Template, which was modified in 1984 in accordance with the USITT Lighting Graphic Standard (see Fig. B-2). This template is made in 1/2", 1/4", and 1/8" scales in both plan and section views.

As a companion to these Theatrical Lighting Templates, Lighting Associates provides a plastic card which describes the USITT Lighting Graphic Standard (see Fig. B-3).

Lighting Associates also makes several special purpose lighting templates, including one for television lighting, one for striplights and other drop lighting instruments (see Fig. B-4), and a template which has rows of 6" ellipsoidal reflector spotlight templates for high speed drafting of heavy shows (see Fig. B-5).

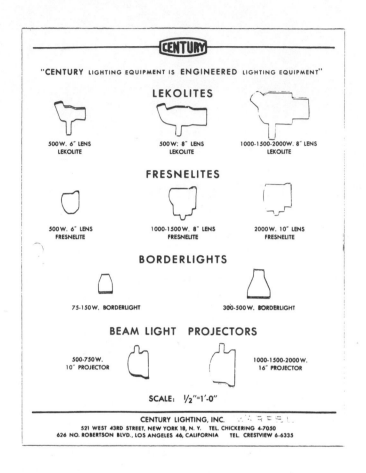

*Fig. B-1: The Century Lighting section template.*

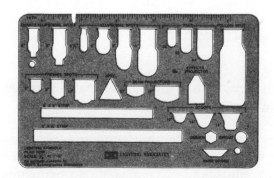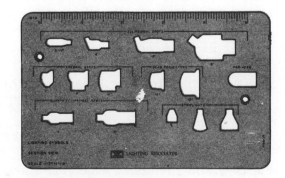

*Fig. B-2: The Lighting Associates Theatrical Lighting
Template in both plan and section views.*

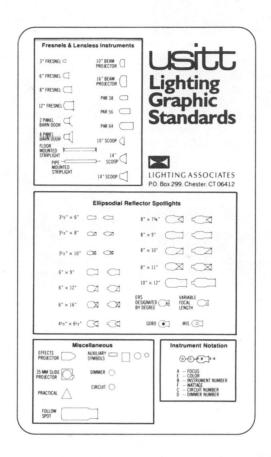

*Fig. B-3: The Lighting Graphic Standard card*

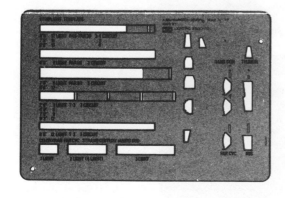

*Fig. B-4: The Striplight and drop lighting template by Lighting Associates*

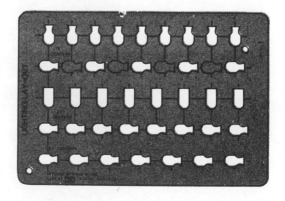

*Fig. B-5: The Lighting Associates Lighting Layout Template*

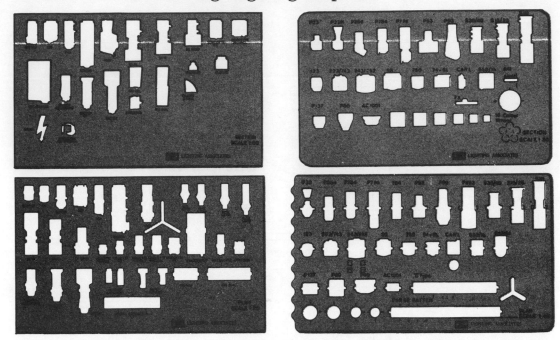

*Fig. B-6: One set of Lighting Associates metric scale templates.*

At the request of Theatre Projects of London, Lighting Associates has produced a set of eight templates that provide profiles in plan and section of 117 different American and European instruments, four each in the metric 1:25 and 1:50 scales (see Fig. B-6). Unless you are disturbed by a tiny scale error, the 1:25 scale is usable as 1/2", and the 1:50 as 1/4".

Finally, a company called End Products, located in Seattle, has produced a special eraser shield which can be used to make corrections inside the most common instrument shapes. This clever device is made from the same thin, rigid stainless steel from which standard eraser shields are made (see Fig. B-7).

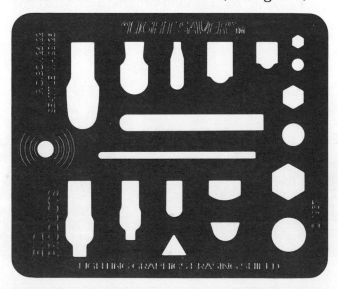

*Fig. B-7: "Lightsaver", an eraser shield intended for
use with 1/2" scale instrument symbols*

At the time this book is being written, Lighting Associates can be contacted at P. O. Box 299, Chester, CT 06412, and End Products at P. O. Box 25122, Seattle, WA 98125.

112

# cocktails

TRADITIONAL AND MODERN COCKTAILS
FOR EVERY OCCASION

## LINDA DOESER

PHOTOGRAPHY BY CHRIS LINTON

This is a Parragon Publishing Book
This edition published in 2003

Parragon Publishing
Queen Street House
4 Queen Street
Bath BA1 1HE, UK

Copyright © Parragon 2002

Original book & cover by
The Bridgewater Book Company Ltd.

*This edition produced by Design Principals*

ISBN: 1-40540-631-3

Printed in China

*NOTE*

*This book uses imperial and metric measurements. Follow the same units of
measurement throughout; do not mix imperial and metric. All spoon measurements
are level: teaspoons are assumed to be 5 ml and tablespoons are assumed to be 15 ml.
Unless otherwise stated, milk is assumed to be whole milk, eggs and individual vegetables
such as potatoes are medium, and pepper is freshly ground black pepper.*

*The times given for each recipe are an approximate guide only because the preparation
times may differ according to the techniques used by different people and include chilling and
marinating times, where appropriate.*

*Recipes using raw or very lightly cooked eggs should be avoided by infants, the elderly,
pregnant women, convalescents, and anyone suffering from an illness.*

# Contents

# Introduction

Precisely where the word 'cocktail' came from is uncertain. A popular piece of folklore describes how a Mexican princess called Xoctl offered a mixed drink to an American visitor to her father's court who confused her name with that of the drink itself. Another suggestion is that the spoon used for mixing drinks reminded

mixed drinks have existed since ancient times and the first recognisable cocktail dates from about the sixteenth century. Indeed, many classics have been around for much longer than most people think. The bourbon-based Old Fashioned, for example, first appeared at the end of the eighteenth century. We know that the

imbibing racegoers of the docked tails of non-thoroughbred horses, called cocktails. There are many other flights of fancy, but modern etymologists mostly agree that the word derives from *coquetel*, a French, wine-based drink. Whatever the origins of the word cocktail,

word cocktail was already in use in 1809 in the United States and, thirty-five years later, when Charles Dickens described Major Pawkins as able to drink 'more rum-toddy, mint-julep, gin-sling, and cock-tail, than any private gentleman of his acquaintance', it had reached Britain, too. Popular among the style-conscious and wealthy in the United States, cocktails were served before dinner in the most exclusive houses and hotels until World

War I made them unfashionable. They have gone in and out of vogue ever since.

Following the war, young people, disillusioned by the elder generation and desperately seeking new experiences, pleasures, stimuli and styles, developed a taste for a new range of cocktails. Ironically, Prohibition in the United States

in the 1920s spurred on their development. Illegally produced liquor frequently tasted poisonous – and sometimes was – so its flavor needed to be disguised with fruit juices and mixers. No doubt, the naughtiness of drinking alcoholic cocktails also added to their appeal to the 'bright young things' of the time. The craze quickly crossed the Atlantic and the best hotels in London, Paris and Monte Carlo, where the quality

of gin and whiskey was more consistent, soon boasted their own cocktail bars.

World War II brought an end to such revelry and, although drunk occasionally, cocktails remained out of style for decades until an exuberant renaissance in the 1970s. This resulted in another new generation of recipes, often featuring white rum and vodka, and tequila, which was just becoming known outside its native Mexico. Inevitably, the pendulum swung against cocktails again until recently. Now, once more, the cocktail shaker is essential equipment in every fashionable city bar.

# Essentials

**Making, serving and, above all, drinking cocktails should be fun. All you
need is some basic equipment, a few ingredients and a sense of adventure.**

## Equipment

Classic cocktails are either shaken or stirred. A shaker
is an essential piece of equipment, consisting of a
container with an inner, perforated lid and an outer
lid. Both lids are secured while the mixture is shaken,
together with cracked ice, and then the cocktail is
strained through the perforated lid into a glass.

A mixing glass is a medium-sized jug in which
stirred cocktails can be mixed. It is usually made of
uncolored glass so you can see what you are doing.

A long-handled bar spoon is perfect for stirring
and a small strainer prevents the ice cubes – used
during mixing – finding their way into the cocktail
glass. Some modern cocktails, including slushes, are
made in a blender or food processor, so if you have
one, by all means make use of it. Any cocktail that is
made by shaking can also be made in a blender.

Measuring cups, sometimes called 'jiggers', and
spoons are essential for getting the proportions right
– guessing does not work. A corkscrew, bottle-
opener and sharp knife are crucial.

## Glasses

You can serve cocktails in any glasses you like. Small,
V-shaped, stemmed glasses may be worth buying,
but it is not essential to have a full range of Old
fashioned, Highball, Collins glasses and so on.
Tumblers, small tumblers and wine glasses cover
most contingencies. As part of their appeal is visual,
cocktails are best served in clear, uncut glass. Chill the
glasses in the refrigerator to ensure cocktails are cold.

## Ingredients

You can stock your bar over a period of time with the
basics – it is not necessary to buy everything at
once. A good, all-round selection of alcoholic drinks
would include whiskey, possibly Scotch and
bourbon, brandy, gin, light and dark rum, triple sec,
sweet and dry vermouth, vodka and tequila. You
could also include Pernod, beer, and red and white
wine. Keep champagne cocktails for special
occasions. Select your stock according to your
tastes – for example, if you never drink whiskey, it
would be extravagant to buy Scotch, Irish,
Canadian, American blended and bourbon.

Standard mixers include soda water, sparkling
mineral water, cola, ginger ale and tonic water.
Freshly squeezed fruit juice is best, but when buying
juice in a bottle or carton, avoid any with added
sugar or extra 'padding'. Cranberry juice, for example,
may be bulked with grape juice. Commercial brands
of grapefruit, orange, cranberry, tomato juice and
lime cordial are useful.

A good supply of fresh lemons, limes and oranges
is essential. Fresh fruit is best, but if you use canned,
buy it in natural juice rather than syrup, and drain
well. Other useful garnishes and condiments include
Angostura bitters, Worcestershire sauce and cocktail
cherries. Finally, you can never have too much ice.

# Techniques

## Cracking and Crushing Ice

Store ice in the freezer until just before use. Cracked ice is used in both shaken and stirred cocktails. To crack ice, put ice cubes into a strong plastic bag and hit it against an outside wall, or put the ice between clean cloths on a sturdy surface and crush with a wooden mallet or rolling pin. Crushed ice is used in cocktails made in a blender. To crush ice, crack it as before but break it into much smaller pieces.

## Frosting Glasses

Glasses can be frosted with sugar – or fine or coarse salt in the case of the Margarita or Salty Dog. Simply rub the rim of the glass with a wedge of lemon or lime, then dip the rim into a saucer of caster sugar or fine salt until it is evenly coated.

## Making Sugar Syrup

To make sugar syrup, put 4 tablespoons water and 4 tablespoons caster sugar into a small saucepan and stir over a low heat until the sugar has dissolved. Bring to the boil, then continue to boil, without stirring, for 1–2 minutes. Cool, then refrigerate in a covered container for up to 2 weeks.

## Shaken or Stirred?

To make a shaken cocktail, put fresh cracked ice into a cocktail shaker and pour over the other ingredients immediately. Secure the lids and shake vigorously for 10–20 seconds, until the outside of the shaker is coated in condensation. Strain into a glass and serve at once. To make a stirred cocktail, again use fresh cracked ice and pour over the ingredients immediately. Using a long-handled spoon, stir vigorously, without splashing, for 20 seconds, then strain into a glass and serve at once.

Classic
Cocktails

# Classic Cocktail

This cannot lay claim to being the first or even the only classic, but it has all the characteristic hallmarks of sophistication associated with cocktails.

### serves 1

wedge of lemon

1 tsp caster sugar

4–6 cracked ice cubes

2 measures brandy

½ measure clear Curaçao

½ measure Maraschino

½ measure lemon juice

lemon peel twist, to decorate

❶ Rub the rim of a chilled cocktail glass with the lemon wedge and then dip in the sugar to frost.

❷ Put the cracked ice into a cocktail shaker. Pour the brandy, Curaçao, Maraschino and lemon juice over the ice and shake vigorously until a frost forms.

❸ Strain into the frosted glass and decorate with the lemon twist.

## Variations

A number of cocktails are the quintessential classics of their type and named simply after the main ingredient.

**Champagne Cocktail**: place a sugar cube in the bottom of a chilled champagne flute and dash with Angostura bitters to douse it. Fill the glass with chilled champagne and decorate with a twist of lemon.

**Tequila Cocktail**: put 4–6 cracked ice cubes into a cocktail shaker. Dash Angostura bitters over the ice and pour in 3 measures golden tequila, 1 measure lime juice and ½ measure grenadine. Shake vigorously until a frost forms, then strain into a chilled cocktail glass.

**Brandy Cocktail**: put 4–6 cracked ice cubes into a cocktail shaker. Dash Angostura bitters over the ice and pour in 2 measures brandy and ½ teaspoon sugar syrup (see page 7). Shake vigorously until a frost forms, then strain into a chilled cocktail glass and decorate with a twist of lemon.

**Bartender's Tip**

Maraschino is a sweet Italian liqueur made from cherries. It is usually white, but may also be colored red. The white version is better for most cocktails, because it does not affect the appearance of the finished drink.

# Sidecar

Cointreau is the best-known brand of the orange-flavored liqueur known generically as triple sec. It is drier and stronger than Curaçao and is always colorless.

*serves 1*

4–6 cracked ice cubes
2 measures brandy
1 measure triple sec
1 measure lemon juice
orange peel twist, to decorate

❶ Put the ice into a cocktail shaker. Pour the brandy, triple sec and lemon juice over the ice and shake vigorously until a frost forms.
❷ Strain into a chilled glass and decorate with the orange peel twist.

## Variations

**Champagne Sidecar**: make a Sidecar, but strain it into a chilled champagne flute and then top it up with chilled champagne.

**Chelsea Sidecar**: put 4–6 cracked ice cubes into a cocktail shaker. Pour 2 measures gin, 1 measure triple sec and 1 measure lemon juice over the ice. Shake vigorously until a frost forms, then strain into a chilled cocktail glass. Decorate with a lemon peel twist.

**Boston Sidecar**: put 4–6 cracked ice cubes into a cocktail shaker. Pour 1½ measures white rum, ½ measure brandy, ½ measure triple sec and ½ measure lemon juice over the ice and shake vigorously until a frost forms. Strain into a chilled cocktail glass and decorate with an orange peel twist.

**Polish Sidecar**: put 4–6 cracked ice cubes into a cocktail shaker. Pour 2 measures gin, 1 measure blackberry brandy and 1 measure lemon juice over the ice. Shake vigorously until a frost forms, then strain into a chilled cocktail glass. Decorate with a fresh blackberry.

## Did you know?

*You can buy 'ice cubes' made from soapstone. Place them in the freezer to chill and use as you would ice cubes. They will not dilute your cocktails and will last forever.*

# Stinger

Aptly named, this is a refreshing, clean-tasting cocktail to tantalize the taste buds and make you sit up and take notice. However, bear in mind that it packs a punch and if you have too many, you are likely to keel over.

*serves 1*

4–6 cracked ice cubes
2 measures brandy
1 measure white crème de menthe

❶ Put the ice cubes into a cocktail shaker. Pour the brandy and crème de menthe over the ice. Shake vigorously until a frost forms.
❷ Strain into a small, chilled highball glass.

## Variations

**Amaretto Stinger**: put 4–6 cracked ice cubes into a cocktail shaker. Pour 2 measures amaretto and 1 measure white crème de menthe over the ice. Shake vigorously until a frost forms, then strain into a chilled cocktail glass.

**Chocolate Stinger**: put 4–6 cracked ice cubes into a cocktail shaker. Pour 1 measure dark crème de cacao and 1 measure white crème de menthe over the ice. Shake vigorously until a frost forms. Strain into a chilled cocktail glass.

**Irish Stinger**: put 4–6 cracked ice cubes into a cocktail shaker. Pour 1 measure Bailey's Irish Cream and 1 measure white crème de menthe over the ice. Shake vigorously until a frost forms, then strain into a chilled shot glass.

## Did you know?

*Bailey's Irish Cream is the world's top-selling liqueur and accounts for one per cent of Eire's export revenue.*

# American Rose

'A rose by any other name...' – this Oscar-winning cocktail has, rightly, inspired roses across the world. It is truly a thing of beauty and a joy forever.

### serves 1

4–6 cracked ice cubes
1½ measures brandy
1 tsp grenadine
½ tsp Pernod
½ fresh peach, peeled and mashed
sparkling wine, to top up
fresh peach wedge, to decorate

❶ Put the cracked ice in a cocktail shaker. Pour the brandy, grenadine and Pernod over the ice and add the peach. Shake vigorously until a frost forms.

❷ Strain into a chilled wine goblet and top up with sparkling wine. Stir gently, then garnish with the peach wedge.

## Variations

**White Rose**: put 4–6 cracked ice cubes into a cocktail shaker. Dash lemon juice over the ice and pour in 3 measures gin, 1 measure Maraschino and 1 measure orange juice. Shake until a frost forms. Strain into a chilled cocktail glass.

**Jack Rose**: put 4–6 cracked ice cubes into a cocktail shaker. Add 2 measures Calvados or applejack brandy, ½ measure lime juice and 1 teaspoon grenadine. Shake vigorously until a frost forms, then strain into a chilled cocktail glass.

**English Rose**: put 4–6 cracked ice cubes into a cocktail shaker. Dash lemon juice over the ice and pour in 2 measures gin, 2 measures dry vermouth and 1 measure apricot brandy. Shake until a frost forms.

Strain into a chilled cocktail glass.

**Russian Rose**: put 4–6 cracked ice cubes into a glass. Dash orange bitters over the ice and pour in 3 measures strawberry-flavored vodka, ½ measure dry vermouth and ½ measure grenadine. Stir gently and strain into a chilled cocktail glass.

**Bermuda Rose**: put 4–6 cracked ice cubes into a cocktail shaker. Pour 2 measures gin, 2 teaspoons apricot brandy, 1 tablespoon lime juice and 2 teaspoons grenadine over the ice. Shake vigorously until a frost forms. Fill a chilled tumbler with crushed ice cubes. Strain the cocktail into the glass and top up with sparkling mineral water. Decorate with a lime slice.

# Mint Julep

A julep is simply a mixed drink sweetened with syrup – but the mere word conjures up images of ante-bellum cotton plantations and a long-gone, leisurely and gracious way of life.

### serves 1

leaves of 1 fresh mint sprig
1 tbsp sugar syrup (see page 7)
6–8 crushed ice cubes
3 measures bourbon whiskey
fresh mint sprig, to decorate

❶ Put the mint leaves and sugar syrup into a small, chilled glass and mash with a teaspoon. Add crushed ice to fill the tumbler, then add the bourbon.
❷ Decorate with the mint sprig.

## Variations

**Frozen Mint Julep**: put 4–6 crushed ice cubes into a blender or food processor. Add 2 measures bourbon whiskey, 1 measure lemon juice, 1 measure sugar syrup (see page 7) and 6 fresh mint leaves. Process at low speed until slushy. Pour into a small, chilled tumbler and decorate with a fresh mint sprig.

**Brandy Julep**: fill a chilled tumbler with cracked ice. Add 2 measures brandy,

1 teaspoon sugar syrup (see page 7) and 4 fresh mint leaves. Stir well to mix and decorate with a fresh mint sprig and a slice of lemon. Serve with a straw.

**Jocose Julep**: put 4–6 crushed ice cubes into a blender or food processor. Pour 3 measures bourbon whiskey, 1 measure green crème de menthe, 1½ measures lime juice and 1 teaspoon sugar syrup (see page 7) over the ice. Add 5 fresh mint leaves. Process until smooth. Fill a chilled tumbler with cracked ice cubes and pour in the cocktail. Top up with sparkling mineral water and stir gently to mix. Decorate with a fresh mint sprig.

## Did you know?

*The word 'julep' is derived from Persian and came to us via Arabic. It means rose-water.*

# Whiskey Sour

Sours are short drinks, flavored with lemon or lime juice. They can be made with almost any spirit, although Whiskey Sour was the original and, for many, is still the flavorite.

### serves 1

4–6 cracked ice cubes
2 measures American blended whiskey
1 measure lemon juice
1 tsp sugar syrup (see page 7)

**To decorate**
cocktail cherry
slice of orange

❶ Put the cracked ice into a cocktail shaker. Pour the whiskey, lemon juice and sugar syrup over the ice. Shake vigorously until a frost forms.

❷ Strain into a chilled cocktail glass and decorate with the cherry and orange slice.

## Variations

**Bourbon Sour**: substitute bourbon for the whiskey and decorate with an orange slice.

**Brandy Sour**: substitute 2½ measures brandy for the blended whiskey.

**Boston Sour**: add 1 egg white to the ingredients and decorate with a cocktail cherry and a slice of lemon.

**Polynesian Sour**: put 4–6 cracked ice cubes into a cocktail shaker. Pour 2 measures white rum, ½ measure lemon juice, ½ measure orange juice and ½ measure guava juice over the ice. Shake vigorously until a frost forms, then pour into a chilled cocktail glass. Decorate with a slice of orange.

**Fireman's Sour**: put 4–6 cracked ice cubes into a cocktail shaker. Pour 2 measures white rum, 1½ measures lime juice, 1 tablespoon grenadine and 1 teaspoon sugar syrup (see page 7) over the ice. Shake until a frost forms. Strain into a cocktail glass and decorate with a cocktail cherry and a slice of lemon.

**Strega Sour**: put 4–6 cracked ice cubes into a cocktail shaker. Pour 2 measures gin, 1 measure Strega and 1 measure lemon juice over the ice. Shake vigorously until a frost forms. Strain into a cocktail glass and decorate with a slice of lemon.

**Double Standard Sour**: put 4–6 cracked ice cubes into a cocktail shaker. Pour 1½ measures blended American whiskey, 1½ measures gin, 1 measure lemon juice, 1 teaspoon grenadine and 1 teaspoon sugar syrup (see page 7) over the ice. Shake vigorously until a frost forms. Strain into a chilled cocktail glass and decorate with a cocktail cherry and a slice of orange.

# Manhattan

Said to have been invented by Sir Winston Churchill's American mother, Jennie, the Manhattan is one of many cocktails named after places in New York. The center of sophistication in the Jazz Age, the city is, once again, buzzing with cocktail bars for a new generation.

*serves 1*

4–6 cracked ice cubes
dash of Angostura bitters
3 measures rye whiskey
1 measure sweet vermouth
cocktail cherry, to decorate

❶ Put the cracked ice into a mixing glass. Dash the Angostura bitters over the ice and pour in the whiskey and vermouth. Stir well to mix.

❷ Strain into a chilled glass and decorate with the cherry.

## City lights

**Harlem Cocktail**: put 4–6 cracked ice cubes into a cocktail shaker. Pour 2 measures gin, 1½ measures pineapple juice and 1 teaspoon Maraschino over the ice and add 1 tablespoon chopped fresh pineapple. Shake vigorously until a frost forms, then strain into a small, chilled tumbler.

**Brooklyn**: put 4–6 cracked ice cubes into a mixing glass. Dash Amer Picon and Maraschino over the ice and pour in 2 measures rye whiskey and 1 measure dry vermouth. Stir to mix, then strain into a chilled cocktail glass.

**Broadway Smile**: pour 1 measure chilled triple sec into a small, chilled tumbler. With a steady hand, pour 1 measure chilled crème de cassis on top, without mixing, then pour 1 measure chilled Swedish Punsch on top, again without mixing.

**Fifth Avenue**: pour 1½ measures chilled dark crème de cacao into a small, chilled, straight-sided glass. With a steady hand, pour 1½ measures chilled apricot brandy on top, without mixing, then pour ¾ measure chilled single cream on top, again without mixing.

**Coney Island Baby**: put 4–6 cracked ice cubes into a cocktail shaker. Pour 2 measures peppermint schnapps and 1 measure dark crème de cacao over the ice. Shake vigorously until a frost forms. Fill a small, chilled tumbler with cracked ice and strain the cocktail over it. Top up with soda water and stir gently.

# Old Fashioned

So ubiquitous is this cocktail that a small, straight-sided tumbler is known as an old-fashioned glass. It is a perfect illustration of the saying, 'Sometimes the old ones are the best.'

*serves 1*

sugar cube

dash of Angostura bitters

1 tsp water

2 measures bourbon or rye whiskey

4–6 cracked ice cubes

lemon peel twist, to decorate

❶ Place the sugar cube in a small, chilled Old Fashioned glass. Dash the bitters over the cube and add the water. Mash with a spoon until the sugar has dissolved.

❷ Pour the bourbon or rye whiskey into the glass and stir. Add the cracked ice cubes and decorate with the lemon twist.

## 'Not old, but mellow'

**Brandy Old Fashioned**: place a sugar cube in a small, chilled tumbler. Dash Angostura bitters over the sugar to douse and add a dash of water. Mash with a spoon until the sugar has dissolved, then pour in 3 measures brandy and add 4–6 cracked ice cubes. Stir gently and decorate with a lemon twist.

**Old Etonian**: put 4–6 cracked ice cubes into a mixing glass. Dash crème de noyaux and orange bitters over the ice and pour in 1 measure gin and 1 measure Lillet. Stir to mix, then strain into a chilled cocktail glass. Squeeze over a piece of orange peel.

**Old Pal**: put 4–6 cracked ice cubes into a cocktail shaker. Pour 2 measures rye whiskey, 1½ measures Campari and 1 measure sweet vermouth over the ice. Shake vigorously until a frost forms, then strain into a chilled cocktail glass.

**Old Trout**: put 4–6 cracked ice cubes into a cocktail shaker. Pour 1 measure Campari and 2 measures orange juice over the ice. Shake vigorously until a frost forms. Fill a tall glass with ice cubes and strain the cocktail over them. Top up with sparkling water and decorate with a slice of orange.

**Old Pale**: put 4–6 cracked ice cubes into a mixing glass. Pour 2 measures bourbon, 1 measure Campari and 1 measure dry vermouth over the ice. Stir well, then strain into a chilled cocktail glass. Squeeze over a piece of lemon peel.

# Martini

For many, this is the ultimate cocktail. It is named after its inventor, Martini de Anna de Toggia, and not the famous brand of vermouth. The original version comprised equal measures of gin and vermouth, now known as a Fifty-fifty, but the proportions vary, up to the Ultra Dry Martini, when the glass is merely rinsed out with vermouth before the gin is poured in.

### serves 1

4–6 cracked ice cubes
3 measures gin
1 tsp dry vermouth, or to taste
cocktail olive, to decorate

❶ Put the cracked ice cubes into a mixing glass. Pour the gin and vermouth over the ice and stir well to mix.
❷ Strain into a chilled cocktail glass and decorate with a cocktail olive.

## Variations

**Gibson**: decorate with 2–3 cocktail onions, instead of an olive.
**Vodka Martini**: substitute vodka for the gin.
**Tequini**: put 4–6 cracked ice cubes into a mixing glass. Dash Angostura bitters over the ice and pour in 3 measures white tequila and ½ measure dry vermouth. Stir well to mix, strain into a chilled cocktail glass and decorate with a twist of lemon.

**Dirty Martini**: put 4–6 cracked ice cubes into a cocktail shaker. Pour 3 measures gin, 1 measure dry vermouth and ½ measure brine from a jar of cocktail olives over the ice. Shake vigorously until a frost forms. Strain into a chilled cocktail glass and decorate with a cocktail olive.
**Saketini**: put 4–6 cracked ice cubes into a cocktail shaker. Pour 3 measures gin and ½ measure Sake over the ice. Shake vigorously until a frost forms. Strain into a chilled cocktail glass and decorate with a twist of lemon peel.

## Did you know?

*Not only did James Bond always demand that his Martini should be shaken, not stirred, but his creator, Ian Fleming, also followed this practice.*

# Salty Dog

This is another cocktail that has changed since its invention. When it first appeared, gin-based cocktails were by far the most popular, but nowadays, a Salty Dog is more frequently made with vodka. You can use either spirit, but the cocktails will have different flavors.

*serves 1*

1 tbsp granulated sugar
1 tbsp coarse salt
lime wedge
6–8 cracked ice cubes
2 measures vodka
grapefruit juice, to top up

❶ Mix the sugar and salt in a saucer. Rub the rim of a chilled Collins glass with the lime wedge, then dip it in the sugar and salt mixture to frost.
❷ Fill the glass with cracked ice cubes and pour the vodka over them. Top up with grapefruit juice and stir to mix. Serve with a straw.

## Variations

**Bride's Mother**: put 4–6 cracked ice cubes into a cocktail shaker. Pour 1½ measures sloe gin, 1 measure gin, 2½ measures grapefruit juice and ½ measure sugar syrup (see page 11) over the ice. Shake vigorously until a frost forms, then strain into a chilled cocktail glass.

**A. J:** put 4–6 cracked ice cubes into a cocktail shaker. Pour 1½ measures applejack or apple brandy, and 1 measure grapefruit juice over the ice. Shake vigorously until a frost forms, then strain into a chilled cocktail glass.

**Midnight Sun**: put 4–6 cracked ice cubes into a cocktail shaker. Pour 2 measures aquavit, 1 measure grapefruit juice and ¼ teaspoon grenadine over the ice. Shake vigorously until a frost forms, then strain into a chilled cocktail glass. Decorate with a slice of orange.

**Blinker**: put 4–6 cracked ice cubes into a cocktail shaker. Pour 2 measures rye whiskey, 2½ measures grapefruit juice and 1 teaspoon grenadine over the ice. Shake vigorously until a frost forms, then strain into a chilled cocktail glass.

**Woodward**: put 4–6 cracked ice cubes into a cocktail shaker. Pour 2 measures Scotch whiskey, ½ measure dry vermouth and ½ measure grapefruit juice over the ice. Shake vigorously until a frost forms, then strain into a chilled cocktail glass.

# White Lady

Simple, elegant, subtle and much more powerful than appearance suggests, this is the perfect cocktail to serve before an al fresco summer dinner.

*serves 1*

4–6 cracked ice cubes
2 measures gin
1 measure triple sec
1 measure lemon juice

❶ Put the ice into a cocktail shaker. Pour the gin, triple sec and lemon juice over the ice. Shake vigorously until a frost forms.

❷ Strain into a chilled cocktail glass.

## Variations

**Green Lady**: put 4–6 cracked ice cubes into a cocktail shaker. Dash lime juice over the ice and pour in 2 measures gin and 1 measure green Chartreuse. Shake vigorously until a frost forms, then strain into a chilled cocktail glass.

**Creole Lady**: put 4–6 cracked ice cubes into a mixing glass. Pour 2 measures bourbon, 1½ measures Madeira and 1 teaspoon grenadine over the ice. Stir well to mix, then strain into a chilled cocktail glass. Decorate with cocktail cherries.

**Perfect Lady**: put 4–6 cracked ice cubes into a cocktail shaker. Pour 2 measures gin, 1 measure peach brandy and 1 measure lemon juice over the ice. Add 1 teaspoon egg white. Shake until a frost forms. Strain into a chilled cocktail glass.

**Apricot Lady**: put 4–6 cracked ice cubes into a cocktail shaker. Pour 1½ measures white rum, 1 measure apricot brandy, 1 tablespoon lime juice, ½ teaspoon triple sec over the ice and add 1 egg white.

Shake vigorously until a frost forms. Half fill a small, chilled tumbler with cracked ice. Strain the cocktail over the ice and decorate with a slice of orange.

**Blue Lady**: put 4–6 cracked ice cubes into a cocktail shaker. Pour 2½ measures blue Curaçao, 1 measure white crème de cacao and 1 measure single cream over the ice. Shake until a frost forms, then strain into a chilled cocktail glass.

**My Fair Lady**: put 4–6 cracked ice cubes into a cocktail shaker. Dash strawberry liqueur over the ice, pour in 2 measures gin, 1 measure orange juice, 1 measure lemon juice and add 1 egg white. Shake vigorously until a frost forms. Strain into a chilled cocktail glass.

**Shady Lady**: put 4–6 cracked ice cubes into a cocktail shaker. Dash lime juice over the ice and pour in 3 measures tequila, 1 measure apple brandy and 1 measure cranberry juice. Shake until a frost forms. Strain into a chilled cocktail glass.

# Tom Collins

This cocktail combines gin, lemon juice and soda water to make a cooling long drink. This is a venerable cocktail, but the progenitor of several generations of the Collins family of drinks, scattered across the globe, was the popular John Collins cocktail.

*serves 1*

5–6 cracked ice cubes
3 measures gin
2 measures lemon juice
½ measure sugar syrup (see page 7)
soda water, to top up
slice of lemon, to decorate

❶ Put the cracked ice into a cocktail shaker. Pour the gin, lemon juice and sugar syrup over the ice. Shake vigorously until a frost forms.

❷ Strain into a tall, chilled tumbler and top up with soda water. Decorate with a slice of lemon.

## Variations

**John Collins**: substitute Dutch gin or genever for the dry gin.

**Mick Collins**: substitute Irish whiskey for the gin.

**Pierre Collins**: substitute brandy for the gin.

**Pedro Collins**: substitute white rum for the gin.

**Colonel Collins**: substitute bourbon for the gin.

**Mac Collins**: substitute Scotch whiskey for the gin.

**Ivan Collins**: substitute vodka for the gin and decorate with a slice of orange and a cocktail cherry.

**Belle Collins**: crush 2 fresh mint sprigs and place in a tall, chilled tumbler. Add 4–6 crushed ice cubes and pour in 2 measures gin, 1 measure lemon juice and 1 teaspoon sugar syrup (see page 7).

Top up with sparkling water, stir gently and decorate with a fresh mint sprig.

**Juan Collins**: half fill a chilled tumbler with cracked ice and pour in 2 measures white tequila, 1 measure lemon juice and 1 teaspoon sugar syrup (see page 7). Top up with sparkling mineral water and stir gently. Decorate with a cocktail cherry.

**Country Cousin Collins**: put 4–6 crushed ice cubes into a blender. Dash orange bitters over the ice and pour in 2 measures apple brandy, 1 measure lemon juice and ½ teaspoon sugar syrup (see page 7). Blend at medium speed for 10 seconds. Pour into a chilled tumbler and top up with sparkling water. Stir gently and decorate with a slice of lemon.

# Singapore Sling

In the days of the British Empire, the privileged would gather in the relative cool of the evening to refresh parched throats and gossip about the day's events at exclusive clubs. Those days are long gone, but a Singapore Sling is still the ideal thirst-quencher on hot summer evenings.

### serves 1

10–12 cracked ice cubes

2 measures gin

1 measure cherry brandy

1 measure lemon juice

1 tsp grenadine

soda water, to top up

**To decorate**

lime peel

cocktail cherries

❶ Put 4–6 cracked ice cubes into a cocktail shaker. Pour the gin, cherry brandy, lemon juice and grenadine over the ice. Shake vigorously until a frost forms.

❷ Half fill a chilled highball glass with cracked ice cubes and strain the cocktail over them. Top up with soda water and decorate with lime peel and cocktail cherries.

## Variations

**Sweet Singapore Sling**: put 4–6 cracked ice cubes into a cocktail shaker. Dash lemon juice over the ice and pour in 1 measure gin and 2 measures cherry brandy. Shake vigorously until a frost forms. Half fill a chilled tumbler with cracked ice cubes and strain the cocktail over them. Top up with soda water and decorate with cocktail cherries.

**Gin Sling**: put 1 teaspoon sugar in a mixing glass. Add 1 measure lemon juice and 1 teaspoon water and stir until the sugar has dissolved. Pour in 2 measures gin and stir to mix. Half fill a small, chilled tumbler with ice and strain the cocktail over it. Decorate with an orange twist.

**Whiskey Sling**: put 1 teaspoon sugar in a mixing glass. Add 1 measure lemon juice and 1 teaspoon water and stir until the sugar has dissolved. Pour in 2 measures American blended whiskey and stir to mix. Half fill a small, chilled tumbler with ice and strain the cocktail over it. Decorate with an orange twist.

# Long Island Iced Tea

Like many other classics, this cocktail dates from the days of the American Prohibition when it was drunk from tea cups in an unconvincing attempt to fool the FBI that it was a harmless beverage. It started out life as a simple combination of vodka colored with a dash of cola, but has evolved into a more elaborate, but no less potent, concoction.

### serves 1

10–12 cracked ice cubes

2 measures vodka

1 measure gin

1 measure white tequila

1 measure white rum

½ measure white crème de menthe

2 measures lemon juice

1 tsp sugar syrup (see page 7)

cola, to top up

wedge of lime or lemon, to decorate

❶ Put 4–6 cracked ice cubes into a cocktail shaker. Pour the vodka, gin, tequila, rum, crème de menthe, lemon juice and sugar syrup over the ice. Shake vigorously until a frost forms.

❷ Half fill a tall, chilled tumbler with cracked ice cubes and strain the cocktail over them. Top up with cola and decorate with the lime or lemon wedge.

## Brewing up

**Artillery Punch** (serves 30): pour 1 litre/ 1¾ pints bourbon, 1 litre/1¾ pints red wine, 1 litre/1¾ pints strong, black tea, 475 ml/ 17 fl oz dark rum, 250 ml/9 fl oz gin, 250 ml/9 fl oz apricot brandy, 4 measures lemon juice, 4 measures lime juice and 4 tablespoons sugar syrup (see page 7) in a large bowl. Refrigerate for 2 hours. To serve, place a large block of ice in a punch bowl. Pour the punch over the ice and decorate with thinly sliced lemon and lime.

## Did you know?

*In 1920, there were about 15,000 bars in New York. Following the introduction of Prohibition in 1920, the number of illegal speakeasies rocketed to some 32,000.*

# Piña Colada

One of the younger generation of classics, this became popular during the cocktail revival of the 1980s and has remained so ever since.

## serves 1

4–6 crushed ice cubes
2 measures white rum
1 measure dark rum
3 measures pineapple juice
2 measures coconut cream
pineapple wedges, to decorate

❶ Put the crushed ice into a blender and add the white rum, dark rum, pineapple juice and coconut cream. Blend until smooth.

❷ Pour, without straining, into a tall, chilled glass and decorate with pineapple wedges speared on a cocktail stick.

# Variations

**Lighten Up Piña Colada**: put 4–6 cracked ice cubes into a cocktail shaker. Pour 2 measures white rum, 2 measures Malibu and 3 measures pineapple juice over the ice. Shake vigorously until a frost forms. Half fill a small, chilled tumbler with cracked ice cubes and strain the cocktail over them. Decorate with a pineapple slice.

**Amigos Piña Colada** (to serve 4): put 10–12 crushed ice cubes into a blender and add 250 ml/9 fl oz white rum, 300 ml/10 fl oz pineapple juice, 5 measures coconut cream, 2 measures dark rum and 2 measures single cream. Blend until smooth. Pour, without straining, into tall, chilled tumblers and decorate with pineapple

wedges speared on cocktail sticks.

**Strawberry Colada**: put 4–6 crushed ice cubes into a blender and add 3 measures golden rum, 4 measures pineapple juice, 1 measure coconut cream and 6 hulled strawberries. Blend until smooth, then pour, without straining, into a tall, chilled tumbler. Decorate with pineapple wedges and strawberries speared on a cocktail stick.

**Banana Colada**: put 4–6 crushed ice cubes into a blender and add 2 measures white rum, 4 measures pineapple juice, 1 measure Malibu and 1 peeled and sliced banana. Blend until smooth, then pour, without straining, into a tall, chilled tumbler and serve with a straw.

# Acapulco

This is one of many cocktails that has changed from its original recipe over the years. To begin with, it was always rum-based and did not include any fruit juice. Nowadays, it is increasingly made with tequila, because this has become better known outside its native Mexico.

### serves 1

10–12 cracked ice cubes
2 measures white rum
½ measure triple sec
½ measure lime juice
1 tsp sugar syrup (see page 7)
1 egg white
sprig of fresh mint, to decorate

❶ Put 4–6 cracked ice cubes into a cocktail shaker. Pour the rum, triple sec, lime juice and sugar syrup over the ice and add the egg white. Shake vigorously until a frost forms.

❷ Half fill a chilled highball glass with cracked ice cubes and strain the cocktail over them. Decorate with the mint sprig.

## Variations

**Acapulco Gold**: put 4–6 cracked ice cubes into a cocktail shaker. Pour 1 measure golden tequila, 1 measure golden rum, 2 measures pineapple juice, 1 measure coconut cream and 1 measure grapefruit juice over the ice. Shake vigorously until a frost forms. Half fill a small, chilled tumbler with cracked ice cubes and strain the cocktail over them.

**Acapulco Clam Digger**: put 4–6 cracked ice cubes into a tall tumbler. Dash Tabasco sauce, Worcestershire sauce and lemon juice over the ice and pour in 1½ measures white tequila, 3 measures tomato juice and 3 measures clam juice. Add 2 teaspoons horseradish sauce. Stir well to mix, decorate with a slice of lime and serve with a straw.

## Did you know?

*Rum owes its origin to Christopher Columbus, who is said to have planted the first sugar cane in the islands of the Caribbean.*

# Daiquiri

Daiquiri is a town in Cuba, where this drink was said to have been invented in the early part of the twentieth century. A businessman had run out of imported gin and so had to make do with the local drink – rum – which, at that time, was of unreliable quality. To ensure that his guests would find it palatable he mixed it with other ingredients. This classic has since given rise to almost innumerable variations.

*serves 1*

4–6 cracked ice cubes
2 measures white rum
¾ measure lime juice
½ tsp sugar syrup (see page 7)

❶ Put the cracked ice cubes into a cocktail shaker. Pour the rum, lime juice and sugar syrup over the ice. Shake vigorously until a frost forms.
❷ Strain into a chilled cocktail glass.

# Variations

**Derby Daiquiri**: put 4–6 crushed ice cubes into a blender and add 2 measures white rum, 1 measure orange juice, ½ measure triple sec and ½ measure lime juice. Blend until smooth, then pour, without straining, into a chilled cocktail glass.

**Banana Daiquiri**: put 4–6 crushed ice cubes into a blender and add 2 measures white rum, ½ measure triple sec, ½ measure lime juice, ½ measure single cream, 1 teaspoon sugar syrup (see page 7) and ¼ peeled and sliced banana. Blend until smooth, then pour the mixture, without straining, into a chilled goblet and decorate with a slice of lime.

**Peach Daiquiri**: put 4–6 crushed ice cubes into a blender and add 2 measures white rum, 1 measure lime juice, ½ teaspoon sugar syrup (see page 7) and ½ peeled, stoned and chopped peach. Blend until smooth, then pour, without straining, into a chilled goblet.

**Passionate Daiquiri**: put 4–6 cracked ice cubes into a cocktail shaker. Pour 2 measures white rum, 1 measure lime juice and ½ measure passion fruit syrup over the ice. Shake vigorously until a frost forms. Strain into a chilled cocktail glass and decorate with a cocktail cherry.

**Bartender's Tip**

For other Daiquiri variations, see page 66.

# Cuba Libre

The 1960s and 1970s saw the meteoric rise in popularity of this simple, long drink, perhaps because of highly successful marketing by Bacardi brand rum, the original white Cuban rum (now produced in the Bahamas) and Coca-Cola, but more likely because rum and cola seem to be natural companions.

*serves 1*

4–6 cracked ice cubes
2 measures white rum
cola, to top up
wedge of lime, to decorate

❶ Half fill a highball glass with cracked ice cubes. Pour the rum over the ice and top up with cola.
❷ Stir gently to mix and decorate with a lime wedge.

## Other Cuban classics

**Bacardi Cocktail**: put 4–6 cracked ice cubes into a cocktail shaker. Pour 2 measures Bacardi rum, 1 measure grenadine and 1 measure fresh lime juice over the ice. Shake vigorously until a frost forms. Strain into a chilled cocktail glass.

**Brandy Cuban**: half fill a chilled tumbler with cracked ice cubes. Pour 1½ measures brandy and ½ measure lime juice over the ice. Top up with cola and stir gently. Decorate with a slice of lime.

**Cuban**: put 4–6 cracked ice cubes into a cocktail shaker. Pour 2 measures brandy, 1 measure apricot brandy, 1 measure lime juice and 1 teaspoon white rum over the ice. Shake vigorously until a frost forms. Strain into a chilled cocktail glass.

**Cuban Special**: put 4–6 cracked ice cubes into a cocktail shaker. Pour 2 measures rum, 1 measure lime juice, 1 tablespoon pineapple juice and 1 teaspoon triple sec over the ice. Shake until a frost forms. Strain into a chilled cocktail glass and decorate with a pineapple wedge.

## Did you know?

*Britain's Royal Navy continued to provide sailors with a daily rum ration until 1969 although, by then, the quantity had been reduced from the original 300 ml/10 fl oz.*

# Zombie

The individual ingredients of this cocktail, including liqueurs and fruit juices, vary considerably from one recipe to another, but all zombies contain a mixture of white, golden and dark rum in a range of proportions.

### serves 1

4–6 crushed ice cubes
2 measures dark rum
2 measures white rum
1 measure golden rum
1 measure triple sec
1 measure lime juice
1 measure orange juice
1 measure pineapple juice
1 measure guava juice
1 tbsp grenadine
1 tbsp orgeat
1 tsp Pernod

### To decorate

sprig of fresh mint
pineapple wedges

❶ Put the crushed ice cubes into a blender and add the three rums, triple sec, lime juice, orange juice, pineapple juice, guava juice, grenadine, orgeat and Pernod. Blend until smooth.

❷ Pour, without straining, into a tall, chilled Collins glass and decorate with the mint sprig and pineapple wedges.

## Variations

**Walking Zombie**: put 4–6 cracked ice cubes into a cocktail shaker. Pour 1 measure white rum, 1 measure golden rum, 1 measure dark rum, 1 measure apricot brandy, 1 measure lime juice, 1 measure pineapple juice and 1 teaspoon sugar syrup (see page 7) over the ice. Shake vigorously until a frost forms. Half fill a chilled tumbler with cracked ice cubes and strain the cocktail over them. Decorate with orange and lemon slices.

**Zombie Prince**: put 4–6 cracked ice cubes into a mixing glass. Dash Angostura bitters over the ice, pour in 1 measure white rum, 1 measure golden rum, 1 measure dark rum, ½ measure lemon juice, ½ measure orange juice and ½ measure grapefruit juice and add 1 teaspoon brown sugar. Stir to mix well, then strain into a tall, chilled tumbler.

**Bartender's Tip**

Orgeat is an almond-flavored syrup. If you can't find it, you could substitute the same amount of amaretto, which is more widely available.

# Mai Tai

For some reason, this cocktail always inspires elaborate decoration with paper parasols, a selection of fruit and spirals of citrus rind – sometimes so much so that you can be in danger of stabbing your nose on a cocktail stick when you try to drink it. If you want to go completely over the top with decorations – and why not – serving the drink with one or two long, colorful straws might be a good idea.

### serves 1

4–6 cracked ice cubes
2 measures white rum
2 measures dark rum
1 measure clear Curaçao
1 measure lime juice
1 tbsp orgeat
1 tbsp grenadine

**To decorate**
paper parasol
slices of pineapple
cocktail cherries
orchid, optional

❶ Put the cracked ice cubes into a cocktail shaker. Pour the white and dark rums, Curaçao, lime juice, orgeat and grenadine over the ice. Shake vigorously until a frost forms.

❷ Strain into a chilled Collins glass and decorate with the paper parasol, pineapple and cherries, adding an orchid, if desired.

## Other decorated cocktails

Generally speaking, you can decorate cocktails in any way you like – or not at all, if you prefer. There are some, however, that are traditionally served in a particular way. The Martini and the Gibson (see page 26), for example, are differentiated only because the former is decorated with a cocktail olive, while the latter is always served with a cocktail onion.

**Horse's Neck**: hang a long spiral of lemon rind over the rim of a tall, chilled tumbler. Fill the glass with cracked ice and pour 2 measures American blended whiskey over the ice. Top up with ginger ale and stir.

**Ultimate Beefeater Martini**: put 4–6 cracked ice cubes into a mixing glass. Dash dry vermouth over the ice and pour in 1 measure Beefeater gin. Stir well and strain the mixture into a chilled cocktail glass. Decorate with a sliver of fillet steak.

# Margarita

The traditional way to drink tequila is to shake a little salt on the back of your hand between the thumb and forefinger and, holding a wedge of lime or lemon, lick the salt, suck the fruit and then down a shot of tequila in one. This cocktail, attributed to Francisco Morales and invented in 1942 in Mexico, is a more civilized version.

*serves 1*

lime wedge

coarse salt

4–6 cracked ice cubes

3 measures white tequila

1 measure triple sec

2 measures lime juice

slice of lime, to decorate

❶ Rub the rim of a chilled cocktail glass with the lime wedge and then dip in a saucer of coarse salt to frost.

❷ Put the cracked ice cubes into a cocktail shaker. Pour the tequila, triple sec and lime juice over the ice. Shake vigorously until a frost forms.

❸ Strain into the prepared glass and decorate with the lime slice.

## Variations

**Frozen Margarita**: put 6–8 cracked ice cubes into a blender and add 2 measures white tequila, 1 measure lime juice and ½ measure triple sec. Blend at low speed until slushy. Pour, without straining, into a chilled cocktail glass and decorate with a slice of lime.

**Blue Margarita**: frost the rim of a chilled cocktail glass using a lime wedge and coarse salt (as above). Put 4–6 cracked ice cubes into a cocktail shaker. Pour 2 measures white tequila, 1 measure blue Curaçao, 1½ measures lime juice and 1 tablespoon triple sec over the ice. Shake vigorously until a frost forms. Strain into the prepared glass and decorate with a slice of lime.

**Margarita Impériale**: put 4–6 cracked ice cubes into a cocktail shaker. Dash clear Curaçao over the ice and pour in 1 measure white tequila, 1 measure Mandarine Napoléon and 1 measure lemon juice. Shake vigorously until a frost forms. Strain into a chilled cocktail glass.

**Peach Margarita**: frost the rim of a chilled cocktail glass using a lime wedge and coarse salt (as above). Put 4–6 cracked ice cubes into a cocktail shaker. Pour 2 measures white tequila, 2 measures lime juice, ½ measure peach liqueur and 1 tablespoon triple sec over the ice. Shake vigorously until a frost forms, then strain into the prepared glass. Decorate with a fresh peach slice.

# Tequila Sunrise

This is one cocktail you shouldn't rush when making, otherwise you will spoil the attractive sunrise effect as the grenadine slowly spreads through the orange juice.

### serves 1

4–6 cracked ice cubes
2 parts white tequila
orange juice, to top up
1 measure grenadine

❶ Put the cracked ice cubes into a chilled highball glass. Pour the tequila over the ice and top up with the orange juice. Stir well to mix.

❷ Slowly pour in the grenadine and serve with a straw.

## Variations

**Blinding Sunrise**: put 4–6 cracked ice cubes into a cocktail shaker. Pour 1 measure white tequila, 1 measure vodka, 3 measures orange juice and 1 teaspoon triple sec over the ice. Shake vigorously until a frost forms. Half fill a tumbler with cracked ice cubes and strain the cocktail over them. Slowly pour in 1 measure grenadine.

**Pacific Sunrise**: put 4–6 cracked ice cubes into a cocktail shaker. Dash Angostura bitters over the ice and pour in 1 measure white tequila, 1 measure blue Curaçao and 1 measure lime juice. Shake vigorously until a frost forms, then strain into a chilled cocktail glass.

**Mint Sunrise**: put 4–6 cracked ice cubes into a chilled tumbler. Pour 1½ measures Scotch whiskey, ½ measure brandy and ½ measure clear Curaçao over the ice and stir gently. Decorate with a fresh mint sprig and a slice of lemon.

## Did you know?

*The global popularity of tequila took producers by surprise. The agave plant from which it is made takes 8–10 years to mature: due to this long maturation time, and cultivation problems that subsequently developed, a severe shortage arose by the year 2000, which resulted in rocketing prices and a lucrative trade in 'cactus rustling'.*

# Bloody Mary

This classic cocktail was invented in 1921 at the legendary Harry's Bar in Paris. There are numerous versions – some much hotter and spicier than others. Ingredients may include horseradish sauce in addition to or instead of Tabasco sauce, more or less tomato juice, and lime juice instead of lemon. Sometimes the glass is decorated with a sprig of mint. Whatever the version, all experts agree that it is essential to use the highest-quality ingredients.

*serves 1*

4–6 cracked ice cubes
dash of Worcestershire sauce
dash of Tabasco sauce
2 measures vodka
6 measures tomato juice
juice of ½ lemon
pinch of celery salt
pinch of cayenne pepper

**To decorate**
celery stick with leaves
slice of lemon

❶ Put the cracked ice into a cocktail shaker. Dash the Worcestershire sauce and Tabasco sauce over the ice and pour in the vodka, tomato juice and lemon juice. Shake vigorously until a frost forms. ❷ Strain into a tall, chilled glass, add a pinch of celery salt and a pinch of cayenne and decorate with a celery stick and a slice of lemon.

# Variations

**Bloody Maria**: substitute 2 measures white tequila for the vodka and add 1 teaspoon horseradish sauce and a pinch of ground coriander. Decorate with a lime wedge.

**Cold and Clammy Bloody Mary**: substitute 3 measures clam juice for 3 of the measures of tomato juice and decorate with a spring onion curl.

**Bullshot**: substitute 4 measures chilled beef stock for the tomato juice and season with salt and freshly ground black pepper.

# Moscow Mule

This cocktail came into existence through a happy coincidence during the 1930s. An American bar owner had overstocked ginger beer, and a representative of a soft drinks company invented the Moscow Mule to help him out.

## serves 1

10–12 cracked ice cubes
2 measures vodka
1 measure lime juice
ginger beer, to top up
slice of lime, to decorate

❶ Put 4–6 cracked ice cubes into a cocktail shaker. Pour the vodka and lime juice over the ice. Shake vigorously until a frost forms.

❷ Half fill a chilled highball glass with cracked ice cubes and strain the cocktail over them. Top up with ginger beer. Decorate with a slice of lime.

## Other stubborn drinks

**Delft Donkey**: make a Moscow Mule but substitute gin for the vodka.

**Mississippi Mule**: put 4–6 cracked ice cubes into a cocktail shaker. Pour 2 measures gin, ½ measure crème de cassis and ½ measure lemon juice over the ice. Shake vigorously until a frost forms, then strain into a small, chilled tumbler.

**Mule's Hind Leg**: put 4–6 cracked ice cubes into a cocktail shaker. Pour ½ measure apricot brandy, ½ measure apple brandy, ½ measure Bénédictine, ½ measure gin and ½ measure maple syrup over the ice. Shake vigorously until a frost forms, then strain into a chilled cocktail glass.

**Jamaica Mule**: put 4–6 cracked ice cubes into a cocktail shaker. Pour 2 measures white rum, 1 measure dark rum, 1 measure golden rum, 1 measure Falernum and 1 measure lime juice over the ice. Shake vigorously until a frost forms, then strain the mixture into a tall, chilled tumbler. Top up with ginger beer and then decorate with some pineapple wedges and crystallized ginger.

# Screwdriver

Always use freshly squeezed orange juice to make this refreshing cocktail – it is just not the same with bottled juice. This simple, classic cocktail has given rise to numerous and increasingly elaborate variations.

*serves 1*

6–8 cracked ice cubes
2 measures vodka
orange juice, to top up
slice of orange, to decorate

❶ Fill a chilled highball glass with cracked ice cubes. Pour the vodka over the ice and top up with orange juice.

❷ Stir well to mix and decorate with a slice of orange.

## Variations

**Cordless Screwdriver**: pour 2 measures chilled vodka into a shot glass. Dip a wedge of orange into caster sugar. Down the vodka in one go and suck the orange.

**Creamy Screwdriver**: put 4–6 crushed ice cubes into a blender and add 2 measures vodka, 6 measures orange juice, 1 egg yolk and ½ teaspoon sugar syrup (see page 7). Blend until smooth. Half fill a tall, chilled tumbler with cracked ice cubes and pour the cocktail over them without straining.

**Harvey Wallbanger**: make a Screwdriver, then float 1 measure Galliano on top by pouring it gently over the back of a teaspoon.

**Slow Screw**: substitute sloe gin for the vodka.

**Bartender's Tip**
Galliano is a honey- and vanilla-flavored liqueur from Italy. It is sold in tall thin bottles, so bars store it on a top shelf up against the wall to avoid knocking it over.

## Did you know?

*The Harvey Wallbanger is named after a California surfer who took such prodigious delight in drinking Screwdrivers topped with a Galliano float that he ricocheted from wall to wall on leaving the bar.*

# Kir

As with the best mustard, crème de cassis production is centred on the French city of Dijon. This cocktail is named in commemoration of a partisan and mayor of the city, Félix Kir.

*serves 1*

4–6 cracked ice cubes
2 measures crème de cassis
white wine, to top up
twist of lemon peel, to decorate

❶ Put the crushed ice cubes into a chilled wine glass. Pour the crème de cassis over the ice.

❷ Top up with chilled white wine and stir well. Decorate with the lemon twist.

## Wine toppers

**Kir Royale**: substitute champagne for the white wine.

**Osborne** (named after Queen Victoria's Isle of Wight residence and apparently a flavorite tipple of Her Majesty's): pour 3 measures claret and 1 measure Scotch whiskey into a goblet and stir to mix.

**Bellini** (created at Harry's Bar, Venice, and named after the Renaissance artist): fill a goblet with crushed ice and dash over grenadine. Pour in 1 measure peach juice, then top up with chilled champagne. Decorate with a peeled, fresh peach slice.

**Bellinitini**: put 4–6 cracked ice cubes into a cocktail shaker. Pour in 2 measures vodka, 1 measure peach schnapps and 1 measure peach juice.

Shake vigorously until a frost forms, then strain into a chilled goblet. Top up with chilled champagne.

**Rikki-Tikki-Tavi**: put a sugar cube into a chilled champagne flute and dash Angostura bitters over it until red but still intact. Pour in 1 teaspoon brandy and 1 teaspoon clear Curaçao and top up with chilled champagne.

**Champagne Pick-me-up**: put 4–6 cracked ice cubes into a cocktail shaker. Dash grenadine over the ice and then pour in 2 measures brandy, 1 measure orange juice and 1 measure lemon juice. Shake vigorously until a frost forms. Strain the mixture into a wine glass and then top up with chilled champagne.

# Buck's Fizz

Invented at Buck's Club in London, the original was invariably made with Bollinger champagne and it is true that the better the quality of the champagne, the better the flavor.

*serves 1*

2 measures chilled champagne
2 measures chilled orange juice

❶ Pour the champagne into a chilled champagne flute, then pour in the orange juice.

## Variations

**Duck's Fizz**: substitute Canard-Duchêne champagne for the Bollinger.

**Mimosa**: pour the orange juice into the flute and then the champagne. Stir gently. You can use sparkling white wine instead of champagne.

**Black Velvet**: pour 300 ml/10 fl oz chilled champagne or sparkling wine and 300 ml/10 fl oz chilled stout into a chilled tumbler at the same time. Do not stir.

**Soyer au Champagne**: put 1 scoop vanilla ice cream into a wine glass and add ¼ teaspoon brandy, ¼ teaspoon triple sec

and ¼ teaspoon Maraschino. Stir to mix, then top up with chilled champagne. Stir gently and decorate with a cocktail cherry.

**Champagne Cup**: pour ½ measure brandy and ½ measure clear Curaçao into a chilled wine glass. Add 1 ice cube and top up with champagne. Decorate with a sprig of fresh mint and a slice of orange.

**Spritzer**: fill a wine glass with cracked ice cubes and pour in 3 measures white wine. Top up with soda water or sparkling mineral water and decorate with a twist of lemon peel.

## Did you know?

*In spite of his ruthless ambition and Prussian earnestness, Otto von Bismarck must have had a more frivolous side to his nature because he is reputed to have created the Black Velvet.*

# Contemporary
# Cocktails

# Frozen Daiquiri

One of the great classic cocktails, the Daiquiri (see page 42) has moved on. It's not just mixed with fresh fruit or unusual ingredients, it's entered the twenty-first century with a whole new future, as slushes take on a leading role in fashionable cocktail bars.

## serves 1

6 crushed ice cubes
2 measures white rum
1 measure lime juice
1 tsp sugar syrup (see page 7)
slice of lime, to decorate

❶ Put the crushed ice into a blender and add the rum, lime juice and sugar syrup. Blend until slushy.
❷ Pour into a chilled champagne flute and decorate with the lime slice.

## Variations

**Frozen Pineapple Daiquiri**: put 6 crushed ice cubes into a blender and add 2 measures white rum, 1 measure lime juice, ½ teaspoon pineapple syrup and 60 g/2 oz finely chopped fresh pineapple. Blend until slushy, then pour into a chilled cocktail glass. Decorate with pineapple wedges.

**Frozen Mint Daiquiri**: put 6 crushed ice cubes into a blender and add 2 measures white rum, ½ measure lime juice, 1 teaspoon sugar syrup (see page 7) and 6 fresh mint leaves. Blend until slushy, then pour into a chilled cocktail glass.

**Frozen Strawberry Daiquiri**: put 6 crushed ice cubes into a blender and add 2 measures white rum, 1 measure lime juice, 1 teaspoon sugar syrup (see page 7) and 6 fresh or frozen strawberries. Blend until slushy. Pour into a chilled cocktail glass. Decorate with a strawberry.

**Frozen Peach Daiquiri**: put 6 crushed ice cubes into a blender. Add 2 measures white rum, 1 measure lime juice, 1 teaspoon sugar syrup (see page 7) and ½ peeled, stoned and chopped peach. Blend until slushy. Pour into a chilled cocktail glass. Decorate with a slice of peach.

# Tequila Slammer

Slammers, also known as shooters, are currently very fashionable. The idea is that you pour the different ingredients directly into the glass, without stirring (some slammers form colorful layers). Cover the top of the glass with one hand to prevent spillage, then slam the glass on the bar or a table to mix and drink the cocktail down in one. It is essential to use a strong glass that is unlikely to break under such treatment.

*serves 1*

1 measure white tequila
1 measure lemon juice
chilled sparkling wine, to top up

❶ Put the tequila and lemon juice into a chilled glass and stir to mix. Top up with sparkling wine.
❷ Cover the glass with your hand and slam.

## 'Those little shooters, how I love to drink them down...'

**Alabama Slammer**: put 4–6 cracked ice cubes into a mixing glass. Pour 1 measure Southern Comfort, 1 measure amaretto and ½ measure sloe gin over the ice and stir to mix. Strain into a shot glass and add ½ teaspoon lemon juice. Cover and slam.

**B52**: pour 1 measure chilled dark crème de cacao into a shot glass. With a steady hand, gently pour in 1 measure chilled Bailey's Irish Cream to make a second layer, then gently pour in 1 measure chilled Grand Marnier. Cover and slam.

**B52** (second version): pour 1 measure chilled Kahlúa into a shot glass. With a steady hand, gently pour in 1 measure chilled Bailey's Irish Cream to make a second layer, then gently pour in 1 measure chilled Grand Marnier. Cover and slam.

**Banana Slip**: pour 1 measure chilled crème de banane into a shot glass. With a steady hand, gently pour in 1 measure chilled Bailey's Irish Cream to make a second layer. Cover and slam.

# Wild Night Out

Tequila has a reputation for being an extraordinarily potent spirit, but most commercially exported brands are the same standard strength as other spirits, such as gin or whiskey. 'Home-grown' tequila or its close relative, *mescal*, may be another matter.

*serves 1*

4–6 cracked ice cubes
3 measures white tequila
2 measures cranberry juice
1 measure lime juice
soda water, to top up

❶ Put the cracked ice cubes into a cocktail shaker. Pour the tequila, cranberry juice and lime juice over the ice. Shake vigorously until a frost forms. ❷ Half fill a chilled highball glass with cracked ice cubes and strain the cocktail over them. Add soda water to taste.

## The wild bunch

**Buttafuoco**: put 4–6 cracked ice cubes into a cocktail shaker. Pour 2 measures white tequila, ½ measure Galliano, ½ measure cherry brandy and ½ measure lemon juice over the ice. Shake vigorously until a frost forms. Half fill a tumbler with cracked ice cubes and strain the cocktail over them. Top up with soda water and decorate with a cocktail cherry.

**Magna Carta**: rub the rim of a wine glass with a wedge of lime, then dip in caster sugar to frost. Put 4–6 cracked ice cubes into a mixing glass. Pour 2 measures white tequila and 1 measure triple sec over the ice and stir well to mix. Strain into the prepared glass and top up with chilled sparkling wine.

**Tequila Fizz**: put 4–6 cracked ice cubes into a cocktail shaker. Pour 3 measures white tequila, 1 measure grenadine and 1 measure lime juice over the ice and add 1 egg white. Shake vigorously until a frost forms. Half fill a chilled tumbler with cracked ice cubes and strain the cocktail over them. Top up with ginger ale.

**Changuirongo**: half fill a tall, chilled tumbler with cracked ice cubes. Pour 2 measures white tequila over the ice and top up with ginger ale. Stir gently and decorate with a slice of lime.

# Carolina

White tequila is most commonly used for mixing cocktails, but some require the more mellow flavor of the amber-colored, aged tequilas, which are known as golden tequila or *añejo*.

### serves 1

4–6 cracked ice cubes
3 measures golden tequila
1 tsp grenadine
1 tsp vanilla essence
1 measure single cream
1 egg white

**To decorate**
ground cinnamon
cocktail cherry

❶ Put the cracked ice cubes into a cocktail shaker. Pour the tequila, grenadine, vanilla and cream over the ice and add the egg white. Shake vigorously until a frost forms.
❷ Strain into a chilled cocktail glass. Sprinkle with cinnamon and decorate with a cocktail cherry.

## The golden touch

**Grapeshot**: put 4–6 cracked ice cubes into a cocktail shaker. Pour 2 measures golden tequila, 1 measure clear Curaçao and 1½ measures white grape juice over the ice and shake vigorously until a frost forms. Strain into a chilled cocktail glass.

**Montezuma**: put 4–6 crushed ice cubes into a blender and add 2 measures golden tequila, 1 measure Madeira and 1 egg yolk. Blend until smooth, then pour into a chilled cocktail glass.

**Chapala**: put 4–6 cracked ice cubes into a cocktail shaker. Pour 2 measures golden tequila, 2 measures orange juice, 1 measure lime juice, ½ measure triple sec and ½ measure grenadine over the ice. Shake vigorously until a frost forms. Half fill a chilled tumbler with cracked ice cubes and strain the cocktail over them.

**Piñata**: put 4–6 cracked ice cubes into a cocktail shaker. Pour 2 measures golden tequila, 1 measure crème de banane and 1½ measures lime juice over the ice and shake vigorously until a frost forms. Strain the mixture into a chilled cocktail glass.

# Crocodile

This is certainly a snappy cocktail with a bit of bite. However, it probably gets its name from its spectacular color – Midori, a Japanese melon-flavored liqueur, which is a startling shade of green.

*serves 1*

4–6 cracked ice cubes

2 measures vodka

1 measure triple sec

1 measure Midori

2 measures lemon juice

❶ Put the cracked ice cubes into a cocktail shaker. Pour the vodka, triple sec, Midori and lemon juice over the ice. Shake vigorously until a frost forms.

❷ Strain into a chilled cocktail glass.

## Variations

**Alligator**: put 4–6 cracked ice cubes into a cocktail shaker. Pour 2 measures vodka, 1 measure Midori, ½ measure dry vermouth and ¼ teaspoon lemon juice over the ice. Shake vigorously until a frost forms. Strain into a chilled cocktail glass.

**Melon Ball**: put 4–6 cracked ice cubes into a mixing glass. Pour 2 measures vodka, 2 measures Midori and 4 measures pineapple juice over the ice and stir well to mix. Half fill a chilled tumbler with cracked ice cubes and strain the cocktail over them. Decorate with a melon wedge.

**Melon Balls**: put 4–6 cracked ice cubes into a cocktail shaker. Pour 1 measure vodka, 1 measure Midori and 1 measure pineapple juice over the ice. Shake vigorously until a frost forms, then strain into a chilled cocktail glass.

**Melon State Balls**: put 4–6 cracked ice cubes into a cocktail shaker. Pour 2 measures vodka, 1 measure Midori and 2 measures orange juice over the ice cubes. Shake vigorously until a frost forms, then strain the mixture into a chilled cocktail glass.

# Vodga

As a rule, classic cocktails based on vodka were intended to provide the kick of an alcoholic drink with no tell-tale signs on the breath and they were usually fairly simple mixes of fruit juice, sodas and other non-alcoholic flavorings. By contrast, contemporary cocktails based on vodka often include other aromatic and flavorsome spirits and liqueurs, with vodka adding extra strength.

## serves 1

4–6 cracked ice cubes

2 measures vodka

1 measure Strega

½ measure orange juice

❶ Put the cracked ice cubes into a cocktail shaker. Pour the vodka, Strega and orange juice over the ice. Shake vigorously until a frost forms.

❷ Strain into a chilled cocktail glass.

## Variations

**Golden Frog**: put 4–6 crushed ice cubes into a blender and add 1 measure vodka, 1 measure Strega, 1 measure Galliano and 1 measure lemon juice. Blend until slushy, then pour into a chilled cocktail glass.

**Genoese**: put 4–6 cracked ice cubes into a cocktail shaker. Pour 1 measure vodka, 1 measure grappa, ½ measure Sambuca and ½ measure dry vermouth over the ice. Shake vigorously until a frost forms, then strain into a chilled cocktail glass.

**White Spider**: put 4–6 cracked ice cubes into a mixing glass. Pour 1 measure vodka and 1 measure white crème de menthe over the ice. Stir well to mix, then strain into a chilled cocktail glass.

**Tailgate**: put 4–6 cracked ice cubes into a mixing glass. Dash orange bitters over the ice and pour in 2 measures vodka, 1 measure green Chartreuse and 1 measure sweet vermouth. Stir well to mix, then strain into a chilled cocktail glass.

# Full Monty

The expression 'full monty', meaning not holding anything back, has been around for a long time, but was given a new lease of life by the highly successful British film of the same title. However, you can keep your clothes on when mixing and drinking this cocktail.

*serves 1*

4–6 cracked ice cubes
1 measure vodka
1 measure Galliano
grated ginseng root, to decorate

❶ Put the cracked ice cubes into a cocktail shaker. Pour the vodka and Galliano over the ice. Shake vigorously until a frost forms.
❷ Strain into a chilled cocktail glass and sprinkle with grated ginseng root.

## Cinematic cocktails

**Back to the Future**: put 4–6 cracked ice cubes into a cocktail shaker. Pour 2 measures gin, 1 measure slivovitz and 1 measure lemon juice over the ice. Shake vigorously until a frost forms. Strain into a chilled cocktail glass.

**Star Wars**: put 4–6 cracked ice cubes into a cocktail shaker. Pour 2 measures gin, 2 measures lemon juice, 1 measure Galliano and 1 measure crème de noyaux over the ice. Shake vigorously until a frost forms. Strain into a chilled cocktail glass.

**Titanic**: put 4–6 cracked ice cubes into a cocktail shaker. Pour 3 measures Mandarine Napoléon and 2 measures vodka over the ice. Shake vigorously until a frost forms. Half fill a chilled tumbler with cracked ice cubes and strain the cocktail over them. Top up with sparkling mineral water.

**Last Mango in Paris**: put 4–6 cracked ice cubes into a blender and add 2 measures vodka, 1 measure crème de framboise, 1 measure lime juice, ½ peeled, stoned and chopped mango and 2 halved strawberries. Blend until slushy. Pour into a chilled goblet and decorate with a slice of lime and a strawberry.

# What the Hell

Cheer yourself up when you are at a loose end, or when everything seems to have gone wrong, with this simple but delicious concoction.

*serves 1*

4–6 cracked ice cubes
dash of lime juice
1 measure gin
1 measure apricot brandy
1 measure dry vermouth
twist of lemon peel, to decorate

❶ Put the cracked ice cubes into a mixing glass. Dash the lime juice over the ice and pour in the gin, apricot brandy and vermouth. Stir well to mix.

❷ Strain into a chilled cocktail glass and decorate with a twist of lemon peel.

## Silly questions and answers

**Why Not**: put 4–6 cracked ice cubes into a mixing glass. Dash lemon juice over the ice. Pour in 2 measures gin, 1 measure peach brandy and 1 measure Noilly Prat. Stir to mix. Strain into a chilled cocktail glass.

**Is This All**: put 4–6 cracked ice cubes into a cocktail shaker. Pour 2 measures lemon vodka, 1 measure triple sec and 1 measure lemon juice over the ice and add 1 egg white. Shake until a frost forms. Strain into a chilled cocktail glass.

**What The Dickens**: pour 2 measures gin into a heatproof tumbler and stir in 1½ teaspoons icing sugar. Top up with hot water.

**This Is It**: put 4–6 cracked ice cubes into a cocktail shaker. Pour 2 measures gin, 1 measure triple sec and 1 measure lemon juice over the ice and add 1 egg white. Shake vigorously until a frost forms, then strain the mixture into a chilled cocktail glass.

## Did you know?

*French vermouth, of which Noilly Prat is the leading brand, is almost always dry, whereas sweet red vermouth is still the most popular type in Italy, although all the well-known brands – Martini, Cinzano and Gancia – also include a dry version. Each firm keeps its own formula secret.*

# Non-alcoholic Cocktails

# Lip Smacker

So many delicious ingredients are available today that non-alcoholic cocktails really have come into their own. This one has all the kick of an alcoholic cocktail.

### serves 1

4–6 crushed ice cubes

1 small tomato, peeled, deseeded and chopped

1 measure orange juice

2 tsp lime juice

1 spring onion, chopped

1 small, fresh, red chilli, deseeded and chopped

pinch of caster sugar

pinch of salt

dash of Tabasco sauce

### To decorate

slice of lime and a chilli rosette (see below)

❶ Put the crushed ice, tomato, orange juice, lime juice, spring onion and chilli in a blender and process until smooth.

❷ Pour into a chilled glass, and stir in sugar, salt and Tabasco sauce. Decorate with a lime slice and a chilli rosette. To make a rosette, use a sharp knife to make 5 or 6 cuts 1 cm/ ½ inch from the stalk end to the tip of a long, thin chilli. Place in iced water for 30 minutes, until fanned out.

## Variations

**Hot Lips**: substitute the flesh of ¼ small avocado for the tomato and a deseeded and chopped green chilli for the red chilli. **Open Prairie Oyster**: dash Tabasco sauce and white wine vinegar into a wine glass and pour in 1 teaspoon Worcestershire sauce and 1 measure tomato juice. Stir gently and add 1 egg yolk. Drink down in one, without breaking the egg yolk.

## Did you know?

*Sun-ripened tomatoes have a much sweeter and more concentrated flavor than those grown under glass or in polytunnels. Home-grown varieties are best, but those sold on the vine are a good buy.*

# Little Prince

Sparkling apple juice is a particularly useful ingredient in non-alcoholic cocktails because it adds flavor and color, as well as fizz. Try using it as a substitute for champagne in non-alcoholic versions of such cocktails as Buck's Fizz (see page 62).

*serves 1*

4–6 cracked ice cubes
1 measure apricot juice
1 measure lemon juice
2 measures sparkling apple juice
twist of lemon peel, to decorate

❶ Put the cracked ice cubes into a mixing glass. Pour the apricot juice, lemon juice and apple juice over the ice and stir well.
❷ Strain into a chilled highball glass and decorate with the lemon twist.

## An apple a day

**Apple Frazzle**: put 4–6 cracked ice cubes into a cocktail shaker. Pour 4 measures apple juice, 1 teaspoon sugar syrup (see page 7) and ½ teaspoon lemon juice over the ice. Shake vigorously until a frost forms. Strain into a chilled tumbler and top up with sparkling mineral water.

**Bite of the Apple**: put 4–6 crushed ice cubes into a blender and add 5 measures apple juice, 1 measure lime juice, ½ teaspoon orgeat and 1 tablespoon apple sauce or apple purée. Blend until smooth, then pour into a chilled tumbler. Sprinkle with ground cinnamon.

**Prohibition Punch** (to serve 25): pour 900 ml/1½ pints apple juice, 350 ml/ 12 fl oz lemon juice and 125 ml/4 fl oz sugar syrup (see page 7) into a large jug. Add cracked ice cubes and 2.25 litres/ 4½ pints ginger ale. Stir gently to mix. Serve in chilled tumblers, decorated with slices of orange and with straws.

**Red Apple Sunset**: put 4–6 cracked ice cubes into a cocktail shaker. Dash grenadine over the ice and pour in 2 measures apple juice and 2 measures grapefruit juice. Shake until a frost forms. Strain into a chilled cocktail glass.

# Grapefruit Cooler

This is a wonderfully refreshing drink that is ideal for serving at a family barbecue. Start making this at least two hours before you want to serve it to allow plenty of time for the mint to infuse in the syrup.

### serves 6

60 g/2 oz fresh mint

2 measures sugar syrup (see page 7)

475 ml/17 fl oz grapefruit juice

4 measures lemon juice

about 30 cracked ice cubes

sparkling mineral water, to top up

sprigs of fresh mint, to decorate

❶ Crush the fresh mint leaves and place in a small bowl. Add the sugar syrup and stir well. Set aside for at least 2 hours to macerate, mashing the mint with a spoon from time to time.

❷ Strain the syrup into a jug and add the grapefruit juice and lemon juice. Cover with saranwrap and chill in the refrigerator for at least 2 hours, until required.

❸ To serve, fill six chilled Collins glasses with cracked ice. Divide the cocktail between the glasses and top up with sparkling mineral water. Decorate with fresh mint sprigs.

## Cool it

**Bright Green Cooler** (serves 1): put 4–6 cracked ice cubes into a cocktail shaker. Pour 3 measures pineapple juice, 2 measures lime juice and 1 measure green peppermint syrup over the ice. Shake the mixture vigorously until a frost forms. Half fill a tall chilled tumbler with cracked ice cubes and then strain the cocktail over them. Top up with ginger ale and then decorate with a slice of cucumber and a slice of lime.

## Did you know?

*There is a green-skinned grapefruit variety called 'Sweetie' that is less sharp than the yellow-skinned fruits. Pink grapefruit is also slightly milder in flavor.*

# Shirley Temple

This is one of the most famous of classic non-alcoholic cocktails. Shirley Temple Black became a respected diplomat, but this cocktail dates from the days when she was an immensely popular child film star in the 1930s.

*serves 1*

8–10 cracked ice cubes
2 measures lemon juice
½ measure grenadine
½ measure sugar syrup (see page 7)
ginger ale, to top up

**To decorate**
slice of orange
cocktail cherry

❶ Put 4–6 cracked ice cubes into a cocktail shaker. Pour the lemon juice, grenadine and sugar syrup over the ice and shake vigorously.

❷ Half fill a small, chilled glass with cracked ice cubes and strain the cocktail over them. Top up with ginger ale. Decorate with an orange slice and a cocktail cherry.

## Other classics

**St Clements**: put 6–8 cracked ice cubes into a chilled tumbler. Pour 2 measures orange juice and 2 measures bitter lemon over the ice. Stir gently and decorate with a slice of orange and a slice of lemon.

**Black and Tan**: pour 150 ml/5 fl oz chilled ginger ale into a chilled tumbler. Add 150 ml/5 fl oz chilled ginger beer. Do not stir. Decorate with a wedge of lime.

**Tea Punch**: put 4–6 cracked ice cubes into a mixing glass. Pour 3 measures cold black tea, 3 measures orange juice, 3 measures sparkling apple juice and 1½ measures lemon juice over the ice. Stir well to mix, then pour into a tall, chilled tumbler. Decorate with a slice of lemon.

**Beachcomber**: put 4–6 cracked ice cubes into a cocktail shaker. Pour 150 ml/5 fl oz guava juice, 2 measures lime juice and 1 measure raspberry syrup over the ice. Shake vigorously until a frost forms, then pour into a chilled tumbler.

# Melon Medley

Choose a very ripe, sweet-fleshed melon, such as a cantaloupe, for this lovely, fresh-tasting cocktail. This drink is perfect for sipping on a hot evening.

### serves 1

4–6 crushed ice cubes
60 g/2 oz diced melon flesh
4 measures orange juice
½ measure lemon juice

❶ Put the crushed ice cubes into a blender and add the diced melon. Pour in the orange juice and lemon juice. Blend until slushy.

❷ Pour into a chilled Collins glass.

## Sweet and juicy

**River Cruise** (to serve 6): put 450 g/1 lb diced cantaloupe melon flesh into a blender or food processor and process to a smooth purée. Scrape the purée into a jug. Put the peel and juice of 2 lemons and 2 tablespoons sugar into a small pan. Heat gently, stirring until the sugar has dissolved. Pour the lemon syrup over the melon purée and set aside to cool, then cover with saranwrap and chill in the refrigerator for at least 2 hours.
To serve, half-fill 6 chilled tumblers with cracked ice. Stir the melon mixture and divide it between the glasses. Top up with sparkling mineral water and decorate with melon wedges and cocktail cherries.

**Kool Kevin**: put 4–6 crushed ice cubes into a blender and add 60 g/2 oz diced cantaloupe melon flesh, 1 measure grenadine and 1 measure double or heavy whipping cream. Blend until smooth then pour into a chilled tumbler. Add 1 measure ginger ale and stir gently. Sprinkle with ground ginger and decorate with a wedge of melon.

# Glossary

**Amaretto**: almond-flavored liqueur from Italy

**Amer Picon**: French apéritif bitters, flavored with orange and gentian

**Angostura bitters**: rum-based bitters from Trinidad

**Anisette**: French liqueur, flavored with anise, coriander and other herbs

**Applejack**: North American name for apple brandy (see Fruit Brandies)

**Aquavit**: Scandinavian grain spirit, usually flavored with caraway

**Armagnac**: French brandy produced in Gascony – it is rarely used for cocktails

**Bacardi**: leading brand of white rum, originally from Cuba and now produced in Bermuda – also the name of a cocktail

**Bailey's Irish Cream**: Irish, whiskey-based, chocolate flavored liqueur

**Bénédictine**: French, monastic liqueur flavored with herbs, spices and honey

**Bitters**: a flavor-enhancer made from berries, roots and herbs

**Bourbon**: American whiskey made from a mash that must contain at least 51 per cent corn

**Brandy**: spirit distilled from fermented grapes, although many fruit brandies are based on other fruits (see Fruit brandy)

**Calvados**: French apple brandy from Normandy

**Campari**: Italian bitters flavored with quinine

**Champagne**: French sparkling wine from La Champagne, produced under strictly controlled conditions

**Chartreuse**: French monastic liqueur flavored with a secret recipe of herbs – green Chartreuse is stronger than yellow

**Cobbler**: long, mixed drink traditionally based on sherry but now made from spirits and other ingredients

**Coconut liqueur**: coconut-flavored, spirit-based liqueur – Malibu is the best-known brand

**Coffee liqueur**: coffee-flavored, spirit-based liqueur – Tia Maria, based on Jamaican rum, and Kahlúa from Mexico are the best-known brands

**Cointreau**: best-selling brand of triple sec (see Triple sec), flavored with sweet Mediterranean oranges and Caribbean bitter orange peel

**Collins**: a spirit-based cocktail topped up with a carbonated soda, such as ginger ale

**Crème de banane**: banana-flavored liqueur

**Crème de cacao**: French, chocolate-flavored liqueur, produced in various strengths and colors

**Crème de cassis**: blackcurrant-flavored liqueur, mainly from France

**Crème de framboise**: raspberry-flavored liqueur

**Crème de menthe**: mint-flavored liqueur – may be white or green

**Crème de noyaux**: liqueur made from apricot and peach kernels

**Crème violette**: violet-flavored liqueur

**Crème Yvette**: American Parma violet-flavored liqueur

**Curaçao**: orange-flavored liqueur, produced mainly in France and the Netherlands, but originating from the Caribbean – available in a range of colors including white, orange and blue

**Drambuie**: Scotch whiskey-based liqueur, flavored with honey and heather

**Dry gin**: see Gin

**Dubonnet**: wine-based apéritif, flavored with quinine – available red and blonde

**Eau-de-vie**: spirit distilled from fruit – tends to be used (wrongly) as interchangeable with fruit brandy

**Falernum**: Caribbean syrup flavored with fruit and spices

**Fernet Branca**: Italian liqueur with a bitter flavor

**Fizz**: long, mixed drink, based on spirits and made fizzy with soda water

**Flip**: spirit based, creamy mixed drink made with egg

**Fruit brandy**: strictly speaking, brandy is distilled from fermented grapes, but many fruit brandies are distilled from whatever the fruit type is, such as apple and apricot – plum brandy, also known as slivovitz, is usually made from Mirabelle and Switzen plums

**Galliano**: Italian liqueur, flavored with honey and vanilla

**Genever**: also known as Hollands and Dutch gin, the original gin, which is sweeter and fuller-flavored than London, Plymouth or dry gin – rarely used in cocktails (see Gin)

**Gin**: a colorless, grain-based spirit, strongly flavored with juniper and other herbs. London, Plymouth and dry gin are most commonly used for cocktails

**Gomme Syrup**: sweet syrup from France

**Grand Marnier**: French, orange flavored, Cognac-based liqueur

**Grappa**: fiery, Italian spirit distilled from wine must

**Grenadine**: non-alcoholic, pomegranate-flavored syrup –

used for sweetening and coloring cocktails

**Irish whiskey**: unblended spirit made from malted or unmalted barley and some other grains – suitable for many cocktails

**Julep**: originally a sweet syrup, now a family of spirit-based cocktails, flavored and decorated with fresh mint

**Kahlúa**: popular Mexican brand of coffee liqueur

**Kirsch**: colorless cherry-flavored eau-de-vie, mainly from France and Switzerland

**Kümmel**: colorless Dutch liqueur, flavored with caraway

**Lillet**: French herb-flavored liqueur, based on wine and Armagnac

**Liqueur**: distilled spirit flavored with such things as fruit, herbs, coffee, nuts, mint and chocolate

**London gin**: the driest gin (see Gin)

**Madeira**: fortified wine from the island of the same name

**Malibu**: leading brand of coconut liqueur – based on rum

**Mandarine Napoléon**: Belgian, brandy-based liqueur flavored with tangerines

**Maraschino**: Italian, cherry-flavored liqueur - usually colorless, but may be red

**Martini**: popular Italian brand of vermouth produced by Martini and Rossi and also the name of a classic cocktail

**Melon liqueur**: spirit-based, melon-flavored liqueur – Midori is the leading brand

**Midori**: Japanese liqueur (see Melon Liqueur)

**Noilly Prat**: leading French brand of very dry vermouth

**Orgeat**: almond-flavored syrup

**Pastis**: aniseed-flavored liqueur from France

**Plymouth gin**: a less dry type of gin than London gin (see Gin)

**Port**: Portuguese fortified wine that may be white, ruby or tawny – white and inexpensive ruby are most appropriate for cocktails

**Pousse-Café**: a drink poured in layers to float on top of one another, which gives its name to a narrow, straight-sided stemmed glass

**Quinquina**: French, wine-based apéritif, flavored with quinine

**Rickey**: a spirit-based cocktail including lemon or lime juice and soda water

**Rum**: spirit distilled from fermented sugar cane juice or molasses – light, golden and dark have distinctive flavors and all are widely used, together and severally, in cocktails and punches

**Rye whiskey**: mainly American and Canadian whiskey which must be made from a mash containing at least 51 per cent rye

**Sake**: Japanese rice wine

**Sambuca**: Italian, liquorice- flavored liqueur

**Schnapps**: grain-based spirit – available in a range of flavors, including peach and peppermint

**Scotch whiskey**: blends are a mixture of about 40 per cent malt and 60 per cent grain whiskey and are most suitable for cocktails – single malts should be drunk neat or diluted with water

**Slammer**: a cocktail mixed by slamming it on the bar

**Slivovitz**: plum brandy (see Fruit brandy)

**Sloe gin**: Liqueur made by steeping sloes in gin – previously homemade but now available commercially

**Sour**: a spirit-based cocktail containing sugar, and lemon or lime juice

**Southern Comfort**: American whiskey-based, peach-flavored liqueur

**Strega**: Italian, herb-flavored liqueur

**Sugar syrup**: a sweetener for cocktails, made by dissolving sugar in boiling water (see page 7)

**Swedish Punsch**: aromatic rum-based drink, flavored with wines and syrups

**Tequila**: Mexican spirit distilled from pulque from fermented maguey cacti

**Tia Maria**: popular, Jamaican rum-based coffee liqueur

**Triple sec**: colorless, orange-flavored liqueur

**Vermouth**: wine-based apéritif flavored with extracts of wormwood – both sweet and dry vermouths are widely used in cocktails

**Vodka**: colorless, grain-based spirit, originally from Russia and Poland. Flavored vodkas, such as lemon, raspberry and chilli, are becoming increasingly popular

**Whiskey**: spirit distilled from grain or malted barley – the main types are bourbon, rye, Irish and Scotch

# Cocktail List

# THE NEW
# CROSS
# STITCHER'S
# BIBLE

# THE NEW
# CROSS
# STITCHER'S
# BIBLE

**THE DEFINITIVE MANUAL OF
ESSENTIAL CROSS STITCH AND
COUNTED THREAD TECHNIQUES**

JANE GREENOFF

D&C
David and Charles

# CONTENTS

*To Bill, my husband
and best friend,
with love always.*

A DAVID & CHARLES BOOK
Copyright © David & Charles Limited 2007

David & Charles is an F+W Publications
Inc. company, 4700 East Galbraith Road
Cincinnati, OH 45236

First published in the UK in 2007

Text and designs copyright © Jane Greenoff 2007
Photography and layout copyright ©
David & Charles 2007

Stitch Library artworks © David & Charles 2007
adapted from originals supplied by the Cross Stitch Guild

Jane Greenoff has asserted her right to be identified as
author of this work in accordance with the Copyright,
Designs and Patents Act, 1988.

A catalogue record for this book is available from the
British Library.

ISBN-13: 978-0-7153-2545-2 hardback
ISBN-10: 0-7153-2545-0 hardback

Printed in Singapore by KHL Printing Co Pte Ltd
for David & Charles
Brunel House     Newton Abbot     Devon

Executive Editor  Cheryl Brown
Desk Editor  Bethany Dymond
Project Editor  Lin Clements
Senior Designer  Charly Bailey
Chart Preparation  Ethan Danielson
Production Controller  Ros Napper

Visit our website at www.davidandcharles.co.uk

David & Charles books are available from all
good bookshops; alternatively you can contact
our Orderline on 0870 9908222 or write to us at
FREEPOST EX2 110, D&C Direct, Newton Abbot,
TQ12 4ZZ (no stamp required UK only);
US customers call 800-289-0963 and
Canadian customers call 800-840-5220.

# INTRODUCTION

Since the extraordinary success of *The Cross Stitcher's Bible* published in 2000 (now in ten languages), I felt it was time to look at the book again, particularly in the light of my teaching experiences over the past few years. My classes are now almost without exception dedicated to cross stitch plus additional counted stitches. I still feel that pure cross stitch, worked perfectly, is beautiful to look at and simple to do but many stitchers are moving on and adding Hardanger, blackwork, hemstitch and other counted techniques to their projects, and these techniques require more detailed explanations. This unique book aims to provide you with useful, accessible information in an easy-to-use format.

Cross stitch is often our first love but I hope that by referring to *The New Cross Stitcher's Bible* you will be able to add to and enhance your cross stitch patterns and perhaps design for yourself. The book will add to your armoury of counted techniques whilst allowing you to pursue the pleasure of pure cross stitch.

I hope this book, with its clear instructions, computer-generated charts and extensive chart and stitch libraries, will become your essential manual, allowing you to perfect existing techniques and also explore other exciting companions to cross stitch, such as the use of beads, ribbons and embellishments and many other decorative stitches. The instructions and explanations in this book are the result of over 20 years of designing and stitching and I hope you enjoy sharing my experiences.

*Jan Greenoff*

## HOW TO USE THIS BOOK

The book has been divided into sections with colour-coded pages to enable you to find the information you require easily and to provide a clear and comprehensive approach to all aspects of cross stitching.

❖ Getting Started is colour coded blue and gives advice on choosing and using equipment, fabric and threads, plus all the practical aspects of how to cross stitch on Aida and evenweave fabrics.

❖ Creative Options is colour coded yellow and describes cross stitching techniques using some of the many different fabrics and threads available.

❖ Exploring Choices is colour coded red and features exciting designs that show how easy it is to combine cross stitch with other counted embroidery techniques.

❖ In Getting Started, Creative Options and Exploring Choices, I have included boxes called Stitch Perfect, which focus on the important points in each section. There are also mini technique boxes to assist you.

❖ In Creative Options you will see illustrations of worked designs, many of which combine a number of techniques fully explained elsewhere. For example, the Anemone Floral Cushion (opposite) includes cross stitch with stranded cottons (floss) and linen threads on linen, crossed cushion stitch in space-dyed threads and French knots in pure silk and blending filament (full instructions on page 53).

❖ The extensive Stitch Library includes the stitches you need to work any of the designs in the book, with clear, coloured diagrams and explanatory text.

❖ In addition to the extensive Chart Library I have included some scrumptious samplers so you can create heirloom masterpieces, combining some of the techniques and stitches explained in the book.

❖ Most of the designs are charted in the Chart Library starting on page 166. Colour charts with black/white symbols have been used so you can photocopy and enlarge them. Most of the designs can be stitched on Aida or evenweave. Where evenweave is essential it is indicated in the picture caption. All the cross stitch designs have been stitched with DMC stranded cotton (floss) unless stated otherwise. When fabrics are specified, the thread counts are indicated as threads or blocks to 2.5cm (1in) i.e., 28-count or 14-count. All stitches are worked over two fabric threads or one fabric block unless stated otherwise.

❖ Measurements are given in metric with imperial conversions in brackets. Use either metric or imperial when working, do not combine them.

# GETTING STARTED

You should find this section very useful as it contains a great deal of invaluable information on cross stitch basics, including how to choose equipment, use charts, manage threads and all the instruction you'll ever need on creating beautiful cross stitch on Aida and evenweave fabric.

Counted cross stitch is most commonly worked using stranded cottons (floss), often incorrectly referred to as 'silks'. This is probably the simplest way to start your stitching, adding different threads as you become more experienced. As you can see from the gorgeous pictures here, cross stitch is one of the most rewarding kinds of embroidery and the images that can be created are simply stunning. The kingfisher picture below is worked in stranded cottons and almost all full cross stitches. I have added some optional blending filament to the bird's plumage (see page 46) to make it glisten but the design could be worked even more simply on Aida with just stranded cottons. The two colourful kitchen tile pictures shown opposite use full cross stitch, with half cross stitch for the pale background.

**KINGFISHER**

**Stitch count:** 44h x 41w
**Design size:** 8 x 7.5cm
(3⅛ x 3in)
**Fabric:** Zweigart Cashel ivory linen 28-count or 14-count Aida
**Needle:** Tapestry size 24
**Chart:** Page 167

*This lovely bird has been stitched using two strands of stranded cotton (floss) for cross stitch and one strand for backstitch. The water was stitched in half cross stitch using one strand of stranded cotton together with one strand of Kreinik Blending Filament 095. I used two strands of the blending filament with the stranded cotton to add a slightly frosted appearance to the bird's plumage.*

**GREEN CABBAGE AND RED PEPPER TILES**

**Stitch count:** 56h x 56w (each design)
**Design size:** 11cm (4¼in) square
**Fabric:** Zweigart Dublin ivory 26-count linen
**Needle:** Tapestry size 24
**Charts:** Pages 166 and 169

*These striking kitchen tiles are both worked in the same way. Use two strands of stranded cotton (floss) for cross stitch and one strand for backstitch. Stitch the light-coloured background in half cross stitch using one strand. The designs could be worked on 14-count Aida fabric but would be fractionally smaller.*

# FOLLOWING A CHART

I will never forget the day I discovered counted cross stitch, staring at the fabric expecting to find the design printed! Looking at blank fabric and not knowing what to do next was a bit scary – the secret is to take it in easy, bite-size pieces.

The designs in this book are counted designs and are worked from charts. A chart is really just a detailed map to be followed and if you follow these guidelines you will not get lost. The charts and keys for the majority of the projects are in the Chart Library (pages 166–209). The four celebration samplers have their charts included with the instructions. The charts are easy to follow as they are all in colour with a black and/or white symbol to aid colour identification (see Types of Charts, opposite).

## CHART AND KEY BASICS

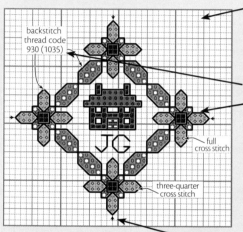

backstitch
thread code
930 (1035)

full
cross stitch

three-quarter
cross stitch

JANE'S TIP
*Check your position regularly to discover counting mistakes early and avoid lots of stitches to unpick – often referred to as reverse stitching!*

◆ Each square on a chart, both occupied and unoccupied, represents two threads of linen or one block of Aida unless otherwise stated. Each occupied square equals one stitch unless otherwise stated.

◆ Backstitch thread code – DMC (Anchor).

◆ Cross stitch charts generally consist of whole squares representing complete cross stitches, but you will see additional stitches added to some charts in the Chart Library indicating three-quarter cross stitches (sometimes called fractional stitches), French knots and so on. These stitches are labelled in the key or included on the chart. The Sampler Key Keeper chart (instructions on page 41) is shown here with the main parts identified.

◆ Traditionally cross stitchers begin to stitch from the middle of the chart and the middle of the fabric to ensure that the design is centred when it is mounted and framed. Find the middle by following the little arrows at the sides.

◆ Some counted thread stitches can be worked over any number of fabric threads although the stitch construction will stay the same e.g., Rhodes stitch may be formed over four, six or eight threads, so check the chart to clarify the number of fabric threads involved.

◆ The count of a fabric (the number of stitches to 2.5cm or 1in) affects the size of a finished piece even when worked from the same chart. This is useful when faced with a frame or card that is slightly too small for the chosen motif. You can increase the fabric count from, say, 14-count to 18-count, which reduces the design so it fits.

◆ To prevent serious counting errors, use a coloured pen to rule a line on the chart from arrow to arrow to find the centre and then add

a line of tacking (basting) to the fabric. If working a band sampler, work tacking lines down either side of the first band, to prevent your project wandering right or left.

◆ When looking at a chart, try to plan the direction in which you are going to stitch. If you count across the shortest distances of empty fabric each time you will avoid making counting mistakes. This sometimes means counting diagonally, vertically or horizontally across a pattern. Mistakes most often occur when counting across long sections of blank fabric. You can turn your work and the chart upside down if you prefer to work towards you, but never turn halfway – your stitches will end up facing the wrong way!

## TYPES OF CHARTS

When stitching cross stitch designs from books, magazines and kits you may find different types of charts but don't panic they all give the same information in a slightly different way. This Green Cabbage Tile could have been worked from a chart presented in various ways, as shown below. See also page 122, Computer-Aided Design.

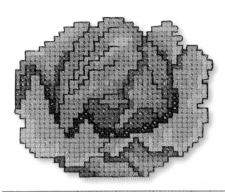

Coloured squares only

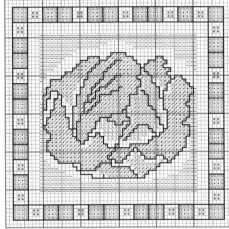

Black and/or white symbols

Coloured squares with black and/or white symbols

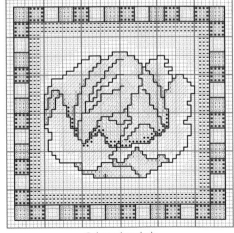

Coloured symbols

### JANE'S TIP

*I make a photocopy of a black and white chart so I can colour it in as I go to avoid looking at the wrong section. You may find a metal board with magnetic strips helpful. It keeps the chart in position and marks your place.*

# EQUIPMENT

The equipment needed for cross stitch couldn't be simpler – essentially just blunt tapestry needles and some sharp, pointed scissors. You will need other items for making up projects but these are given under the relevant finishing instructions at the back of the book. Remember that cross stitch need not be displayed as just cards and framed pictures: as you will see from the purse on the next page and from the photographs throughout, cross stitch can be transformed into all sorts of lovely decorative and useful items.

## NEEDLES

◆ When working counted cross stitch you will need blunt tapestry needles of various sizes, depending on your fabric. A blunt needle is required because you should be parting the threads of the fabric rather than piercing the material. Aim to avoid splitting the fibres as you stitch.

◆ Occasionally I use a 'sharp' needle when adding backstitch outlining or when creating fractional stitches on Aida fabric. A 'sharp' size 10 is useful for this and will double as a small beading needle.

◆ The most commonly used tapestry needles for cross stitch are sizes 24 and 26, although needles are also available in sizes 20, 22 and 28. When using a size 28, use only the equivalent of one strand of stranded cotton (floss) because the eye is very delicate and will break. Adjust the needle size to match the project.

◆ Discard old needles with marks or rough areas as these can damage your threads and fabric.

◆ Avoid leaving your needle in the fabric when it is put away as it may leave a mark (unless you are working with gold-plated needles). The nickel plating on needles varies and some stitchers find they are allergic to the nickel and therefore prefer gold-plated needles.

◆ I only use gold-plated needles as I find they slip through the fabric perfectly and are essential if creating lots of French knots or bullion knots.

◆ If you are working on a floor-standing frame, you may find a double-ended needle helpful, where the eye of the needle is in the middle rather than the end. This means that the needle goes up and down rather like a shuttle in a loom.

◆ When the use of beads is suggested in a project they may be attached using a special beading needle or 'sharp' size 10. A blunt gold-plated beading needle size 26 has been specially developed for cross stitchers (see Suppliers).

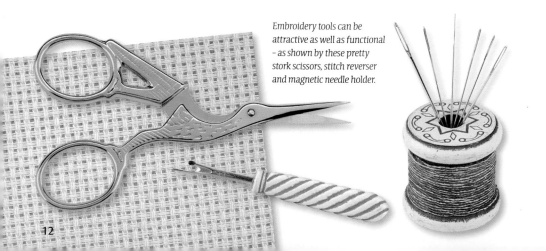

*Embroidery tools can be attractive as well as functional – as shown by these pretty stork scissors, stitch reverser and magnetic needle holder.*

---

### THREADING A NEEDLE OR NEEDLING A THREAD?

Sometimes threading a needle can defeat you, usually when you are tired or distracted or when you have been stitching too long! So try needling the thread instead. Pass the thread across your index finger and hold it quite firmly. With your other hand holding the pointed end of the needle, rub the eye of the needle up and down the thread. The thread will pop up through the eye of the needle is if by magic.

---

## SCISSORS

◆ Keep a small, sharp pair of pointed scissors exclusively for your embroidery. I wear mine around my neck on a ribbon so I know where they are at all times. There are magnets available to attach your scissors to the embroidery frame if you use one.

◆ Use dressmaker's shears for cutting fabric.

## FRAMES AND HOOPS

◆ Frames or hoops are not essential for cross stitchers and I have worked without them for many years. I prefer to work my cross stitch in my hand as this allows a sewing action (see How to Hold Fabric page 22) but this is a matter of personal preference. I do use a frame when a project includes satin stitch.

◆ Generally, I avoid embroidery hoops as I find that they tend to mark the fabric but if you must use one, choose one large enough to hold the complete design – moving a hoop across your beautifully formed stitches is criminal!

◆ When I use a frame (such as when working the crossed cushion stitch and the spider's webs on the Anemone Floral Cushion on page 53), I use a padded, upholstered frame with a sandbag weight, shown below (see Sue Hawkins in Suppliers).

◆ Frames and hoops are useful when you are working in miniature and also when adding beads or combining cross stitch with silk ribbon.

An upholstered
needlework frame
with sand-bag weight
is a useful accessory
(see Suppiers).

## PINK MALLOW PURSE

**Stitch count:** 33h x 32w
**Design size:** 6 x 5.8cm
(2⅜ x 2¼in)
**Fabric:** Zweigart Cashel
ivory 28-count linen
**Needle:** Tapestry size 24
**Chart:** Page 167

*This pretty purse makes a feature of a simple design and could be used for items of stitching equipment. Work this floral motif over two linen threads, using two strands of stranded cotton (floss) for cross stitch and French knots and one strand for backstitch. If working this project on Aida fabric you may prefer to work the three-quarter stitches using a sharp needle. I made the embroidery into a folded purse using Liberty lawn fabric but do feel free to experiment. To make up as a purse see page 217.*

## MAGNIFIERS

There are a number of different types of magnifying contraptions on the market, some of which will make you look like something from the planet Zog but you will be among friends! There are various factors that will affect your choice.

♦ If you already wear glasses for close work you may be able to find a cheap and simple pair of magnifying spectacles that will be just right for your stitching. There are also small clip-on lenses that can be worn in addition to your glasses. Lenses can be worn around the neck and the position adjusted with side cords. The success or failure of these also depends on your bust size as they do seem to need an adequate 'shelf' to be in the correct position!

♦ If you feel the need for something more substantial you will be able to find many excellent lenses with flexible arms which clip to the table, chair or embroidery frame. Some of these may be combined with a lamp (see picture opposite).

♦ Do make sure you hold your work at the correct distance from your eyes. To find this distance, hold your work at arm's length then gradually bring it towards you until you can see it clearly. If you then continue to bring it nearer, you will find another point where it starts to become indistinct again. Hold your work at a distance between these two points where you can naturally see it most clearly. When they reach their forties, many people start to find that this position gets further and further away from their eyes. If this is happening to you, you probably need reading glasses, so consult an optician.

> ### JANE'S TIP
> *When choosing magnifiers or magnifying spectacles, take some stitching with you as you may well hold your needlework in a different position to that of a book.*

## LAMPS AND DAYLIGHT BULBS

Your requirements here will vary depending on when you have the opportunity to stitch.

◆ An old-fashioned standard lamp is probably the most suitable as the soft light drops on your work from above and you are unlikely to burn yourself on the bulb!

◆ Some stitchers have great success with head torches (from camping shops). They vary but the most successful type seems to be those with an adjustable beam, which can be angled on your stitching.

◆ The list of lamps available grows daily but Daylight bulbs and Ott Lite are very helpful, particularly as domestic light bulbs distort colours, which can be very trying and lead to colour matching mistakes. I use Ott Lite, as the bulbs create a very clear light and do not get too hot.

*You will find magnifiers and lamps very useful when working projects in miniature, such as this pansy key ring (instructions on page 58), where the finished design is less than 2.5cm (1in) square!*

15

# CHOOSING AND MANAGING THREADS

The most commonly used thread for counted embroidery is stranded cotton (floss) but you will see flower threads, linen threads, rayons, perlé cottons, assorted metallics and spaced-dyed specialist threads used throughout this book.

All the charts in the Chart Library were stitched using DMC stranded cotton (floss) unless stated otherwise. Anchor alternatives are given in brackets. If you do change to Anchor or another brand of thread, bear in mind that an exact colour match is not always possible. The following guidelines apply to stranded cotton (floss) as information about other yarns will be found in the relevant sections.

## CHECKING FOR COLOURFASTNESS

Ensuring that threads are colourfast is important, particularly if you need to launder the piece or are planning to tea-dye it (see page 33). I have had experience of threads not just running but galloping! You should have no trouble with well-known reputable brands such as DMC, Anchor and Madeira but take extra care with Christmas reds.

To check for colourfastness, place the work face down on a clean surface and press the back of the stitches with a clean, damp white tissue. Any trace of colour on the tissue means the thread colours are not fast, so do not wash or tea-dye.

## USING STRANDED COTTON

◆ When selecting threads, always have the fabric you are intending to use close at hand, because the colour of the background fabric will affect your choice of thread colours. When in a shop, check the colour of the thread in daylight as electric light can 'kill' some shades. Buy a daylight bulb to use in normal spotlights to help when working in the evening.

◆ Cross stitch is generally worked using two strands of stranded cotton when working on 14-count and 16-count Aida. It is perfectly acceptable to mix the number of threads used within the same project. You could alter the texture by working in one, two and even three strands.

◆ When using two strands or more for cross stitch, you will need to separate the strands and then realign them before threading your needle and beginning to stitch.

◆ If you're not sure how many strands to use on Aida, stitch a few complete cross stitches and look at the stitching in daylight. Some colours may need the number of strands adjusting to suit the project.

◆ If you are working on evenweave and do not know how many strands to use, carefully pull a thread from the edge of the fabric and compare the thread with the strands of cotton. Generally, the strands on the needle should be a similar weight, unless you want a more striking effect.

### JANE'S TIP
*In some cases there are no alternatives to the threads I've used but this should not hinder you in any way! Experiment with some of the many gorgeous threads available! See pages 38–50 for some mouth-watering examples.*

## TWEEDING

Where two shade numbers are quoted for one stitch this is known as tweeding. This straightforward practice is a simple way to increase the numbers of colours you have without buying more thread.

To tweed, simply combine more than one coloured thread in the needle at the same time and work as one – as I have for this little hedgehog (stitching instructions on page 66). You can also apply the tweeding technique to working French knots and bullion bars to great effect. Metallic threads and blending filaments can also be tweeded with stranded cotton.

## ORGANIZING YOUR THREADS

It really does pay to start with good habits and have an organizer system for your threads. You will then be able to find a shade when you need it and you will be surprised by how many projects you will be able to stitch using left-over threads. There are many excellent organizer systems on the market but I make my own cards as shown here.

**1** Take a piece of stiff card (I use the card from a packet of tights or panty-hose) and punch holes down each side of the card. Take a skein of stranded cotton (floss), cut the cotton into manageable lengths of about 80cm (30in), double them and thread them through the holes as shown. It is quite simple to remove one length of thread without disturbing the rest.

**2** Label the card with the manufacturer's name and shade number. When the project is complete all the threads will be labelled ready for another project.

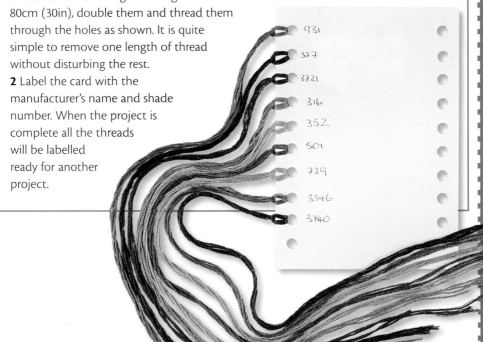

# STARTING TO STITCH

This section of the book creates a background for the later sections, Creative Options and Exploring Choices. Whether you are an expert cross stitcher or just beginning, please read this section in case there are tips and hints you may not have heard before. You may be able to see the reasons for some of the things you do or perhaps the reasons why you should! Much of the advice here is from a personal perspective, so feel free to do your own thing. When stitching the designs, beginners might find Working Projects (page 30) useful as it provides a checklist to get your project started.

## CROSS STITCH FABRICS

When I started to stitch back in the 1980s there was very little choice of fabric available for stitchers. In the UK, it was either fine linen or 14-count Aida fabric and that was about it! Now there is so much choice it can be quite confusing and leave the stitcher, particularly a newcomer, quite at a loss.

Counted cross stitch, and in fact any type of counted embroidery, can be worked on a variety of materials – not just popular fabrics like linen or Aida, but also Hardanger fabric (22-count), canvas, stitching paper, magic canvas and Afghan material. I describe fabric choices and uses in more detail in Creative Options (pages 32–36).

**BUTTERFLIES AND BUDDLEIA**

**Stitch count:**
71h x 60w
**Design size:**
12.7 x 11cm (5 x 4in)
**Fabric:** Aida ivory
14-count or Zweigart
Cashel ivory linen
28-count
**Needle:** Tapestry
size 24
**Chart:** Page 168

*This picture is worked on Aida using cross stitch and backstitch only – see page 27 for a version on linen using massed French knots for the flower and the butterflies stitched over one thread. Use two strands of stranded cotton (floss) for cross stitch (and French knots if using) and one strand for backstitch.*

## STITCHING ON AIDA

All Aida fabrics are woven with threads grouped into bundles to form a square pattern, which creates obvious holes. The stitches are formed using these holes. Aida is available in many different colours and counts and is also available made of linen threads, which is lovely to handle.

Aida is wonderful for cross stitch as it creates very square stitches and projects seem to grow quickly. Beginners like it because it is so easy to see the holes and therefore where to put the needle. It is perfect for checks, tartan and gingham designs. It frays less than evenweaves, unless encouraged.

Aida has some disadvantages. You are limited to using the holes created by the fabric manufacturer, which can make fractional stitches more difficult to form. In addition, some counted stitches need more fabric threads for formation.

## STITCHING ON EVENWEAVE

This range of fabrics, which includes linen, has threads woven singly rather than in blocks and are available in many colours and counts.

Many people like using evenweave for the aged-linen look and the way it handles. Working on evenweave is not difficult, just different. The blue posy design below illustrates this: the finished pieces are the same size on evenweave as on Aida because each stitch is formed over two threads instead of one block, therefore a 28-count evenweave has the same stitch count as a 14-count Aida – 28 threads to 2.5cm (1in) = 14 blocks to 2.5cm (1in). See overleaf for a more detailed explanation of fabric counts and working out design sizes.

Evenweave can be worked over one thread or for fine detail. See also Working with Linen on page 28.

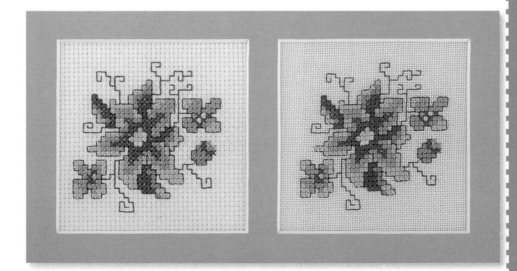

**PRETTY BLUE POSY**

**Stitch count:** 32h x 32w    **Design size:** 5.8cm square (2¼in)    **Fabric:** Zweigart cream 28-count Cashel linen and/or 14-count cream Aida    **Needle:** Tapestry size 24
**Chart:** Page 169

*The posy has been worked twice – on Aida over one block and on linen over two threads but the designs are the same size. Use two strands of stranded cotton (floss) for cross stitch and one for backstitch.*

## WHAT IS THREAD COUNT?

All fabrics are sold by the yard or metre or part thereof and are described by the number of threads to 1in (2.5cm), i.e., their gauge or count. To check the count of a fabric, lay a ruler on the fabric and count the number of blocks or threads in 1in (2.5cm) – use a needle to help you follow the threads. If there are 14 blocks to 1in (2.5cm) then the fabric is 14-count. A 28-count linen will have 28 threads to 1in (2.5cm).

You can work counted cross stitch on anything that has a grid or is made up of squares. To translate a squared chart or pattern on to fabric accurately, you need material that is itself made up of squares. Therefore fabrics used for counted needlework are all woven in even squares. These fabrics are divided into two main groups: Aida, which is woven in blocks with obvious holes; and evenweave, which is woven in single threads. (See also Choosing and Using Fabrics page 32.) The butterflies and buddleia design on page 18 was worked on 14-count Aida.

## HOW MANY STRANDS?

The number of strands of stranded cotton (floss) used depends mainly on the stitch count of the fabric you are using. When in doubt, work a few cross stitches in the fabric margin and decide how many strands you prefer. If the chart does not indicate how many strands to use, check by pulling a thread from the edge of the fabric and compare it with the strands of cotton. They should be a similar weight to the threads in the fabric. As you experiment with your stitching you will be able to combine different threads in the same project with remarkable effects. (See also Mixing Thread Types page 52.)

## HOW IS DESIGN SIZE CALCULATED?

If you are going to progress from purchased cross stitch kits to working from charts or better still, your own designs, you must know how to work out the finished size of the design. It is this calculation that decides how much fabric you will need to stitch your project or whether a particular motif will fit in a card aperture. There is nothing worse than working a project and realising belatedly that the whole design will not fit on the fabric!

All that determines the finished size of a cross stitch design is the number of stitches up and down and the thread count of the fabric. Calculate the size of a design as follows.

**1** Look at your chart and count the number of stitches in each direction.

**2** Divide this number by the number of stitches to 2.5cm (1in) on the fabric of your choice and this will determine the completed design size. For example, 140 stitches divided by 14-count Aida results in a design size of 10in (25.5cm).

**3** Now add a margin for stretching, framing or finishing. I always add 13cm (5in) to both dimensions for a picture or sampler. This can be reduced to 7.5cm (3in) for smaller projects.

When calculating design sizes on linen or evenweave, remember that you will be working over two threads, so divide the count of the evenweave by two before you start calculating.

### JANE'S TIP

*Remember when creating a card or trinket pot to allow the extra margin on the aperture size not the stitch count.*

## Stitch Perfect – PREPARING YOUR FABRIC

❖ Press the fabric before you start, to remove creases and check for marks and blemishes.

❖ Find the middle of the fabric by folding in four and pressing lightly. Open out and work a line of tacking (basting) stitches following the threads to mark the fold and the centre. Remove these stitches when work is completed. Now rule a line on the chart (if using a copy) to match the arrows and the tacking.

❖ Sew a narrow hem or oversew raw fabric edges to prevent fraying. This can be removed on completion. Avoid using adhesive tape or glue as they can 'creep' and attract grime.

❖ Work one large cross stitch at the top of your fabric some distance away from the stitching area – this will remind you which is the top of the work and which way the work is facing.

# STITCHING FROM A KIT

Good quality cross stitch kits will supply you with enough fabric and thread to complete the whole design (see picture below). This will be based on you sorting the threads correctly and keeping them in a safe place away from cats and coffee! See also page 120.

◆ Always read all the instructions in the kit pack before starting to stitch.

◆ If the kit threads are supplied as a bundle or swatch, sort them before you start stitching and try to do this is daylight. I have mistaken blues, greys and greens many times when working under domestic electric light. Check that you have all the colours you need and mount all the threads on a thread organizer alongside its shade number (see page 17).

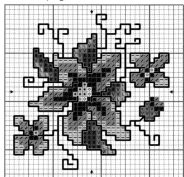

◆ Unless indicated otherwise by the kit designer, start stitching in the middle of a design to ensure an adequate margin for making up.

◆ Find the centre of the chart by following the little arrows at the sides to the centre stitch or the stitch nearest the centre point. You could circle this with a pencil.

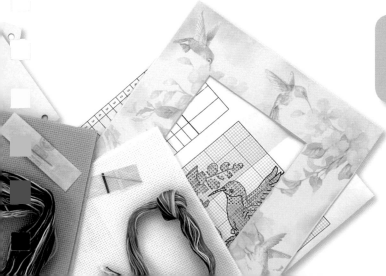

### JANE'S TIP

Be aware that the physical size of a chart doesn't bear any resemblance to the completed size of the project.

Cross stitch kits vary a little in their contents, depending on the manufacturer, but you should have a chart, embroidery threads, fabric and a needle, and perhaps also a thread organizer and a picture mount or card blank, if appropriate.

# How to Start Stitching

It is important to start and finish your stitching neatly, avoiding the use of knots which would create ugly lumps and bumps in your finished work.

## Knotless Loop Start

Starting this way (Fig 1) can be very useful with stranded cotton (floss), but only works if you are intending to stitch with an even number of strands, i.e. 2, 4, or 6.

**1** Cut the stranded cotton to 80cm (31.5in) long and separate out one strand. Double this strand and then thread your needle with the two ends.

**2** Pierce your fabric from the wrong side where you intend to place your first stitch, leaving the looped end at the back of the work. Return your needle to the wrong side after forming a half cross stitch and pass the needle through the waiting loop. The stitch is now anchored and you may begin to stitch.

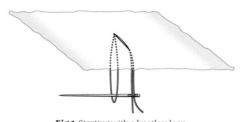

**Fig 1** *Starting with a knotless loop.*

### Jane's Tip

*I don't think that the back has to be as perfect as the front but if you keep it neat you will not have to spend hours sorting out the spaghetti on the back.*

## Away Waste Knot Start

Start this way (Fig 2) if working with an odd number of strands or when tweeding threads (where you use one strand each of two or more colours to achieve a mottled, tweedy appearance – see page 17), or if you are a real perfectionist!

**1** Thread your needle and make a knot at the end. Take the needle and thread through from the front of the fabric to the back and come up again about 2.5cm (1in) away from the knot.

**2** Now either begin cross stitching and work towards the knot, cutting it off when the threads are anchored, or thread the end into your needle and finish off under some completed stitches. Avoid using this method with black thread as it may leave a shadow on the fabric.

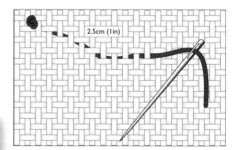

**Fig 2** *Starting with an away waste knot.*

---

## How to Hold Fabric

If you are working on a frame or hoop this doesn't really apply but if you are using a sewing action it may be helpful. With a large piece of fabric, I roll the material towards the centre of the area where I am stitching so I'm holding the wrong side of the material.

# WORKING A CROSS STITCH

A cross stitch has two parts and can be worked in one of two ways – a complete stitch can be worked, or a number of half stitches may be stitched in one line and then completed on the return journey. Your cross stitch may face either direction but the one essential rule is that all the top stitches should face the same direction to produce the neatest result.

To create perfect cross stitches the strands of thread first need to be aligned. Take two strands of stranded cotton (floss), separate the strands completely and then realign them before threading your needle.

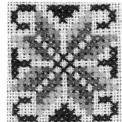

## JANE'S TIP

When using some fibres it is helpful to pass the threads through a lightly dampened sponge to help remove unwanted static from the threads.

## FORMING A SINGLE CROSS STITCH ON AIDA OR EVENWEAVE

Bring the needle up from the wrong side of the fabric at the bottom left of an Aida block or to the left of a vertical evenweave thread (see Fig 11 page 29). Cross one block of Aida or two threads of evenweave and insert the needle into the top right-hand corner (see Fig 3 and Fig 4 below). Push through and come up at the bottom right-hand corner. Complete the stitch in the top left-hand corner. To work an adjacent stitch, bring the needle up at the bottom right-hand corner of the first stitch.

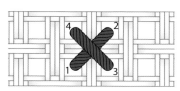

**Fig 3** Working a single, whole cross stitch on Aida fabric.

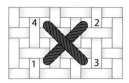

**Fig 4** Working a single, whole cross stitch on evenweave fabric.

## FORMING CROSS STITCH IN TWO JOURNEYS

Work the first leg of the cross stitch as usual but instead of completing the stitch, work the next half stitch and continue to the end of the row (Fig 5). Complete the cross stitches on the return journey. I recommend this method as it forms neater vertical lines on the back of the work. This method isn't suitable for cross stitching over one fabric thread (see Stitch Perfect – Evenweave in Miniature page 59).

**Fig 5** Working cross stitches in two journeys (on evenweave).

## JANE'S TIP

If you prick yourself whilst stitching (or should I say when) and mark your fabric, a dab of your own saliva will remove the stain.

23

## FRACTIONAL CROSS STITCHES

Quarter and three-quarter cross stitches enable us to create curves and smoother lines. Three-quarter cross stitch creates a triangular shape allowing for more detail within small motifs (see examples in the picture below). These stitches are less easy to form on Aida because the needle passes down the central hole in the thread group. When forming these stitches on Aida, a 'sharp' needle is helpful.

Work the first half of the cross stitch as usual, sloping the stitch in the direction shown on the chart. Work the second, quarter stitch over the top and down into the central hole to anchor the first half of the stitch (Fig 6).

### STITCH & PARK

When working with a number of different shades you can use several needles at a time to avoid stopping and starting over again. Work a few stitches in one shade, bring the needle out to the front of the work and 'park' it above where you are stitching. Introduce another colour, work a few stitches and then park that colour. Bring back the previous colour, working under the back of the stitches. Use a gold-plated needle to avoid any risk of the needle marking the fabric.

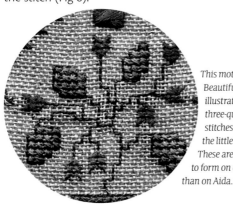

This motif from the Beautiful Band Sampler illustrates the use of three-quarter cross stitches very clearly on the little pink flowers. These are always easier to form on evenweave than on Aida.

**Fig 6** Working three-quarter cross stitch on evenweave.

## *Stitch Perfect* – CROSS STITCH

❖ Use the correct size needle for the fabric and number of strands of thread required.

❖ When stitching on evenweave fabric, start to the left of a vertical thread (see Fig 11 page 29) to prevent counting mistakes.

❖ Start with a knotless loop start or away waste knot (see page 22), avoiding knots on the back of the work.

❖ Work the cross stitch in two journeys (see Fig 5 on previous page) forming neat vertical lines on the back of the work. Use a sewing movement – half cross stitch in one direction, covering these original stitches with the second row.

❖ To prevent thread twisting when working cross stitch in two journeys, either turn the work upside down and let the needle spin, or twist the needle as you stitch.

❖ Work cross stitch with all the top stitches facing the same direction.

❖ Come up through unoccupied holes to help keep stitches beautifully formed.

❖ Plan your route around a chart, counting over short distances to avoid mistakes.

❖ Do not travel across the back of the fabric for more than two stitches as trailing thread will show on the front of the work (see Stitch & Park above).

# BACKSTITCH OUTLINING

Backstitching is a personal thing. Sometimes it is essential to the project because without it, you wouldn't be able to recognize the finished piece! It is used to add definition to a motif or for details like a cat's whiskers or a ship's rigging.

## *Stitch Perfect* – BACKSTITCH

❖ Try using subtle shades for backstitch to avoid a hard edge to the cross stitches and avoid black unless needed for wrought iron or similar motifs.

❖ Generally, use one strand of stranded cotton and a slightly smaller needle size for backstitch outlining.

❖ Work backstitch after all cross stitching has been completed, to avoid breaking up the backstitch line.

❖ Work backstitch over individual blocks on Aida or pairs of threads on evenweave and avoid working long stitches, unless it is

appropriate or unless you are deliberately aiming for a 'sketchy' backstitch style which does not follow the cross stitch neatly.

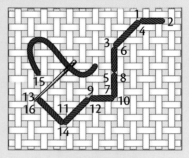

**Fig 7** *Working backstitch.*

**GOOSE AND PIG**

**Stitch count:** 32h x 71w
**Design size:** 5.8 x 12.7cm
(2¼ x 5in)
**Fabric:** Zweigart cream
14-count Aida
**Needle:** Tapestry size 24
**Chart:** Page 171

*These two animals are from the Farmyard Fun Cushion on page 37, with the pig reversed to make a pleasing shape. The motif has been worked twice to show the use of backstitch. The lower version has backstitch added and you can see that the creatures have more character once outlined. Work the design using two strands of stranded cotton (floss) for cross stitch and the French knot, and then one strand for backstitch.*

# WORKING FRENCH KNOTS

French knots are small but important little stitches often used for eyes and other details. In this book they are shown as coloured circles or knots, with colour and code given in the chart key or on the chart. The design opposite uses massed French knots to great effect.

French knots can cause some distress as they can disappear to the back of the work or end up as a row of knots on the thread in the needle! To work perfect French knots, follow Fig 8. Bring the needle through to the front of the fabric and wind the thread around the needle twice. Begin to 'post' the needle partly through to the back, one thread or part of a block away from the entry point (to stop the stitch being pulled to the wrong side). Now gently pull the thread you've wound, so it sits snugly at the point where the needle enters the fabric. Pull the needle through to the back to have a perfect knot in position.

For bigger French knots, add more thread to the needle as this gives better results than winding more times around the needle.

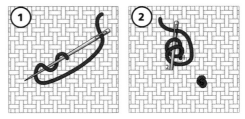

**Fig 8** *Creating a French knot.*

# CHANGING THREADS AND FINISHING OFF

Changing threads and finishing your work off correctly will pay dividends, creating a neat appearance and a safe, lasting piece of stitching.

At the back of the work, pass the needle under several stitches of the same or similar colour and snip off the loose end close to the stitching (see Fig 9). Small loose ends have a nasty habit of pulling through to the right side! If you are a perfectionist, try finishing the stitches in the direction that you are working – this is particularly relevant when working band samplers, where you don't want to distort the fabric or create a gap in the centre of a band.

When the thread needs replacing, stop stitching and 'park' the needle above the design. Thread a new needle with the replacement thread and form a few stitches. Now un-park the needle and finish the old thread under the new stitches. This will prevent any stitch distortion on the front of the work.

**Fig 9** *Finishing off a thread neatly.*

*This buddleia and butterfly design is the same as the one on page 18 but has been worked over two threads of a 28-count linen, with the buddleia flower stitched in massed French knots instead of cross stitch, effectively imitating the many small flowers of the plant. The butterflies have been worked over just one linen thread and so are half the size of those in the previous design. To ensure the butterflies are worked in the correct position, stitch them from the flower outwards.*

# WORKING WITH LINEN

Linen is made from the fibres of the flax plant *Linium usitatissimum*. Unlike other fabrics, linen increases in strength when wet and it is the perfect choice for cross stitch on table or bed linen and for pulled and drawn thread work. Today, linen fabric is used extensively by the fashion industry as pure linen clothing is in great demand. I wear linen clothing and as a result spend plenty of time clutching a steam iron!

Linen manufactured for embroidery is generally an evenweave fabric, which means there are the same number of vertical and horizontal threads to 2.5cm (1in); it does not mean that the threads are all the same thickness or that there are no slubs or wobbly threads! These naturally occurring irregularities can dissuade some stitchers from using it but stitching on linen is not difficult, just different. It is also the fabric of choice when working pulled thread embroidery (see page 106) because you *want* the threads to stay pulled or creased. It is also possible to stitch poems or other text within a small sampler if the border is worked over two threads and the text over one thread.

**ROSY APPLES**

**Stitch count:** 45h x 51w    **Design size:** 8.8 x 10cm (3½ x 4in)    **Fabric:** Zweigart Dublin ivory 26-count linen    **Needle:** Tapestry size 24    **Chart:** Page 185

*This charming little picture is worked over two threads of linen, using two strands of stranded cotton (floss) for cross stitch and then one for backstitch.*

## RAILROADING

This technique is used to force two strands of stranded cotton (floss) to lie flat and parallel to each other (Fig 10). When pushing the needle through the fabric, pass it in between the two strands of stranded cotton. You can railroad both parts of the cross stitch or only the top stitch.

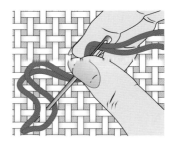

**Fig 10** *Using the railroading technique.*

## STITCH PERFECT – EVENWEAVE/LINEN

The general instructions for working on evenweave fabrics also apply to linen.

❖ Use the correct size needle for the fabric (see page 12).

❖ Separate each strand of stranded cotton (floss) and then re-combine them, ensuring the twist is running in the same direction on each strand.

❖ To avoid reversing the twist, start stitching with an away waste knot (page 22) rather than the loop start method.

❖ On linen and evenweave start stitching to the left of the vertical thread (Fig 11) as this will help prevent counting mistakes.

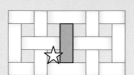

**Fig 11** *Starting to the left of a vertical thread on linen/evenweave.*

❖ Work cross stitches over two threads in each direction to even out any discrepancies. If more detail is required, stitches can be formed over one thread.

❖ When stitching over one thread, work the stitches singly rather than in two journeys, to prevent the stitches sliding under the fabric threads.

❖ Learn to railroad (see above): although time-consuming, it produces effective results. Even simpler, as you take the needle out of the fabric, give it a half turn: this will keep the thread from twisting and the stitches will lie flat.

❖ When working across the fabric, for example, on a band sampler, it is good practice to finish the stitches in the direction that you are working.

# WORKING PROJECTS

This book is full of projects you can stitch, some of which are shown opposite. This page gives stitching information in a nutshell, which will be particularly helpful for less experienced stitchers. The idea of stitching a project from scratch is sometimes daunting but these basic instructions will get you on track. See also Getting Started pages 10–29.

## WHAT THREADS DO I NEED?

The majority of the project designs in this book are charted in the Chart Library (with a few in the main chapters), with the colour keys listing the colours and threads needed. You can use different colours to the ones listed but remember to check that all the colours work well together.

## WHICH FABRIC AND HOW MUCH?

The fabric used, the stitch count and the finished design size are given in the caption under the colour pictures of the projects. If you are working the design as photographed just add a margin of 12.5cm (5in) to the design size and you can move on to 'Where Do I Start' (below).

If using alternative fabrics, check the stitch count of the material and if this is different to that of the stitched sample you must work out the finished design size – refer to page 20. A higher thread count will produce a smaller stitched design.

## WHERE DO I START?

Start stitching in the middle of the design to ensure an adequate margin for stretching and framing. To find the middle of the fabric, fold it in four and press lightly. Open out the fabric and work a narrow line of tacking (basting) stitches following the threads to mark the fold and the centre. These tacking stitches should be removed on completion of the work.

## HOW MANY STRANDS?

If the design you wish to stitch does not indicate in the chart or stitching instructions how many strands of stranded cotton to use, check by carefully pulling a thread from the edge of the fabric and comparing it with the strands of cotton – they should be a similar weight. If using alternative threads to the ones used in the stitched sample, work a few stitches in the fabric margin to check the effect.

## BEFORE YOU START

◆ Prepare your fabric for work – see also page 21. Sew a narrow hem or oversew the raw edges to prevent fraying. This can be removed on completion of the project.

◆ Rule a line on the chart (if using a copy) to match the tacking (basting) stitches on your piece of fabric.

◆ Check you have all the thread colours you need and mount all the threads on a piece of card or a thread organizer, adding the shade numbers beside the threads.

◆ Work one large cross stitch at the top of your work away from the stitching to remind you which is the top and which way the work is facing.

*This selection of projects gives you some idea of the exciting designs you can create using the comprehensive advice in this book. From the top, clockwise: Hardanger and Honesty Picture (stitching instructions on page 51); Zigzags and Ladders Sampler (page 110); Hellebore Card (page 132); Assisi Dragonfly Sachet (page 93); Blue Ribbon Flower Card (page 86) and Rainbow Alphabet Sampler (page 49).*

# CREATIVE OPTIONS

This section takes a closer look at some of the fabric and thread options open to the cross stitcher. You will see how easy and rewarding it is to cross stitch on a variety of materials, including perforated paper, silk, waste canvas, non-evenweave fabric and double canvas. Some of the many threads available are explored, showing how effective cross stitching is with yarns other than stranded cotton (floss), such as flower threads, space-dyed threads, rayons, metallics and blending filaments.

## CHOOSING AND USING FABRICS

Today there is so much choice, both in fabric thread count and colour, and the next few pages show you a variety of fabrics to whet your appetite and encourage you to look further – the only limit is your imagination and perhaps your eyesight!

The important message is to remind you to choose the appropriate fabric for the job in hand i.e., soft washable cotton Afghan fabric for a baby rather than crisp, crunchy linen and so on. Another example of this would be using pure linen for pulled thread embroidery, as you are creating the holes and therefore the decorative effect by creasing the fabric threads. This would not be as satisfactory if worked on an easy-care material that does not crease!

Bear in mind whether the fabric is for decoration or a more functional use, and select a thread count you can manage without the frustration of working on material that strains your eyes. Most charted designs will adapt to suit different fabrics, for example, you can transfer cross stitch patterns on to canvas and vice versa.

**CLIMBING CREEPER BOOKMARK**

**Stitch count:** 98h x 23w
**Design size:** 18 x 4cm (7 x 1½in)
**Fabric:** 4.5cm wide (1¾in) ivory 28-count linen band
**Needle:** Tapestry size 26
**Chart:** Page 173

*This pretty bookmark has been worked on a length of linen band. Work the design over two linen threads, using two strands of stranded cotton (floss) for cross stitch and one for backstitch. I used a simple hemstitch across the top edge (see page 119) and folded the lower edge to a point and stitched it in place invisibly, adding a twisted cord (see page 41).*

I would add a note of warning: if you are going to spend hours stitching personal masterpieces – do resist the temptation to economize on fabric quality. I prefer Zweigart and use all the fabrics across their range. I have visited their factory in Germany and have seen how the fabric is woven, dyed and the quality controls that are in place.

## LINEN AND AIDA BANDS

Fabric is woven in a variety of widths, but one specialist area is that of bands. Linen band is widely used in Europe for home decorations, door bow embellishments, shelf edging and so on. Linen and Aida bands are also ideal for creating small projects, such as the bookmark opposite, as only two raw edges need to be finished.

*You will see in this section that fabrics for counted thread embroidery are excitingly varied. Evenweave linens are available in some lovely colours, from soft and subtle to deep and vibrant, as you can see by the picture here. The range of linen and Aida bands also continues to improve. See page 60 for examples of canvas fabrics.*

## AGEING LINEN

It is easy to add the appearance of age to linen by dipping it in black tea. The fabric must be a pure, natural fabric such as 100% cotton or linen. Tea-dyeing can be done on the fabric before you start stitching or to the completed embroidery, although you need to make sure that threads used are colourfast (see page 16). After dipping the fabric or needlework in the tea, dry naturally and then press.

### JANE'S TIP
*To avoid waste and keep fabric costs down, try to buy a 'fat quarter', which is generally 50 x 70cm (20 x 27½in).*

# COLOURED AND PATTERNED FABRICS

The range of fabrics available to the stitcher is quite overwhelming and I can't illustrate them all here, but hopefully will set you thinking about some of the options available to you. There are fabrics that combine damask fabric with Aida patches forming stitchable areas; others are hemmed as tablecloths and in a myriad of colours, textures and fibre content.

## COLOURED FABRICS

Some of the fabric colours just make your fingers itch to stitch, but there are factors to consider. When selecting threads you do need daylight and the fabric of choice at hand as the background fabric colour will have a profound effect on the finished piece. Some of the new, bright colours are simply wonderful to look at, as these bold pincushions show. Take care though with some unusual colours to select threads carefully.

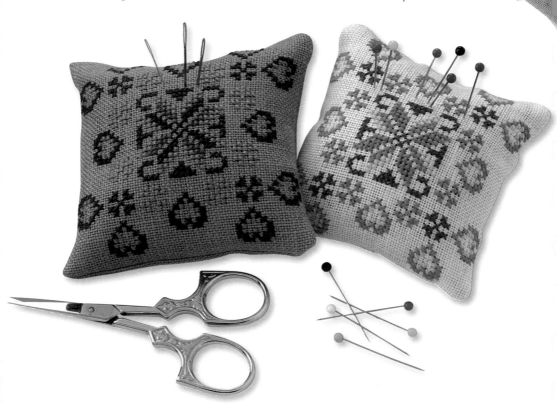

### CROSS STITCH HEART PINCUSHIONS

**Stitch count:** 46h x 45w each   **Design size:** 8.5cm (3¼in) square
**Fabric:** Zweigart Annabelle 28-count shade 487 (peach) or Zweigart
Cashel linen 28-count shade 227 (lemon)   **Needle:** Tapestry size 24   **Charts:** Page 175

*These two bright pincushions are worked on different fabrics but both have the same
thread count so the projects are the same size. Use two strands of stranded cotton (floss)
for cross stitch. See page 216 for making up a pincushion.*

## PATTERNED FABRICS

These fabrics have been woven using different coloured threads rather than weaving in white and then dyeing to suit and this offers us all sorts of options. You could use the pattern as part of your project, incorporating it into your design as I have done in this Baby Photograph Keepsake. Alternatively, ignore the pattern and use it as a background, as in the Bouquet and Buttons picture below.

### BABY PHOTOGRAPH KEEPSAKE

**Stitch count:** 15h x 15w
(maximum for each patterned square)
**Design size:** 2.5cm (1in) square (for each square)
Overall size of case 9 x 11.5cm (3½ x 4½in)
**Fabric:** Zweigart blue check 14-count Aida, 30 x 18cm (12 x 7in) approx
**Needle:** Tapestry size 24
**Chart:** Page 183

*This little case is perfect for photos. Change the blue shades to pinks if you prefer. If using the fabric as part of your design, centre the motif within each square. If working on plain fabric, fold the fabric into three to gauge where to place the motifs – see diagram on page 217. Use two strands of stranded cotton (floss) for cross stitch and one for backstitch. To make up the case see page 217.*

### BOUQUET AND BUTTONS

**Stitch count:** 41h x 44w
**Design size:** 7.5 x 8cm
(3 x 3⅛in)
**Fabric:** Zweigart pink check 14-count Aida
**Needle:** Tapestry size 24
**Chart:** Page 171

*This charming design uses two strands of stranded cotton (floss) for cross stitch and French knots and one strand for backstitch. Add four mother-of-pearl buttons with contrasting thread.*

# AFGHAN FABRICS

Afghan fabrics are generally used for making decorative throws or cot blankets although the fabrics do lend themselves to lovely cushions, as shown opposite. I use pure cotton fabrics when making throws as I like the way they handle and wash.

When working an Afghan intended as a throw, remember that the back of the project will be in view so try to be tidy as you work. I work all the design over two fabric threads so that I can work the crosses in two journeys (see page 23) thus forming nice straight lines on the back of the work. It will also grow satisfyingly quickly.

Afghan fabrics do vary – some restrict the areas that can be stitched while others allow you to extend your stitching over the squares. On the two folk-art cushions, I have worked the central parts of the design over two threads within the Afghan squares and the smaller border motifs over one thread.

Cross stitching over one fabric thread (unless on interlocked fabric) is not satisfactory when worked in two journeys; so form each cross stitch individually or perhaps work the border motifs in tent stitch. (See also Stitching in Miniature on page 59.)

I have included a corner of an Afghan throw (the Black-Eyed Susan design, below) to illustrate the frayed edge possible with this fabric. You would need to either hand stitch or use a sewing machine to work a line of stitches invisibly to avoid fraying too far. The frayed edge may then be knotted to create a more decorative effect.

## JANE'S TIP

*If working on an Afghan fabric with a high acrylic content (which many of the 'easy care' ones have), you may need to use hand cream prior to stitching to smooth your skin and help avoid snagging the fabric.*

### FARMYARD FUN AND HEARTS AND HOUSES CUSHIONS

**Stitch count:** 38h x 42w maximum motif size  **Design size:** 10.7 x 11.8cm (4¼ x 4½in) maximum motif size    **Fabric:** Zweigart pure cotton Anne 18-count  **Needle:** Tapestry size 22
**Charts:** Pages 170–173

*These cushions are both made in the same way. Work the larger motifs over two fabric threads, centring each design within an Afghan square (although this Afghan fabric allows you to extend your stitching further than 44 x 44 stitches if desired). Use three strands of stranded cotton (floss) for cross stitch and two for backstitch. Work the smaller border motifs repeatedly over one fabric thread, using two strands of stranded cotton and completing each cross stitch individually. Work a heart in each corner. Add a grid around the large motifs in cross stitch or double cross stitch over four threads using two strands of Appletons crewel wool.*

### BLACK-EYED SUSAN

**Stitch count:** 43h x 48w
**Design size:** 12cm (4¾in) square
**Fabric:** Zweigart pure cotton Anne 18-count
**Needle:** Tapestry size 22
**Chart:** Page 183

*Work the design over two fabric threads, using three strands of stranded cotton (floss) for cross stitch and two for backstitch. Before fraying, work a row of backstitch in thread matching the fabric to define the frayed edge.*

# EMBROIDERY THREADS

There is now a vast range of thread types available for cross stitch embroidery and some of the most common are shown here. Threads may be supplied in hanks, skeins or wound on to cards or spools and this can be a bit confusing for the less experienced if you do not know what the thread is going to look like.

There are no rules about what you can and cannot do with which threads: the trick is to try the thread on the fabric you intend to use, experiment with the number of strands if appropriate and then see what happens.

It is worth keeping left-over threads clearly marked with the manufacturer and shade number (see page 17) but all is not lost if you have not done this. You can create a sampler using odds and ends (although you won't be able to repeat the project when it is much admired by friends and family!).

*A mouth-watering selection of embroidery threads from various manufacturers to tempt you – and there are lots more to choose from!*

*STRANDED COTTON – Mercerized, divisible, six-ply cotton thread with a soft sheen. Available as solid colours, variegated and multicolour.*
*STRANDED RAYON – Very shiny, non-metallic, divisible four-ply thread.*
*PERLÉ COTON OR PEARL COTTON – Glossy single-ply pure cotton thread often used in Hardanger embroidery. They have different names depending on manufacturer. Available as solid colours, space-dyed and in hanks or balls.*
*SPACE-DYED THREADS – Generally made from cotton or silk and may be stranded or supplied as single threads. They have different colours (or shades of one colour) along their length and are sometimes referred to as hand painted.*
*FLOWER THREADS – Pure cotton with a matt appearance, available in solid or space-dyed colours.*

SPACE-DYED
SILKS

STRANDED RAYONS

SPACE-DYED
FLOWER
THREAD

STRANDED
PERLE RAYON

HAND-PAINTED
SYNTHETIC
THREAD

VARIEGATED
RAYONS

SPACE-DYED
THREADS

SOLID COLOUR
STRANDED
COTTONS

LINEN
THREADS

MULTICOLOURED
STRANDED COTTONS

MULTICOLOURED
PERLE COTTONS

39

# STRANDED COTTONS

Choosing and Managing Threads (page 16) gave detailed information on the use of stranded cotton (floss) in cross stitch embroidery. The pictures on the previous page and the bright needlecase below show you some of the colour range available. Stranded cottons are also perfect for making twisted cords, as shown by the little key keeper opposite. The major thread manufacturers produce solid and variegated stranded cottons. Some Variations threads are shown here.

## *Stitch Perfect* – STRANDED COTTON

- ✤ Before starting to stitch, separate the strands and realign them before threading your needle.
- ✤ Work with a length of stranded cotton about 80cm (30in).
- ✤ If you are not sure how many strands to use, stitch a few complete cross stitches and look at the stitching in daylight – see also page 20.
- ✤ Cross stitch is generally worked using two strands of stranded cotton on 14-count and 16-count Aida but you can, of course, mix the number of threads used within the same project. For example, you could alter the texture of a piece by working in one, two and even three strands. Try working French knots with different strands..
- ✤ Before laundering a piece of work, ensure that the threads are colourfast by following the advice on page 16.

**BRIGHT NEEDLECASE**

**Stitch count:** 32h x 37w
(front flap, cross stitch only)
**Design size:** 6.3 x 6.7cm (2½ x 2¾in)
**Fabric:** Zweigart 14-count cream Aida
**Needle:** Tapestry size 24
**Chart:** Page 174

*Remember to allow extra fabric for the back flap of the needlecase. Work the design using two strands of stranded cotton (floss) for cross stitch. Use two strands to work the hemstitch (page 119) around three sides of the design and then use two strands to work the two rows of four-sided stitches (page 154) down the 'spine' of the case. My version was completed by stitching two flannel 'pages' to the inside of the four-sided stitches, with a twisted cord (see opposite) added to finish.*

## SAMPLER KEY KEEPER

**Stitch count:** 34h x 34w     **Design size:** 6.2cm (2½in) square     **Fabric:** Zweigart Cashel 28-count tea-dyed linen     **Needle:** Tapestry size 24     **Chart:** Page 174

*This little project illustrates how a twisted cord made from stranded cottons can add a perfect finishing touch. The ends of the cord can be teased out to make a little tassel. Work the design using two strands of stranded cotton for full and three-quarter cross stitches and one strand for the backstitch outline and initials. Change the initials using the backstitch alphabet on page 198.*

## MAKING A TWISTED CORD

A twisted cord is perfect for embellishing projects as you can see by the key keeper above, and they are very easy to make.

**1** Choose a colour or group of colours in stranded cottons (floss) (or other threads) to match your embroidery.

**2** Cut a minimum of four lengths at least four times the finished length required and fold in half. Ask a friend to hold the two ends while you slip a pencil through the loop at the other end.

**3** Twist the pencil and continue twisting until kinks appear. Walk slowly towards your partner and the cord will twist.

**4** Smooth out kinks from the looped end and secure with a knot at the other end.

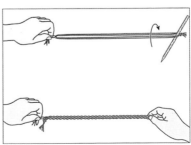

*Making a length of twisted cord from embroidery threads.*

# METALLIC THREADS AND BLENDING FILAMENTS

There are now dozens of wonderfully vibrant metallic, sparkly and glow-in-the-dark threads available to the cross stitcher. The Christmas Bell Pull (overleaf) has been stitched combining metallics and stranded cottons (floss). In the past, metallic threads have been regarded as rather difficult threads to use but there are now metallics that are much more user friendly. I have included tips from Kreinik, who produce the largest range of metallic and blending filaments – so they should know!

*This eyecatching selection of dazzling and colourful metallic threads, braids and blending filaments is sure to make your fingers itch to stitch!*

FINE METALLIC THREADS

STRANDED
LIGHT EFFECTS
THREADS

## STITCH PERFECT – METALLIC THREADS

❖ When using metallic threads stitch more slowly and more attentively, and use a needle large enough to 'open' the hole in the fabric sufficiently to allow the thread to go through easily.

❖ Use short lengths of thread 46cm (18in) or less to avoid excessive abrasion when pulling the thread through the fabric.

❖ Let your needle hang frequently (after one or two stitches) so the thread can untwist.

❖ Stitch using the 'stab' method rather than the 'hand sewing' method, working your stitches in two movements – up vertically, and down vertically through the fabric.

❖ To vary the amount of shine, change the number of strands of metallic thread – more strands give a greater sheen.

❖ If using DMC Light Effects threads, treat these as space-dyed threads (see page 48) to avoid disrupting the colour pattern.

❖ When using blending filaments, instead of combining the thread with stranded cotton you could overstitch existing cross stitched areas with the filament.

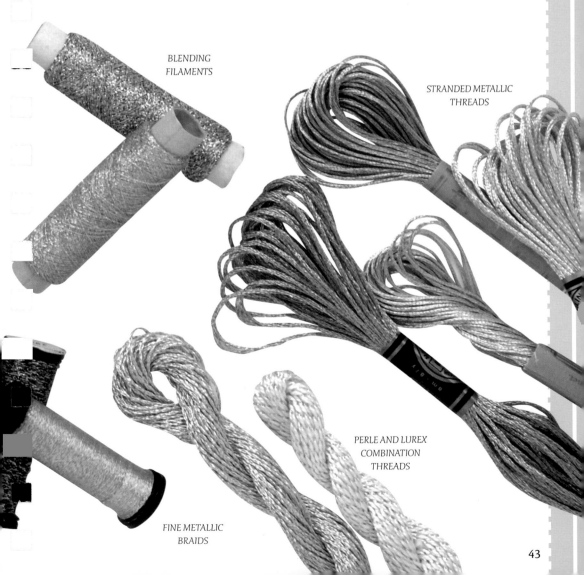

BLENDING
FILAMENTS

STRANDED METALLIC
THREADS

PERLE AND LUREX
COMBINATION
THREADS

FINE METALLIC
BRAIDS

# Using Metallic Threads

The projects on these two pages will allow you to explore metallic threads and their effects on different fabrics, and also create some attractive gifts and keepsakes.

I think the secret of using metallic threads is to find the style and thickness needed for the project by looking at the threads when you make your selection. Some fine yarns are referred to as 'braids' but look like normal thread, so it is much easier to select by eye, unless you have a specific list of requirements from the designer.

Some yarns are stitched using a needle and some are thicker, so are added to the surface of the design and then stitched or couched in place, so be prepared to experiment. (Silk ribbon and fine lace may also be treated in this way.)

When using very glossy metallic gold or silver threads, it is vital that you work with short lengths, about 46cm (18in), and a needle large enough help the threads through the fabric. If you work with long lengths you will find that the gold or silver flakes away from the core thread as you work and you lose the metallic effect.

## JANE'S TIP

*Metallic braids, such as Kreinik #4 braid, can be moistened with a damp sponge to help relax the thread and reduce twisting and knotting.*

### CHRISTMAS BELL PULL

**Stitch count:** 62h x 30w
**Design size:** 11.3 x 5.5cm (4½ x 2⅛in)
**Fabric:** Zweigart Cashel linen 28-count shade 513
**Needle:** Tapestry size 24
**Chart:** Page 180

*This pretty little project could be stitched on sparkly Aida fabric if preferred. Work using two strands of stranded cotton (floss) for cross stitch, double cross stitch and French knots. Where the Anchor Lamé metallic thread is used, divide and use as described on the chart. Work the backstitch using one strand. See page 214 for making up the bell pull. Make a hanging cord using the left-over threads (see page 41), teasing out the ends into little tassels.*

## CHRISTMAS PARCEL NAPKIN RING

**Stitch count:** 27h x 20w
**Design size:** 5 x 3.6cm (2 x 1½in)
**Fabric:** Zweigart 14-count Star Aida
**Needle:** Tapestry size 24
**Chart:** Page 179

*Work the cross stitch using three strands of DMC Light Effects. Work the darker area of the bow with three strands of Anchor Lamé. Work the lighter part with one strand of stranded cotton and three strands of the lamé together. Add backstitch with one strand of navy blue stranded cotton. To make up as a napkin ring, fold in the raw edges, hem them invisibly and join them at the back to make a continuous ring.*

## BLUE BOW AND BERRIES

**Stitch count:** 40h x 40w
**Design size:** 7.5cm square (3 x 3in)
**Fabric:** Zweigart 14-count linen Aida
**Needle:** Tapestry size 24
**Chart:** Page 179

*Work the design using two strands of stranded cotton (floss) and six strands of Anchor Lamé for cross stitch and one strand of stranded cotton for backstitch. The card was made using handmade blue paper, red card and a decorative ribbon. See page 215 for making cards.*

*A sparkly cube like this makes an interesting scissor or key keeper or a decoration for a Christmas tree and is a great way to experiment with metallic threads. It is worked as a flat embroidery on single canvas and is shown on page 61 in a red/green/gold colourway, where you will also find the stitching instructions.*

# USING BLENDING FILAMENTS

Blending filaments are light, delicate threads intended to be combined with other fibres, usually with stranded cotton (floss) to add a glisten or sparkle. For example, pearl blending filament is ideal combined with white stranded cotton to create snow effects, as you can see in the exquisite little Snowy Bird House Card opposite. You can see blending filament used alone to create delicate spider's webs on the Anemone Floral Cushion on page 53. Refer to the Stitch Perfect box on page 43 for advice on working with metallic threads.

**JANE'S TIP**
Blending filament is perfect for adding reflective highlights to areas of sunlight, moonlight, dew and water. It was used in this way for the water in the kingfisher design on page 9.

## THREADING BLENDING FILAMENT

When combining blending filament with stranded cotton (floss) in one needle, follow the four-part diagram here, as this method anchors the thread firmly in the needle.

**1** Loop the thread and pass the loop through the eye of the needle, leaving a short tail.

**2** Now pull the loop of thread over the point of the needle.

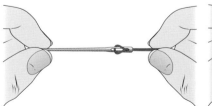
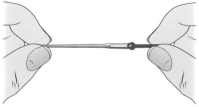

**3** Tighten the loop at the end of the eye of the needle by pulling the two ends of the thread.

**4** Gently stroke the knotted thread to 'lock' it in place. Add the stranded cotton by threading it on to the needle in the usual way.

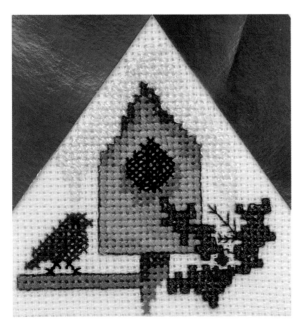

## SNOWY BIRD HOUSE

**Stitch count:** 39h x 38w
**Design size:** 7cm (2¾in) square
**Fabric:** Zweigart 14-count ivory linen Aida
**Needle:** Tapestry size 24
**Chart:** Page 174

*Work this charming motif using two strands of stranded cotton (floss) for cross stitch, adding three strands of Balger Blending Filament to the stranded cotton when working the snow on the roof. Use two strands of DMC Light Effects E321 for the holly berries and robin's breast. Add the backstitch in one strand of stranded cotton. Make up into a card by framing the embroidery with strips of gold card secured with double-sided adhesive tape and add a festive bow to finish.*

## SPACE-DYED THREADS

One of the joys of working cross stitch is that the stitch stays the same throughout the project but the effect can be changed by clever use of different fibres. Space-dyed threads, sometimes called variegated threads, have different colours (or shades of one colour) along their length. They change colour at regular, spaced intervals so you can decide where you want a particular shade to appear in your stitching. It is a very relaxing way to stitch as a whole project is worked from just the one skein of thread. Follow the basic guidelines below for using space-dyed threads and the effects will be stunning – and sometimes surprising! Your work will definitely not be the same as any other stitcher.

In a way, working with space-dyed threads is a type of designing without the angst! There are dozens of manufacturers of these specialist fibres so feel free to experiment and some are shown here and overleaf to give you some idea of the yummy colours available. If you can't find the exact version used in my projects do try something else – there will be dozens of alternatives.

The Rainbow Band Sampler opposite has been stitched using space-dyed threads throughout, with the addition of a little gold metallic. In this instance I have used De Haviland Flower Thread and the sampler was very relaxing to stitch as the whole project was worked from the same skein. I have used space-dyed threads in other parts of this book and love to combine them with other fibres, for example, the Hardanger and Honesty design shown on page 51 uses Anchor Multicolour Pearl thread, and you will see space-dyed thread used in the blackwork section later in the book.

> ### JANE'S TIP
> Not all space-dyed threads are colourfast so you need to consider the end use when selecting them. After spending dozens of hours on a Hardanger tablecloth, it would be heartbreaking to ruin it in the first wash (see Checking for Colourfastness on page 16).

## *Stitch Perfect* – SPACE-DYED THREADS

- ❖ When combining stranded cottons (floss) with space-dyed threads, compare the colours along the length of the thread to check that the shades tone successfully.
- ❖ Look at the skein and cut the thread to see where colours start and finish.
- ❖ Irrespective of the number of strands used for the project, always start with an away waste knot and not the loop start, as the colour order will be disrupted.

- ❖ When threading the needle, check the colour you intend to use is near the away waste knot.
- ❖ When working cross stitches always complete each cross as you go and do not form cross stitches in two journeys.
- ❖ Use a length of thread only whilst the colours suit the project. Do not attempt to use the whole length of thread if the colour of that section is not appropriate.

## RAINBOW ALPHABET SAMPLER

**Stitch count:** 69h x 28w
**Design size:** 12.5 x 5cm
(5 x 2in)
**Fabric:** Zweigart 14-count
linen Aida
**Needle:** Tapestry size 24
**Chart:** Page 181

*Work the cross stitches using one
strand of De Haviland English
Flower Thread in rainbow shades,
adding twirls in backstitch. Work
Rhodes stitches with one strand.
Use one strand of Madeira gold
metallic for the adapted double
cross stitch. Frame as desired.*

# *Stitch Perfect*
## – FLOWER THREADS

❖ Experiment with the thread thickness of Flower
  Thread as it varies slightly.
❖ Use the correct number of strands for the fabric in
  question (see page 20).
❖ You may need to use stranded cotton (floss) rather
  than the Flower Thread for backstitch as it may be
  too heavy for the project.
❖ Use shorter lengths when working with Flower
  Thread as it becomes rather fluffy if pulled through
  the fabric too many times.

## Unusual Threads

Space-dyed or variegated threads vary enormously, not only in price but also in fibre content and colour variation. Some have quite simple colour patterns, while others have more complex or subtle arrangements of colour. The Hardanger and Honesty picture opposite uses a pretty Anchor variegated thread for the Kloster blocks. Your local needlecraft shop will probably have examples of interesting and unusual threads from many different manufacturers, perhaps including Caron, Stef Francis, Thread Gatherers and Oliver

Twists. A word of warning though: some manufacturers do not always give their colour ranges different code numbers, which makes it rather difficult to find more of a thread you have been working with – so make sure you buy enough for your project!

Using variegated threads to introduce a different look to your work is great fun. Some are completely randomly dyed, so choosing different sections of colour and predicting how they will change as the thread is used is not always possible but they can be useful for working mixed greenery, brick walls etc.

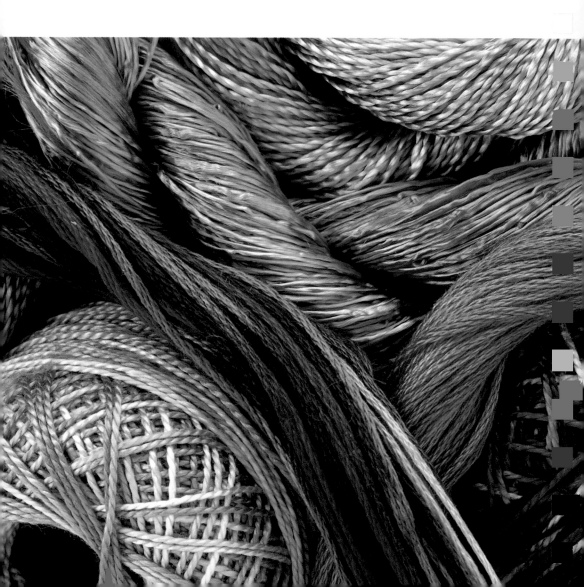

### HARDANGER AND HONESTY PICTURE

**Stitch count:** 54h x 50w   **Design size:** 9.8 x 9cm (3¾ x 3½in)   **Fabric:** Zweigart cream 28-count linen (not suitable for Aida)   **Needle:** Tapestry size 22 and 24   **Chart:** Page 182

*Work the design using two strands of stranded cotton (floss) for cross stitch and one for backstitch. Use one strand of Anchor Multicolour Pearl No.5 for the Kloster blocks and one strand of cream Pearl No.12 for the filling stitches (see pages 96–105 for Hardanger instructions). Mount and frame as preferred.*

*These two details show the Kloster blocks formed in a pretty variegated thread, with various filling stitches added in a similar colour to the fabric, including dove's eyes, corner dove's eyes, spider's webs and corner needleweaving.*

# MIXING THREAD TYPES

There are no rules about which threads go with which and there's no limit to what you can achieved by mixing fibres. This has been common practice in the machine embroidery and free embroidery worlds but perhaps has been slower coming to those who count!

A chart is the map we use to transfer the design from the paper to the fabric and the key may be simply a list of shades or in the case of the Anemone Floral Cushion shown opposite, the key also refers to types of thread and thread thicknesses. The idea of this design is to tempt you to look at charts in a different way and try new threads with at least a little gay abandon. Stitchers who enjoy counted thread embroidery are by their nature used to following patterns, or in our case charts, and hopefully this pretty cushion will tempt you to push the boundaries, just a little.

## ANEMONE FLORAL CUSHION

**Stitch count:** 69h x 69w    **Design size:** 12.5cm (5in) square    **Fabric:** Zweigart ivory 28-count linen
**Needle:** Tapestry size 24 and 26    **Chart:** Page 178

*The central panel on this cushion has been stitched using stranded cotton (floss), linen thread, Pearsall silk, Kreinik blending filament and De Haviland Tudor Twist. Refer to the Stitch Library for working the stitches. Work the cross stitch first using two strands of stranded cotton, Pearsall silk and linen thread. Work the outer border of crossed cushion stitch in one strand of Tudor Twist, adding the spider's web in Kreinik blending filament 034. It might help to use a frame when adding the web. Add a dragonfly charm (see Suppliers) using one strand of matching thread and make up as a cushion (see page 219).*

*The central panel of the Anemone Floral Cushion uses an attractive combination of mixed threads, including a variegated blending filament for the delicate cobwebs. The crossed cushion stitch border is very colourful.*

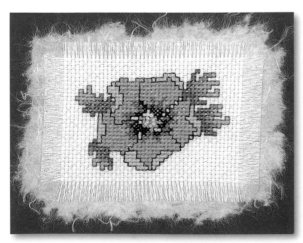

### ANEMONE CARD

**Stitch count:** 26h x 39w
**Design size:** 4.6 x 7cm
(1¾ x 2¾in)
**Fabric:** Zweigart Star
14-count Aida
**Needle:** Tapestry size 24
**Chart:** Page 178

*This card uses the flower from the chart on page 178 (with a few ad libs!). Use two strands of stranded cotton (floss) for cross stitch and one for backstitch. The card is made by layering a fluffy, handmade paper on green card using double-sided tape.*

# STITCHING ON NON-EVENWEAVE

So far we have seen how cross stitching looks on evenweave fabrics but non-evenweave or un-evenweave linen was used to create samplers and counted masterpieces long before the concept of evenweave had been invented, and it is exciting to attempt to recreate a design on non-evenweave material. The little violet card below has been stitched on linen scrim, a non-evenweave but pure linen fabric, which usually ends up as tea-towels or dish-cloths and isn't normally intended for embroidery.

The term 'evenweave' refers to the method used to manufacture the fabrics we use for cross stitch and does not mean that the material will have no lumps and bumps! This misunderstood term means that when the fabric is woven, the number of warp and weft threads (along the length and across the width) are the same. This is why when you work a cross stitch on evenweave fabric, the stitch appears square rather than squashed, shortened or elongated. However, cross stitches worked on non-evenweave fabric *will* be affected by the uneven weave, becoming slightly shortened or elongated; therefore you will need to experiment with the characteristics of the fabric to achieve the best results. And the results can be wonderful, especially if you are aiming to replicate the authentic look of antique samplers. If you love that aged look, as I do, refer to *Cross Stitch Antique Style Samplers* (D&C, 2005) for a wealth of designs.

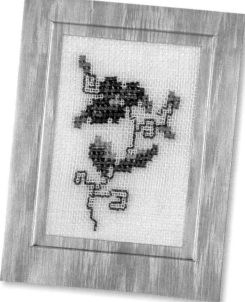

## VIOLET CARD

**Stitch count:** 29h x 19w
**Design size:** 7.5 x 4.5cm (3 x 1¾in)
**Fabric:** linen scrim 22/24-count
**Needle:** Tapestry size 24
**Charted motif:** Page 177

*This card uses the left-hand violet from the Willow Tree Sampler chart. Use three strands of stranded cotton (floss) for cross stitch and two for backstitch. Mount into a double-fold card.*

## BUMBLEBEE FLY SWAT

**Stitch count:** 18h x 34w
**Design size:** Depends on your swat or item being used!
**Fabric:** Use your imagination
**Needle:** Tapestry size 24
**Chart:** Page 173

*I have added this amusing little project just to make the point that you can add stitching to anything with a grid! Use four strands of stranded cotton (floss) for cross stitch and two strands for backstitch.*

**WILLOW TREE SAMPLER**

**Stitch count:** 67h x 66w     **Design size:** 11.5 x 9.5cm (4½ x 3¾in) approx
(will vary depending on the non-evenweave)     **Fabric:** Cross Stitch Guild non-evenweave 28/32 linen
**Needle:** Tapestry size 28     **Chart:** Page 177

*If you look at the stitch count of this project it would be square on an evenweave fabric but you can see that it is portrait shaped. Work the design on Cross Stitch Guild non-evenweave fabric, using two strands of stranded cotton (floss) for cross stitch and one for backstitch. Use two shades of green and two strands for the random French knots added to the willow. Frame as desired.*

## *Stitch Perfect* – NON-EVENWEAVE

❖ To know non-evenweave fabric and its foibles, work a square of 20 tacking stitches counting over two threads, to see whether a landscape (long) or portrait (tall) shape is created.

❖ Work a small test piece on the fabric and check you have the effect you require.

❖ If you are planning a traditional sampler, it is important to select motifs that are of the right style and weight and which will benefit from the effect produced by non-evenweave fabric e.g., a rabbit when stitched may look more like a hare!

❖ Don't be afraid to experiment with different motifs that will alter depending on the fabric direction. Trial and error is the way you will achieve the most successful results.

❖ If you want the design to fit a certain frame, be aware that design size may vary as the thread count may not be constant.

❖ Non-evenweaves can be given a lovely aged look by tea-dyeing (see page 33).

# USING STITCHING PAPER

Fabric isn't the only material you can cross stitch on. Stitching paper (perforated paper) can be stitched, folded, glued and cut to make pretty cross stitch projects and used to fill scrapbooks and treasure albums. I have collected items stitched on early perforated paper for many years, including samplers, bookmarks and needle cases.

Stitching paper is based on early Victorian punched paper, also called Bristol Board, made in England as early as 1840. The Victorians used it to work bookmarks, needle cases, pincushions, glove and handkerchief boxes, notebook covers and greetings cards.

Stitching paper is generally the equivalent of a 14-count fabric, so you can transfer cross stitch charts on to this medium as long as the design does not include three-quarter cross stitches. I have used stitching paper here to create a gift card and a hollyhock design.

I have also included an example of Stitching Cards produced by Tokens & Trifles (see Suppliers), which are the closest examples of the ready-formed bookmarks and paper scraps available during Victorian times (see opposite). These stitching cards are available in different stitch counts.

## HELLEBORE GIFT CARD

**Stitch count:** Not appropriate here
**Design size:** 8 x 12cm (3¼ x 4¾in)
**Fabric:** Stitching paper gold 14-count
**Needle:** Tapestry size 24
**Chart:** Page 183 (elements charted separately)

*Work the motifs using three strands of stranded cotton (floss) for cross stitch, one strand of gold metallic for the centre detail and two strands of stranded cotton for the backstitch outline. To make up, cut out the motifs leaving a small margin around the edge as shown in the hollyhock detail photograph below and then arranged on a double-fold card with a green insert, fixing the various parts in place with double-sided adhesive tape.*

## HOLLYHOCK

**Stitch count:** 29h x 34w
**Design size:** 5 x 6.2cm (2 x 2½in)
**Fabric:** Stitching paper black 14-count
**Needle:** Tapestry size 24
**Chart:** Page 180

*Work an individual flower using three strands of stranded cotton (floss) for cross stitch. I have started to cut out the flower leaving one row of paper at the edge. You could create a remarkable effect by working individual flowers on paper, cutting them out and applying them to a cross-stitched stem.*

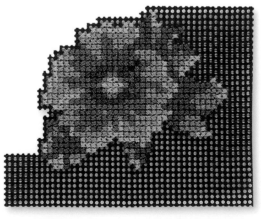

## *Stitch Perfect* – STITCHING PAPER

- Stitching paper is quite strong but it does need to be handled with care.
- There is a right and a wrong side to the paper: the smoother side is the right side.
- Avoid folding the paper unless this is part of the design.
- Find the centre of the paper with a ruler and mark with a pencil. Pencil lines can be removed with a soft rubber.
- On stitching paper, use three strands of stranded cotton (floss) for the cross stitch and two strands for backstitch outlining and lettering.
- Complete all stitching before any cutting.
- Draw the cutting lines on the back of the completed stitching using a soft pencil.
- Use small, sharp-pointed scissors or a good craft knife to cut out the design and any decorative elements of the pattern.
- Where appropriate, stick completed sections together using double-sided adhesive tape, unless stitching is required.

**TUDOR ROSE HEART**

**Stitch count:** 40h x 49w
**Design size:** 5.6 x 7cm (2½ x 2¾in)
**Fabric:** Heart-shaped stitching card 18-count (see Suppliers)
**Needle:** Tapestry size 28
**Chart:** Page 184

*Work the motif using one strand of stranded cotton (floss) for cross stitch, half cross stitch and backstitch. Join the two cards together using a running stitch around the existing perforations using one strand of DMC 3685 (Anchor 1028).*

## *Stitch Perfect* – STITCHING CARDS

- Stitching Cards are often much finer than stitching paper.
- Check your stitch count before you start – you do not want to run over the edge!
- When using Stitching Cards you can use the ivory side or the antique finish on the reverse.
- Use a size 28 needle to avoid distorting the ready-made holes in the cards.
- Use one strand of stranded cotton (floss) for cross stitch and backstitch.
- The cards are supplied with an un-perforated blank which may be used to cover the wrong side of the stitching.
- If you are tempted to add beads you will need to select Petite Glass beads because of the finer stitch count.

# Stitching in Miniature

I mentioned on page 20, the connection between stitch counts and design size and you can see by the photographs below and opposite the scale change achieved by working a charted design on very fine fabric. I have used silk gauze and evenweave linen to create some tiny counted projects. Indeed, in the dolls' house world stitching in miniature is the norm. Little samplers, pictures, pole screens, cushions and so on can be created from using counted charts and fine-count fabrics. Look in dolls' house embroidery books and you'll see what I mean.

Silk gauze is very expensive but you only need small amounts and it can be purchased in small squares ready mounted. Cross stitchers generally think stitching on silk gauze 40 stitches to 2.5cm (1in) is out of the question because it sounds so fine but it is much less taxing than first imagined. Silk gauze is constructed in such a way that although the stitch count is high, the holes in the fabric are large and easier to see than you think! The secret is to prepare the fabric as described right and work in a good light with the correct size gold-plated needle. I use a size 28 needle and work under a standard lamp which gives a wonderful light but doesn't get too hot.

I have included two flower motifs that have been stitched in miniature using two different stitches to suit the specific fabric – the pansy has been cross stitched on silk gauze and mounted into a key ring, while the rose card is worked on linen in tent stitch.

## Mounting Silk Gauze

When working on silk gauze you will need to use a simple mount-board frame.
1 Cut two pieces of stiff mount board to the size of your fabric.
2 Cut two sections or windows out of the centre of each piece of board – these sections need to be just big enough to work the embroidery.
3 Using double-sided adhesive tape, sandwich the silk gauze piece between the two boards. The frame can easily be removed once stitching is completed.

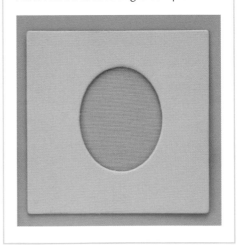

**PANSY KEY RING**

**Stitch count:** 25h x 25w
**Design size:** 1.6cm (⅝in) square
**Fabric:** 40-count silk gauze
**Needle:** Tapestry size 28
**Chart:** Page 179

*Work the design using one strand of stranded cotton (floss) for cross stitch and mount into a purchased key ring (see Suppliers).*

# *Stitch Perfect* – SILK GAUZE IN MINIATURE

❖ Silk gauze is constructed in a similar way to interlock canvas, to ensure that the threads will not slide.

❖ Silk gauze should be worked in a small mount-board frame to prevent the fabric distorting (see opposite).

❖ Half cross stitch or full cross stitch may be used successfully.

❖ Try stitching a small section to check your tension because you may find that half cross stitch is adequate.

❖ Avoid carrying threads across the back of work because it will show from the front.

❖ You can work long stitches and half cross stitches on silk gauze without distortion because it is interlocked.

**ROSE CARD**

**Stitch count:** 32h x 23w
**Design size:** 3 x 2cm (1⅛ x ¾in)
**Fabric:** Zweigart Cashel antique white 28-count linen
**Needle:** Tapestry size 28
**Chart:** Page 179

*Work the rose over one thread using one strand of stranded cotton (floss) for the tent stitch (rather than half cross stitch) and then add the backstitch in one strand. Mount the design into a double-fold card with a circular aperture to fit the embroidery. The partly worked rose is cross stitched over two fabric threads, showing the change in design size by working over two threads not one.*

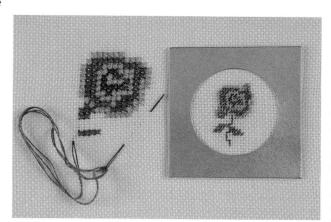

# *Stitch Perfect* – EVENWEAVE IN MINIATURE

❖ If working cross stitch over one thread on evenweave, work each cross stitch individually rather than in two journeys to stop the stitches sliding under neighbouring fabric threads.

❖ If working over one thread on linen (or any evenweave) use tent stitch rather than half cross stitch, as tent stitch will give

better coverage of the fabric and keep the stitches in position. If half cross stitch is used the threads will slide under neighbouring fabric threads.

❖ Select your evenweave fabric with care, with the minimum of slubs and imperfections, which are less easily disguised when working over one thread.

# WORKING ON CANVAS

I enjoy the contrast of working cross stitch designs on canvas for a change of effect and have designed projects commercially using canvas as an alternative to Aida or evenweave. Stitchers are sometimes nervous of transferring designs on to canvas when they were designed for fabric but the principles are the same. Early French samplers were generally stitched on canvas with the background left unstitched, to great effect – so have a go! Just remember to count the thread of the canvas and not the holes.

Canvas can be made from cotton, linen and plastic and is available in four mesh sizes – 10-, 12-, 14- and 18-count (threads to 2.5cm/1in). Any gauge of canvas can be used with any chart. Canvas is available in two main types: double-thread (duo) canvas and single-thread (mono) canvas. See page 63 for working on single canvas. The material with blue lines shown below is waste canvas, a removable background fabric – see page 66.

> ### JANE'S TIP
> Your choice of fabric to stitch on will depend on the stitches you plan to use, your eyesight and whether the project is decorative or functional. For example, canvas is perfect for cushions, chair seats and so on, which need to be harder wearing.

*Some of the types of canvas are shown here. From the top: Congress cloth (an evenweave canvas); plastic canvas with its distinctive blue lines; Magic Canvas; single canvas and a selection of plastic canvas shapes (on blue evenweave to show the mesh more clearly).*

**SPARKLY CHRISTMAS CUBE**

**Stitch count:** 16h x16w each face    **Design size:** 2.5cm (1in) cube    **Fabric:** 18-count single canvas
**Needle:** Tapestry size 22    **Chart:** Page 176

*A sparkly cube (made by Sue Hawkins as a Christmas tree decoration) would make an interesting scissor or key keeper. It is shown on page 45 in a blue/silver colourway. Work the design as a flat embroidery over different numbers of canvas threads as shown on the chart. Use six strands when working with stranded cotton (floss) and six strands of Anchor Lamé for all the counted stitches, referring to the Stitch Library for working the rice stitch, tent stitch, satin stitch and Rhodes stitch. Make up into a cube as described on page 213. See page 41 for making a twisted cord and page 218 for making a tassel.*

*The Sparkly Christmas Cube features three designs, each stitched twice: these three pictures show the different faces of the cube.*

## WORKING ON DOUBLE CANVAS

This type of canvas, also called Duo or Penelope is the same as mono canvas except that the threads are grouped in pairs in each direction and are usually finer. As with an evenweave fabric, stitches are worked over the double threads but if you want to put more detail into part of a design, you can make four times as many stitches by using every canvas thread. Half cross stitch, full cross stitch and tent stitch can be worked on double canvas.

Cross stitch charts may be used to work designs on canvas and vice versa as I have done with this pretty bluebell motif, worked once on Aida and mounted as a book patch and once on double canvas.

 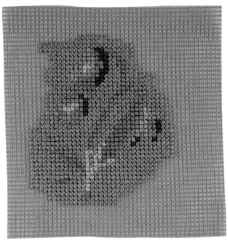

**BLUEBELL ON AIDA AND DOUBLE CANVAS**

**Stitch count:** 36h x 28w    **Design size:** 5.7 x 4.5cm (2¼ x 1¾in) on 16-count Aida
**Fabric:** Cream 16-count Aida or double canvas 10-count    **Needle:** Tapestry size 22    **Chart:** Page 185

*This motif has been worked on Aida and also on double canvas to show that charts may be transferred on to canvas if preferred. The cross stitch version uses two strands of stranded cotton (floss) for cross stitch. The canvas version uses six strands for cross stitch and DMC 352 (Anchor 9) for the tent stitch background colour.*

## *Stitch Perfect* – CANVAS

- ❖ Before stitching on double canvas, use a thick tapestry needle to push apart the double threads. This is known as pricking out the canvas and will make stitching easier if you intend to combine working one and two threads.
- ❖ Using double canvas when adding beads to a design creates the most satisfactory results as the beads stay nicely in position, not wobbling as they tend to do on single canvas.
- ❖ When counting canvas, always count the *threads* and not the holes, because your stitches are made over threads and not in holes. This is a common stumbling block but you will always get it right if you remember it this way – holes in canvas cannot be counted because they are empty and therefore do not exist!
- ❖ When working on single canvas it is best to use continental or diagonal tent stitch because if you use half cross stitch some of them may slip under the weave of the canvas and will be very uneven.

## WORKING ON SINGLE/MONO CANVAS

Single-thread or mono canvas is constructed of simple, even weaves and is also available in a deluxe quality, where the threads are polished before the canvas is woven and so the yarn passes smoothly through the canvas as you stitch. Single-thread canvas is suitable for any piece of work but especially upholstery, such as seat covers where the embroidery will be stretched unevenly when the seat is in use. The canvas threads are free to move a little on each other and so adjust to the stress rather than tearing. You will find both ordinary and deluxe canvas in white or brown (the latter is known as antique) and you should choose according to the colours of yarn that you will be using.

A word of warning: some commercial kits tell you to work half cross stitch on single canvas. A much better result is obtained by using tent stitch, but you will probably run out of wool as tent stitch uses about half as much yarn again as half cross stitch. You have to decide whether to buy more wool or settle for a rather thin-looking finished piece with inferior wearing qualities.

> ### JANE'S TIP
> *Deluxe canvas is always worth the extra expense as the polished threads help to prevent the yarn snarling up.*

## WORKING ON INTERLOCK CANVAS

Single/mono canvas is also available as interlock canvas, with the threads along the length doubled and twisted together to hold the cross threads firmly in place. This produces a more stable canvas, ideal for designs that include long stitches, which might otherwise pull loose canvas threads together and make holes in your work. The Topiary Trees Needlecase, with its satin stitch,

benefitted from being stitched on interlock canvas. The disadvantage of interlock canvas is that it is only available in white so you must take care not to stitch too tightly or the white will show through. Interlock is easy to make up once the embroidery is finished because it does not fray, unlike mono deluxe canvas which will very quickly fray right to the edge of the stitching unless great care is taken.

### TOPIARY TREES NEEDLECASE AND PENDANT

**Stitch count:** 53h x 46w for case;
21h x 21w for pendant
**Design size:** 7.5 x 6.5cm (3 x 2½in) for case;
3cm (1⅛in) square for pendant
**Fabric:** 18-count single canvas
**Needle:** Tapestry size 22
**Chart:** Page 184

*Work the satin stitch borders with one strand of Anchor Multicolour Pearl No.5 and the rest of the pattern with two strands in tent stitch, with a cream tent stitch background. (You could omit the background and work the design as cross stitch on evenweave or Aida.) Work the spine and outside edge of the case in long-legged cross stitch and attach the pendant with a twisted cord (see page 41). Line the case and pendant with dark green felt invisibly hemmed with matching thread.*

# USING MAGIC CANVAS

This specialized product is a treated interlock single canvas that does not fray. It can be folded and so is excellent for three-dimensional projects. It has an attractive appearance, so it isn't necessary to cover the background with stitching. I have used a sparkly version for some window light catchers but Magic Canvas is also available in a variety of colours, including white, red, yellow, green, blue, black, gold and silver.

### LIGHT CATCHERS

**Stitch count:** 28h x 28w
(each project including eyelets)
**Design size:** 4cm (1½in) square
**Fabric:** Zweigart Magic Canvas 18-count
in white and silver
**Needle:** Tapestry size 22    **Chart:** Page 185

*Work the motif on one half of the canvas then fold the other half to cover the back of the stitching. Cross stitch the darker blue and brown in two strands of stranded cotton (floss) and work the lighter blue in half cross stitch in two strands. Add the eyelets in two strands and the backstitch in one.*

### BEADED PICTURE FRAME

*This fun project takes no time at all and you can use the frame for a little photo or a tiny piece of stitching. I keep a jar of assorted glass beads in a glorious array of colours for just such a project. No chart is needed – just do your own thing. Fold a 10cm square (4in) of Magic Canvas into four and then fold in all four corners and press firmly. Now fold out the points to meet the outside edge. I joined the seams at the sides with matching threads and assorted Mill Hill seed beads, adding a few to the folded points. You could use Nymo thread to attach the beads, a specialized beading thread.*

## USING PLASTIC CANVAS AND PERFORATED CANVAS

These materials are very popular and are used in great quantities and in many ways, particularly in the United States of America. Plastic canvas is made from sheets of plastic punched with a mesh of holes and you use these holes to stitch a design just as you would on Aida. Perforated plastic canvas is very similar to stitching paper (see page 56).

Because these materials are stiffer than Aida they are often used for three-dimensional projects, such as festive decorations, napkin rings, picture frames, boxes and trinket pots. The plastic pieces can be trimmed to a shape with sharp scissors, joined together by stitching and can also be used to support a design already stitched on Aida or evenweave. Plastic canvas is available in 7-, 10- and 14-count and as pre-cut shapes. I have used a ready-made plastic canvas heart for the project shown below, concealing the edge of the canvas with blanket stitch.

> ### JANE'S TIP
> *If you accidentally cut a bar on your plastic canvas, it can be repaired with superglue or a hot glue gun.*

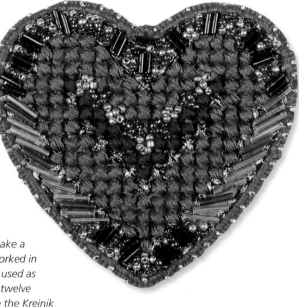

### BEADED CHRISTMAS HEART

**Stitch count:** 18h x 19w
**Design size:** 7.6 x 7.6cm (3 x 3in)
**Fabric:** Plastic canvas heart 7-count
**Needle:** Tapestry size 22
**Chart:** Page 181

*This project is fun to do and would make a pretty Christmas tree decoration. If worked in cross stitch without beads it could be used as a coaster. Work the cross stitch using twelve strands of stranded cotton (floss). Use the Kreinik ⅛in Ribbon to add the backstitch and the cross stitch as shown on the chart. Work blanket stitch around the edge of the heart, adding the Mill Hill Petite beads (using one strand of stranded cotton) to cover any gaps. Add the seed and bugle beads at random in the remaining spaces on the canvas (see picture for guidance).*

> ### JANE'S TIP
> *If you want the edge of the plastic canvas to be well covered, use more strands of thread when working the blanket stitch edging.*

# USING WASTE CANVAS

Waste canvas is a really useful material that enables the cross stitcher to transfer charted designs on to fabrics that were not intended for that purpose and therefore do not have an even, countable weave. Today, the most commonly used application for this technique is to add designs to sweatshirts, T-shirts and baby clothes. Before waste canvas was produced commercially this technique was worked using linen as the waste fabric and if a very fine stitch count is needed this would still be the fabric of choice.

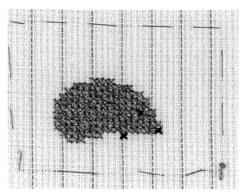

Waste canvas is a double canvas treated with a water-soluble starch product, which makes it simple to remove the threads after stitching but is therefore unsuitable for any other type of use. It is easily distinguished by the blue line running through the fabric. The waste material is applied to the garment or fabric and the grid is used to count whilst the design is stitched and then the threads of the canvas are removed.

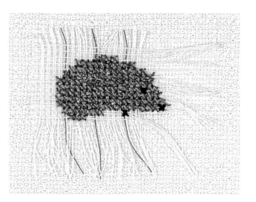

As you can see by the photographs here, the technique is worked in three stages and is described fully in Stitch Perfect opposite.

**1** Tack the waste fabric in position.
**2** Stitch the design from the chart.
**3** Remove the waste threads.

Once all the waste threads have been removed, check for any missed stitches and add any additional backstitch outlining that might be needed to complete the design. Press the finished piece of stitching from the wrong side on soft towels (see page 210).

### LITTLE HEDGEHOG

**Stitch count:** 11h x 18w    **Design size:** 2 x 3.3cm (¾ x 1¼in)
**Fabric:** 14-count waste canvas and viscose dress fabric in cream (or your garment)
**Needle:** Tapestry size 26 and crewel size 5    **Chart:** Page 167

*This little creature has been stitched to illustrate the process of working with waste canvas. He is also a good example of tweeding threads – combining more than one shade in the needle to add texture and shading (see page 17). His prickles are worked at random using two thread combinations. Use one strand each of two shades of stranded cotton (floss) in the needle at any one time, with the exception of the eye, nose and foot.*

# Stitch Perfect – WASTE CANVAS

❖ Select the correct stitch count waste fabric for the design and if unsure, work a small test piece confirming the number of strands of stranded cotton (floss) required.

❖ Use the best quality thread (e.g., DMC, Anchor or Madeira) to avoid colour runs.

❖ Cut waste canvas at least 5cm (2in) larger than the completed design size.

❖ Tack (baste) the waste fabric in position carefully using horizontal and vertical tacking lines – it must stay put whilst you work.

❖ Work the cross stitch design from a chart, working each stitch individually though the grid of the canvas and the ground fabric.

❖ When working on a large count waste material, work through the small holes on the canvas to keep the stitches firmly in position and prevent variable tension.

❖ When the stitching is complete, trim away any excess waste canvas and lightly spray with cold water. This releases the starch and makes removing the threads easier.

❖ The starch released can be very sticky so use tweezers to remove the fabric threads and wash your hands regularly.

❖ Pull out the threads one at a time, varying the direction from which you are working to avoid any distortion.

❖ When all the waste canvas has been removed check for missed stitches, which may be added carefully with a sharp needle.

❖ If using this technique on clothing, wash on the normal wash cycle for the garment but press the stitched section on the wrong side where possible.

**BLUE BUTTERFLY ON SILK**

**Stitch count:** 29h x 24w
**Design size:** 5 x 4.5cm (2 x 1¾in)
**Fabric:** 14-count waste canvas and raw silk background fabric
**Needle:** Tapestry size 26 and crewel size 5
**Chart:** Page 168

*I have added this decorative butterfly to a piece of hand-dyed raw silk. The silk has been washed to remove excess dye and to give an antique appearance. The motif has been worked in two distinct sections. The body has been worked through the small holes in the waste canvas using three strands of stranded cotton (floss). The wings are then worked through the large holes on the canvas thus forming a slight gap between the wings and body. The legs and antennae were added in backstitch in one strand of Kreinik Fine #8 Braid 393 and the backstitch added in two strands of stranded cotton (floss).*

# EXPLORING CHOICES

This section features a range of exciting designs showing how easy it is to combine cross stitch with other counted embroidery techniques. You will discover how much fun it is to bring a whole new dimension to your embroidery with the addition of buttons, charms, beads and ribbon, and how simple it is to enhance your cross stitch with other techniques such as blackwork, pulled work, drawn thread work, Hardanger embroidery and hemstitching.

I love adding different stitches to my cross stitch projects and using unusual threads, lace, ribbon, buttons and charms. The limit to choosing embellishments is really only your imagination, and successful treasure hunting. I trawl through bric-a-brac stalls, antique markets and junk shops and have used French paste jewellery, hand-painted Venetian glass and even the odd real pearl! Do experiment with embellishments and search for alternatives if you can't source the charm or button that I've used.

This section also includes advice on adapting cross stitch kits and designing projects, either on the computer or using paper and coloured pencils.

## USING EMBELLISHMENTS

Charms, buttons and other embellishments may be added to a completed piece of stitching to great effect, although there are pitfalls to avoid. The scale of a charm or button needs to be correct for the project, and look good together if combined on the same piece of stitching (see the tiny bee charm on the card below). I have included a charm on my Anemone Floral Cushion (page 53) in addition to some of the projects in this section. In some cases I've used buttons alone or combined with charms and silk ribbon embroidery.

### CHARMS

When selecting metal charms, avoid cheap, stamped versions as your work deserves the best. Brass charms are manufactured using strong processes and there will be chemical residues left on a charm if it has not been 'finished'. A process of 'dip, tub and roll' is the scouring method used to clean charms for use on embroidery, which prevents potential damage. If a completed piece of stitching is exposed to a damp atmosphere, a chemical reaction may cause the fabric to discolour. It is possible for blue fabric to have an orange patch where the charm touches the fabric. Where I have used antique embellishments to my own pieces, I have cleaned them very thoroughly, as virdigris marks may be impossible to remove.

## SUMMER FLOWER CARD (left)

**Stitch count**: 25h x 21w including button
**Design size**: 4 x 3.5cm (1½ x 1⅜in)
**Fabric**: 14-count white Aida
**Needle**: Gold-plated tapestry size 24
**Chart**: Page 202
**Embellishments**: Flowerpot button and gold-plated charm

*Work cross stitch, bullion knots, French knots and lazy daisy stitches with two strands of stranded cotton (floss) and a gold-plated needle. Refer to the chart for the length of the bullion knots and lazy daisies. Sew on the button and charm with cream sewing cotton and complete the card with a gold card frame and coloured card. See page 215 for making up a card.*

## STORK SCISSOR SAMPLER

**Stitch count**: 90h x 80w
**Design size**: 16.5 x 14.5cm (6½ x 5¾in)
**Fabric**: Zweigart Cashel 28-count
**Needle**: Tapestry size 24
**Chart**: Page 195
**Embellishments**: Five pewter charms, two brass charms, a novelty button and gold-plated needle

*This charming design has a real antique look. It is worked over two threads of linen (or one block of a 14-count Aida), using two strands of stranded cotton (floss) for cross stitch and French knots and the backstitch in one strand. Sew on the assorted charms, button and needle with matching thread. Mount and frame as preferred.*

# BUTTONS

There is an increasing array of buttons available, in the craft shops and through mail order, and some decorative buttons were used on the Summer Flower Card (page 68) and the Tea for Two Picture (overleaf). Mother-of-pearl or shell buttons create a lovely effect added to cross stitch and may also be combined with charms and beads. A charming result is created in the Stitcher's Treasure Picture (page 73) by using a combination of ribbon, lace, buttons and charms, which transform the small cross stitch motif into a much more complex project.

> **JANE'S TIP**
> Even if you do not have a computer at home, they are available in local libraries, allowing you to search for decorative items on the Internet.

> **JANE'S TIP**
> To tear handmade paper, place a ruler against the edge and tear. Dampening the paper before you tear will create a nice fluffy edge.

## LILAC BOOT CARD

**Stitch count**: 31h x 31w
**Design size**: 5.6cm (2¼in) square
**Fabric**: Zweigart Dublin 25-count ivory linen
**Needle**: Tapestry size 24
**Motif charted**: Page 193
**Embellishments**: six mother-of-pearl buttons

*The motif for this card is from the Little Shoe Sampler opposite (see chart key on page 193 for the changed colours). You could make an exquisite card for a bride by altering the colours to suit the bridal flowers. Work over two threads of linen, using two strands of stranded cotton (floss) for cross stitch and one for backstitch. Sew on the buttons using strong sewing thread. I completed the card with a tattered patch, some handmade paper and a ribbon trim. See page 215 for making up a card.*

## LITTLE SHOE SAMPLER

**Stitch count:** 53h x 74w

**Design size:** 9.5 x 13cm (3¾ x 5¼in)

**Fabric:** Zweigart 14-count pale qrey Aida

**Needle:** Tapestry size 24

**Chart:** Page 193

**Embellishments:** Heart button, six mother-of-pearl buttons and a gold-plated charm

*Work over one block of Aida, using two strands of stranded cotton (floss) for cross stitch and backstitch in one. Sew on the buttons and charm with strong sewing thread and mount and frame.*

> ### Jane's Tip
> *When adding buttons use a strong thread that matches the button rather than the ground fabric, so the decorative effect is not spoiled.*

## OTHER EMBELLISHMENTS

Other embellishments, such as lace and ribbon, are fun to use with cross stitch. You could also use ribbon roses, tiny artificial flowers and even doll's house miniatures. Why not try adding cutlery charms to a kitchen sampler, with buttons for plates on a dresser and flowerpot charms on the fireplace? The Tea for Two Picture below could have the addition of coloured lace or broderie anglaise above and below the design if desired. Unless the lace or other embellishment is added with decorative stitches as part of the design, it should be attached invisibly with tiny stitches and matching thread, using a sharp needle if necessary.

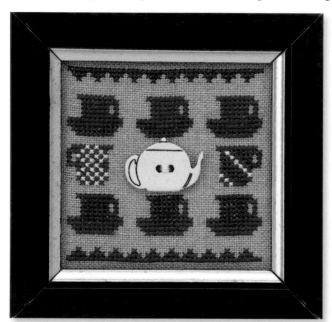

### TEA FOR TWO PICTURE

**Stitch count**: 43h x 42w
**Design size**: 8cm (3¼in) square
**Fabric**: Zweigart Dublin
25-count unbleached linen
**Needle**: Tapestry size 24
**Chart**: Page 194
**Embellishments**: Teapot button

*This little kitchen project is worked in pure cross stitch over two fabric threads (or one block of 14-count Aida). Use two strands of stranded cotton (floss) for cross stitch. Sew on the button with strong sewing thread. Mount and frame the design as preferred.*

## *Stitch Perfect* – EMBELLISHMENTS

✦ The size and scale of charms and buttons should match or balance with the scale of the cross stitch design.

✦ Clean a metal charm thoroughly with a paper towel before applying it to your stitching and if concerned, coat the back of the charm with clear nail varnish.

✦ Attach charms and buttons using a thread colour that matches the fabric.

✦ To attach a button or charm, starting with a loop start (see page 22), position the charm or button and pass the needle through the hole in the charm from the right side, thus marking the position. Slip the charm off the eye of the needle and pass the needle in and out of the fabric and then through the loop on the right side.

✦ When stitching a charm into position, ensure that the threads on the needle stay taut and do not form an unsightly loop in the hole of the charm.

✦ If additional stitches are to be added in direct relationship to the charm or button, stitch the button in position first and then carefully add the additional stitches (see the flowers on the Summer Flower Card).

✦ When adding lace and ribbons to a cross stitch design, use invisible thread or a colour that matches the ribbon or lace, and use tiny stitches.

### STITCHER'S TREASURE PICTURE

**Stitch count**: 31h x 32w (cross stitch only)
**Design size**: 5.8cm (2¼in) square (12cm / 4¾in finished frame size)
**Fabric**: Zweigart 28-count Cashel unbleached linen
**Needle**: Tapestry size 24   **Chart**: Page 194
**Embellishments**: Assorted mother-of-pearl buttons and
ivory lace and a gold-plated bow charm

*Work the cross stitch over two threads of linen (or one block of 14-count Aida) with two strands of stranded cotton (floss). Add the backstitch outline in one strand. Arrange the lace and ribbon in a pleasing way and stitch in position using tiny running stitches and matching or invisible thread. Add the buttons and charm with strong sewing thread. Frame as preferred.*

### JANE'S TIP
*I try to use ivory or antique white cotton lace rather than manmade fabrics, as nylon and polyester tend to be a bright white with an unattractive sheen.*

# COUNTING WITH BEADS

Using beads is one of the most satisfying embellishment techniques when you are straying away from pure cross stitch. Their use is highly effective, whether you intend to combine the beads with your cross stitches or completely replace the stitches with beads, like the gorgeous Beaded Iris Chatelaine opposite. You will find designs using beads instead of stitches or beads complementing stitched areas elsewhere in this book, but the basic guidelines are included in this section.

The best bit about counted embroidery is that you have so many choices and are free to express your artistic tendencies, and nowhere is this more evident than when stitching with beads. In many cases you will simply be exchanging beads for stitches, because you can adapt any cross stitch chart to allow the use of beads, as long as the chart does not contain fractional cross stitches – it's not possible to attach half a bead!

Substituting beads for stranded cottons on parts of a charted design as in the Sunflower Card overleaf is a wonderful way to explore your creative powers. Working with beads in this way is easier than you can imagine: as all the beads are stitched on using only one colour thread you can work across the pattern row by row instead of working blocks of colour as you would for cross stitch.

---

## BASIC BEAD TYPES

There is a huge range of beads available today and obtaining catalogues from some suppliers will reveal an irresistible array. For the cross stitch designs in this book I have used the smaller types of beads and some of the basic ones are described here. Beads are measured at the widest point and they do vary slightly.

 **Seed beads** – these are small beads, between 1.8–2.5mm. The Mill Hill range includes petite glass beads, glass seed beads and seed beads with special finishes, such as antique and frosted.

 **Magnifica beads** – these are very uniform, cylindrical beads, about 2.25mm in diameter, with larger holes than seed beads and thin walls. They are commonly used for bead weaving but also look good with cross stitch.

 **Bugle beads** – these are rods of cut glass in a variety of lengths, colours and finishes. The sizes vary between 2–30mm long and they are usually 2.5mm wide.

**Pebble beads** – these are larger than seed beads and almost round in shape, about 5.5mm in diameter. Being a little heavier than seed beads, they can be attractive added to tassels and fringes.

---

### JANE'S TIP

*Select the correct size bead for the fabric of your choice. If the beads are too large, they will crowd on top of each other and the design will distort. Most seed beads are perfect for 14-count Aida and 28-count evenweave. If unsure, work a small square in beads to see if the beads fit the space.*

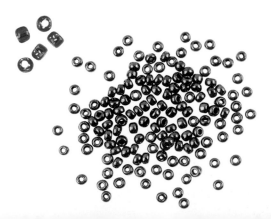

## BEADED IRIS CHATELAINE

**Stitch count:** 46h x 79w
**Design size:** 14.3 x 8.3cm (5½ x 3¼in)
**Fabric:** Zweigart Cashel linen 28-count shade 224
**Needle:** Tapestry size 24 and beading needle or size 10 sharp
**Chart:** Page 186

*This iris chatelaine was designed by Sue Hawkins (see Suppliers) using a combination of beads to create an exquisite effect. Sue stitched this motif by working the flower and decorative top border in Mill Hill glass seed beads using one strand of matching thread. A simple twisted cord (see page 41) and beaded tassel completes the project (see page 218 for making up).*

### JANE'S TIP
*You could attach beads using Nymo thread, a strong, waxed thread created especially for beadwork. It is available in various colours.*

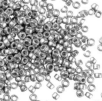

# DIFFERENT EFFECTS

You can see two very different effects created by beads in this section. The Sunflower Card below is worked with all the beads attached in rows, all facing the same direction and creating a very formal effect, whereas the Lily of the Valley opposite is a copy of an early Victorian piece (taken from a hand-painted Berlin pattern) and here the beads were added in a less formal fashion. This gives a rather attractive aged appearance.

## JANE'S TIP

*Beads are lively things and will end up all over the floor if you are not careful. There are excellent bead holders on the market but putting the beads on a square of cotton velvet on the table is the ideal solution, making them easy to pick up with your needle.*

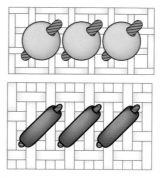

## ATTACHING BEADS

Attach seed beads and bugle beads with a fine 'sharp' needle or a beading needle using half cross stitch and thread that matches the fabric background. Bugle beads make excellent flower stamens and, because they are longer, are best attached after the cross stitch has been completed.

## SUNFLOWER CARD

**Stitch count:** 31h x 23w
**Design size:** 5.6 x 4.1cm
(2¼ x 1¾in)
**Fabric:** Zweigart Cashel antique white linen 28-count
**Needle:** Tapestry size 24 and beading needle or size 10 sharp
**Chart:** Page 187

*This sunflower motif has been embellished by working the flower head in Mill Hill glass seed beads, leaving the leaf and stem in pure cross stitch. Work the cross stitch over two threads of linen with two strands of stranded cotton (floss). Attach beads with matching thread and a beading needle.*

**BEADED LILY OF THE VALLEY**

**Stitch count:** 58h x 54w    **Design size:** 9.8 x 10.5cm (3¾ x 4⅛in)
**Fabric:** Zweigart Cashel cream linen 28-count    **Needle:** Tapestry size 24 and beading needle or size 10 sharp    **Chart:** Page 186

*Work the leaves and stems in cross stitch over two linen threads using two strands of stranded cotton (floss). Add the beads using one strand of matching thread. I used a combination of shiny (silver-lined) and opaque beads to create an antique effect.*

## *Stitch Perfect* – BEADS

❖ To substitute beads for stranded cottons (floss) on a chart design, gather together the stranded cottons and match the beads to the threads. Choosing beads in isolation can be difficult.

❖ Treat bright yellow and orange beads with a little caution as they can outshine more subtle colours.

❖ Use a size 10 'sharp' needle instead of a blunt tapestry needle to attach beads. Specialist beading needles are available, which are longer and thinner.

❖ Apply beads using ordinary sewing thread matched to the fabric colour. To make sure

you cannot see the thread through the beads, experiment by stitching a few on the corner of the fabric.

❖ Polyester mixture threads are stronger than pure cotton and thus are useful for attaching beads securely.

❖ Choose your fabric carefully. Beads will sit better on evenweave fabric than Aida, and on double canvas than on a single weave canvas.

❖ Consider using a frame or a hoop when working with beads. This will keep the fabric taut and you can pull the thread firmly as you work to keep the beads in position.

# INTRODUCING BLACKWORK

I have called this section an introduction to blackwork because it would take a much larger book than this one to cover the subject properly. I hope this will give you a real taste for this fascinating technique.

The name blackwork is very misleading as the technique may be worked in any colour or combination of colours. Blackwork is often used to depict flowers or stylized historical patterns but, as you can see by the elephant on page 81, the technique is very versatile. Blackwork consists of geometric patterns built up using Holbein stitch (double running stitch) and was traditionally worked in black thread against a contrasting (usually white) background with gold metallic highlights added for extra impact. During Tudor Elizabethan times blackwork was used to decorate clothing to imitate the appearance of lace. Many different effects can be achieved by varying the thickness of the thread, and careful selection of patterns with dark, medium and light tones. You will see from the blackwork designs on page 83 that you can select different patterns to create the dark and light effects.

Modern blackwork can make good use of different colours and even space-dyed threads can be used with great effect – see the Blackwork Poppy on page 82.

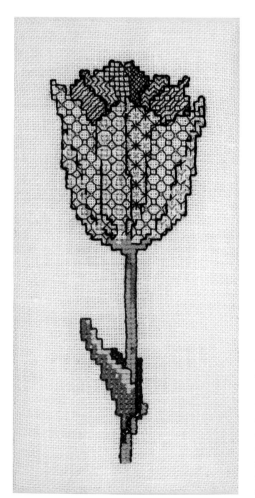

### JANE'S TIP

When designing band samplers, I sometimes include a section of holbein stitch as this creates a striking contrast to the areas of cross stitch.

### BLACKWORK TULIP

**Stitch count:** 82h x 31w
**Design size:** 14.9 x 5.6cm (5¾ x 2¼in)
**Fabric:** Zweigart Cashel ivory linen 28-count
**Needle:** Tapestry size 26
**Chart:** Opposite

*The charts show an outline and then a version complete with blackwork patterns. You could use any of the patterns on page 83 to make your own version. The motif was stitched in a combination of cross stitch and blackwork over two threads of linen. Work the cross stitch with two strands of stranded cotton (floss) and the black backstitch outline with one strand. Outline the tulip head in two strands of black and then use a selection of green and gold filling stitches in one strand to complete the design. Make up as desired.*

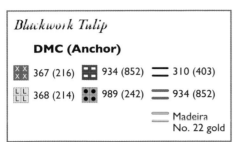

**Blackwork Tulip**

**DMC (Anchor)**

367 (216)  934 (852)  310 (403)

368 (214)  989 (242)  934 (852)

Madeira
No. 22 gold

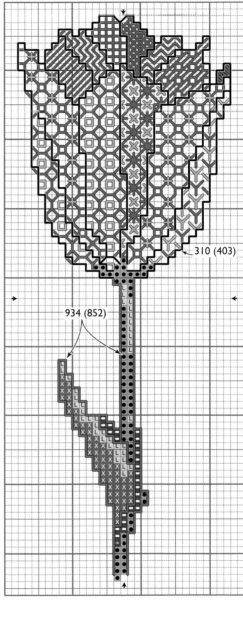

310 (403)

934 (852)

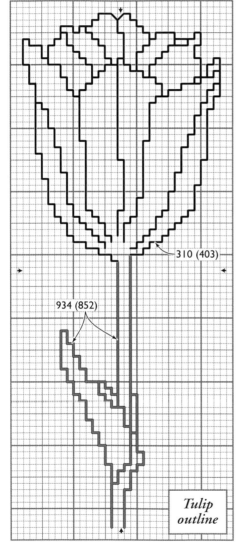

310 (403)

934 (852)

*Tulip outline*

I'm often asked to explain the difference between blackwork and backstitch and the answer is to look at the back of the stitching. As I have said before, I'm not of the strict school that suggests that the back of your work should look like the front, but in the case of blackwork I do make the exception. If you work the stitches correctly, you will not know the back from the front. In truth, you may find it necessary to combine backstitch and Holbein as you can end up at the end of a row with nowhere to go!

Traditionally the outline of the pattern is worked first, often in a heavier thread weight (i.e., two strands) and then the filling patterns are worked from the middle of any section using Holbein stitch (double running) – see diagram below. The blackwork tulip design charted on the previous page, shows the outline separately, and then with the blackwork filling patterns.

The clever thing about blackwork is that you can use cross stitch patterns and adapt them to blackwork very simply. All you need is a clear outline. The tulip design occurs later in the book as a darning pattern (see page 84), where I have used the same outline and altered the filling technique. The Blackwork Elephant opposite has a very distinctive outline, with easy filling stitches.

## WORKING HOLBEIN STITCH

To work this stitch, also called double running stitch, begin by working a running stitch under and over two fabric threads if working on evenweave or one block if working on Aida (a). Now stitch the return journey, filling in the gaps (b).

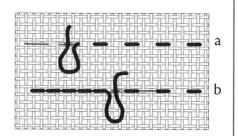

a

b

## *Stitch Perfect* – BLACKWORK

❖ Blackwork is traditionally worked using double running stitch or Holbein stitch, rather than backstitch.

❖ Holbein stitch will give a smoother effect and the back of your work will look almost as good as the front, so it is particularly useful for table linen.

❖ Before starting to stitch you will need to plan the direction you are working so that you can return to fill the gaps without ending up a blind alley!

❖ You may find it useful to use a finer needle than usual – I use a size 28 gold-plated tapestry needle for the filling stitches.

❖ Use slightly shorter threads, particularly when using one strand of black. The thread tends to fluff up as it is used and this can spoil your lacy effect.

❖ When stitching blackwork, aim to create a stitched line like a thin, pen-drawn line; split the thread if necessary and work with a small, sharp needle.

## BLACKWORK ELEPHANT

**Stitch count:** 36h x 41w
**Design size:** 6.5 x 7.5cm (2½ x 3in)
**Fabric:** Zweigart Cashel ivory linen 28-count
**Needle:** Tapestry size 26
**Chart:** Page 193

*This fun design would be an easy project to begin to explore the joys of blackwork. Work over two linen threads, stitching the outline first in two strands of stranded cotton (floss) and then adding the filling stitches in black and gold in one strand.*

## MULTICOLOURED BLACKWORK POPPY

**Stitch count:** 117h x 100w    **Design size:** 21.5 x 18cm (8½ x 7⅛in)
**Fabric:** Zweigart Dublin 26-count ivory linen    **Needle:** Tapestry size 26
**Chart:** Pages 190–191

*Stitch the poppy outline over two strands of linen using two strands of black stranded cotton (floss). Work the areas of multicoloured cross stitch with one strand. Add the blackwork filling stitches in the multicoloured stranded cotton and gold thread in one strand. Work the cross stitched stems in two strands of black. Work the blackwork border of leaves in two strands of multicoloured stranded cotton.*

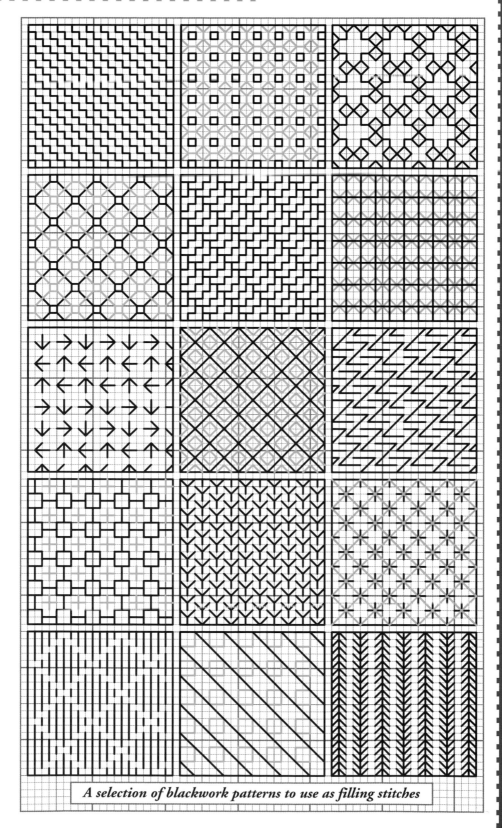

*A selection of blackwork patterns to use as filling stitches*

# PATTERN DARNING

This decorative counted technique isn't new and was, in fact, taught to girls in schools in England in the mid 19th century. With modern textiles, much of our clothing is more durable than in earlier times so darning isn't considered a necessary skill, but in the past it was highly valued. The idea of darning, particularly socks, leaves me cold but pattern darning for fun is so satisfying. The trick is to follow the pattern very carefully to begin with and then, as you see the pattern begin to take shape and how the repeats occur, you will need the chart less. In a similar style to blackwork, the outline of the motif is created first and then the darning patterns are worked from the centre of each section.

The projects in this section are very pretty: you could start with the Flowerpot Button darn design opposite and then move on to the elegant tulip and stylized flower.

## Stitch Perfect –
### PATTERN DARNING

❖ This is a difficult technique to work on Aida, so use evenweave.
❖ You will find it helpful to use a frame to hold the fabric taut.
❖ Work all darning patterns in running stitch, working in one direction only.
❖ Avoid the temptation to use satin stitch as it will spoil the effect.
❖ Count the fabric threads carefully as some patterns will use a variety of stitch lengths.
❖ Use shorter lengths of thread to avoid the thread fluffing, which will spoil the look of the patterns.
❖ If you make a mistake, it is easier to cut out the offending thread than attempt to unpick the error.

**PATTERN DARN TULIP**

**Stitch count:** 83h x 31w
**Design size:** 15 x 5.6cm (6 x 2¼in)
**Fabric:** Zweigart Cashel 28-count ivory linen
**Needle:** Tapestry size 26–28
**Chart:** Page 204

*Work over a variety of fabric threads, as indicated on the chart, stitching the stem and leaves with two strands of stranded cotton (floss) for the cross stitch and one strand for the backstitch outline. Outline the flower head in two strands of stranded cotton and then add the filling stitches with one strand.*

## FLOWERPOT BUTTON DARN

**Stitch count:** 58h x 58w    **Design size:** 10.5cm square (4⅛in)
**Fabric:** Zweigart Dublin 26-count ivory linen    **Needle:** Tapestry size 26–28    **Chart:** Page 187

*Work over a variety of fabric threads, as indicated on the chart, stitching cross stitch with two strands of stranded cotton (floss) and backstitch outlining with one strand. Work all the darning patterns with one strand. Add the lattice flowerpot button with matching thread when the stitching is complete.*

### PATTERN DARN FLOWER

**Stitch count:** 43h x 41w
**Design size:** 7.8 x 7.5cm
(3 x 2⅞in)
**Fabric:** Zweigart Cashel
28-count cream linen
**Needle:** Tapestry size 26–28
**Chart:** Page 202

*Work over a variety of fabric threads, as indicated on the chart, stitching the stem with two strands of stranded cotton (floss) for the cross stitch and one strand for the backstitch outline. Outline the flower head with two strands of stranded cotton and then add the filling stitches with one strand.*

# Silk Ribbon and Cross Stitch

Adding silk ribbon embroidery to cross stitch can introduce a wonderful new dimension and variety to a piece of stitching, creating a fresh, three-dimensional look. Silk ribbon embroidery grows quickly, so it is also a very speedy way to produce the emergency card needed for a special friend. I use YLI silk ribbons (see Suppliers).

Silk ribbon is used as it comes, as it is fine enough to pass through the fabric in the same way as thread does. Other ribbons made from rayon and viscose can be used for surface stitches, like gathered ribbon stitch in this Peach Blossom Card, but are not suitable for some stitches.

If you wish to develop the use of silk ribbon embroidery in your work make the Blue Ribbon Flower Card and the Wedding Shower Card shown here. Try other stitches using silk ribbon, such as tent stitch, satin stitch or bullion stitches, and invest in a good ribbon embroidery book.

## PEACH BLOSSOM CARD

**Stitch count**: 21h x 11w
**Design size**: 5 x 3cm (2 x 1¼in) including flowers
**Fabric**: Zweigart Cashel 28-count cream linen
**Needle**: Tapestry size 24 and gold-plated chenille size 7   **Chart**: Page 176
**Embellishments**: Heart button, 2mm and 7mm YLI silk ribbon and Madeira No.8 colour 8011

*This pretty card was stitched over two fabric threads, using two strands of stranded cotton (floss) for cross stitch. Add the silk ribbon embroidery using 2mm ribbon in pale peach and dark rose for French knots and 7mm ribbon in pale peach for the gathered ribbon stitch (see overleaf). Mount the design in a silver card, then into a gold card and trim with gold thread.*

## BLUE RIBBON FLOWER CARD

**Stitch count**: 32h x 29w including button and flowers
**Design size**: 5.7 x 5cm (2¼ x 2in)
**Fabric**: Zweigart Cashel 28-count cream linen
**Needle**: Tapestry size 24 and gold-plated chenille size 7
**Chart**: Page 197
**Embellishments**: Lattice flowerpot button and silk ribbon

*This ribbon-trimmed card was fun to make. Create the blue flower first in silk ribbon lazy daisy stitches (see page 89). Add random French knots to the flower centre and stem stitch stalks with two strands of stranded cotton (floss). Work the leaves in ribbon stitch (page 89), sew on the button and add ribbon French knots. Fray the edges of the linen and mount on blue card, adding a silk ribbon running stitch around half of the blue card and then mount on a single-fold card. See page 215 for making cards.*

### WEDDING SHOWER CARD

**Stitch count**: 31h x 16w including silk ribbon flowers
**Design size**: 5.7 x 3cm (2¼ x 1⅛in)
**Fabric**: Zweigart Cashel 28-count cream linen
**Needle**: Tapestry size 24, gold-plated chenille size 7 and size 10 sharp
**Chart**: Page 195
**Embellishments**: Seed pearls and 7mm YLI silk ribbon

*Work over two linen threads (or one block of 14-count Aida), using two strands of stranded cotton (floss) for cross stitch and one for backstitch. Using the pink and peach ribbon add the ribbon flowers in gathered ribbon stitch (diagrams overleaf). Add the seed pearls at random using a 'sharp' needle and cream thread. Mount the finished design in a silver card frame, trim diagonally and then mount on a pink card, cutting off two corners for a decorative effect.*

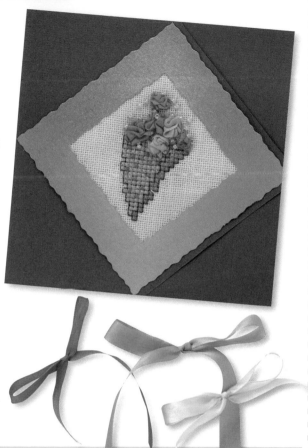

## *Stitch Perfect* – SILK RIBBON EMBROIDERY

❖ The use of an embroidery hoop is recommended for silk ribbon embroidery.

❖ Use a large chenille needle (size 20) for ribbon embroidery, and size 24 tapestry needle when using stranded cotton (floss).

❖ If working silk ribbon French knots you will find a gold-plated needle helpful.

❖ Work over two threads of the fabric or as stated on the chart.

❖ Use pure silk ribbon, readily available in 2mm, 3mm, 4mm and 7mm widths.

❖ Work with 30cm (12in) lengths of ribbon, cutting the ends at an angle to prevent fraying and make needle threading easier.

❖ To begin, make a knot at one end of the ribbon and come up through the fabric from the back. Remove any twists in the ribbon before stitching.

❖ Work with a loose tension to give the required effect – as a guide, the eye of the size 20 needle should pass under the ribbon with ease.

❖ When finishing off silk ribbon embroidery, take the ribbon through to the back of the fabric and using sewing thread, backstitch the end of the ribbon to the nearest stitch of ribbon to secure it and then cut off close to the fabric.

❖ When framing ribbon embroidery, you must ensure that it does not get squashed by the underside of the glass, which would spoil the effect. Insert very narrow strips of board (spacers) into the edges of the frame, between the glass and the mounted embroidery to hold them apart, before you assemble the frame.

## GATHERED RIBBON ROSE

I have used this stitch in the Wedding Shower Card and it creates a beautiful effect. You can also create a two-tone rose by placing two ribbons, in different colours and widths, one on top of the other and then working a running stitch through them both, before creating the rose by following the steps below.

**1** Cut a piece of ribbon long enough to complete the whole rose. Using a sewing thread with a knotted end, work small running stitches along one edge, leaving the thread end long.

**2** Thread one end of the ribbon on to a chenille needle and take the ribbon through to the back of the fabric.

**3** Now use a new length of sewing thread to secure the ribbon to the back of the fabric, bringing the thread out to the front.

**4** Start to pull up the gathers and begin to couch the ribbon in place.

**5** Carry on gathering, forming a spiral and continuing to couch the ribbon as you go.

**6** When the end of the ribbon is reached, tuck the end under the rose, couch in place and then take the thread through to the back of the work and secure.

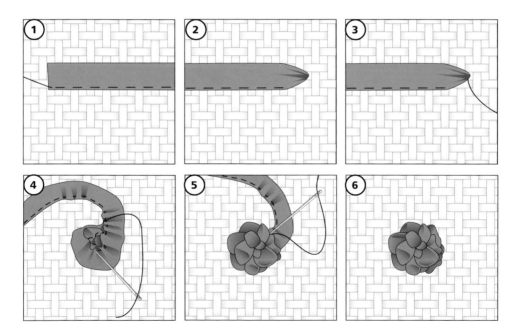

*Gathered ribbon roses create a lovely effect on the Wedding Shower Card and are very easy to create. Try using multicoloured or variegated ribbons for a different effect. The picture also shows French knots worked with silk ribbon.*

## LAZY DAISY STITCH

This stitch worked in silk ribbon is very effective when combined with cross stitch in the Blue Ribbon Flower Card. The stitch can also be worked in stranded cotton or other threads.

**1** Bring the ribbon to the front of the fabric (at point 1 on the first diagram), and then take it to the back of the fabric, close to where it first emerged, and re-emerge some distance away (at point 2). Leave the ribbon as a slack loop.

**2** Now loop the ribbon behind the tip of the needle and begin to pull the needle and ribbon through the fabric.

**3** Carry on pulling until the loop is the shape you want.

**4** Take the needle to the back of the fabric, just beyond the loop, making a little anchoring stitch.

**5** Pull the needle through to the back of the fabric to complete the stitch.

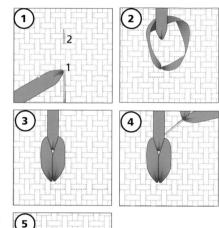

## RIBBON STITCH

This stitch is very simple to do and is ideal for creating leaves, as you can see on the Blue Ribbon Flower Card shown on page 86.

**1** Bring the ribbon to the front of the fabric, where you want the base of the stitch to be (at point 1).

**2** Hold the ribbon flat against the fabric.

**3** Put the needle under the ribbon and ease it upwards, smoothing and spreading the ribbon.

**4** Put the tip of the needle in the centre of the ribbon, in the place where you want the tip of the stitch to be (at point 2).

**5** Take the needle through to the back of the fabric, using your thumb to keep the stitch untwisted. Now slowly and gently pull the ribbon through.

**6** The ribbon will fold back on itself, curling at the edges. Secure the stitch at the back of the work.

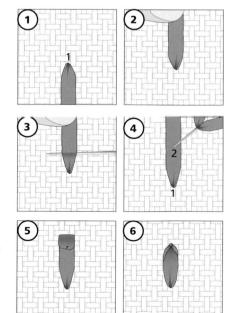

# COUNT ANYTHING BUT CROSS STITCH

This is an unusual section to find in a cross stitch book but it demonstrates that counted embroidery is not just cross stitch but lots, lots more. The three projects here illustrate some of the variety of stitches included in the counted repertoire. Some of these stitches can be worked on Aida fabric, as you can see from the Tiny Band Sampler opposite, while others need the additional fabric threads available on evenweave fabric. Working the Little Floral Garden or the Queen Stitch Sampler will be the perfect opportunity to try evenweave.

The trick when working rows of these counted stitches is to be consistent and to construct the stitches in the same way each time. When you refer to the Stitch Library you will see that some stitches may be worked over different numbers of fabric threads even though the construction stays the same; for example, Algerian eye may be worked over two, four or more threads. Refer to the chart you are working from each time to confirm the number of fabric threads involved.

### LITTLE FLORAL GARDEN

**Stitch count:** 32h x 24w    **Design size:** 6.2 x 5cm (2½ x 2in)
**Fabric:** Zweigart Dublin 25-count cream linen    **Needle:** Tapestry size 24    **Chart:** Page 197

*This design is worked with two strands of stranded cotton (floss) for all the stitches except the Madeira No.22 gold, which is used as supplied. Work the Algerian eye, adapted double cross stitch, rice stitch and four-sided stitch (worked last) over four fabric threads. Work the long-legged cross stitch over two threads. Work the three satin stitch flowers following the chart for stitch length.*

**QUEEN STITCH SAMPLER**

**Stitch count**: 34h x 38w, including four-sided stitch border     **Design size:** 6.2 x 7cm (2½ x 2¾in)
**Fabric:** Zweigart Cashel 28-count cream linen     **Needle:** Tapestry size 24     **Chart:** Page 196

*Work this pretty sampler using two strands of stranded cotton (floss) over four fabric threads for Queen stitch, double cross stitch, Rhodes stitch, Algerian eyes, rice stitch and four-sided stitch (worked last). Work the half Rhodes stitches over six threads and backstitch in one strand over two threads. The Queen stitch, Algerian eyes and four-sided stitch are pulled stitches and should form holes if pulled firmly – see page 106 for more advice.*

**TINY BAND SAMPLER**

**Stitch count**: 36h x 12w
**Design size:** 6.5 x 2.2cm (2½ x ⅞in)
**Fabric:** Zweigart 14-count cream Aida
**Needle:** Tapestry size 24
**Chart:** Page 196

*This is about the smallest band I have ever stitched and was great fun to do – perfect for practising some new stitches, and only a few of each to make! I used eyelets, half Rhodes stitch, rice stitch, long-legged cross stitch, double cross stitch, satin stitch and Algerian eyes. Work all the stitches with two strands of stranded cotton (floss) and the backstitch with one strand. I bordered the design with some simple hemstitch (see page 119) and then trimmed away the excess fabric to the edge of the stitching.*

91

# Assisi Embroidery

This style of cross stitch takes its name from embroideries made in Assisi, Italy during the 13th and 14th centuries. Early examples can still be seen in Italian churches and museums and were worked by nuns and monks. The altar cloths they made were worked on white linen with a single colour silk thread, usually red, blue, yellow, green or brown. Designs included stylized birds, animals, flowers, foliage and also classical and biblical scenes.

In the last 20 years, a modern version of Assisi embroidery has evolved. Many different colours and patterns are used for the background, and the motifs are extremely varied. However, the traditional version is still practised in the town of Assisi, where the local women can be seen sitting in front of their houses and embroidering items for the local co-operative embroidery shop, which was established in 1902 to give employment to poor women to supplement their income.

Assisi work can be described as pure cross stitch although in reverse. The design is transferred to the fabric by working a backstitch outline first, and then the background of the design is stitched, leaving the motif void, remaining as blank fabric. In the past, stitches other than pure cross stitch were used, for example long-legged cross stitch and even four-sided stitch.

The Assisi Dragonfly Sachet shown opposite illustrates the versatility of a cross stitch chart, showing how the outline used for the motif can be used as the framework for the Assisi embroidery. I have worked the original design in cross stitch for the little pill box below and then taken the dragonfly motif and completed that as Assisi embroidery. You can see that I have used a slightly darker outline colour for the Assisi version as I wanted to be able to see the dragonfly's legs clearly. You could choose almost any design from the Chart Library and work it in the same way.

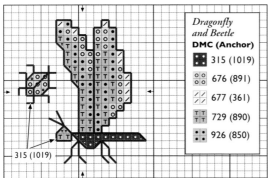

**Dragonfly and Beetle**

**DMC (Anchor)**

| | |
|---|---|
| ▦ | 315 (1019) |
| ○○ | 676 (891) |
| ╱╱ | 677 (361) |
| TT | 729 (890) |
| ∶∶ | 926 (850) |

315 (1019)

## JANE'S TIP
Zweigart make an antique-effect fabric with a mottled look, which would give your Assisi work an extra dimension.

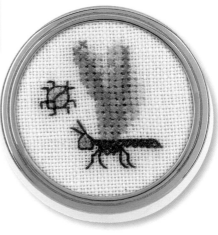

### DRAGONFLY AND BEETLE PILL BOX

**Stitch count**: 19h x 17w    **Design size**: 2.5cm (1in) square    **Fabric**: Zweigart Newcastle 40-count ivory linen    **Needle**: Tapestry size 28    **Chart**: above

*Work this design over two fabric threads, using one strand of stranded cotton (floss) for the cross stitch and the backstitch. The insect's wings are not outlined. This tiny project was finished by mounting it into a tiny enamel pill box following the manufacturer's instructions.*

## Stitch Perfect – ASSISI EMBROIDERY

❖ Work the outline in backstitch or Holbein stitch (see page 80), carefully counting from the chart

❖ Experiment with the number of strands needed to create the effect required.

❖ Work the cross stitch in two journeys to keep a neat tension throughout and perfect vertical lines on the reverse. If using a brighter coloured variegated thread with more distinctive colour changes, it would be best to work the cross stitches individually to maintain the colour sequence.

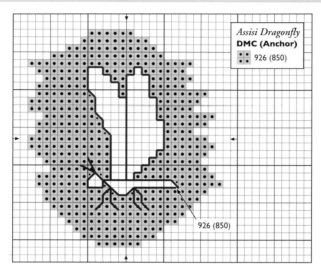

*Assisi Dragonfly*
**DMC (Anchor)**
926 (850)

926 (850)

### ASSISI DRAGONFLY SCENTED SACHET

**Stitch count:** 29h x 26w
**Design size:** 5 x 4.5cm (2 x 1¾in)
**Fabric:** Zweigart Cashel 28-count in ivory
**Needle:** Tapestry size 24
**Chart:** Above

*Work this design over two fabric threads, beginning with the outline of the dragonfly's body in Holbein stitch using one strand of stranded cotton (floss) only. Work the cross stitch around the edge of the outline as shown on the chart using one strand of stranded cotton, adding the legs and antennae in the darker colour as shown on the chart. Fray the edges of the finished stitching and sew it on to a sachet (see page 213 for making a bag). The sachet was made from patterned linen and finished with a simple hemstitch across the raw top edge (see page 119). Make a twisted cord made for a tie (see page 41) and fill the bag with scented pot-pourri to finish.*

# Decorated Initials

Decorated initials are an ideal way of giving an emergency gift or card to a special friend. One of these initials could be stitched in an evening and made in to a simple patch to attach to a card or you could create a very different look if you work the initial on fine silk gauze and mount it in a pretty pot or pendant. I have designed a traditional alphabet and embellished it with a daisy head and poppy face but you could add your preferred flower to a favourite alphabet.

Decorative initials have a myriad of uses, as either single motifs or grouped together as a word, name or phrase. Try some of the following project ideas.

♦ Plan the letters of your name on graph paper and then stitch and make up as a door plate or book cover.

♦ Stitch a child's initial and mount it into a pretty frame for their bedroom.

♦ Stitch a friend's initial and mount it into a coaster for when they call round for a cup of tea.

♦ Work the whole alphabet as a sampler and frame it or make up as a cushion.

♦ See the illustrated suggestions below for changing the fabric or design colours.

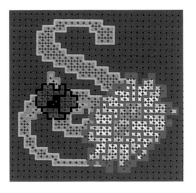

The charted letters from the Daisy Alphabet could be worked on different, perhaps bolder-coloured fabrics to change the look, as shown above. You could also experiment with changing the thread colours completely to others of your choice, as the picture below shows.

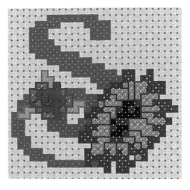

## CRYSTAL POT

**Stitch count:** 33h x 25w
**Design size:** 4.5 x 6.5cm (1¾ x 2½in)
**Fabric:** Zweigart cream 28-count Cashel linen
**Needle:** Tapestry size 24
**Chart:** Pages 206–209

*Work this design using two strands of stranded cotton (floss) for cross stitch and one for the backstitch. Mount into the pot following the manufacturer's instructions.*

## WOODEN POT

**Stitch count:** 27h x 34w
**Design size:** 5 x 6.5cm (2 x 2½in)
**Fabric:** Zweigart cream 14-count Aida
**Needle:** Tapestry size 24
**Chart:** Pages 206–209

*Work the design using two strands of stranded cotton (floss) for cross stitch and one for the backstitch. Mount into your pot to finish.*

### Jane's Tip

*Remember that alphabet letters vary in physical size so check the letter of choice fits the pot or card in question. The W is much wider than the letter B in my stitched examples. See page 20 for calculating design size.*

# Hardanger Embroidery

Hardanger, a town in Norway, gave its name to this type of counted embroidery, where cut work was a feature of the local dress. Hardanger embroidery or cut work is easy to do and is extremely effective when combined with cross stitch but it seems to strike terror in the hearts of cross stitchers, possibly because they have snipped a fabric thread in error whilst unpicking!

As with many of the techniques covered in this book I can only give you taste of Hardanger, sure in the knowledge that once you have had a go at this deceptively easy range of stitches you will, like me, become hooked! The Multicolour Hardanger Bookmark shown below would be a perfect starter project. To experiment further, go on to create the three other stunning projects in this section, and see page 51 for another Hardanger project.

When you work the basic stitches that make up Hardanger embroidery your stitching will not disintegrate and fall apart! When done correctly this type of embroidery can be machine washed if need be. Hardanger embroidery can be worked on evenweave fabric of any thread count or on Hardanger fabric which is supplied with 22 blocks to 2.5cm (1in). If working on Hardanger fabric, treat each block as one thread. At its simplest, Hardanger work consists of three stages which are described over the next few pages:

**1** Stitching Kloster blocks.

**2** Cutting threads.

**3** Decorating the remaining threads and spaces.

The secret of successful cut work embroidery is working Kloster blocks (the framework needed for the decorative filling stitches) and to count these blocks correctly. If they are in the right place the threads may be cut out and the stitching will not fall to pieces!

> ### Jane's Tip
> *When you are working up the second side of the Kloster block pattern, run your needle across the fabric to check that your stitches are still in line.*

### MULTICOLOUR HARDANGER BOOKMARK

**Stitch count:** 87h x 18w
**Design size:** 15.8 x 3.3cm (6¼ x 1¼in)
**Fabric:** Unbleached 28-count linen band
**Needle:** Tapestry size 24 and 22
**Chart:** Page 204

*Stitch the Kloster blocks with one strand of Anchor Multicolour Pearl No.8. Check the Kloster blocks are in the correct positions and then cut the threads as shown on page 98. Withdraw the loose threads and then stitch the needleweaving and dove's eyes with one strand of Pearl No.12 in ecru. Work the backstitch in one strand of stranded cotton (floss). Neaten the top of the bookmark with one row of hemstitch in cream Pearl No.12 and trim to the stitching (see page 119). Make a simple tassel (see page 218) with the remaining multicolour threads and see page 214 for making up.*

## STITCHING KLOSTER BLOCKS

Kloster blocks form the framework for the cut areas in Hardanger embroidery. You will be, in fact, binding the fabric edges prior to cutting. Start with an away waste knot, far enough away so as not to interfere with your progress. When you need a fresh thread finish off under a number of blocks and then cut very close to the stitching. If you make a small counting error on a cross stitch project it's often possible to hide the fact but this is **not** the case when working the Kloster blocks. If you make an error you will need to find the problem and put it right. I will give some tips as you work through this section.

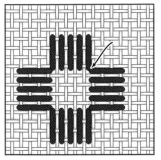

### Working Kloster blocks

These are worked in patterns, formed with 5 vertical or 5 horizontal straight stitches, each of them over 4 threads on evenweave or 4 blocks on Hardanger fabric. The stitches are worked side by side, following the grain of the fabric. When counting Hardanger, count the threads never the holes. To see why, hold up four fingers – if you count the gaps between fingers you could count five or three depending on where you started counting!

> ### JANE'S TIP
>
> *When forming Kloster blocks, take the time to snip off the knot and weave in the remaining trailing threads as you go. This is much better than having dozens to sort out before you can cut the fabric threads.*

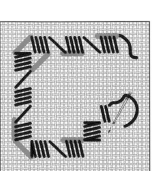

### Kloster blocks from the back

When travelling to the next block (if it is not immediately next door to your last stitch) do not travel across the surface of the material, as this trailing thread on the back may be cut in error and you'll have to waste time on repair work! To move between the blocks, pass your needle under the back of the Kloster block (through the tunnel) and not only will the whole thing look neat and tidy but you will also avoid potential panic! In this diagram, the blue route is to be avoided.

## *Stitch Perfect*   KLOSTER BLOCKS

✤ Count the threads **not** the holes.

✤ To form Kloster blocks, work the stitches side by side so that they look the same on the wrong side of the fabric. The back stitches will have a very slight slant.

✤ The vertical and horizontal blocks must meet at the corners, sharing the corner hole. Check as you work to avoid unpicking.

✤ Check that you have counted correctly as you stitch and check that each block is in the correct position.

✤ Check that vertical Kloster blocks are opposite one another and horizontal blocks are opposite horizontal ones.

✤ Work all Kloster blocks in a pattern, checking the blocks meet where they should.

✤ Never start cutting until all Kloster blocks are completed and match everywhere.

✤ Do not travel between blocks at the back unless under existing Kloster blocks.

# CUTTING THREADS

When the Kloster blocks have been stitched, the threads between them are cut and pulled out. The secret to successful cutting is to work all the Kloster blocks, checking that you have counted correctly and that all the blocks are exactly opposite each other. Looking at the photographs of the Hardanger projects in this section you can see that the Kloster blocks are formed in vertical and horizontal lines.

**Cutting threads** Once you have completed the first set of Kloster blocks, study this diagram to see where to cut the fabric threads. The threads should be cut in pairs, with very sharp, pointed scissors at the end of the Kloster blocks, not at the side. Remember to cut where the needle has pierced the fabric. You will see the reason the horizontal lines are opposite each other and why the Kloster block stitches have to be in the correct place. You will be cutting two ends of the same thread.

### JANE'S TIP
*Before cutting a pair of threads, check that you can see both points of the scissors and then count the threads on the blade – this way you cannot make a cutting mistake.*

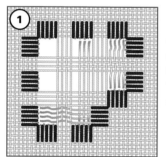

**Removing threads**
Pull out the cut threads carefully. This diagram shows Kloster blocks stitched with some threads cut and some awaiting removal.

*This detail shows part of the Christmas Hardanger Heart (shown in full opposite), with the Kloster blocks completed, the needleweaving worked and the filling stitches completed. You can also see the silver calligraphy paper I used as a background beneath the embroidery to complement the Hardanger.*

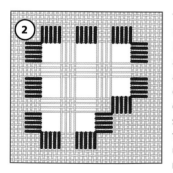

**Threads removed** This diagram shows the Kloster blocks stitched and with all the correct threads cut and pulled out, ready for decorating. After cutting, don't worry if you can see some small whiskers at the cut sides. Leave these until the piece is finished: many will disappear as the work is handled, but if necessary they can be carefully trimmed when all the stitching is complete.

## CHRISTMAS HARDANGER HEART

**Stitch count:** 48h x 54w
**Design size:** 8.7 x 9.8cm (3½ x 3¾in)
**Fabric:** Zweigart Cashel antique white
28-count linen
**Needle:** Tapestry size 24 and 22
**Chart:** Page 203

*Stitch the Kloster blocks with one strand of Anchor Pearl No.5 (with metallic silver). Work the filling stitches with one strand of Pearl No.12 in ecru. Work the cross stitch with two strands of stranded cotton (floss) over two fabric threads, with the backstitch candle wick in one strand. Mount and frame as desired.*

### JANE'S TIP

*Be disciplined at the cutting stage and avoid distraction. Start at a shared corner hole and cut two threads away from you. Cut the second two threads and then turn your work so you continue to cut in the same direction – two threads at a time because then you cannot cut three!*

### REPAIR WORK

If you do make a mistake and cut a thread unintentionally it is easy to correct this.

**1** Remove the fabric thread you've cut by mistake.

**2** Take a strand of stranded cotton (floss) the same colour as your fabric or a fabric thread if working on linen, and darn it in and out so that it replaces the accidentally cut thread, leaving a long thread hanging on the wrong side.

**3** Needleweave or wrap this section next to anchor the threads, then the loose thread can be trimmed.

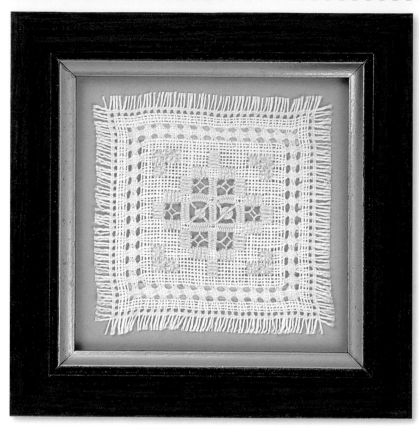

**MINI HARDANGER SAMPLER**

**Stitch count:** 26h x 26w    **Design size:** 5cm (2in) square
**Fabric:** Zweigart Dublin 26-count antique white linen
**Needle:** Tapestry size 24 and 22    **Chart:** Page 205

*Stitch the Kloster blocks with one strand of DMC Perlé No.5 in cream and the filling stitches in one strand of Perlé No.8 in cream. Work the double cross stitch with one strand of Perlé No.5 in cream and the four-sided stitch in one strand of Perlé No.8 in cream. Hemstitch around the edge using one strand of Perlé No.8 in cream. Fray the raw edge, trim to shape and frame.*

## *Stitch Perfect* – Cutting Threads

- ❖ Work slowly, in a good light and with small, sharp, pointed scissors.
- ❖ The cutting side is where the long straight stitches enter the fabric. Never cut alongside the long edges of the stitches.
- ❖ Cut the threads at the end of each Kloster block, working from a corner out. You need to cut four threads, but cut them in pairs.
- ❖ Pass the point of the scissors into the corner-shared hole and lift the threads. Check that you can see both points of

the scissors and that you are only cutting two threads, then lean slightly towards the Kloster block and cut.
- ❖ It is easier to cut all the relevant threads in one direction first then turn the fabric to cut in another direction.
- ❖ Pull out the loose threads using tweezers if necessary. The stitching should look like the final diagram on page 98, with groups of four threads vertically and horizontally left to decorate.

## DECORATING THREADS AND VOIDS

When Kloster blocks are completed and the threads are cut and removed, you are left with groups of threads and spaces or void areas to decorate. It is also an important function of this decorative element that the remaining fabric threads are reinforced and strengthened after cutting. There are dozens of ways to do this but I have worked a few examples for you to see the finished effect. Traditionally, all these decorative filling stitches are worked in a finer thread than the Kloster blocks. To work any of these filling stitches, follow the sequence in the diagrams provided over the next few pages, ensuring that you work each section in the same manner, counting the wraps or weaves.

## NEEDLEWEAVING

This is one of the most commonly used methods of embellishing threads left after cutting, especially over larger areas, and creates covered bars, which can be worked alone or be combined with filling stitches such as dove's eye and picots. The stitch is formed by starting from a void area and weaving in and out of two pairs of fabric threads – see the stages below. The aim is not to distort the bar but to form a neatly woven or plaited appearance. If adding dove's eye or picots these are traditionally worked during the needleweaving process rather than afterwards.

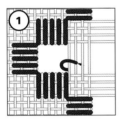 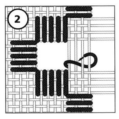 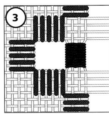 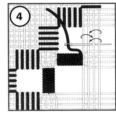

**1** Start by anchoring the thread under adjacent cross stitch or hemstitch on the back of the work.

**2** Beginning from a cut area, bring the needle up through a void area.

**3** Weave the needle under and over pairs of threads to form a plaited effect. The stitches should not distort or bend the threads.

**4** When one set of threads has been woven, move on to the next set.

## CORNER NEEDLEWEAVING

As the name implies, corner needleweaving is the same stitch as needleweaving but instead of working across a bar (a set of four threads), the stitch is formed across a corner and depending on where you choose to do this the effects can be stunning.

Use an away waste knot and start by wrapping a pair of threads until you are a few stitches away from an intersection. Needleweave the wrapped bar and the bar running at right angles for a few stitches, then continue with the wrapping. Keep a record of how many weaves you work so that they all look the same.

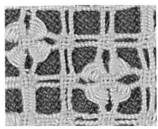

## WRAPPED BARS

Wrapping bars simply means that the thread is wound round and round two or four threads after cutting. After Kloster blocks have been formed and the threads have been cut and removed, the four remaining threads may be wrapped in pairs and possibly embellished with spider's webs or corner dove's eyes. As you wrap each bar you will need to hold the threads you are wrapping quite firmly to prevent them from unravelling as you work. It does take a little practise – follow the stages below.

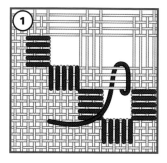
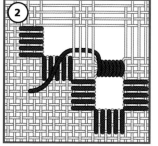
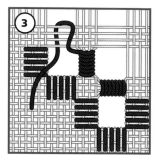

**1** Start by anchoring your thread under adjacent stitches and then begin wrapping, working horizontally across the fabric.

**2** Wind the thread around and around the remaining fabric threads, then travel to the next group of threads and repeat. As you wrap each bar, hold the threads you are wrapping quite firmly, to prevent them unravelling as you work.

**3** Continue wrapping the bars, noting how many times each set is wrapped and keeping the stitches consistent.

## DOVE'S EYE STITCH

Dove's eye stitch is a traditional Hardanger stitch that is usually constructed whilst needleweaving or wrapping bars. It is possible to add it afterwards but this is not recommended. The stitch creates a diamond-shaped hole in the centre of the void left by cutting. When forming the stitch, watch for the last twist as without this the diamond will look rather strange. Forming a dove's eye takes a little practise and a little 'pinching and pulling' will be needed to achieve perfect results – follow the stages below.

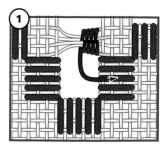
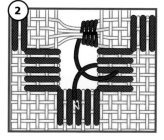
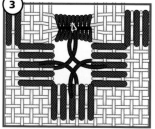

**1** Whilst working the last side of a square, needleweave to the centre of the bar, bringing the needle out through a void area.

**2** Pierce the neighbouring needlewoven bar (or wrapped bar) halfway along its length, bringing the needle up through the void and through the loop formed by the thread.

**3** Continue around the square, but before resuming needleweaving or wrapping, loop the needle under the first stitch to form the final twist in the dove's eye.

## CORNER DOVE'S EYE

An adaptation of the dove's eye previously described, this stitch is formed across the corners of the square rather than through the side bars.

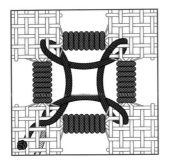

To create a corner dove's eye, follow the route taken by the needle in the diagram and remember to make the last twist to complete the square.

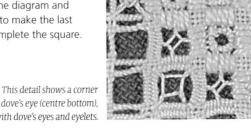

*This detail shows a corner dove's eye (centre bottom), with dove's eyes and eyelets.*

## SPIDER'S WEB STITCH

Spider's web is a traditional filling stitch used to decorate the voids left by cutting threads and it is often used with wrapped bars – follow the stages below. As with all these stitches, although they are not counted it is a good idea to keep notes of the numbers of winds and weaves to ensure that the stitches are uniform.

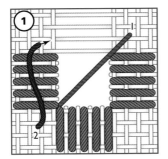

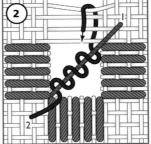

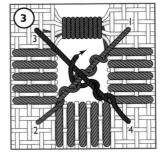

**1** Work three sides in Kloster blocks, wrapped bars or a combination of both, bringing the needle out at the position marked 1 on the diagram. Cross the square, bringing the needle out at 2.

**2** Return to position 1, winding the thread around the diagonal just formed, ready to complete the final side (shown as a wrapped bar in next diagram).

**3** Bring the needle up at 3 and pass diagonally to 4, then wind the thread around the diagonal to the centre (as shown in the previous diagram).

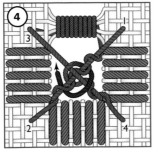

**5** After three winds you may need to tighten and adjust the position of the winds to ensure that they are even and in the centre of the square. When the web is complete, leave the stitch by winding around the diagonal, as before.

**4** Start weaving the web around the diagonals.

# Picots

These pretty, decorative elements (rather like a sideways French knot) are worked as you wrap or needleweave the remaining threads after cutting. Take care to work each section in a uniform style. It will take a little practise to perfect these stitches but when worked they are very effective.

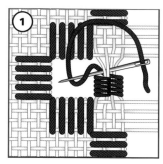

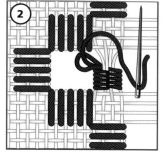

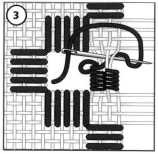

**1** Needleweave halfway along a set of four threads and bring the needle out at the side to form the picot. Pass the needle under two threads on the same side and wrap the thread around the needle as shown.

**2** Pull the needle through carefully, holding the wrapped thread in position – don't pull too tightly. Pass the needle through the centre of the four fabric threads, ready to make another picot along the other edge in the same way.

**3** Once both picots have been formed, complete the needleweaving. To keep all the stitches consistent, make a record of how many weaves you make either side of the picots.

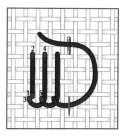

## Buttonhole Edging

Buttonhole stitch is a very useful and versatile stitch and has been used to edge the Hardanger Diamond project (opposite). Once all the Hardanger embroidery and any cross stitch has been completed, the buttonhole stitches are worked around the perimeter, so the shape can be cut out without fear of the design falling to pieces!

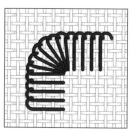

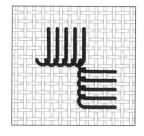

To work buttonhole stitch, start with an away waste knot (see page 22) and work long stitches over four threads (similar to Kloster blocks). Keep the stitches flat against the fabric and as consistent as possible. From the back, the stitches will look like a series of straight lines.

When you turn outer corners in buttonhole stitch, note that the corner hole holds seven threads.

When turning internal corners, note the way that the corner stitches are connected.

# COMPLETING HARDANGER PROJECTS

The very nature of Hardanger embroidery means that you can see through it and so the final challenge is to use a complementary background to the piece. You may be surprised by what does and doesn't look good when you come to mount and frame. I have tried all sorts of background fabrics and was amazed at how effective Hardanger looked on tartan! In the projects in this chapter I have used some plum-coloured linen, stone-coloured card and some decorative parchment covered in Latin script written in silver pen.

### HARDANGER DIAMOND

**Stitch count:** 58h x 62w (excluding buttonhole edge)
**Design size:** 10.5 x 11.3cm (4⅛ x 4¼in)
**Fabric:** Zweigart Cashel 28-count linen shade 224
**Needle:** Tapestry size 24 and 22
**Chart:** Page 192

*Stitch Kloster blocks with one strand of ecru DMC Perlé No.8 and the filling stitches and eyelets in one strand of ecru Perlé No.12. Work the buttonhole edge in one strand of ecru DMC Perlé No.8 and then trim to the edge of the stitching. Mount and frame as desired.*

## *Stitch Perfect* – HARDANGER FILLING STITCHES

❖ For all filling stitches, use a slightly finer thread than for stitching the Kloster blocks.

❖ To weave a bar, bring the needle up in a void area and work over and under pairs of threads. After completing one bar, weave the next one at right angles to it, working around the design, taking care not to run threads across the back of the cut areas.

❖ Needleweaving shouldn't alter the shape of the bar, which should stay flat and straight.

❖ When wrapping a pair of threads, hold the wrapped thread firmly so it doesn't unravel.

❖ When working filling stitches, plan your route around the project and if necessary pass the needle under Kloster blocks but never across voided areas.

❖ When working dove's eyes, work in the same direction every time and remember to make the last twist.

❖ Count the number of winds of the spider's webs to keep them consistent.

❖ Finish off waste ends as you progress.

# Pulled and Drawn Thread Embroidery

These are techniques that can cause a little confusion so I am going to look at them in detail in this section of the book. The two techniques can create such wonderful effects that they are well worth exploring. Both drawn and pulled thread embroidery are counted thread techniques and so they combine very well with traditional cross stitch. If you look at early antique band samplers you will find a myriad of counted stitches as well surface embroidery stitches combined, with stunning effects.

---

## Pulled Thread Embroidery

In this technique the decorative effect on the fabric is created by forming stitches that are pulled to form holes in the fabric.

## Drawn Thread Embroidery

In this technique fabric threads are withdrawn from the fabric prior to decorating remaining threads with counted stitches.

---

## Pulled Thread Embroidery

This is a type of embroidery where the pattern is created by pulling the fabric threads together using the construction of the stitch to create the effect. No fabric threads are removed to create the holes – it is all done by the tension in the embroidery. The holes produced by the pulled work stitches form patterns that are, perhaps confusingly, referred to as fillings! For this reason, some cross stitchers can find this technique a little difficult to master simply because they do not pull the stitches tightly enough. This habit comes from working pure cross stitch beautifully and not allowing the stitches to create holes!

Another secret to producing lovely pulled thread embroidery is to work on pure linen. Linen creases: if you wear linen clothes, you will know that it is not easy-care and creases very easily. When working pulled thread embroidery, you *want* the fabric to crease where the stitches are pulled and you want them to *stay* creased!

Traditionally, pulled thread embroidery is worked in the same colour as the fabric, as it is the holes that you create which are of interest, rather than the stitch itself. Pulled stitches, such as four-sided stitch, Algerian eye and Queen stitch can be worked alone or combined with cross stitch to create very pretty decorated motifs, as in the Strawberries and Cream Sampler opposite. They can also be used as filling stitches, as shown in the Lacy Flower Face on page 109. Using satin stitch in different formations can create very decorative pulled effects as long as the stitch is pulled firmly.

> ### Jane's Tip
> If you work on an evenweave with a lot of synthetic content, the tendency is for the fabric to spring back to its original position. These easy-care materials are ideal for baby clothes or bibs that need constant washing and ironing but are less successful when working pulled stitches.

### STRAWBERRIES AND CREAM SAMPLER

**Stitch count**: 54h x 54w    **Design size**: 10.5cm (4¼in) square
**Fabric**: Zweigart Dublin 26-count ivory linen    **Needle**: Tapestry size 24
**Chart**:  Page 198

*To work this delicate-looking sampler, work the cross stitch and queen stitch centre panel first using two strands of stranded cotton (floss). Now work the framework in four-sided stitch and cross stitch. Use filling stitches to complete each section: I used pulled satin stitch, Greek cross stitch, honeycomb stitch, double faggot stitch and coil stitch over four threads (refer to the Stitch Library). Work the eyelets over eight fabric threads using two strands of pink. All the pulled stitches are worked in two strands of stranded cotton (floss), with the backstitch added in one strand only.*

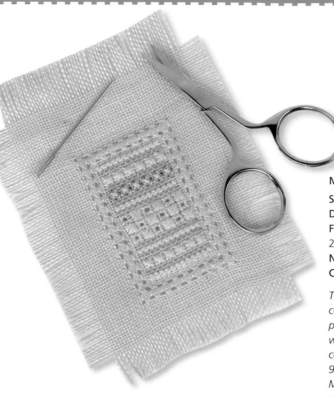

## MINI CREAM SAMPLER

**Stitch count:** 30h x 18w
**Design size:** 5.5 x 3.3cm (2⅛ x 1¼in)
**Fabric:** Zweigart Cashel ivory
28-count linen
**Needle:** Tapestry size 24
**Chart:** Page 199

*This tiny band sampler is worked in a combination of counted stitches and pulled threads. All stitches have been worked in two strands of stranded cotton (floss) (DMC 712 or Anchor 926), with the exception of the Madeira No.22 gold thread, which is used as supplied. Stitches used include long-legged cross stitch, double cross stitch, rice stitch and satin stitch (refer to the Stitch Library). The Algerian eyes and the four-sided stitch border are the pulled elements in this project (shown in the detail below).*

### JANE'S TIP

*Pulled thread embroidery is generally worked in thread the same colour as the fabric, but you could try using the stitches as decorative elements, as I did for the hemstitch edge in the needlecase on page 40. I also enjoy using linen thread for pulled thread embroidery.*

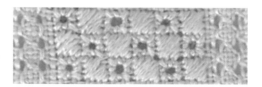

## Stitch Perfect – PULLED THREAD EMBROIDERY

❖ Use linen for pulled thread work, particularly for table linen, samplers and pillow covers.

❖ Pull the stitches so that the threads of the fabric are drawn together to form holes.

❖ With some stitches in pulled work, e.g., Algerian eye, the central hole is formed by pulling the thread firmly and always passing down the central hole in the stitch.

❖ Examples of special pulled stitches are described in the Stitch Library but you can produce very effective pulled thread embroidery by using the same stitch repeated in different formations. Satin stitch is a versatile stitch to try this with.

❖ Hemstitch is another pulled stitch (covered on page 111) and is used in conjunction with thread removal.

**LACY FLOWER FACE**

**Stitch count**: 38h x 38w  **Design size**: 7.5cm (3in) square
**Fabric**: Zweigart Dublin 26-count ivory linen
**Needle**: Gold-plated tapestry size 24
**Chart**: Page 199

*To work this simple flower face, backstitch the outline of the flower first in two strands of stranded cotton (floss). Now, using a variety of pulled stitches, fill each petal with a different stitch: I used pulled satin stitch, coil stitch over two threads, double faggot stitch, Greek cross stitch and honeycomb stitch (refer to the Stitch Library). Using two strands of thread, add random bullion and French knots to the flower centre. Border the flower with four-sided stitches worked over four fabric threads. Frame as desired.*

# DRAWN THREAD EMBROIDERY

Drawn thread embroidery is one of my personal favourites – it looks so clever but is in fact very simple to do. The trick is to take it in small stages, use a fabric you can see clearly and work in a good light. Drawn threads may be worked in bands, as shown in the samplers below and overleaf; in squares, as in the Corner Flowers and Hemstitch Square on page 115; or as part of a decorative hem around a project. The lovely Rose and Violet Sampler on page 116 uses all of these techniques, as well as some pulled stitches.

Essentially, a number of fabric threads are removed and/or re-woven and the remaining threads are then decorated. Withdrawing fabric threads is often combined with hemstitching of one sort or another. You will see examples of decorative hemstitch bands on the sampler on page 136 as well as some small examples in this section of the book.

Drawn thread work may superficially look like pulled work but their methods are quite different because in drawn thread work, fabric threads are cut and drawn out from the ground fabric.

**ZIGZAGS AND LADDERS SAMPLER**

**Stitch count**: 46h x 23w    **Design size**: 9 x 4.5cm (3½ x 1¾in)
**Fabric**: Zweigart Dublin 26-count ivory linen    **Needle**: Tapestry size 24 and 22    **Chart**: Page 200

*Work cross stitch with two strands of stranded cotton (floss) and backstitch with one. Referring to the chart, withdraw the fabric threads using Method 2 described opposite. Work ladder hemstitch, simple hemstitch and zigzag hemstitch using two strands of stranded cotton DMC 712 (Anchor 926). Mount with a contrasting background fabric to display the drawn thread work and then frame as preferred.*

## PREPARING TO HEMSTITCH

I describe two ways here of removing fabric threads, prior to stitching hemstitch bands: Method 1 is suitable for wider bands, while Method 2 is better for narrower bands.

### Method 1

**1** On a wide band you can work roughly from the centre of the band because the cut threads will be long enough to work with. Carefully snip two horizontal fabric threads and gently unravel these threads to the edge of the band sampler.

**2** Working in pairs, re-weave these threads as follows. Remove one fabric thread entirely, creating a ladder in the fabric. Using a size 22 needle, weave the needle in and out of the fabric threads as if to replace the missing thread.

**3** Slip the loose fabric thread into the eye of the needle and pull gently.

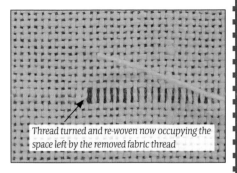

*Thread turned and re-woven now occupying the space left by the removed fabric thread*

### Method 2

If you are working on a narrow band, it is easier to remove the fabric threads from the edge of the band because this leaves longer fabric ends to work with and re-weave.

**1** Carefully snip *one* horizontal fabric thread at the margin of the band. Unravel it across the band to the other side, where you cut another adjacent fabric thread and unravel in the opposite direction. You will now have a ladder in the fabric and two fabric whiskers, one at either edge.

**2** Working in pairs, re-weave these threads as follows: lift the fabric thread carefully and you will see the cut end of the other whisker. Remove this completely. Using a needle, weave the point in and out of the fabric threads and slip the loose fabric thread into the eye of the needle and pull gently. When done satisfactorily, you cannot tell where the linen threads have gone.

**3** Repeat this process until all fabric threads are gone. Refer to the chart for the number of threads to remove. When the threads are re-woven, you will have created a new selvedge. The final picture would look the same on a wide band.

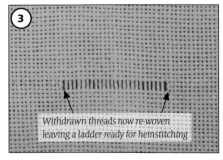

*1*   *Cut end*

*Cut end*

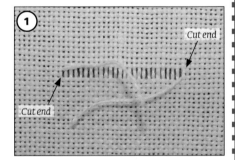

*2*   *Thread in the needle, ready to be re-woven into the margin of the band*

*Cut end pulled back to make room for the reweave*

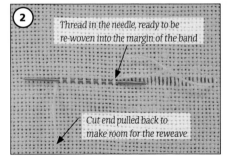

*3*

*Withdrawn threads now re-woven leaving a ladder ready for hemstitching*

## SIMPLE HEMSTITCH

Once you have prepared the fabric by removing and re-weaving threads, as previously described in Method 1 or Method 2, you can begin to work a simple hemstitch band. Follow the steps and diagrams below, using two strands of stranded cotton (floss).

**1** This hemstitching is over two threads in each direction. Work a straight stitch across two threads, turning the needle to face horizontally.

**2** Make another straight stitch across two

threads, at right angles to the first, then pass the needle down diagonally under two threads.

**3** Repeat the straight stitches along the row, counting carefully.

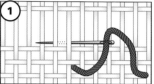

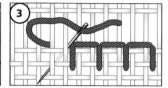

## LADDER HEMSTITCH

This is the simplest decorative hemstitch. Cut the horizontal threads, as described in Method 1 or Method 2 and re-weave the threads. Now work two rows of hemstitch, as described above and shown in this diagram: the vertical threads that remain form a ladder pattern.

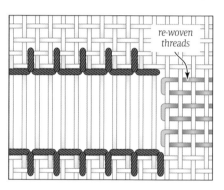

re-woven threads

### JANE'S TIP

*When working hemstitch bands, try to avoid running out of thread halfway across as it is difficult to hide where you start the new threads. If you need to change the thread, leave a long end, work a few stitches with the new thread and then finish the trailing end in the same direction that you are stitching thus avoiding an unsightly pull.*

### WHITE HEMSTITCH SAMPLER

**Stitch count**: 42h x 24w
**Design size**: 8.5 x 4.5cm (3¼ x 1⅞in)
**Fabric**: Zweigart Dublin 26-count ivory linen 26-count
**Needle**: Tapestry size 24 and 22
**Chart**: Page 201

*This project features some straightforward hemstitch bands, as well as pulled stitches in the four-sided stitch border. Using stranded cotton (floss) DMC 712 (Anchor 926), work all the counted stitch bands on the sampler leaving the hemstitched bands until last. Use two strands for the long-legged cross stitch, rice stitch, adapted double cross stitch and large crosses. Use Madeira No.22 gold thread as supplied. Using Method 2 (page 111) and referring to the chart, withdraw four fabric threads for each hemstitch band. Add the hemstitch to the top and bottom band and somersault stitch to the middle one. I completed the design with a border of four-sided stitch and a hemstitch edge cut to the stitching (see page 119 for instructions).*

## Working a Hemstitch Square

The Corner Flowers and Hemstitch Square project is an ideal one to stitch if you haven't yet created a hemstitch square. The threads remaining in the centre of this square have been wrapped and decorated with eight dove's eye stitches. The central detail (right) from the picture, shows how attractive the finished effect is.

**1** Using two strands of DMC 712 (Anchor 926), work a square of simple hemstitch, following the chart and taking care to count each side carefully. As you turn a corner, count the last stitch on one row as the first on the next – otherwise you will end up with the wrong number of threads. Finish off carefully underneath the hemstitches on the wrong side of the stitching.

**2** You can now cut the fabric threads. To ensure that you cut the correct ones it's helpful to run a line of tacking (basting) threads through the square (as shown by the blue dashed lines in the diagram below). Count to the centre of the hemmed area and snip alternate pairs. Carefully unravel the cut threads from the middle to the hemstitched edge, leaving a two-thread border at the sides. When each side is unravelled, tack (baste) these threads out of the way on the back of the work or they will get in the way.

**3** To decorate the remaining threads, wrap each pair with one strand of DMC 712 (Anchor 926) adding dove's eye stitches as you wrap. To complete the square, use two strands of DMC 712 (Anchor 926) to work one row of satin stitch all around the square – as shown by the red stitches in the diagram below. Remove the tacking and cut away loose fabric whiskers.

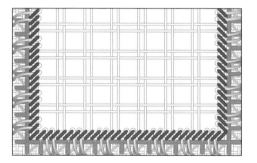

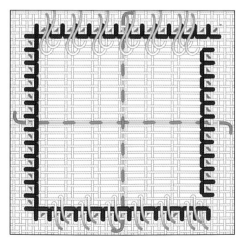

### Jane's Tip

*If you work the hemstitches with two strands of stranded cotton but wrap threads and add dove's eyes with only one strand, you will create a more delicate finish.*

114

**CORNER FLOWERS AND HEMSTITCH SQUARE**

**Stitch count:** 25h x 25w   **Design size:** 4.5cm (1¾in) square
**Fabric:** Zweigart Cashel linen 28-count shade   **Needle:** Tapestry size 24   **Chart:** Page 201

*Work the cross stitch over two linen threads, using two strands of stranded cotton (floss).
Now use two strands of DMC 712 (Anchor 926) to work a square of hemstitch – see opposite
for instructions. Once all stitching is complete, mount and frame your picture. The addition of
a contrast fabric beneath the embroidery will show the hemstitch square to best advantage.*

## Stitch Perfect – DRAWN THREAD EMBROIDERY

❖ Always study the chart well and count the site very carefully so you know exactly how many threads need to be cut.

❖ Work slowly and methodically when cutting and re-weaving threads. Take it in small stages, use a fabric you can see clearly and work in a good light.

❖ If you are new to drawn thread work and a little nervous, work a line of tacking (basting) threads over and under two threads of the linen prior to thread withdrawal.

❖ If working on a wide band, work roughly from the centre of the band when cutting and re-weaving threads. If working on a narrow band, remove the fabric threads from the edge of the band to leave longer fabric ends to re-weave.

❖ When working hemstitch bands, try to avoid running out of thread halfway across as it is difficult to hide where you start the new threads.

❖ Work the hemstitches as indicated on the chart you are following, taking care to count two threads carefully.

## ROSE AND VIOLET SAMPLER

**Stitch count**: 128h x 66w
**Design size**: 23 x 12cm (9 x 4¾in) excluding folded hem
**Fabric**: Zweigart Cashel linen 28-count
**Needle**: Tapestry size 24 and 22
**Chart**: Pages 188–189

*This exquisite band sampler has a satisfying mixture of pulled thread and drawn thread techniques for you to try and includes a decorative folded hem (see overleaf). Work the sampler from the top down. Work the counted stitches in two strands of stranded cotton (floss) referring to the chart for the numbers of fabric threads involved and the Stitch Library for stitch instructions. Work backstitch with one strand. Work the various hemstitch bands with two strands of DMC 712 (Anchor 926), with the optional use of Mill Hill beads as embellishment. Use Method 1 (page 111) for the thread withdrawal and refer to the diagrams in this section as needed. Wrapped bars and dove's eyes decorate the hemstitch square (see page 114 for hemstitch square instructions).*

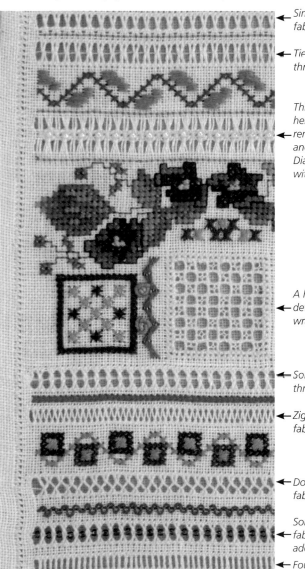

← Simple hemstitch worked after four fabric threads have been removed.

← Tied hemstitch worked after six fabric threads have been removed.

← This slightly more complicated hemstitch band has four threads removed, four threads left, then another four threads removed. Diamond hemstitch is then worked with the inclusion of pearl seed beads

← A hemstitch square (see page 114 for detailed instructions) is decorated with wrapped bars and dove's eyes.

← Somersault stitch worked after six fabric threads have been removed.

← Zigzag hemstitch worked after four fabric threads have been removed.

← Double tied hemstitch worked after six fabric threads have been removed.

← Somersault stitch worked after six fabric threads have been removed, with added beads.

← Four threads removed to create ladder hemstitch.

## FOLDED HEMS

When using a folded hem as a border around a piece of stitching, you can decide on the margin you prefer. You can see an example of a narrow margin from the close-up photograph of the Rose and Violet Sampler, right and the Beautiful Band sampler, below.

The steps below and opposite describe how to create a simple folded hem. If you wish you can make a folded hem even more complicated by withdrawing extra fabric threads from around the edge of the project, so that the hem is still the same width but there is room to add decorative hemstitching in the gap.

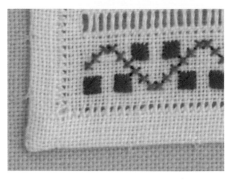

The detail picture above shows the narrow folded hem border on the Rose and Violet Sampler (shown in full on page 116), which finishes the project off beautifully. The Beautiful Band sampler (see page 136) also has a folded hem border on all sides.

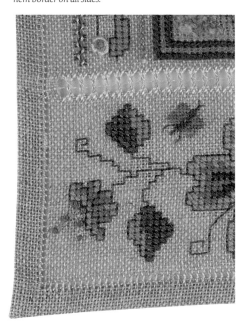

> ### JANE'S TIP
>
> *When scoring fabric prior to folding a hem, try using a glossy magazine cover for an excellent working surface.*

## SCORING FABRIC

To form a perfect fold when stitching a hem, it is essential to score the fabric so that your hem will follow the fabric threads.

**1** Place the fabric on a clean, flat surface (not French polished) and place the needle in a line of threads that will form the fold.

**2** Carefully pull the fabric not the needle, which will create a score mark on the fabric making turning the material simple. This score line will need pressing with a steam iron to remove!

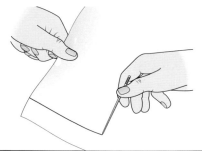

> ### JANE'S TIP
>
> *When planning a folded hem use a little spray starch whilst pressing the embroidery (on the back of area to be scored) and this will help the folding and rolling of the fabric edges.*

## CREATING A FOLDED HEM

**1** From the middle of the long side of the stitching count five threads out from the edge of the stitching and cut the sixth thread. Carefully unravel this thread back to the corner and re-weave it into the margin. Repeat on all four sides. Now lay the fabric wrong side up on a hard surface and count out from the missing thread to the ninth and tenth threads.

**2** Place a tapestry needle between these threads and pull the fabric (not the needle) to score a line that will form a crease – this will form the fold at the edge of the work (see box opposite for how to score fabric). Repeat on all four sides.

**3** Score the fabric again, nine threads further out (line 2 on the diagram). Score another line seven threads out and cut the fabric carefully following this line of threads.

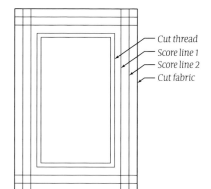

- Cut thread
- Score line 1
- Score line 2
- Cut fabric

**4** Fold the fabric piece at the corners and cut as shown in the diagram. Now fold in all the edges, mitring the corners.

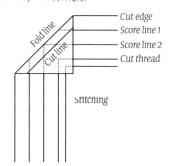

Fold line
Cut line

- Cut edge
- Score line 1
- Score line 2
- Cut thread

Stitching

**5** Using an away waste knot start, hemstitch the folded edge in place. At the corners, stitch the mitres with invisible stitching up the seam.

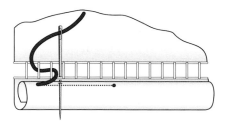

## HEMSTITCH EDGING

It is possible to work a row of hemstitch as shown in the diagram below and then cut the excess fabric away without the fabric fraying. This is an ideal way to create bookmarks if you do not have linen or Aida band. This stitch may be worked on Aida fabric, as you can see from the needlecase on page 40, and can be effective when worked in a contrasting colour if you want to create a more striking effect.

If you are nervous of the result, stitch as shown in the diagram but work each stitch twice, thus forming an even stronger edge. You can see this type of cut edge used here on the Heart and Stork Sachet. If the project is going to require regular washing I prefer to use the folded hem described above.

cut along this line

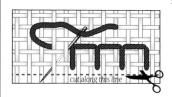

# ADAPTING AND DESIGNING CROSS STITCH

This section is an introduction to creating your own cross stitch designs. One easy way to start is to adapt an existing cross stitch kit, perhaps by changing some of the colours used, replacing a motif with something else or using different stitches. Once you start to think outside the box, it is easier to move on to designing from scratch – and you will find plenty of advice here. See also Stitching from a Kit on page 21.

## USING PURCHASED KITS

There can be no better introduction to cross stitch than working one of the many small kits available. However, there is no reason why the more experienced embroiderer should not enjoy these too. They are still the cheapest way to collect the essentials to complete a project, and they can provide the perfect opportunity to develop simple designing techniques using the chart from the kit as a starting point. A counted needlework kit will contain the fabric and threads for the project, sometimes with the addition of special threads, charms or beads.

It is possible, with just a little imagination, to create many new designs from the original provided, and the joy of counted embroidery is that there is no printing on the fabric so you can decide where and how you want to make changes. Generally, people buy ready-made kits partly for convenience and partly to avoid making design decisions. This section will start you thinking of ways to change and personalize kits – the beginning of designing for yourself.

## ADAPTING A KIT

There are many ways that you can adapt a cross stitch kit – here are a few suggestions.

◆ Consider adding names and dates to the finished piece to make it unique. To add wording, draw the letters on to a sheet of graph paper, mark the centre and then stitch in position.

◆ Look at the picture of the kit design and try a simple change of colour. For example, you may prefer a blue and silver border rather than pink and gold.

◆ Make a copy of the original chart and write notes on this. Keep the notes simple, e.g., 'French knots here' or 'change these cross stitches to seed beads' – the colours and details can come as you stitch.

◆ Keep a record of what colour was used for each change so that you can ensure that both sides of the design match, if this is crucial.

◆ Avoid adding too many different colours to a pattern: instead use different shades of the same colour.

### JANE'S TIP
*Keep your store of threads organized and labelled so that when you are ready to give full vent to your artistic bent you will have all you need to work your own design.*

# DESIGNING A SAMPLER

There are many books devoted to sampler design so this section can only give you some basic tips on how to start designing your own work. A sampler usually features certain elements: the Stork Birth Sampler on page 125 is a straightforward cross stitch design (with a little backstitch), which contains the following basic elements.

◆ A border around the design, which may be wide or narrow, single or double.

◆ An alphabet, sometimes an upper case and a lower case one, and perhaps numbers too.

◆ A selection of motifs or patterns within the border, which may be single or mirror image and may reflect a specific theme.

◆ Some initials or a name and a date, either of the stitcher or the intended recipient of the stitched piece.

## DESIGN CONTENT

When designing for the first time, whether on the computer or using graph paper and coloured pencils, the idea may seem daunting but try dealing with it in small, bite-sized pieces. You will need to make fairly basic decisions before you start work and considering the following points should help.

**Do some research:** Is the design for a family member or special friend and is it a secret? Ask older or more distant relatives for family details. If planning a local design to include maps or plans, use libraries to collect information. Make lists of the receiver's hobbies and favourite pastimes to help you decide what motifs or theme to use.

**Choose the motifs:** Don't be afraid to experiment with using different motifs as trial and error often achieve the most successful results. Use a master chart on which you can temporarily stick motifs to judge the overall effect. When selecting a house motif, relate the size and style of the house to any figures included and adjust the choices of flowers and trees to suit the overall plan. Aim for a balance between the motifs and the overall design size.

**Decide on style:** Are you designing a traditional piece or one with a more modern feel? This will affect what motifs you choose and how you combine them, particularly for a traditional sampler, where it is important to select motifs of the right style and weight. An extreme example would be adding a Ferrari car to a traditional border and stylized trees and flowers!

**Choose the stitches:** Are you planning to work the design entirely in cross stitch or use additional stitches as well? Some stitches are not as successful on Aida as on evenweave.

**Select the fabric:** The following factors are important when choosing fabric. If the design is very traditional (and also includes lots of three-quarter cross stitches), it might suit an evenweave rather than an Aida fabric. You may also want to work some lettering over one fabric thread (for longer verses). If your design is a large one you may need to work it on a higher stitch count, i.e., an 18-count Aida, which would result in a smaller finished size. If working on a finer fabric though, consider your eyesight and the amount of time you have to complete the stitching.

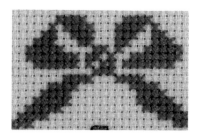

**Decide on size:** What size do you want your work to be? A sampler can be any size or shape, generally determined by how much time you have and if you have a deadline.

**Think about borders:** When designing a large sampler, deep, strong borders work better than narrow, rather mean ones. Use simple narrow borders around smaller projects.

**Choose lettering:** Is the design intended to be read like a verse or a prayer? If so, keep the style simple or the text may be difficult to read. A large alphabet may be better on its own rather than part of a mixed sampler.

**Consider the making up:** What is the end use of your piece of stitching? A sampler doesn't have to be a picture – a small design might look well as a card or bag. You may have to allow more fabric for some making up techniques.

**Sign and date your work:** Why not write a paragraph about the design, its date and how it came to be, plus your own details to put inside the back of the frame? Alternatively, draw a label to stick on the back, with details such as: Designed and stitched by . . . Completed and presented on . . .

# COMPUTER-AIDED DESIGN

Since I started using a computer to help with my cross stitch design, people (not stitchers) have asked me what I do with the spare time! When designing a lovely, complicated border I can spend time perfecting the pattern repeat rather than copying or tracing mirror images. I do not use a scanner to produce cross stitch patterns because I would be breaking any number of copyright laws, and I can always tell when a design is scanned, so I use a computer to remove the drudgery out of designing. The computer replaces the pen, paper, scissors, correction fluid and eraser but does not 'produce' designs by magic. You still need to draw the images on the screen and position the coloured squares.

## DESIGN DEVELOPMENT

I use my own computer programme to design all my counted embroidery (see page 220) and I have included some pictures of the computer screen opposite so you can see the development of a cross stitch chart. The programme enables you to create different counted stitches, draw Hardanger, pulled and drawn thread embroidery in addition to cross stitch and canvaswork charts. You can, of course, scan in your own photographs and import them into the programme to create cross stitch charts for your own use. It is possible to draw in backstitch, copy and paste, flip, reverse and mirror image your motifs. In addition you can create text in cross stitch and look at the chart in black and white symbols, colour and in a combination of both (see page 11).

*Some charting software programmes (including my own), allow you to see what a design would look like if worked on different types of fabrics and different colours. Here, this little violet is shown on green Aida, mauve linen and white stitching paper.*

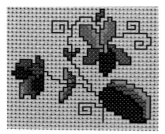 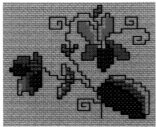 

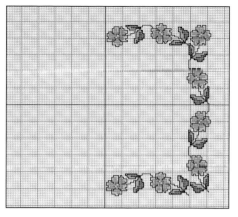

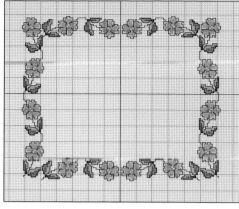

At this stage, I have designed the right-hand side of the border for the Forget-Me-Not Wedding Sampler (stitching instructions on page 128).

Here, the border for the sampler has been completed by copying the right side, pasting it and flipping the image to create a mirror half.

At this point in the designing process one of the main flower motifs has been drawn outside the border, and then copied and pasted into position within the design area.

Other elements of the design are created and added in a similar way until at last the chart is complete and ready for stitching to begin.

# CELEBRATION SAMPLERS

This section has a bonus collection of four large samplers – a birth sampler, a wedding sampler, a festive sampler and a traditional band sampler. These designs are perfect to stitch for special celebrations and can either be stitched as shown or adapted and personalized to suit events and occasions in your life. Colours can be changed, messages added and motifs substituted. You can also use smaller parts from the charts to create quick-stitch projects, such as the sachet and cards shown. Full stitching instructions are given for each of the four designs and their charts are also contained within this section.

## STORK BIRTH SAMPLER

A birth sampler is often the starting point for a new cross stitcher. Whether a new mum or doting grandparent, many stitchers have discovered cross stitch by working a celebratory sampler and this project would be ideal. Worked on Aida fabric, it is simple to stitch, has very few fractional stitches and grows quickly. The design was stitched on a soft peachy-pink fabric but you use blue or a brighter candy pink.

**Stitch count:** 121h x 91w
**Design size:** 22 x 16.5cm (8¾ x 6½in)
**Fabric:** Zweigart 14-count Aida shade 406
**Needle:** Tapestry size 24
**Chart:** Overleaf

*1 Prepare your fabric for work and stitch over one block of Aida, using two strands of stranded cotton (floss) for cross stitch and then one strand for backstitch.*
*2 Use the alphabet and the numbers to personalize the design, adding initials and a date. Plan the letters and numbers on graph paper first, to ensure they fit the space.*
*3 When all the stitching is complete, mount and frame your sampler.*

### HEART AND STORK SACHET

**Stitch count:** 38h x 33w
**Design size:** 7 x 6cm (2¾ x 2½in)
**Fabric:** Zweigart Cashel 28-count washed unbleached linen
**Needle:** Tapestry size 24

*This little sachet uses motifs from the Stork Birth Sampler but you could make up your own combination, and change the colours too if you wish. Use two strands of stranded cotton for cross stitch and one for backstitch. The design was made into a sachet (see page 213) with the top edge hemstitched and trimmed to the stitching (see page 119). Fill with scented pot-pourri or perhaps a little christening gift and tie with a ribbon.*

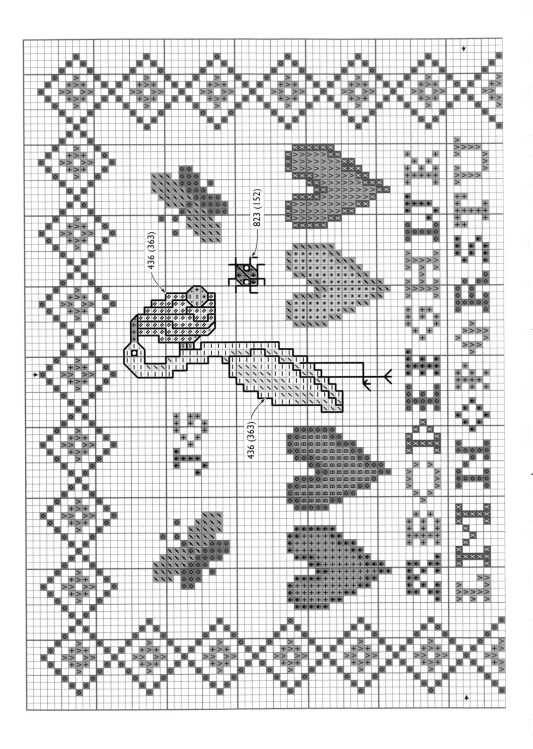

823 (152)

436 (363)

436 (363)

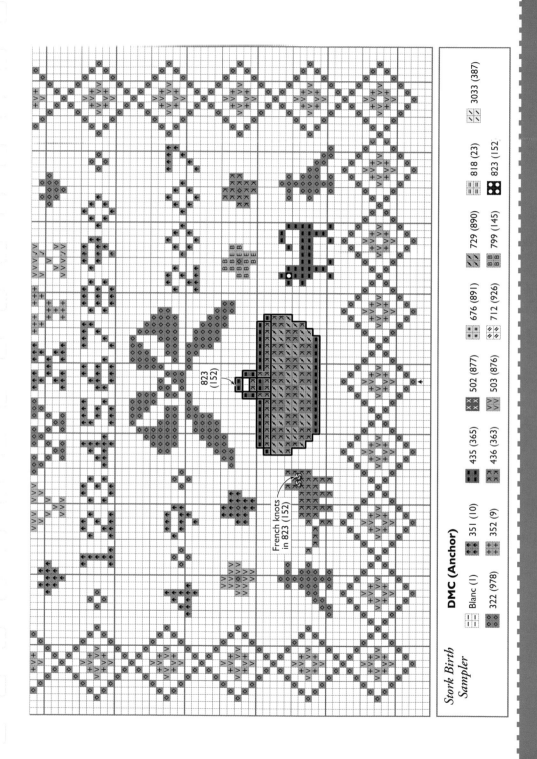

*Stork Birth Sampler*

**DMC (Anchor)**

| | | |
|---|---|---|
| Blanc (1) | 351 (10) | 3033 (387) |
| 322 (978) | 352 (9) | 818 (23) |
| | 435 (365) | 823 (152 |
| | 436 (363) | 729 (890) |
| | 676 (891) | 799 (145) |
| | 712 (926) | 712 (926) |
| | 502 (877) | |
| | 503 (876) | |

823 (152)

French knots in 823 (152)

# FORGET-ME-NOT WEDDING SAMPLER

This pretty sampler could be adapted for a wedding or anniversary, perhaps altering the colour of the hearts to suit the occasion. I have worked some pulled satin stitches in the two heart motifs to add interest and texture but if you prefer not to work these then the design could be stitched on a 14-count Aida. The illustrations on page 123 show this chart being developed by computer software.

**Stitch count:** 103h x 128w (excluding alphabet)
**Design size:** 18.5 x 23cm (7¼ x 9in)
**Fabric:** Zweigart Cashel 28-count linen, shade 224
**Needle:** Tapestry size 24
**Chart:** Overleaf

*1 Prepare fabric for work and stitch over two threads of linen, using two strands of stranded cotton (floss) for cross stitch and one for backstitch. Work pulled satin stitch with two strands of DMC 712 (Anchor 926).*
*2 Use the alphabet and numbers on page 205 to personalize the design, adding initials and a date. Plan the letters and numbers on graph paper first, to ensure they fit.*
*3 When all the stitching is complete, mount and frame your sampler.*

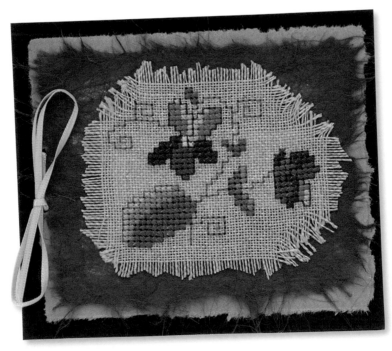

### VINTAGE VIOLA CARD

**Stitch count:** 29h x 35w    **Design size:** 5.5 x 6.5cm (2¼ x 2¾in)
**Fabric:** Zweigart Dublin 26-count washed unbleached linen    **Needle:** Tapestry size 24

*This pretty motif was taken from the Forget-Me-Not Wedding Sampler. Stitch using two strands of stranded cotton for cross stitch and one for backstitch. Prepare as a tattered patch, mount on handmade paper and card and trim with a narrow ribbon. See page 215 for making cards. This motif is shown on different coloured computer-generated fabrics on page 122.*

3740 (872)

501 (878)

3834 (100)

Pulled
satin stitch
in 712 (926)

200.

501 (878)

**Forget-Me-Not Wedding Sampler**

**DMC (Anchor)**

- 351 (10)
- 352 (9)
- 353 (8)
- 501 (878)
- 502 (877)
- 503 (876)
- 676 (891)
- 677 (361)
- 712 (926)
- 3740 (872)
- 3834 (100)
- 3838 (177)
- 3839 (176)
- 3840 (120)

Use the alphabet and numbers on page 205 to personalize the design

Pulled satin stitch in 712 (926)

3834 (100)

501 (878)

501 (878)

3740 (872)

501 (878)

# HOLLY AND HELLEBORE GARLAND

This festive design makes a lovely sampler to be brought out each year to herald the arrival of Christmas. Instead of working the alphabet you could use the charted letters to create a greeting – perhaps 'Happy Christmas to One and All'.

**Stitch count:** 105h x 125w
**Design size:** 19 x 23cm (7½ x 9in)
**Fabric:** Zweigart Cashel 28-count linen shade 638
**Needle:** Gold-plated tapestry size 24
**Chart:** Overleaf

1 *Prepare your fabric for work and stitch over two threads of linen (or one block of 14-count Aida), using two strands of stranded cotton (floss) for cross stitch and French knots, and one strand for backstitch. There are some tweeded cross stitches in the cottage – use one strand of each colour together in the needle (see page 17). Work eyelets in Madeira No.22 gold thread.*
2 *Use the alphabet to change the initials or personalize the design in some other way.*
3 *When all the stitching is complete, mount and frame your sampler.*

### POINSETTIA GIFT TAG

**Stitch count:** 12h x 16w
**Design size:** 2 x 3cm (¾ x 1⅛in)
**Fabric:** Zweigart linen Aida with Lurex 14-count
**Needle:** Tapestry size 24

*This motif was taken from the Holly and Hellebore Garland. Stitch over one block of Aida, using two strands of stranded cotton (floss) for cross stitch and one for backstitch. Fray the patch and make up as a folded gift tag trimmed with metallic thread. See page 215 for making up cards.*

### HELLEBORE CARD

**Stitch count:** 22h x 35w
**Design size:** 4 x 6.5cm (1½ x 2½in)
**Fabric:** Zweigart 14-count Star Aida
**Needle:** Tapestry size 24

*Another motif taken from the Holly and Hellebore Garland. Stitch over one block of Aida, using two strands of stranded cotton (floss) for cross stitch and one for backstitch. Add French knots in two strands, with two twists around the needle. Prepare the design as a patch, mount it on handmade card and trim with silk ribbon. See page 215 for making up cards.*

Eyelets in gold thread

934 (852)

840 (1084)

3830 (5975)

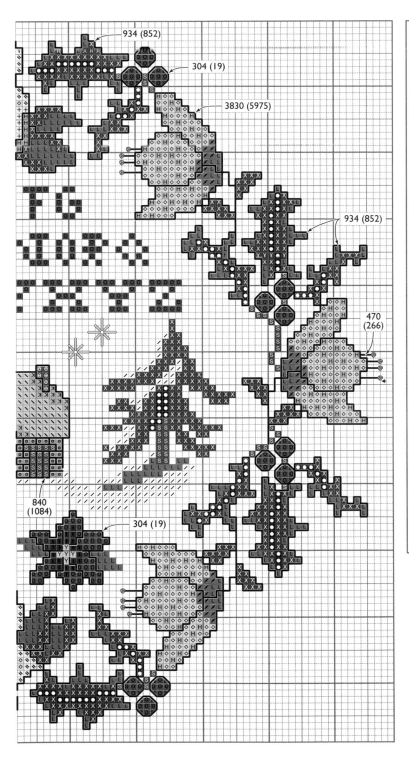

Holly and
Hellebore
Garland

**DMC
(Anchor)**

934 (852)

304 (19)

3830 (5975)

934 (852)

470
(266)

840
(1084)

304 (19)

| | |
|---|---|
| Blanc (1) |
| 223 (1027) |
| 224 (895) |
| 225 (894) |
| 304 (19) |
| 437 (362) |
| 470 (266) |
| 666 (46) |
| 712 (926) |
| 725 (305) |
| 738 (361) |
| 840 (1084) |
| 934 (852) |
| 937 (268) |
| 3072 (397) |
| 3830 (5975) |
| 758 (9575) + 3830 (5975) |

French knots
in 470 (266)

Eyelets in
Madeira
No.22 gold

# BEAUTIFUL BAND SAMPLER

Band samplers were originally stitched as learning and remembering tools long before pen and paper were used to record stitches and techniques. A stitcher would copy a row of a stitch or pattern on to a narrow piece of linen and then roll the fabric up and keep it as a reference work.

As a self-confessed addict of band samplers I always find a way of including one in my books. This exquisite sampler is not difficult to stitch as all the techniques are explained within this book, but I would not recommend it as a project for a beginner! Work this project on evenweave as some of the stitches cannot be constructed on Aida – see the extensive Stitch Library or relevant techniques within the body of the book. This design is also a treasury of small motifs that could be used in smaller projects for quick gifts and cards.

**Stitch count:** 60w x 259h    **Design size:** 11.5 x 50.5cm (4½ x 20in)    **Fabric:** Zweigart 26-count Dublin linen washed unbleached    **Needle:** Gold plated size 26

*Press the fabric to remove creases and oversew the edges to prevent fraying (particularly important if finishing the project with a folded hem). Start at the top of the sampler, leaving at least 6.5cm (2½in) at the top of the fabric. The chart occurs over six pages, with the key on each spread. You will find the design easier to work if you colour photocopy the parts and carefully tape them together.*

## BAND 1

*Work the cross stitch motifs using two strands of stranded cotton (floss) and two strands of Caron Waterlilies silk. Use one strand for backstitch. Once you have established the width of the sampler, work a line of tacking (basting) stitches down each side (under and over two fabric threads) to help keep you in position as you work down the project. This also helps when removing*

*fabric threads in preparation for working the various hemstitch bands. See also page 111.*

*Use two strands of stranded cotton for half Rhodes stitch, braided cross stitch, crossed cushion stitch, threaded herringbone, double cross stitch and rice stitch, combining the latter with one strand of gold metallic thread. Use three strands of Caron Waterlilies for the large Rhodes stitch.*

## BAND 2

Work the vertical satin stitch bands in three strands of Caron Waterlilies (don't pull stitches too tight – they should lie smoothly side by side). For the double tied hemstitch, remove six threads (see page 111) and then work two rows of hemstitch with two strands of 712 (926) across either side of the fabric ladder. Use one strand to work the double tied hemstitch.

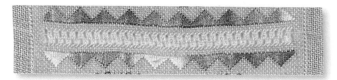

## BAND 3

Use two strands of stranded cotton for the cross stitch and one for backstitch. Use two strands to work the red berry motifs in detached buttonhole stitch and then outline in counted chain stitch. Use one strand to backstitch outline the area for braid stitch and then work the braid stitch with one strand of De Haviland Flower Thread. Couch a strand of metallic gold in place with one strand of stranded cotton. Work satin stitch with two strands, in two shades of pink. Work two rows of Montenegrin stitch with two strands of stranded cotton prior to removing and re-weaving four fabric threads. Work hemstitch on one side of the ladder, grouping the fabric threads in fours.

## BAND 4

Use two strands of stranded cotton for cross stitch, French knots and four-sided stitch and one strand for backstitch. Work the hemstitch square (see page 114) with two strands of 712 (926). Fill with wrapped bars and dove's eyes with one strand. Remove and re-weave four fabric threads, leave four, and remove and re-weave another four before working the diamond hemstitch in two strands, adding beads as you go. Work a line of backstitch with gold metallic.

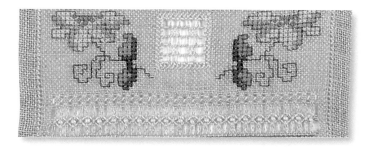

## BAND 5

Use two strands of stranded cotton for cross stitch, half Rhodes stitch, queen stitch, eyelets, Algerian eyes, French knots, four-sided stitch, hemstitch and needlelace petals (the needlelace is shown in a detail beside the chart). Work tied hemstitch after removing and re-weaving six fabric threads.

## BAND 6

Use two strands of stranded cotton for cross stitch, long-legged cross stitch and threaded herringbone (with one strand of Caron Waterlilies). Use one strand of Caron Waterlilies for Pekinese stitch, bullion roses, half cross stitch and French knots. Use one strand of Madeira Lana wool for velvet stitch in the 'pond' and one strand of stranded cotton for half cross stitch background. Remove and re-weave six fabric threads and work somersault stitch with two strands of 712 (926).

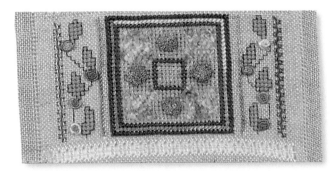

## BAND 7

Use two strands of stranded cotton for cross stitch, counted chain stitch and bullions. Use one strand of Caron thread for French knots. Use one strand for backstitch. Work the insects in tent stitch, with one strand over just one fabric thread.

Finish the sampler with a folded and stitched hem (see page 118). Remove all tacking. Alternatively, mount and frame your sampler.

# Beautiful Band Sampler

DMC (Anchor)

| | | | | |
|---|---|---|---|---|
| 315 (1019) | 930 (1035) | | Caron Waterlilies Far Horizon | Queen stitch in 3687 (68) |
| 316 (1017) | 931 (1034) | | De Haviland Green Flower Thread | All hemstitching in 712 (926) |
| 470 (255) | 932 (1033) | | Velvet stitch in Madeira Lana Wool 3396 | Mill Hill antique glass beads 03021 pearl |
| 471 (265) | 3041 (871) | | Half cross in one strand of 932 (1033) | |
| 676 (891) | 3042 (870) | | | |
| 729 (890) | 3051 (845) | | | |
| 778 (361) | 3778 (1013) | | | |
| | 3346 (267) | | | |
| | 3347 (266) | | | |
| | 3721 (896) | | | |
| | 3740 (872) | | | |
| | 3772 (1007) | | | |
| | 3777 (1015) | | | |

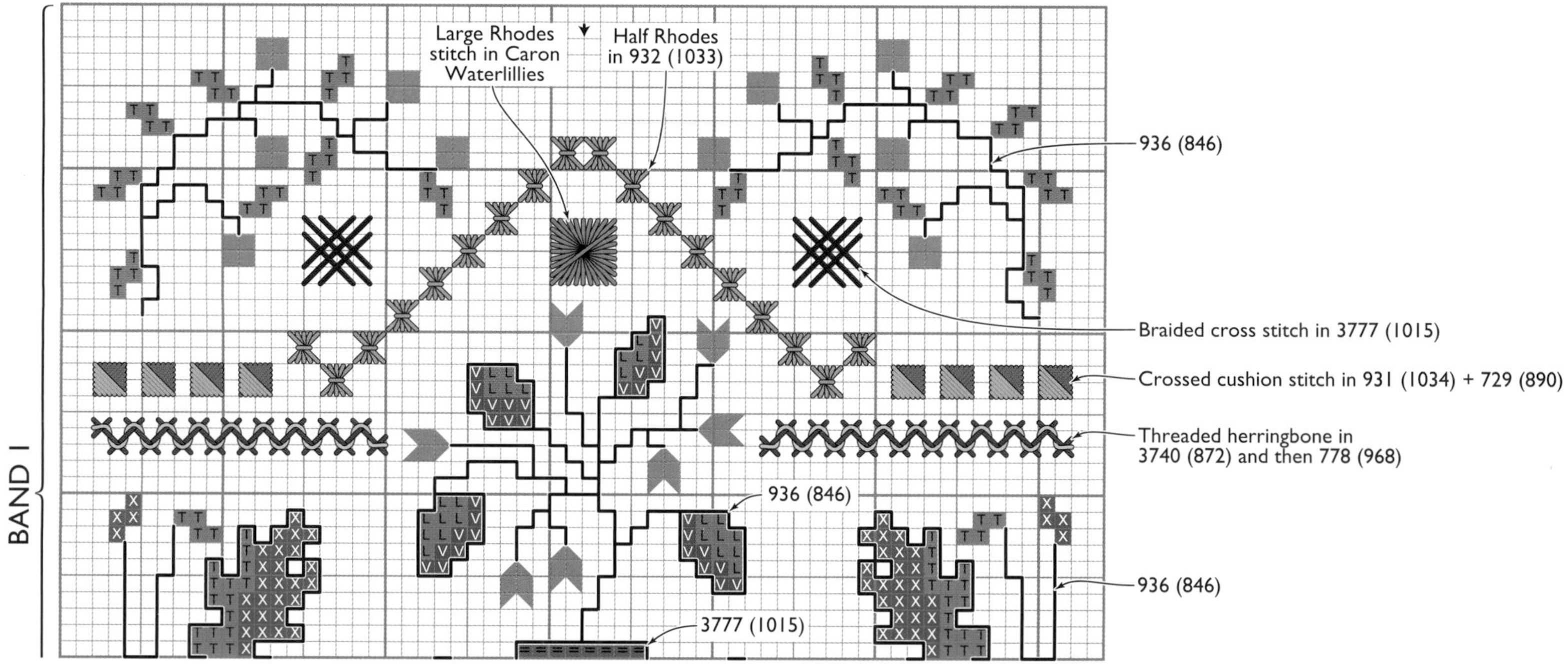

936 (846)

Braided cross stitch in 3777 (1015)

Crossed cushion stitch in 931 (1034) + 729 (890)

Threaded herringbone in 3740 (872) and then 778 (968)

936 (846)

Half Rhodes in 932 (1033)

Large Rhodes stitch in Caron Waterlillies

936 (846)

3777 (1015)

BAND I

140

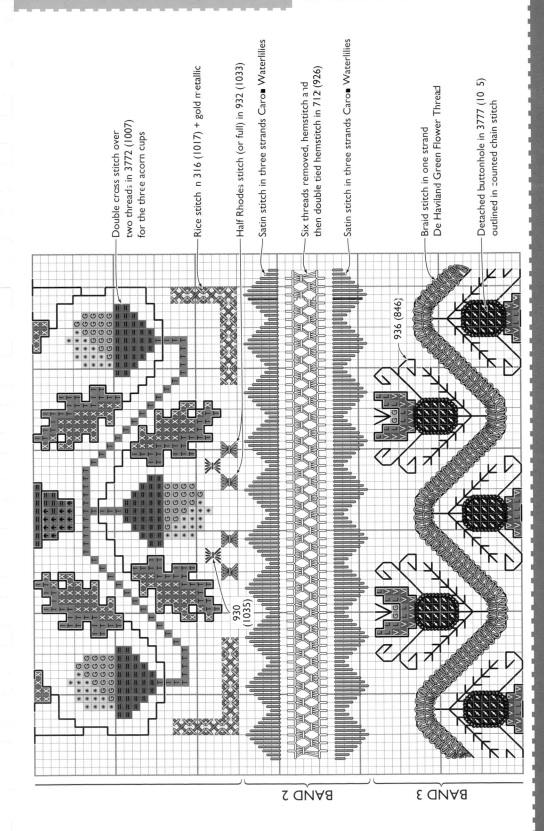

Double cross stitch over two threads in 3772 (1007) for the three acorn cups

Rice stitch in 316 (1017) + gold metallic

Half Rhodes stitch (or full) in 932 (1033)

Satin stitch in three strands Caro■ Waterlilies

Six threads removed, hemstitch and then double tied hemstitch in 712 (926)

Satin stitch in three strands Caro■ Waterlilies

Braid stitch in one strand De Haviland Green Flower Thread

Detached buttonhole in 3777 (10 5) outlined in counted chain stitch

936 (846)

930 (1035)

BAND 2

BAND 3

# Beautiful Band Sampler

## DMC (Anchor)

| | |
|---|---|
| ▨ 315 (1019) | ▨ 930 (1035) |
| ⅴⅴ 316 (1017) | ⅴⅴ 931 (1034) |
| ⊤⊤ 470 (255) | ⊝⊝ 932 (1033) |
| △△ 471 (265) | ⊹⊹ 3041 (871) |
| ** 676 (891) | ⬚⬚ 3042 (870) |
| GG 729 (890) | ✕✕ 3051 (845) |
| ‖‖ 778 (361) | |

| | |
|---|---|
| ▨ 3346 (267) | ◈ Queen stitch in 3687 (68) |
| ⅴⅴ 3347 (266) | |
| ⊏⊏ 3721 (896) | ⊔⊔ All hemstitching in 712 (926) |
| GG 3740 (872) | |
| ⊞⊞ 3772 (1007) | ⬤⬤ Mill Hill antique glass beads 03021 pearl |
| ⁄⁄ 3777 (1015) | |
| ◄◄ 3778 (1013) | |

▨ Caron Waterlilies Far Horizon

▨ De Haviland Green Flower Thread

▨ Velvet stitch in Madeira Lana Wool 3396

▨ Half cross in one strand of 932 (1033)

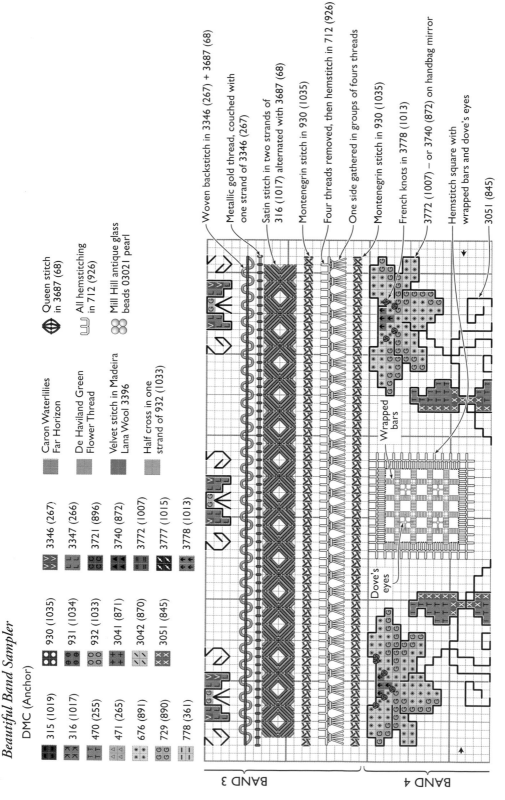

Woven backstitch in 3346 (267) + 3687 (68)

Metallic gold thread, couched with one strand of 3346 (267)

Satin stitch in two strands of 316 (1017) alternated with 3687 (68)

Montenegrin stitch in 930 (1035)

Four threads removed, then hemstitch in 712 (926)

One side gathered in groups of fours threads

Montenegrin stitch in 930 (1035)

French knots in 3778 (1013)

3772 (1007) – or 3740 (872) on handbag mirror

Hemstitch square with wrapped bars and dove's eyes

3051 (845)

Wrapped bars

Dove's eyes

BAND 3

BAND 4

Four-sided stitch over four threads in 712 (926)

Four threads removed

Diamond hemst tch in 712 (926) embellished with pearl beads

Four threads removed

Backstitch in gold metallic thread

Half Rhodes stitch with a bar in 932 (1233)

Woven leaves in 315 (1019)

French knots in 316 (1017)

Queen stitch in 3687 (68)

Eyelets and Algerian eyes in 932 (1033)

Four-sided stitch over four threads in 712 (926)

936 (846)

3740 (872)

BAND 5

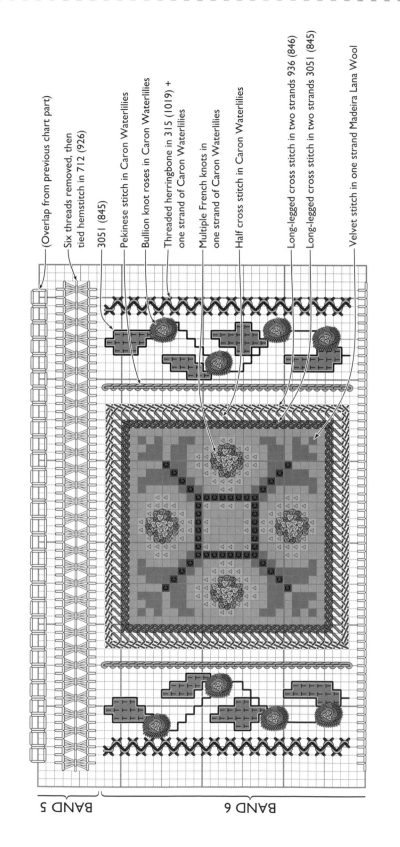

(Overlap from previous chart part)

Six threads removed, then
tied hemstitch in 712 (926)

3051 (845)

Pekinese stitch in Caron Waterlilies

Bullion knot roses in Caron Waterlilies

Threaded herringbone in 315 (1019) +
one strand of Caron Waterlilies

Multiple French knots in
one strand of Caron Waterlilies

Half cross stitch in Caron Waterlilies

Long-legged cross stitch in two strands 936 (846)

Long-legged cross stitch in two strands 3051 (845)

Velvet stitch in one strand Madeira Lana Wool

BAND 5

BAND 6

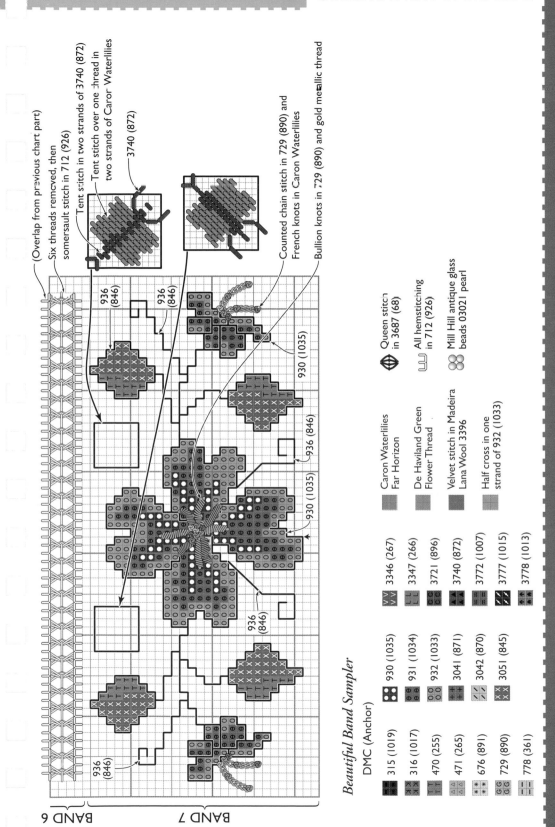

(Overlap from previous chart part)

Six threads removed, then somersault stitch in 712 (926)

Tent stitch in two strands of 3740 (872)

Tent stitch over one thread in two strands of Caron Waterlilies

3740 (872)

936 (846)

936 (846)

930 (1035)

936 (846)

930 (1035)

936 (846)

936 (846)

Counted chain stitch in 729 (890) and French knots in Caron Waterlilies

Bullion knots in 729 (890) and gold metallic thread

BAND 6

BAND 7

*Beautiful Band Sampler*

DMC (Anchor)

| | | | |
|---|---|---|---|
| 315 (1019) | 930 (1035) | 3346 (267) | |
| 316 (1017) | 931 (1034) | 3347 (266) | |
| 470 (255) | 932 (1033) | 3721 (896) | |
| 471 (265) | 3041 (871) | 3740 (872) | |
| 676 (891) | 3042 (870) | 3772 (1007) | |
| 729 (890) | 3051 (845) | 3777 (1015) | |
| 778 (361) | | 3778 (1013) | |

Caron Waterlilies Far Horizon

De Haviland Green Flower Thread

Velvet stitch in Madeira Lana Wool 3396

Half cross in one strand of 932 (1033)

Queen stitch in 3687 (68)

All hemstitching in 712 (926)

Mill Hill antique glass beads 03021 pearl

145

# STITCH LIBRARY

This is a very personal library of stitches collected over more than 20 years of my own enjoyment of counted thread embroidery. The term 'counted thread' can strike terror in the heart of the cross stitcher but it is only the generic name for the type of embroidery that we do. It just means working from a chart rather than the design being printed on the fabric.

I continue to be an avid cross stitcher but having discovered all these lovely stitches I can't resist using them! Many of the stitches in this collection can be worked on Aida fabric but some need the additional threads available on evenweave. This will become easier to grasp as you look at the diagrams. The clear stitch diagrams will lead you through the construction of the stitches in easy stages. Some of the diagrams are numbered to indicate that there are several steps to working the stitch. Remember that the construction of a stitch remains the same but may be worked over a variety of fabric threads so it is important to check the chart each time.

The stitches are alphabetical and are also indexed. If the stitch you require is not included in this section you will find it within the relevant chapter of the book; for example, Kloster blocks are in the Hardanger section.

## ALGERIAN EYE

This pretty, star-shaped stitch is a pulled stitch, which means that when formed correctly holes are pulled in the fabric. It usually occupies the space taken by four cross stitches and is an ideal stitch to combine with cross stitch as it can add a delicate lacy appearance without the anxiety of cutting threads. Algerian eye can be worked over two or four threads of evenweave as shown and is more successful worked on evenweave than Aida. (See also eyelet variations on page 153.)

> ### JANE'S TIP
> When trying new stitches, I use a piece of 20-count Cork linen so I can master the stitch on a large-count material before working it on my project. There is no point learning a new stitch and fighting your eyesight at the same time.

**1** Start to the left of a vertical thread and work from left to right around each stitch in an clockwise direction (or vice versa but keeping each stitch the same).

**2** Always work the stitch by passing the needle down through the central hole, pulling quite firmly so that a small hole is formed in the centre. Take care that trailing threads do not cover this hole as you progress to the next stitch.

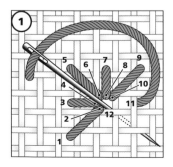

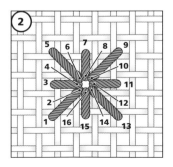

## BACKSTITCH – SEE PAGE 25

## BRAID STITCH

This very decorative stitch seen on early band samplers was often stitched using metallic threads. The stitch may be formed filling an area surrounded by cross stitch or be worked after marking the fabric with a backstitch line, which gives a framework to create the stitch.

**1** Work the backstitch line on the chart using one strand of stranded cotton (floss). On the back of the embroidery, at the right-hand end of the band, form a loop start through the back of the backstitch just completed and bring the needle to the front of the work at the bottom of the backstitched line. Pass the thread across to the left and hold in place with your thumb.

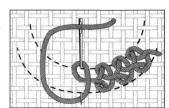

**2** Pass the needle under the held thread towards you and twist to the left so that it is pointing in the opposite direction. The needle should now have the thread twisted around it.

**3** Now pass the needle through the top backstitch and out again through the bottom row. Wrap the thread around the point of the needle and pull through. Work across the backstitch band keeping the stitches as even as you can.

## BRAIDED CROSS STITCH

This is a very decorative stitch that can be worked over a number of fabric threads and is effective when worked in one or two colours. The secret is to work the stitch in one direction at a time and then weave the second set of stitches through the first.

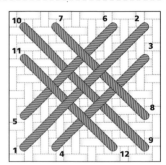

Following the number sequence in the diagram, work one long stitch from bottom left to top right. Work two further stitches facing the same direction. Now complete the stitch by working from right to left, weaving in and out of the first set of long stitches.

## BULLION STITCH

This unusual stitch, also called a knot or bar, is not a counted stitch but is useful as it adds a three-dimensional texture to a design. It can be formed in straight lines, be adapted to make a raised bar, and can also be made to curve for petal shapes and for building up roses (see overleaf). Bullion bars are easier to form using a gold-plated needle. Don't panic when you reach the end – careful teasing with a needle will rescue any apparent disaster.

**1** Begin the stitch by working an incomplete backstitch, leaving the needle in the fabric. It is vital that the point of the needle exits from the hole where it started.

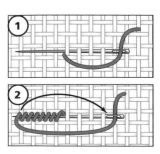

**2** With the needle still in the fabric, wind the thread around the needle as many times as necessary to make the coil the length of the incomplete backstitch. Hold the needle and coil of thread firmly against the fabric, then gently pull the needle through the coil and fabric. To finish the stitch turn the coil back on itself and push the needle through the fabric at the rear of the backstitch.

## BULLION ROSE

Working bullion stitch this way can create roses or cabbages or cauliflowers, depending on the colours you choose!

**1** First work a few French knots.

**2** Now work a bullion bar, adding extra winds to the needle to force the bar to bend. Begin to build up the rose, adding more tightly curved bullions around the first two.

**3** A completed bullion rose can have as many curved bullions as you like. The final diagram here shows six, with the colour changed to a deeper shade on the final two.

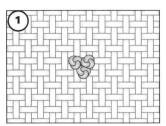

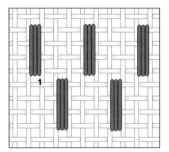

## BUTTONHOLE STITCH

This very old stitch is very simple to work and extremely versatile. See also buttonhole edging on page 104.

Start with an away waste knot and follow the number sequence in the diagram. Buttonhole stitches are usually worked closely together but may be spaced more widely according to the pattern you are working.

## COIL STITCH

This pulled stitch is simple but very pretty and is most effective when worked in the same colour as the fabric and pulled fairly firmly.

Beginning at 1, work three satin stitches over the required number of horizontal fabric threads (in this case four). Leave a gap of the same number of vertical fabric threads. Repeat to the end. Take a small stitch into the back of the last cluster of each row to secure it. Work the next row staggered midway between the stitches of the pervious row, as shown.

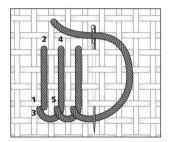

## COUCHING

This is not a counted stitch as such but can be very effective, particularly on a band sampler. Couching is often worked with a metallic thread laid on the fabric, held down by small vertical stitches. Start by bringing the laid thread up through the fabric and laying it across the fabric. Using the couching thread, work small vertical stitches, as shown. When working on linen, I try to come up and go down the same holes in the fabric to avoid long stitches spoiling the effect.

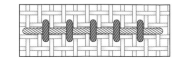

## COUNTED CHAIN STITCH

This stitch is very versatile as it may be used on Aida or evenweave fabric, as part of a pattern or to join sections of stitching together. It can be used as an outline stitch or worked in close rows when filling in a pattern. If using counted chain stitch to join sections of stitching you normally use the same colour thread for the join but you could use a contrasting colour.

**1** To work chain stitch on evenweave, start to the left of a vertical thread, bringing the needle up through the fabric and down through the same hole, forming a loop on the surface. Pass the point of the needle under two threads and up to the surface forming another loop. Each new stitch thus anchors the previous stitch.

**2** If chain stitch is worked as a border, then the last stitch will anchor the first. If not, the last stitch may be anchored with a small stitch over one thread, as shown in the second diagram.

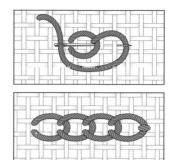

## CROSS STITCH – SEE PAGE 23

## THREE-QUARTER CROSS STITCH – SEE PAGE 24

# CROSS STITCH VARIATIONS

Basic cross stitch can be altered in various ways to produce interesting new stitches. Try some of the variations shown here and overleaf. The diagrams are shown in two colours as the stitches look most effective this way.

## DOUBLE CROSS STITCH

Double cross stitch, also known as Smyrna or Leviathan stitch, may be worked over two or four threads of an evenweave fabric or over two blocks of Aida, to create a series of bold crosses or 'stars'. Tiny double cross stitches may be formed over two threads of evenweave but they are difficult to work on one block of Aida.

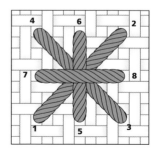

## ADAPTED DOUBLE CROSS STITCH

This stitch can be worked vertically or diagonally but is more difficult on Aida as the second stage of the stitch needs to be carefully placed. To keep all double cross stitches uniform make sure that the direction of the stitches within them is the same. Adapted double cross stitch looks particularly effective when the second stage of the stitch is added in metallic thread.

Work the stitch in the same way as double cross stitch but with the first large cross over twice as many threads as the second smaller cross.

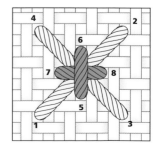

## VERTICAL DOUBLE CROSS STITCH

This stitch is worked in a similar way to double cross stitch and can also be worked in two colours, or with the second stage worked in metallic thread.

## BOXED VERTICAL CROSS STITCH

For this cross stitch variation, work a vertical cross stitch and then add four smaller stitches at the top, bottom and both sides to create a box-like appearance.

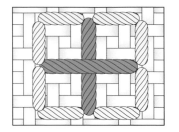

## TACKED CROSS STITCH

Work a cross stitch over four evenweave threads or two blocks of Aida, and then add a single stitch across the centre of the cross over two threads or one block.

## CUSHION STITCH

This is really an adaptation of satin stitch and is very straightforward. It is most effective when worked in small even squares and reversing the stitch direction as shown here. You may find this stitch easier to form using an embroidery frame.

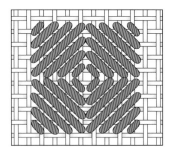

## CROSSED CUSHION STITCH

Crossed cushion stitch is formed by working the satin stitch square and then crossing the stitch in the other direction in a different colour thread covering half the base stitch completely. Again these can be most effective when the direction of the stitch is reversed.

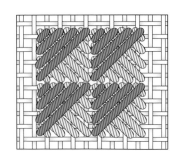

## DETACHED BUTTONHOLE STITCH

This stitch can be used to fill shapes. The stitches should lie closely together but are shown widely spaced in the second diagram below to explain the stitch more clearly. The rows are worked to and fro, with the first and last stitches of each row worked into the fabric, to anchor all the buttonhole stitches.

**1** Begin by outlining the motif in backstitch, then work two long stitches across the width of the shape. Work the first row of buttonhole stitch (see page 148) over this satin stitch line.

**2** When you come to the end of the row, reverse direction and work the next row into the previous row, with the stitches close together. Continue working to and fro, reducing the length of the rows to follow the shape being filled.

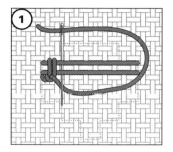
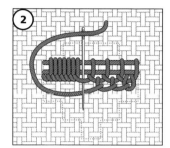

## DIAMOND HEMSTITCH

This is an attractive hemstitch variation (see simple hemstitch page 112), which can be formed over two, four or other combinations of threads. Withdraw threads either side of a solid fabric area (see withdrawing and re-weaving page 111) and then work the hemstitch in two journeys. The stitches will form diamond shapes on the front of the work and if pulled firmly will create small holes in the solid fabric area. This stitch is formed on the front of the fabric, so if you find yourself with the needle on the back you know something is wrong!

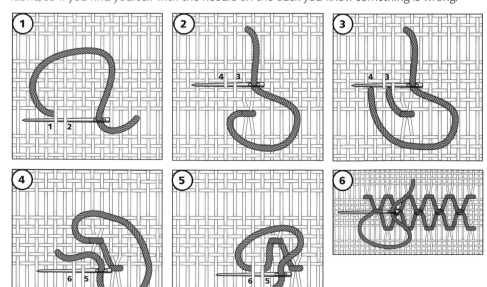

## DOUBLE FAGGOT STITCH

This stitch is used almost exclusively as a pulled stitch and it is intended to create a decorative, lacy effect on the fabric. As with all pulled stitches, it is better formed on linen. The stitch creates textured areas in a design and can be worked as a border or in a regular pattern for filling in larger areas. The effect created looks particularly good if worked in thread the same colour as the fabric.

**1** Bring the thread through the fabric at position 1, then insert the needle at 2 (four threads to the right) and bring through at 1 again.

**2** Re-insert the needle at 2, then bring it through at 3 (four threads down and four to the left). Pull stitches firmly to achieve the open effect.

**3** Insert the needle at 1 (four threads up) and bring it through at 3 again.

**4** Re-insert the needle at 1, then bring it through at 4 (four threads down and four to the left).

**5** Continue in this way, following the number sequence to the end of the row. Complete the last stitch 7–8 by re-inserting the needle at 6 and bringing it out at 8 (four threads down and four to the right).

**6** Turn the work around to work the last row. Bring the thread through at 8, insert the needle at 7 and bring through at 8 again. Turn the work and repeat the procedure to create four sides to each stitch.

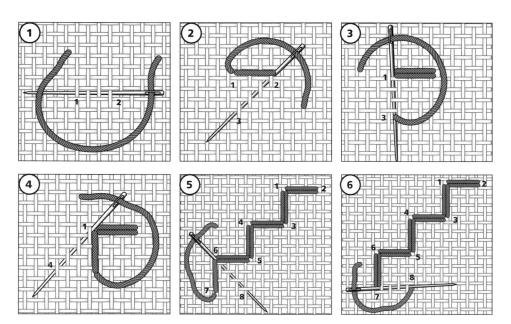

DOUBLE RUNNING STITCH (HOLBEIN STITCH) – SEE PAGE 80

DOVE'S EYE STITCH – SEE PAGE 102

CORNER DOVE'S EYE – SEE PAGE 103

## EYELET VARIATIONS

There are a number of eyelet stitch variations, some of which are shown in the diagrams here. You can choose the shape you like and work it over more or less threads to create larger or smaller eyelets.

The rules are the same for all eyelets. As with Algerian eye you need to work the stitch in the correct order and in one direction to ensure that the hole created is uniform and as round as possible. When following the number sequence on the diagrams always work the stitch by passing the needle down through the central hole each time, and take care that trailing threads do not cover this hole as you progress to the next stitch.

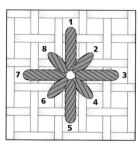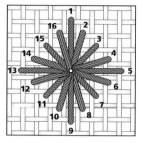

## FLY STITCH

This is a versatile looped stitch that can be used singly or worked in rows as a border or filling.

**1** Bring the needle out at position 1 and hold down the thread. Insert the needle a little to the right at 2 and then out at 3, halfway between 1 and 2 but lower.

**2** Keeping the thread under the needle, pull the thread through. Insert the needle at 4 to make a small tying stitch in the centre – this stitch can be longer if desired.

**3** If working a row of fly stitch, continue on to make the next stitch. The stitch can also be worked in vertical rows, as shown in the final diagram, and in this case the tying stitches should butt up together. The stitch width can also be altered.

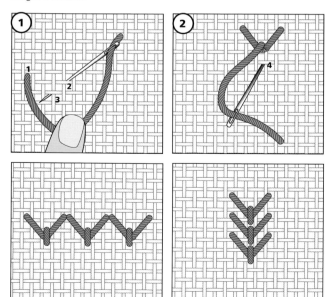

# Four-Sided Stitch

This is traditionally worked as a pulled stitch to create a lacy effect without the removal of fabric threads. It can also be used as a hemstitch when threads are to be cut or removed. The secret of creating a perfect four-sided stitch is to make sure that your needle travels in the correct direction on the back of the stitch. The stitches on the front should be vertical or horizontal but diagonal on the back. It is this tension that forms the small holes as the stitch is worked. The stitch is not recommended for Aida fabric.

**1** Begin to the left of a vertical thread and work a horizontal straight stitch across four threads (or the number indicated on the chart), passing the needle diagonally across four threads at the back of the work.

**2** Bring the needle up and form a vertical straight stitch, again passing the needle diagonally across four threads at the back of the work.

**3** Bring the needle up and form another vertical straight stitch, again passing the needle diagonally across four threads at the back.

**4** Work a horizontal straight stitch to form the last side of the square but this time pass the needle across diagonally to begin the next stitch.

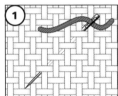
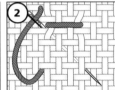
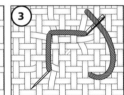
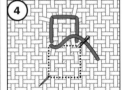

# French Knot – see page 26

# Gathered Ribbon Rose – see page 88

# Gobelin Stitch

Gobelin stitch is a straight stitch often used as a filling stitch as it can mimic the appearance of a woven tapestry. The stitch can be worked to form regular shapes or in encroaching rows to create softer shapes. It can also be worked as long stitches in zigzag rows to form a Florentine pattern or flame stitch. When worked this way it is often known as bargello and is used as a hard-wearing stitch for upholstery. Gobelin stitch can be worked in stranded cotton or in crewel or tapestry wool and should not be pulled too tight.

**1** Work a long, straight stitch over the number of threads indicated on the chart and follow the number sequence in the diagrams. The stitch shouldn't pull or distort the fabric.

**2** Leaving a space for the second row, work along the row, positioning the needle to return to fill the gaps.

**3** Continuing to follow the number sequence, work the second row of stitches, which should encroach on the first row.

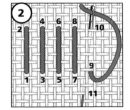
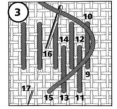

## GREEK CROSS STITCH

This pulled stitch looks very ordinary on its own but creates wonderful patterns when worked on groups. The pattern created will vary depending on the relative position of each stitch. The stitch needs to be pulled fairly firmly to create the correct effect.

**1** Bring the needle and thread through at position 1, go down at 2 (four threads up and four to the right) then up at 3 (four threads down), keeping the thread under the needle.

**2** Pull the thread through then put the needle down at 4 (four threads to the right) and up at 3 as shown (four threads to left), keeping the thread under the needle.

**3** Pull the thread through then put the needle down at 5 (four threads down) and up at 3 as shown (four threads up), keeping the thread under the needle.

**4** Pull the thread through and secure the cross by inserting the needle at 3 to overlap the first and last stitches.

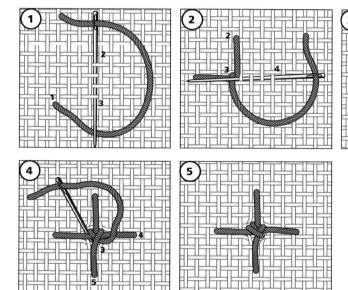

---

## HEMSTITCH – SEE PAGE 112

---

## HEMSTITCH EDGING – SEE PAGE 119

---

## HEMSTITCH RECTANGLE – SEE PAGE 114

---

# HERRINGBONE STITCH

This stitch is also known as plaited stitch, catch stitch, fishnet stitch and witch stitch. It is a simple and decorative stitch often used on band samplers and makes a fine companion to cross stitch. It looks particularly pretty when combined with stitches like long-legged cross stitch. It can also be whipped with a second colour (see also threaded herringbone below). It is shown here worked over four evenweave threads diagonally and under two horizontally. It can be worked over two threads and under one to make it smaller, or over and under more threads to make it larger.

Work the stitch by starting to the left of a vertical thread, across the number of threads indicated on the chart, following the number sequence in the diagram.

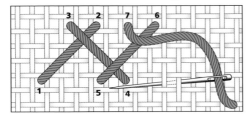

# THREADED HERRINGBONE STITCH

This version of herringbone is usually worked in two different colours. Work herringbone as normal and then weave the second colour through the foundation stitches, without piercing the fabric. The length of these woven stitches can vary to create different effects.

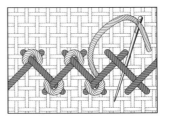

# HONEYCOMB STITCH

As its name suggests, this stitch creates a honeycomb effect, which is more pronounced when the thread colour contrasts with the fabric colour.

**1** Bring the needle out at 1, insert it at 2, two threads to the right, and bring it out at 3, two threads down. Insert the needle at 2 and bring it out at 3 again.

**2** Continue as shown, going down at 4, out at 5, in at 4 again and back out at 5, in at 6 and so on.

**3** To work the second row position the stitches as shown, working the connecting stitches into the same holes. Repeat these two rows to fill an area.

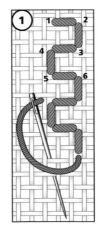
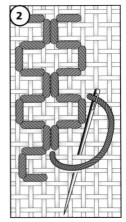

**KLOSTER BLOCKS – SEE PAGE 97**

**LADDER HEMSTITCH – SEE PAGE 112**

**LAZY DAISY STITCH – SEE PAGE 89**

## LONG-LEGGED CROSS STITCH

This stitch, also known as long-armed Slav stitch and Portuguese stitch, seems very uninteresting when first seen but looks wonderful when worked in rows because it forms a plaited effect, which is ideal for borders or for the outside edges of pieces to be made up as a pincushion or scissor keeper. It can also be worked on Aida across two blocks and upwards over one. The stitch may also be used to join sections – see below.

**1** To work the stitch on evenweave, begin to the left of a vertical thread. Following the number sequence, insert the needle four threads forward and two up in a long diagonal 'leg'.

**2** Insert the needle two threads upwards and two backwards diagonally to make the short leg.

**3** If working a row, continue making stitches across the fabric, following the number sequence.

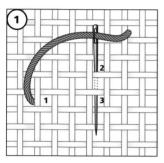

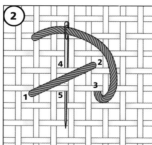

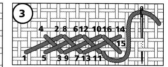

## LONG-LEGGED CROSS STITCH AS A JOINING STITCH

This stitch is easy to do when working on canvas but can also be stitched on Aida or linen effectively. To join two pieces of work, the sections to be joined need to be folded along a row of threads and then stitched, picking up threads from either side of the gap.

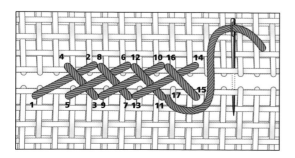

## Montenegrin Stitch

This unusual stitch looks similar to long-legged cross stitch but is constructed in a different way and includes an extra vertical leg, which gives it a richer, fuller appearance. It forms an embossed braid on the front of the stitching and makes a fine, raised edge for folding. It is shown worked on evenweave but can also be worked on Aida fabric by moving two blocks forwards and one block up.

**1** Start to the left of an evenweave thread, and following the number sequence in the diagram, work a long diagonal leg by moving four threads forwards and two threads up. Bring the needle two threads back and two threads down to emerge at position 3.

**2** Insert the needle two threads backwards diagonally to make the short leg at 4. Bring the needle back up at 5 and down at 6 to form the final vertical leg.

**3** Repeat Montenegrin stitch to form the pattern shown in the final diagram.

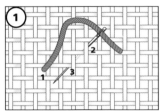
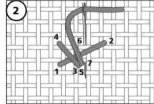
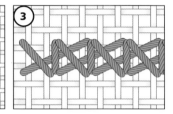

---

## Needleweaving – see page 101

---

## Corner Needleweaving – see page 101

---

## Pekinese Stitch

This looped stitch is worked over a line of backstitch and may use two different types of thread and two colours. To explain the stitch more clearly, the loops are shown loosely worked in the diagram below but can be pulled tighter to achieve different effects.

Work a line of backstitch the width of the area to be stitched. Take the interlaced thread from left to right, passing it beneath the second backstitch, and then looping to pass beneath the third and so on. The fabric is not pierced by the interlaced thread.

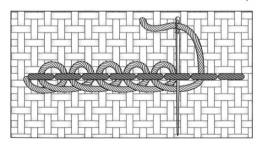

---

## Picots – see page 104

---

## QUEEN STITCH

This is an ancient pulled stitch made of four parts, which forms little dimples in the embroidery by pulling small holes in the fabric. It is also known as Rococo stitch. Although this stitch looks fairly unexciting on its own it is gorgeous when worked as a group. As it is a fairly labour-intensive stitch it is best used in small areas. Following the instructions and diagrams, work the stitch over a square of four threads in four stages. This stitch is traditionally worked from right to left, but if you find this difficult to count, try working the two middle parts first followed by the outer ones.

**1** Work one long stitch over four threads of the fabric, which is then moved two threads to the right by the needle coming up at position 3 and a small stitch worked across one thread.

**2** Repeat the long stitch from the same position as in Fig 1, but this time bending the stitch over one thread only.

**3** Repeat the long stitch from the same position as in Fig 1, but bend the long stitch to the left, re-entering the fabric in the centre position.

**4** The last stage of the stitch is completed to form a lantern shape. Note how the top and bottom hole is shared by each stage of the stitch so forming the distinctive little dimples.

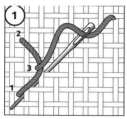
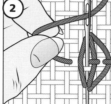
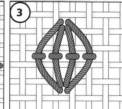
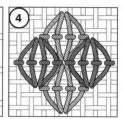

## REVERSIBLE CROSS STITCH

This stitch is truly reversible, although it has the addition of a vertical line at the end of a row which cannot be avoided. The stitch is quite time consuming as each row is worked four times but it is very useful for bookmarks and table linen. The vertical line created at the end of rows can appear as the backstitch outline if you plan your route carefully.

**1** The first journey is across two threads on the front, working diagonally across the back of the next two threads, missing the stitch on the front.

**2** The return journey covers the first diagonal threads on the front and back of the work.

**3** The third journey fills in the missed stitches back and front.

**4** The final journey completes the row.

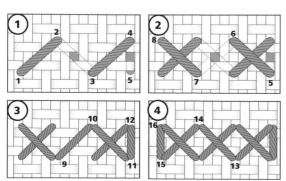

## RHODES STITCH

Rhodes stitch produces a solid, slightly raised, three-dimensional effect, almost like a series of studs on the fabric. The diagrams below illustrate one version but the size of the stitch can be altered – refer to the chart to see how many threads are in each stitch. This stitch doesn't work well on Aida fabric. (See also half Rhodes stitch with a bar, below.)

**1** Begin to the left of a vertical evenweave thread, working each stitch over squares of two, four or more threads.

**2** Following the number sequence, build up the stitch, working in an anticlockwise direction around the square.

**3** A complete Rhodes stitch will have a raised central area. Maintain the same sequence for every stitch to produce a uniform effect.

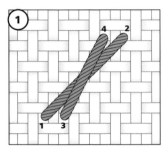

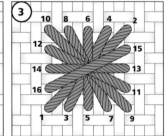

## HALF RHODES STITCH WITH BAR

This is an adaptation of Rhodes stitch, producing a decorative stitch shaped rather like a sheaf of corn, with a straight bar across the centre to tie the threads together. Buttonhole stitches could be added to the bar.

**1** Work over squares of two, four, six or eight threads of evenweave fabric, in a slanting, anticlockwise direction.

**2** Complete the half Rhodes stitch and maintain the same sequence for every stitch to create a uniform effect.

**3** To finish, add a single straight stitch across the centre, holding the threads firmly.

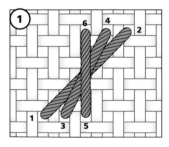
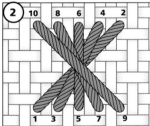
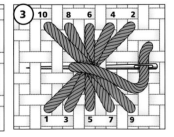

## RIBBON STITCH – SEE PAGE 89

## RICE STITCH

Rice stitch is a cross stitch with an additional stitch worked over each 'leg' or corner of the cross. It can be worked in two stages: a row of normal cross stitches, followed by the additional stitches as a second row. This makes it ideal for working in two colours, which can create very pretty effects. When using two colours, work all large crosses first, followed by the additional stitches in the second colour. Rice stitch is worked over an even number of threads, usually over four threads of an evenweave fabric but it can also be worked to occupy the space of four blocks of Aida. Do not pull the stitch and form holes around the edge.

**1** Start to the left of a vertical thread, working a half cross stitch across four evenweave threads, then returning to complete the cross.

**2** Add the additional stitches across the legs in a second colour. These are traditionally worked as a backstitch into the central side hole in each case.

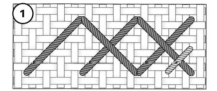

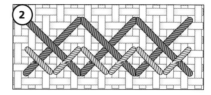

---

## SATIN STITCH

This is a long, smooth stitch, also known as damask stitch, which covers the fabric and is often used to fill in shapes. When worked in a glossy thread like stranded cotton (floss), the stitches have a velvety sheen and can look very effective when worked in blocks facing in different directions. Avoid using very long lengths of thread as this will suffer by being pulled through the fabric too many times. You could experiment with the number of strands of thread used, to vary the effect – many strands can give an almost padded look.

Follow the number sequence in the diagram, laying flat stitches neatly side by side. Don't pull too tightly, unless working pulled satin stitch – see below.

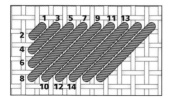

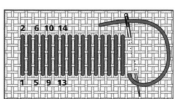

---

## PULLED SATIN STITCH

Working pulled satin stitch is a very different matter to working normal satin stitch as the intention is to make some seriously large holes in the fabric and create a lacy appearance. Pulled thread embroidery is better formed on linen fabric as the stitches once pulled will stay pulled! The stitch may be worked horizontally, vertically or diagonally, in boxes, groups or offset, and over various numbers of fabric threads (keeping the pattern consistent).

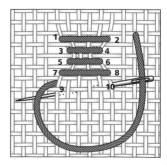

## SOMERSAULT STITCH

This stitch is formed on the vertical threads that remain after hemstitching and thread withdrawal.

**1** Begin the stitch after thread withdrawal and two rows of hemstitch have been completed. Using the hemstitch thread, bring the needle up at the side centre of the hemstitched frame (you will need to snick through the back of the fabric to do this). Count four fabric threads and insert the needle under two threads and up between the two pairs, so the needle is positioned over the second pair of threads. Don't pull the needle through the work yet.

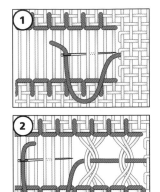

**2** Without removing the needle from these threads, twist the needle until it faces the other way. The threads will twist automatically as you do this. Pinch your fingers together over this stitch and gently pull the needle through, keeping the thread horizontal and taut. Repeat this process down the row, fastening off into the fabric edge.

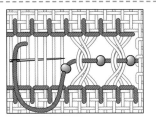

## BEADED SOMERSAULT STITCH

This is worked in the same way as somersault stitch above but slipping a bead on in between each stitch.

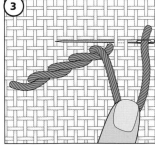

## SPIDER'S WEB STITCH – SEE PAGE 103

## STEM STITCH

Stem stitch is another surface embroidery stitch I have borrowed with success. The secret is to form the stitch in the same manner for the whole project, carefully counting the threads each time. Using spare fabric, experiment with turning gentle corners to perfect your technique. The stitch is most effective on evenweave fabric.

**1** Follow the number sequence in the diagram, working a straight stitch across four threads on evenweave, passing the needle back two threads.

**2** Make the next stitch by holding the thread over and below the previous stitch and working across four threads again.

**3** Repeat the stitching sequence so each stitch is formed in the same manner, checking that each new stitch is on the same side, to create the rope-like effect required.

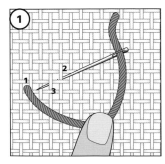

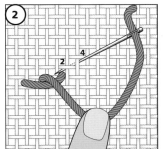

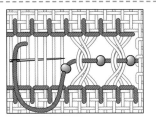

## TENT STITCH

Tent stitch is best known as a canvaswork stitch and is sometimes called continental tent stitch. It has long slanting stitches on the back and even, full stitches on the front. It is the long slanting stitches on the back that cause the distortion of the canvas which is characteristic of this stitch. Tent stitch is sometimes mistaken for half cross stitch but it uses a third more wool than half cross stitch and creates a much thicker and harder-wearing stitch, which makes it ideal for furnishings. This stitch could be used for the little butterflies in the Butterflies and Buddleia picture on page 27.

Tent stitch is a diagonal stitch formed by the needle being taken under the stitches from right to left, supporting the stitches and forming a fuller stitch. Ensure that you don't use tent stitch in one direction and half cross stitch in the other.

*Tent stitch used in a sparkly Christmas decoration (see pages 45 and 61).*

## DIAGONAL TENT STITCH

The alternative name for diagonal tent stitch is basketweave stitch because of the woven effect produced on the reverse.

The stitches are worked diagonally across the canvas threads, so they distort the canvas less than ordinary tent stitch. You could use straight lines of tent stitch for working a design and then complete the background in diagonal tent stitch.

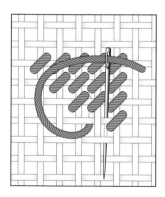
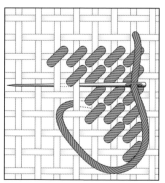

## THREADED BACKSTITCH

This pretty embellishment to backstitch is very simple to work. It is sometimes called woven backstitch or embellished backstitch. Work backstitch, as shown on page 25 and then take the second thread colour and weave it in and out of each backstitch, creating smooth S-shaped loops. The pattern lines can be straight, as shown, or in any pattern you choose.

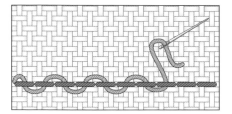

## TIED HEMSTITCH

This pretty hemstitch variation is created by hemstitching two rows, withdrawing the intervening threads and then simply using the needle to tie groups of threads together.

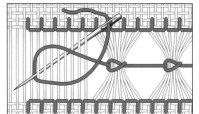

Begin by stitching two rows of simple hemstitch, spaced four threads apart (or as indicated on the chart). Take the needle and thread over a group of eight threads (or as the chart), knotting them around. The secret of perfection is to ensure that the tying thread is as straight as possible.

## DOUBLE TIED HEMSTITCH

Remove at least six fabric threads prior to working ladder hemstitch as shown on page 112. To create the tied effect use one strand of stranded cotton and, coming from the side of the band, tie the first four fabric threads together (or the number indicated on the chart). Slide down these threads and tie these four with the next four. Slide up these four threads and tie these to the next four, and so on.

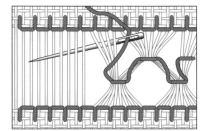

## TIPSY STITCH

This is my variation on Rhodes stitch, which produces an interesting 'tipsy' slant to your stitching. The stitch can be worked over a variety of fabric threads. Follow the number sequence in the diagram.

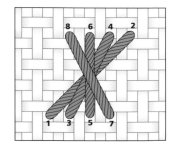

## Velvet Stitch

This stitch, also known as plush or Turkey stitch, was commonly used by Victorian embroiderers who worked in wools: after completing an area of velvet stitch, the loops were cut and sometimes actually sculpted to great effect.

This stitch is basically a cross stitch with an extra loop in it, left long to create a pile on the fabric. The loops can be left as they are or can all be cut to the same length. Work in rows from bottom to top and left to right.

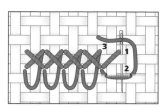

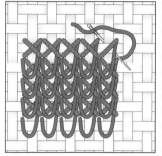

## Woven or Needlelace Flowers

Needlelace flowers are not a modern idea – some samplers from the 17th century included pretty flower petals created this way. Practise on spare fabric before starting your sampler.

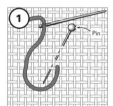
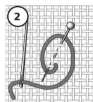
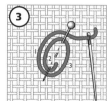
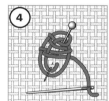

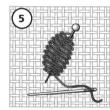
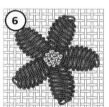

## Wrapped Bars – see page 102

## Zigzag Hemstitch

This is formed in almost the same way as ladder hemstitch (page 112). Cut the horizontal threads (see chart for how many) and then re-weave them as shown. Work one row of hemstitch, as for ladder hemstitch, and then work the second row but offset the stitches by one fabric thread to create a zigzag effect.

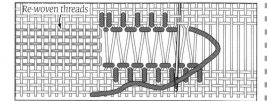

Re-woven threads

# CHART LIBRARY

I have used a variety of projects in the book to illustrate a stitching technique or unusual type of thread and most of the charts can be found in this section of the book.

◆ The charts are in colour with a black or white symbol to aid colour identification. Refer to Following a Chart on page 10.

◆ The DMC range of stranded cotton (floss) was used to stitch the projects, with Anchor alternatives given in brackets (although accurate colour matches may not always be possible).

◆ Some of the designs are charted over two pages: there is no overlap, so just continue the stitching. For your own use you could colour photocopy the parts and tape them together.

◆ The chart keys give the page reference where you can find the stitching instructions captions and pictures of the projects.

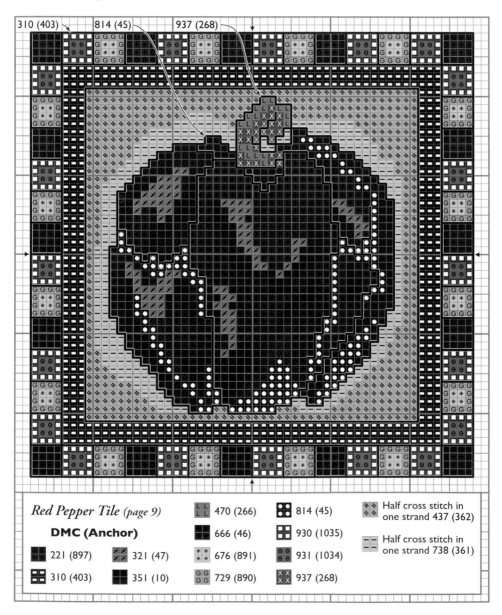

*Red Pepper Tile* (page 9)

**DMC (Anchor)**

| | | | |
|---|---|---|---|
| ▨ 221 (897) | ▨ 321 (47) | LL / LL 470 (266) | ⊞ 814 (45) |
| ⊞ 310 (403) | ■ 351 (10) | ■ 666 (46) | ⊞ 930 (1035) |
| | | **·**/**·** 676 (891) | ⊕⊕ 931 (1034) |
| | | GG/GG 729 (890) | XX/XX 937 (268) |

Half cross stitch in one strand 437 (362)

Half cross stitch in one strand 738 (361)

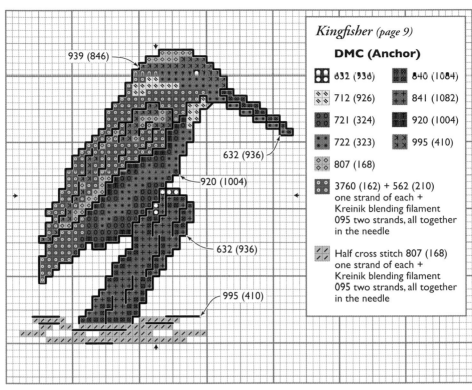

### Kingfisher *(page 9)*

#### DMC (Anchor)

| | | | |
|---|---|---|---|
| 632 (936) | | 840 (1084) | |
| 712 (926) | | 841 (1082) | |
| 721 (324) | | 920 (1004) | |
| 722 (323) | | 995 (410) | |
| 807 (168) | | | |

3760 (162) + 562 (210)
one strand of each +
Kreinik blending filament
095 two strands, all together
in the needle

Half cross stitch 807 (168)
one strand of each +
Kreinik blending filament
095 two strands, all together
in the needle

Labels on chart: 939 (846), 632 (936), 920 (1004), 632 (936), 995 (410)

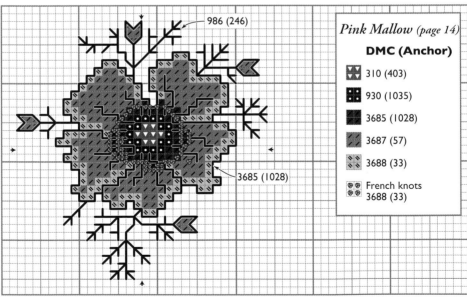

### Pink Mallow *(page 14)*

#### DMC (Anchor)

310 (403)
930 (1035)
3685 (1028)
3687 (57)
3688 (33)

French knots
3688 (33)

Labels on chart: 986 (246), 3685 (1028)

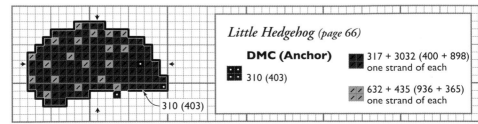

### Little Hedgehog *(page 66)*

#### DMC (Anchor)

310 (403)

317 + 3032 (400 + 898)
one strand of each

632 + 435 (936 + 365)
one strand of each

Label on chart: 310 (403)

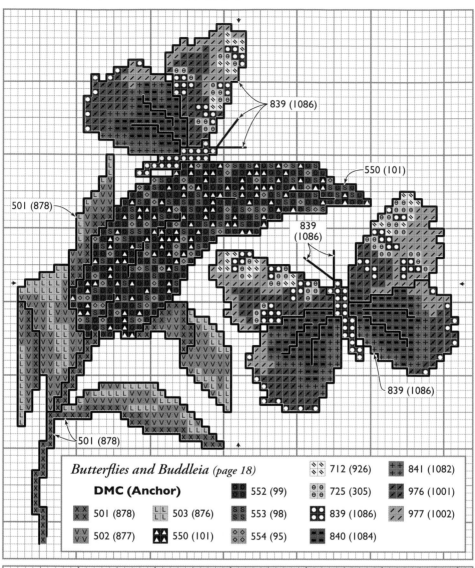

839 (1086)

550 (101)

501 (878)

839
(1086)

839 (1086)

501 (878)

*Butterflies and Buddleia* (page 18)

**DMC (Anchor)**

| | | |
|---|---|---|
| XX 501 (878) | LL 503 (876) | SS 553 (98) |
| VV 502 (877) | ▲▲ 550 (101) | ◇◇ 554 (95) |

| | |
|---|---|
| ▨▨ 552 (99) | ◇◇ 712 (926) |
| | ⊖⊖ 725 (305) |
| | ◘◘ 839 (1086) |
| | ▦▦ 840 (1084) |

| | |
|---|---|
| ++ 841 (1082) | |
| ▨▨ 976 (1001) | |
| ⁄⁄ 977 (1002) | |

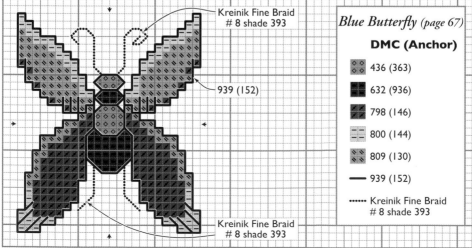

Kreinik Fine Braid
# 8 shade 393

939 (152)

Kreinik Fine Braid
# 8 shade 393

*Blue Butterfly* (page 67)

**DMC (Anchor)**

| | |
|---|---|
| ◇◇ | 436 (363) |
| ■■ | 632 (936) |
| ▨▨ | 798 (146) |
| ⁼⁼ | 800 (144) |
| ▧▧ | 809 (130) |
| — | 939 (152) |
| ••••• | Kreinik Fine Braid # 8 shade 393 |

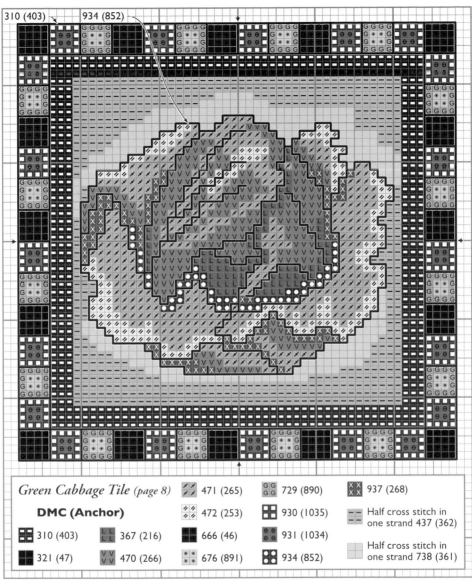

**Green Cabbage Tile** *(page 8)*

**DMC (Anchor)**

| | | | |
|---|---|---|---|
| ▦ 310 (403) | ㏁ 367 (216) | ■ 666 (46) | ◉ 931 (1034) |
| ▦ 321 (47) | ᴠᴠ 470 (266) | ✳ 676 (891) | ▦ 934 (852) |
| ⁄⁄ 471 (265) | GG 729 (890) | ✕✕ 937 (268) | |
| ◇◇ 472 (253) | ▦ 930 (1035) | – Half cross stitch in one strand 437 (362) | |
| | | ▦ 934 (852) | Half cross stitch in one strand 738 (361) |

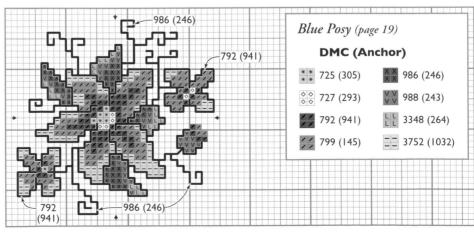

**Blue Posy** *(page 19)*

**DMC (Anchor)**

| | |
|---|---|
| ✳ 725 (305) | ✕✕ 986 (246) |
| ◇◇ 727 (293) | ᴠᴠ 988 (243) |
| ⁄⁄ 792 (941) | ㏁ 3348 (264) |
| ⁄⁄ 799 (145) | – 3752 (1032) |

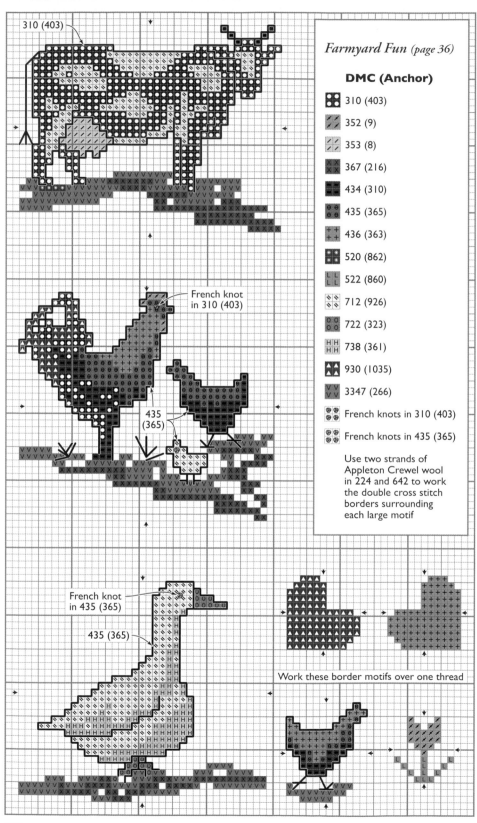

310 (403)

French knot
in 310 (403)

435
(365)

French knot
in 435 (365)

435 (365)

**Farmyard Fun** *(page 36)*

**DMC (Anchor)**

310 (403)

352 (9)

353 (8)

367 (216)

434 (310)

435 (365)

436 (363)

520 (862)

522 (860)

712 (926)

722 (323)

738 (361)

930 (1035)

3347 (266)

French knots in 310 (403)

French knots in 435 (365)

Use two strands of
Appleton Crewel wool
in 224 and 642 to work
the double cross stitch
borders surrounding
each large motif

Work these border motifs over one thread

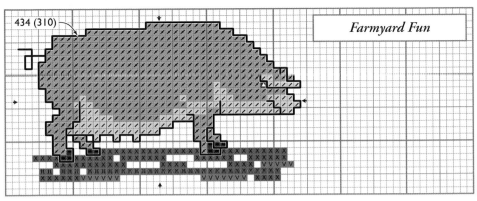

434 (310)

*Farmyard Fun*

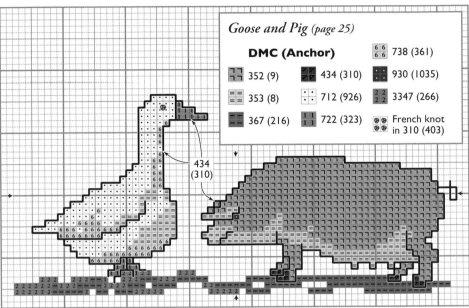

*Goose and Pig* (page 25)

**DMC (Anchor)**

352 (9)
353 (8)
367 (216)
434 (310)
712 (926)
722 (323)
738 (361)
930 (1035)
3347 (266)
French knot in 310 (403)

434 (310)

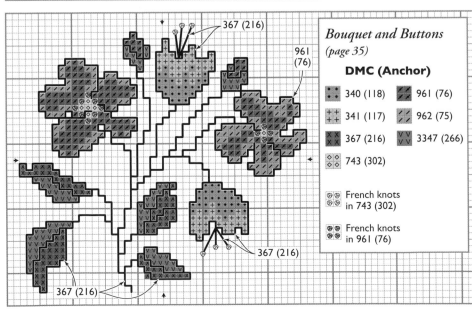

367 (216)

961 (76)

*Bouquet and Buttons*
(page 35)

**DMC (Anchor)**

340 (118)
341 (117)
367 (216)
743 (302)
961 (76)
962 (75)
3347 (266)

French knots in 743 (302)

French knots in 961 (76)

367 (216)

367 (216)

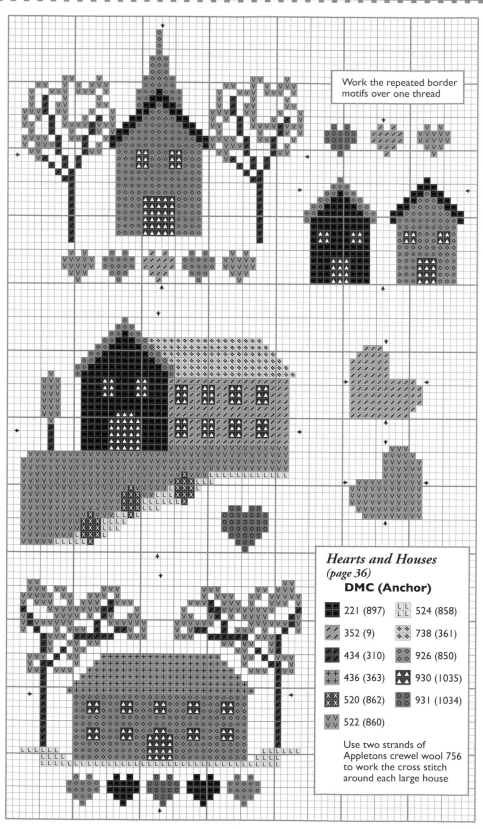

Work the repeated border motifs over one thread

**Hearts and Houses**
*(page 36)*

**DMC (Anchor)**

| | | | |
|---|---|---|---|
| | 221 (897) | | 524 (858) |
| | 352 (9) | | 738 (361) |
| | 434 (310) | | 926 (850) |
| | 436 (363) | | 930 (1035) |
| | 520 (862) | | 931 (1034) |
| | 522 (860) | | |

Use two strands of Appletons crewel wool 756 to work the cross stitch around each large house

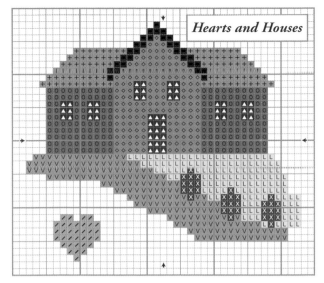

Hearts and Houses

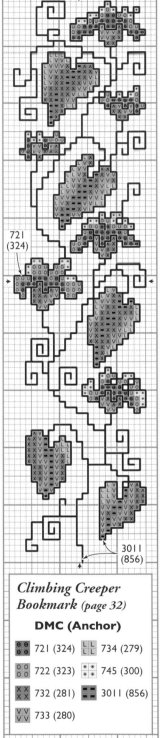

721 (324)

3011 (856)

Climbing Creeper
Bookmark (page 32)

**DMC (Anchor)**

| | | | | |
|---|---|---|---|---|
| ⊕⊕ | 721 (324) | LL | 734 (279) |
| ○○ | 722 (323) | ** | 745 (300) |
| XX | 732 (281) | ▬▬ | 3011 (856) |
| VV | 733 (280) | | |

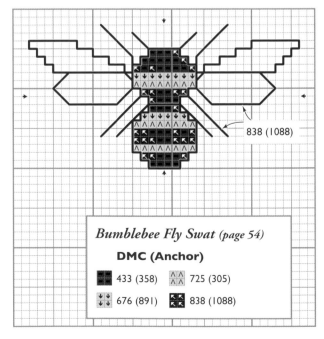

838 (1088)

Bumblebee Fly Swat (page 54)

**DMC (Anchor)**

| | | | | |
|---|---|---|---|---|
| ■■ | 433 (358) | ∧∧ | 725 (305) |
| ↓↓ | 676 (891) | ◥◥ | 838 (1088) |

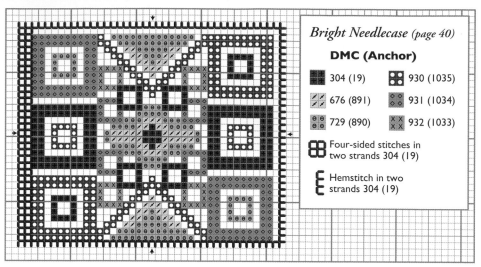

**Bright Needlecase** *(page 40)*

**DMC (Anchor)**

- 304 (19)
- 676 (891)
- 729 (890)
- 930 (1035)
- 931 (1034)
- 932 (1033)

Four-sided stitches in two strands 304 (19)

Hemstitch in two strands 304 (19)

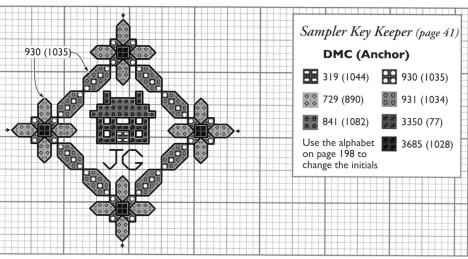

930 (1035)

JG

**Sampler Key Keeper** *(page 41)*

**DMC (Anchor)**

- 319 (1044)
- 729 (890)
- 841 (1082)
- 930 (1035)
- 931 (1034)
- 3350 (77)
- 3685 (1028)

Use the alphabet on page 198 to change the initials

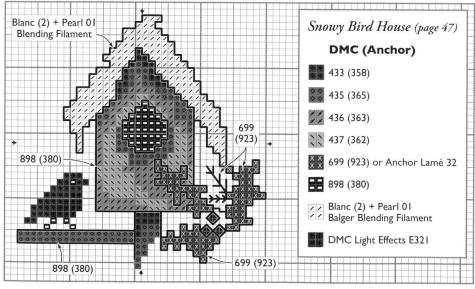

Blanc (2) + Pearl 01 Blending Filament

898 (380)

699 (923)

898 (380)

699 (923)

**Snowy Bird House** *(page 47)*

**DMC (Anchor)**

- 433 (358)
- 435 (365)
- 436 (363)
- 437 (362)
- 699 (923) or Anchor Lamé 32
- 898 (380)
- Blanc (2) + Pearl 01 Balger Blending Filament
- DMC Light Effects E321

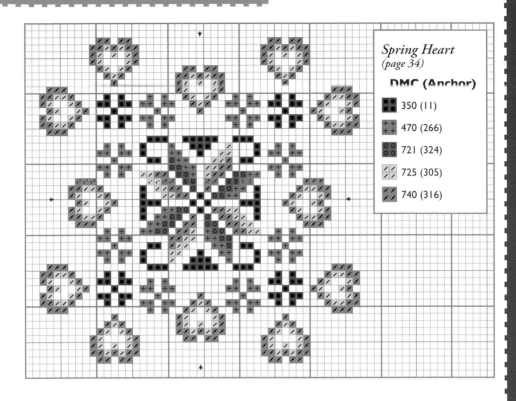

**Spring Heart**
*(page 34)*

### DMC (Anchor)

| | | |
|---|---|---|
| ◼◼ | 350 | (11) |
| ++ | 470 | (266) |
| ◦◦ | 721 | (324) |
| ╱╱ | 725 | (305) |
| ╱╱ | 740 | (316) |

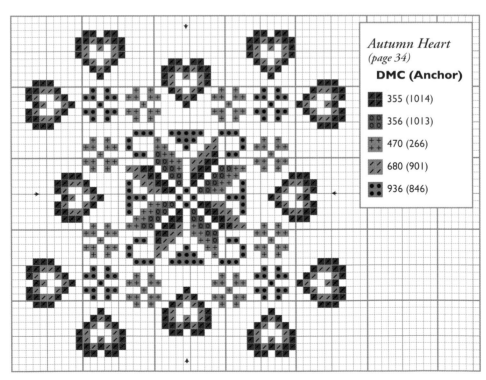

**Autumn Heart**
*(page 34)*

### DMC (Anchor)

| | | |
|---|---|---|
| ◼ | 355 | (1014) |
| ◦◦ | 356 | (1013) |
| ++ | 470 | (266) |
| ╱╱ | 680 | (901) |
| ●● | 936 | (846) |

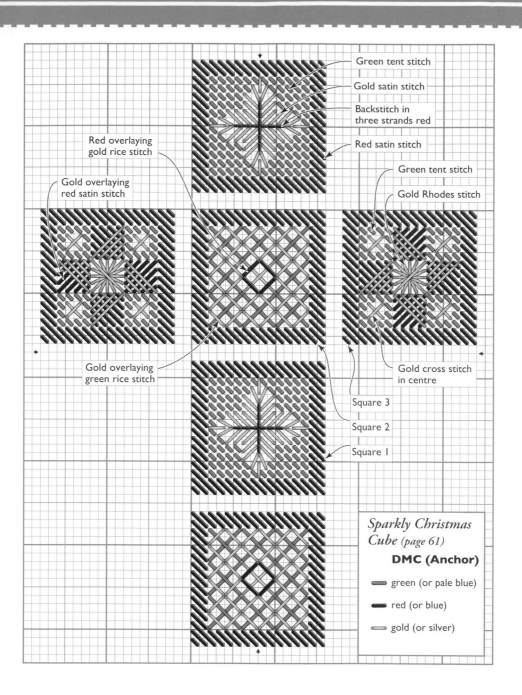

Green tent stitch

Gold satin stitch

Backstitch in three strands red

Red satin stitch

Red overlaying gold rice stitch

Green tent stitch

Gold Rhodes stitch

Gold overlaying red satin stitch

Gold overlaying green rice stitch

Gold cross stitch in centre

Square 3

Square 2

Square 1

*Sparkly Christmas Cube* (page 61)

**DMC (Anchor)**

— green (or pale blue)

— red (or blue)

— gold (or silver)

*Peach Blossom Card* (page 86)

**DMC (Anchor)**

 937 (268)

French knots in 2mm YLI silk ribbon in pale peach and dark rose

Gathered ribbon stitch in 7mm YLI silk ribbon in pale peach

✕ Button position

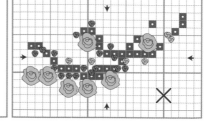

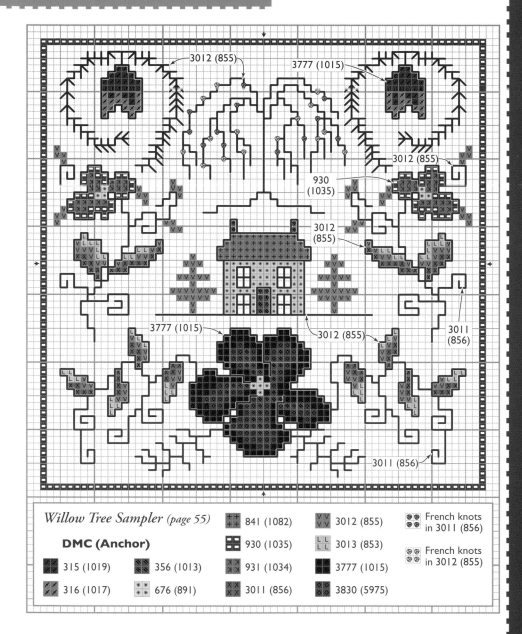

3012 (855)

3777 (1015)

3012 (855)

930
(1035)

3012
(855)

3777 (1015)

3012 (855)

3011
(856)

3011 (856)

*Willow Tree Sampler* (page 55)

**DMC (Anchor)**

315 (1019)  356 (1013)  841 (1082)  3012 (855)  French knots in 3011 (856)

316 (1017)  676 (891)  930 (1035)  3013 (853)  French knots in 3012 (855)

931 (1034)  3777 (1015)

3011 (856)  3830 (5975)

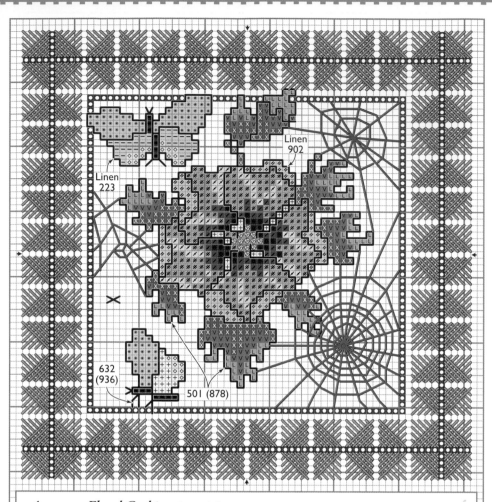

## Anemone Floral Cushion *(page 53)*

### DMC (Anchor)

- X X / 501 (878)
- V V / 502 (877)
- L L / 503 (876)
- 632 (936)
- + + / 772 (259)
- 930 (1035)
- 945 (881)

### DMC Linen Thread

- Linen 778
- Linen 225
- Linen 902
- Linen 223
- ✕ Dragonfly charm
- Work cobwebs with one strand of Kreinik Blending Filament 034 confetti

- ◇ Pearsalls silk thread in cream
- ▬ Pearsalls silk thread in peach
- French knots in Pearsalls silk in cream
- Crossed cushion stitch in one strand of De Haviland Tudor Twist (antique peacock and purple)

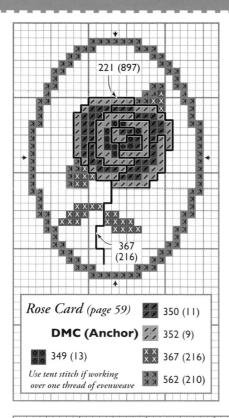

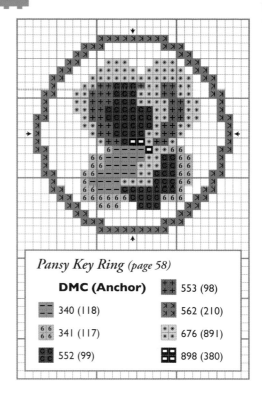

### Rose Card *(page 59)*

**DMC (Anchor)**

| | | | |
|---|---|---|---|
| ▓ | 349 (13) | ▨ | 350 (11) |
| | | ▨ | 352 (9) |
| *Use tent stitch if working over one thread of evenweave* | | X X<br>X X | 367 (216) |
| | | ▨ | 562 (210) |

### Pansy Key Ring *(page 58)*

**DMC (Anchor)**

| | | | |
|---|---|---|---|
| ⊟ | 340 (118) | ✛✛ | 553 (98) |
| 6 6<br>6 6 | 341 (117) | ▨ | 562 (210) |
| ▨ | 552 (99) | ✳✳ | 676 (891) |
| | | ▦ | 898 (380) |

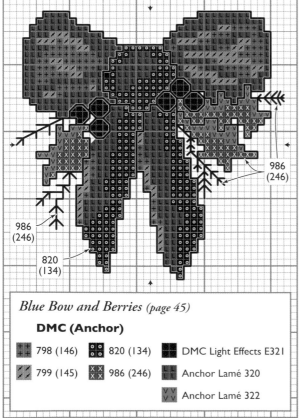

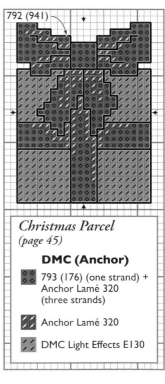

### Blue Bow and Berries *(page 45)*

**DMC (Anchor)**

| | | | | | |
|---|---|---|---|---|---|
| ✛✛ | 798 (146) | ⊙⊙ | 820 (134) | ▓ | DMC Light Effects E321 |
| ▨ | 799 (145) | X X<br>X X | 986 (246) | L L<br>L L | Anchor Lamé 320 |
| | | | | V V<br>V V | Anchor Lamé 322 |

### Christmas Parcel *(page 45)*

**DMC (Anchor)**

| | |
|---|---|
| ⊙⊙ | 793 (176) (one strand) + Anchor Lamé 320 (three strands) |
| ▨ | Anchor Lamé 320 |
| ▨ | DMC Light Effects E130 |

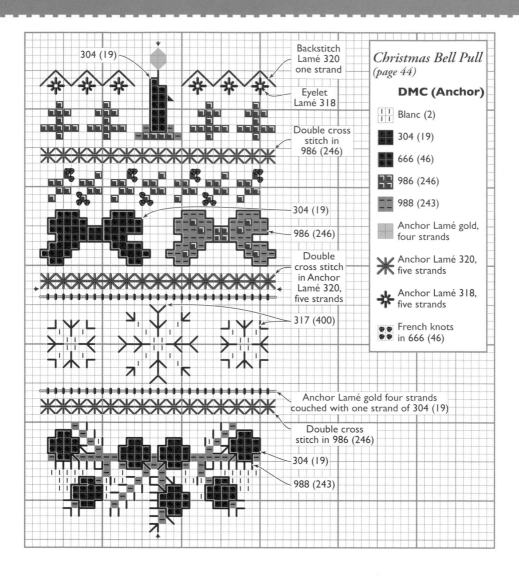

304 (19)

Backstitch
Lamé 320
one strand

Eyelet
Lamé 318

Double cross
stitch in
986 (246)

304 (19)

986 (246)

Double
cross stitch
in Anchor
Lamé 320,
five strands

317 (400)

Anchor Lamé gold four strands
couched with one strand of 304 (19)

Double cross
stitch in 986 (246)

304 (19)

988 (243)

**Christmas Bell Pull**
*(page 44)*

## DMC (Anchor)

| | |
|---|---|
| Blanc (2) | |
| 304 (19) | |
| 666 (46) | |
| 986 (246) | |
| 988 (243) | |
| Anchor Lamé gold, four strands | |
| Anchor Lamé 320, five strands | |
| Anchor Lamé 318, five strands | |
| French knots in 666 (46) | |

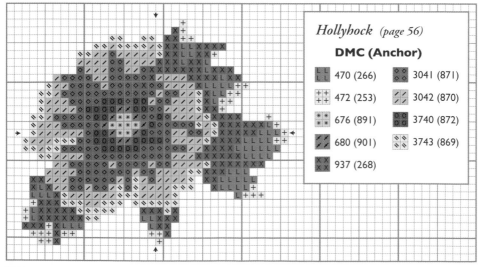

**Hollyhock** *(page 56)*

## DMC (Anchor)

| | |
|---|---|
| 470 (266) | 3041 (871) |
| 472 (253) | 3042 (870) |
| 676 (891) | 3740 (872) |
| 680 (901) | 3743 (869) |
| 937 (268) | |

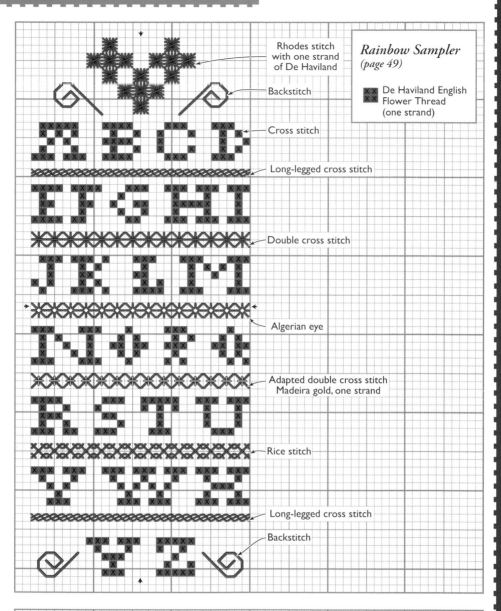

Rhodes stitch with one strand of De Haviland

Backstitch

Cross stitch

Long-legged cross stitch

Double cross stitch

Algerian eye

Adapted double cross stitch Madeira gold, one strand

Rice stitch

Long-legged cross stitch

Backstitch

**Rainbow Sampler** (page 49)

De Haviland English Flower Thread (one strand)

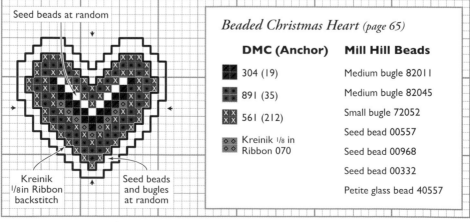

Seed beads at random

Kreinik 1/8in Ribbon backstitch

Seed beads and bugles at random

**Beaded Christmas Heart** (page 65)

| DMC (Anchor) | Mill Hill Beads |
|---|---|
| 304 (19) | Medium bugle 82011 |
| 891 (35) | Medium bugle 82045 |
| 561 (212) | Small bugle 72052 |
| Kreinik 1/8 in Ribbon 070 | Seed bead 00557 |
| | Seed bead 00968 |
| | Seed bead 00332 |
| | Petite glass bead 40557 |

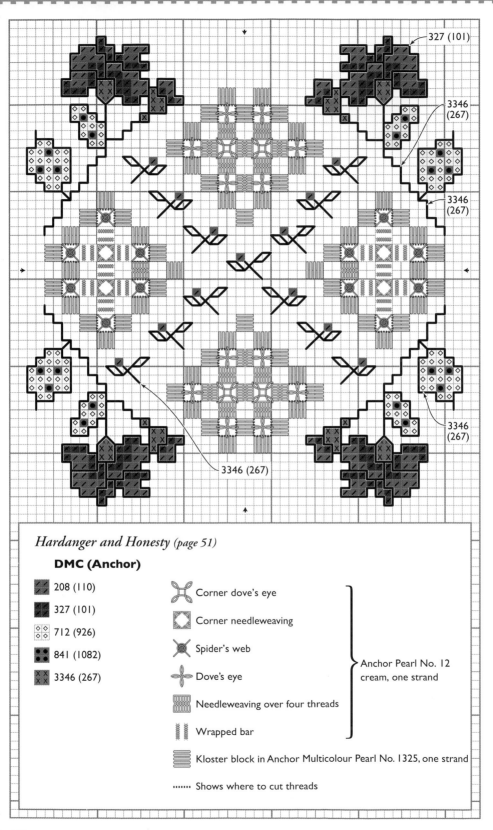

327 (101)

3346 (267)

3346 (267)

3346 (267)

3346 (267)

*Hardanger and Honesty (page 51)*

**DMC (Anchor)**

| | |
|---|---|
| 208 (110) | |
| 327 (101) | |
| 712 (926) | |
| 841 (1082) | |
| 3346 (267) | |

Corner dove's eye

Corner needleweaving

Spider's web

Dove's eye

Needleweaving over four threads

Wrapped bar

Anchor Pearl No. 12 cream, one strand

Kloster block in Anchor Multicolour Pearl No. 1325, one strand

······· Shows where to cut threads

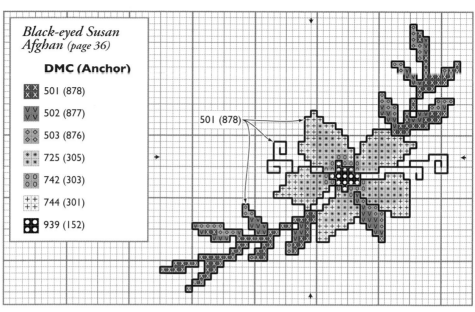

**Black-eyed Susan Afghan** *(page 36)*

**DMC (Anchor)**

| | |
|---|---|
| XX | 501 (878) |
| VV | 502 (877) |
| ◇◇ | 503 (876) |
| ** | 725 (305) |
| oo | 742 (303) |
| ++ | 744 (301) |
| ●● | 939 (152) |

501 (878)

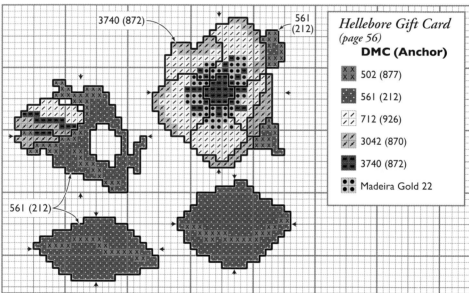

3740 (872)

561 (212)

561 (212)

**Hellebore Gift Card** *(page 56)*

**DMC (Anchor)**

| | |
|---|---|
| XX | 502 (877) |
| ●● | 561 (212) |
| ∕∕ | 712 (926) |
| ∕∕ | 3042 (870) |
| ▦ | 3740 (872) |
| ●● | Madeira Gold 22 |

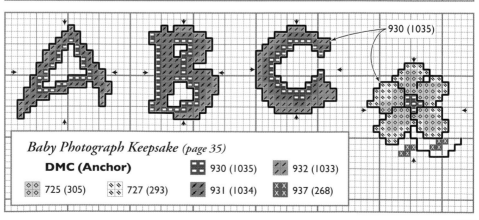

930 (1035)

**Baby Photograph Keepsake** *(page 35)*

**DMC (Anchor)**

| | | | |
|---|---|---|---|
| ◇◇ 725 (305) | ≈≈ 727 (293) | ▦ 930 (1035) | ∕∕ 932 (1033) |
| | | ∕∕ 931 (1034) | XX 937 (268) |

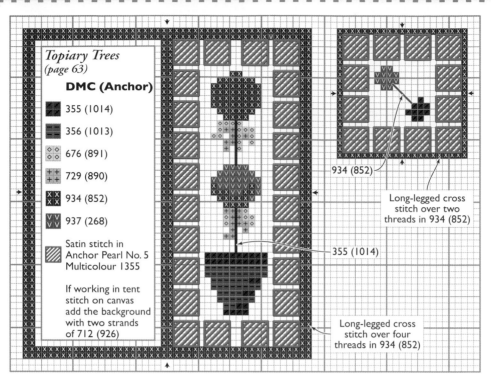

**Topiary Trees**
(page 63)

**DMC (Anchor)**

- 355 (1014)
- 356 (1013)
- 676 (891)
- 729 (890)
- 934 (852)
- 937 (268)

Satin stitch in Anchor Pearl No. 5 Multicolour 1355

If working in tent stitch on canvas add the background with two strands of 712 (926)

934 (852)

Long-legged cross stitch over two threads in 934 (852)

355 (1014)

Long-legged cross stitch over four threads in 934 (852)

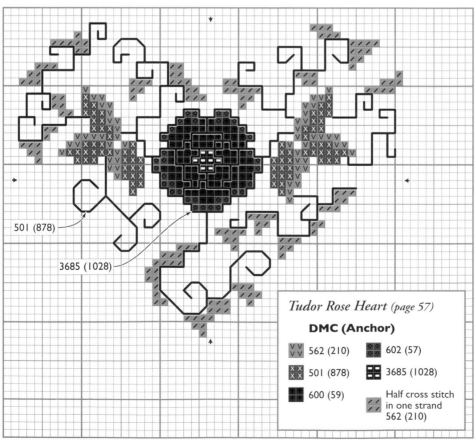

501 (878)

3685 (1028)

**Tudor Rose Heart** (page 57)

**DMC (Anchor)**

- 562 (210)
- 602 (57)
- 501 (878)
- 3685 (1028)
- 600 (59)
- Half cross stitch in one strand 562 (210)

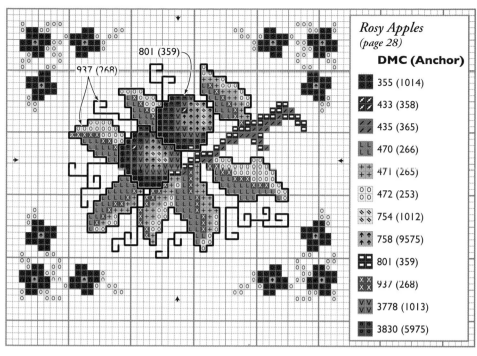

**Rosy Apples**
*(page 28)*

### DMC (Anchor)

- 355 (1014)
- 433 (358)
- 435 (365)
- 470 (266)
- 471 (265)
- 472 (253)
- 754 (1012)
- 758 (9575)
- 801 (359)
- 937 (268)
- 3778 (1013)
- 3830 (5975)

937 (268)

801 (359)

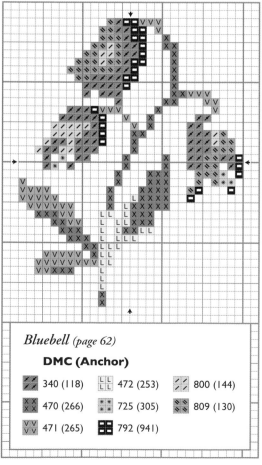

**Bluebell** *(page 62)*

### DMC (Anchor)

| | | |
|---|---|---|
| 340 (118) | 472 (253) | 800 (144) |
| 470 (266) | 725 (305) | 809 (130) |
| 471 (265) | 792 (941) | |

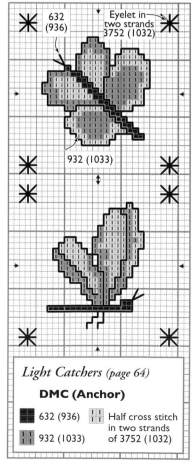

632 (936)

Eyelet in two strands 3752 (1032)

932 (1033)

**Light Catchers** *(page 64)*

### DMC (Anchor)

- 632 (936)
- 932 (1033)
- Half cross stitch in two strands of 3752 (1032)

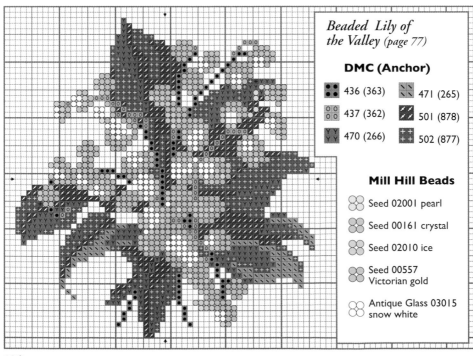

## Beaded Iris Chatelaine *(page 75)*

### Mill Hill Beads

- Seed 02015 sea blue
- Seed 02024 heather mauve
- Seed 00151 ash mauve
- Seed 00330 copper
- Seed 02010 ice
- Seed 00332 emerald
- Seed 00167 Christmas green
- Seed 02008 sea breeze
- Frosted seed 62031 gold

Fold line

## Beaded Lily of the Valley *(page 77)*

### DMC (Anchor)

- 436 (363)
- 437 (362)
- 470 (266)
- 471 (265)
- 501 (878)
- 502 (877)

### Mill Hill Beads

- Seed 02001 pearl
- Seed 00161 crystal
- Seed 02010 ice
- Seed 00557 Victorian gold
- Antique Glass 03015 snow white

562 (210)

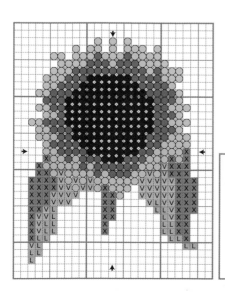

---

### Flowerpot Button Darn *(page 85)*

#### DMC (Anchor)

| | | | |
|---|---|---|---|
| ✕✕ | 561 (212) | ▬▬ | 561 (212) |
| ⌄⌄ | 562 (210) | ▬▬ | 729 (890) |
| ◇◇ | 676 (891) | ▬▬ | 3350 (77) |
| ++ | 729 (890) | ✕ | Button position |
| ▧ | 3350 (77) | | |
| ▨ | 3731 (76) | | |

---

### Sunflower Card *(page 76)*

| DMC (Anchor) | | Mill Hill Beads | |
|---|---|---|---|
| ✕✕ | 3346 (267) | ◌◌ | Seed 02011 Victorian gold |
| ⌄⌄ | 3347 (266) | ✖✖ | Seed 00330 copper |
| ʟʟ | 3348 (264) | ❀❀ | Seed 00557 gold |

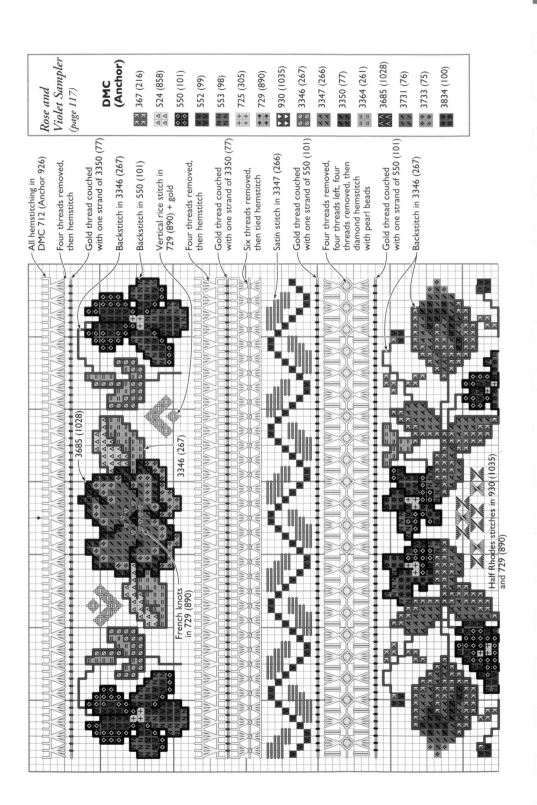

Rose and
Violet Sampler
(page 117)

**DMC
(Anchor)**

367 (216)
524 (858)
550 (101)
552 (99)
553 (98)
725 (305)
729 (890)
930 (1035)
3346 (267)
3347 (266)
3350 (77)
3364 (261)
3685 (1028)
3731 (76)
3733 (75)
3834 (100)

All hemstitching in
DMC 712 (Anchor 926)

Four threads removed,
then hemstitch

Gold thread couched
with one strand of 3350 (77)

Backstitch in 3346 (267)

Backstitch in 550 (101)

Vertical rice stitch in
729 (890) + gold

Four threads removed,
then hemstitch

Gold thread couched
with one strand of 3350 (77)

Six threads removed,
then tied hemstitch

Satin stitch in 3347 (266)

Gold thread couched
with one strand of 550 (101)

Four threads removed,
four threads left, four
threads removed, then
diamond hemstitch
with pearl beads

Gold thread couched
with one strand of 550 (101)

Backstitch in 3346 (267)

3685 (1028)

3346 (267)

French knots
in 729 (890)

Half Rhodes stitches in 930 (1035)
and 729 (890)

188

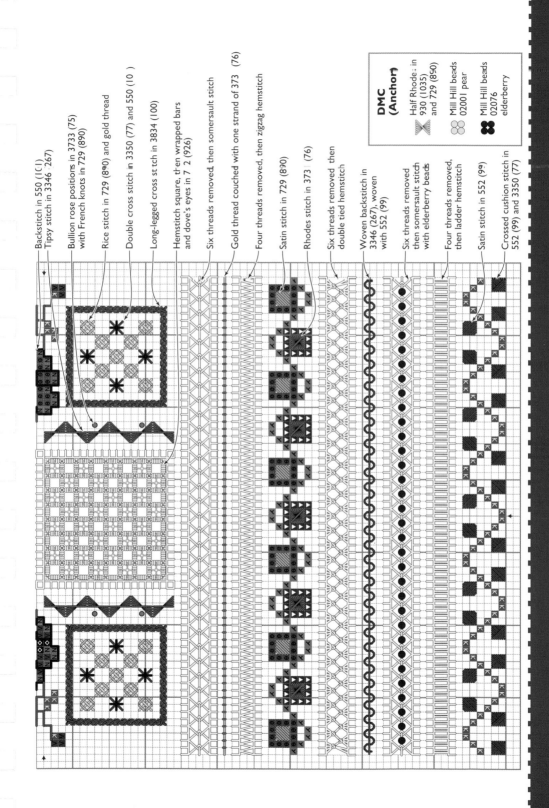

Backstitch in 550 (101)
Tipsy stitch in 3346 (267)

Bullion rose positions in 3733 (75)
with French knots in 729 (890)

Rice stitch in 729 (890) and gold thread

Double cross stitch in 3350 (77) and 550 (101)

Long-legged cross stitch in 3834 (100)

Hemstitch square, then wrapped bars
and dove's eyes in 712 (926)

Six threads removed then somersault stitch

Gold thread couched with one strand of 373 (76)

Four threads removed, then zigzag hemstitch

Satin stitch in 729 (890)

Rhodes stitch in 373 (76)

Six threads removed then
double tied hemstitch

Woven backstitch in
3346 (267), woven
with 552 (99)

Six threads removed
then somersault stitch
with elderberry beads

Four threads removed,
then ladder hemstitch

Satin stitch in 552 (99)

Crossed cushion stitch in
552 (99) and 3350 (77)

**DMC (Anchor)**

Half Rhodes in
930 (1035)
and 729 (890)

Mill Hill beads
02001 pear

Mill Hill beads
02076
elderberry

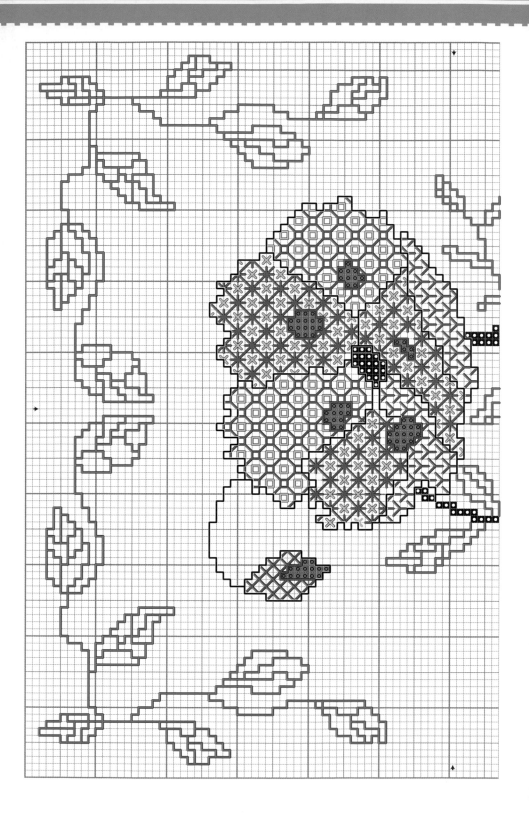

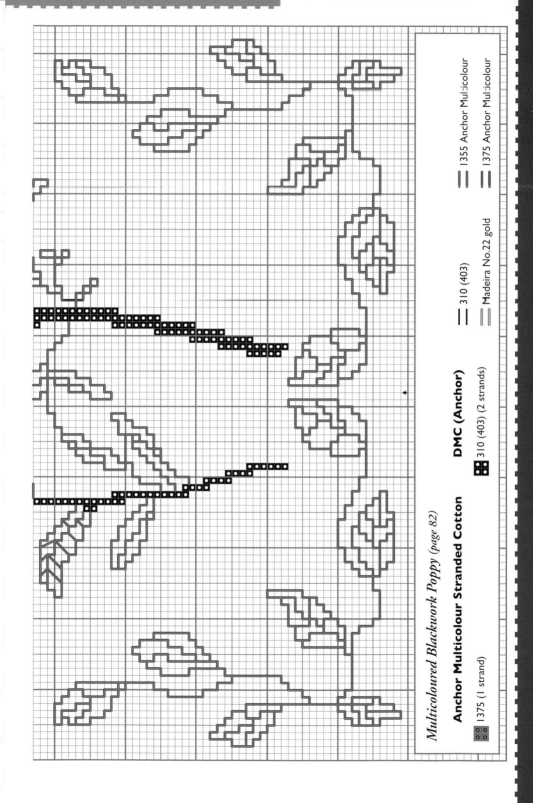

*Multicoloured Blackwork Poppy* (page 82)

**Anchor Multicolour Stranded Cotton**

**DMC (Anchor)**

▓ 310 (403) (2 strands)

━━ 310 (403)
━━ Madeira No.22 gold

═══ 1355 Anchor Multicolour
═══ 1375 Anchor Multicolour

░ 1375 (1 strand)

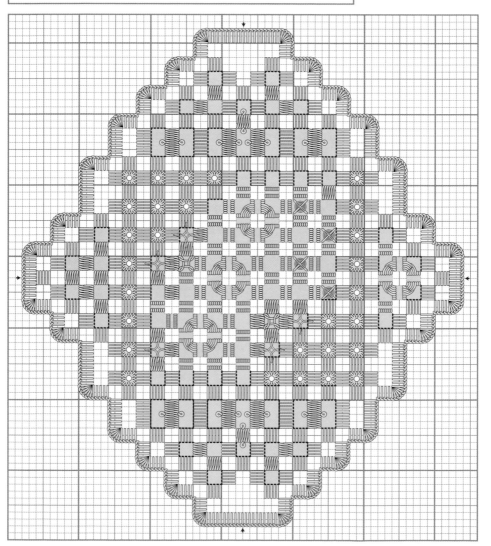

## Hardanger Diamond (page 105)

▦ Kloster blocks DMC Perlé No.8 ecru

◖ Buttonhole edging DMC Perlé No.8 ecru

Filling stitches in DMC Perlé No.12 ecru

▤ Needleweaving

⬚ Needleweaving with picots

◢ Corner needleweaving

◙ Eyelets

✢ Dove's eyes

✕ Corner dove's eyes

⊗ Spider's webs

▥ Wrapped bars

----- Red dotted lines show where to cut threads

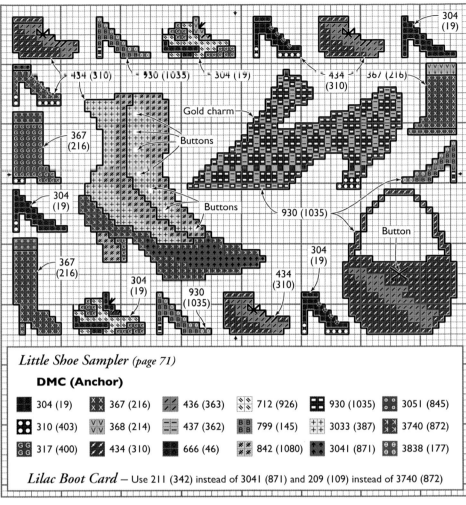

304 (19)
434 (310)
930 (1035)
304 (19)
434 (310)
367 (216)
Gold charm
Buttons
367 (216)
304 (19)
Buttons
930 (1035)
Button
367 (216)
304 (19)
304 (19)
930 (1035)
434 (310)
304 (19)

### Little Shoe Sampler *(page 71)*

#### DMC (Anchor)

| | | | |
|---|---|---|---|
| 304 (19) | 367 (216) | 436 (363) | 712 (926) | 930 (1035) | 3051 (845) |
| 310 (403) | 368 (214) | 437 (362) | 799 (145) | 3033 (387) | 3740 (872) |
| 317 (400) | 434 (310) | 666 (46) | 842 (1080) | 3041 (871) | 3838 (177) |

*Lilac Boot Card* – Use 211 (342) instead of 3041 (871) and 209 (109) instead of 3740 (872)

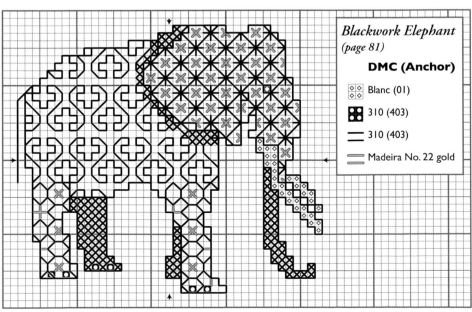

### Blackwork Elephant
*(page 81)*

#### DMC (Anchor)

| | |
|---|---|
| Blanc (01) | |
| 310 (403) | |
| 310 (403) | |
| Madeira No. 22 gold | |

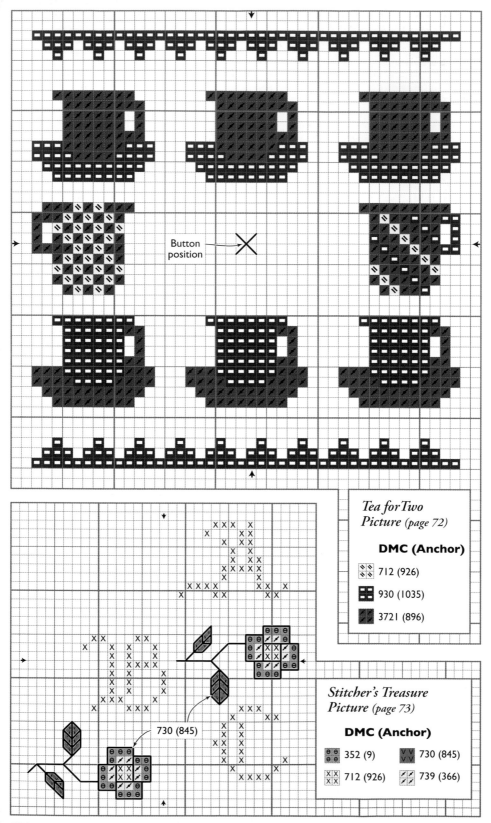

Button position

**Tea for Two**
**Picture** *(page 72)*

**DMC (Anchor)**

712 (926)

930 (1035)

3721 (896)

**Stitcher's Treasure**
**Picture** *(page 73)*

**DMC (Anchor)**

352 (9)

730 (845)

712 (926)

739 (366)

730 (845)

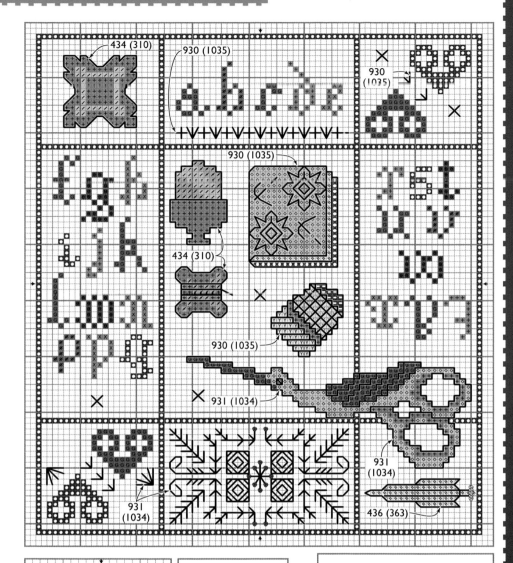

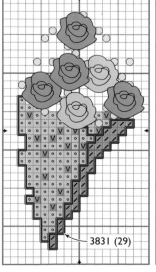

## Wedding Shower Card *(page 87)*

### DMC (Anchor)

- 352 (9)
- 353 (8)
- 962 (75)
- White seed bead
- Gathered ribbon stitch in 7mm YLI silk ribbon in pale peach and dark rose

3831 (29)

## Stork Scissor Sampler *(page 69)*

### DMC (Anchor)

| | |
|---|---|
| 315 (1019) | 738 (361) |
| 316 (1017) | 930 (1035) |
| 434 (310) | 931 (1034) |
| 436 (363) | 3721 (896) |
| 437 (362) | |
| 522 (860) | **French knots** |
| 676 (891) | 712 (926) |
| 677 (301) | 930 (1035) |
| 712 (926) | Positions of charms |

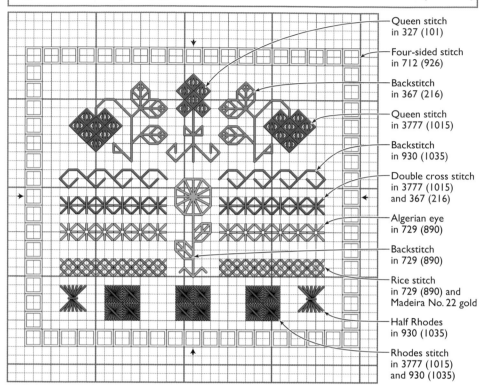

Queen stitch
in 327 (101)

Four-sided stitch
in 712 (926)

Backstitch
in 367 (216)

Queen stitch
in 3777 (1015)

Backstitch
in 930 (1035)

Double cross stitch
in 3777 (1015)
and 367 (216)

Algerian eye
in 729 (890)

Backstitch
in 729 (890)

Rice stitch
in 729 (890) and
Madeira No. 22 gold

Half Rhodes
in 930 (1035)

Rhodes stitch
in 3777 (1015)
and 930 (1035)

*Tiny Band Sampler (page 91)*

**DMC (Anchor)**

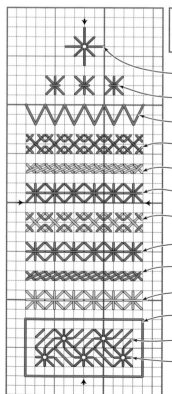

Eyelet in 327 (101)

Half Rhodes in 962 (75)

Backstitch in 522 (860)

Rice stitch in 327 (101) and Madeira No. 22 gold

Long-legged cross stitch in 725 (305)

Double cross stitch in 327 (101) and Madeira No. 22 gold

Rice stitch in 725 (305) and 522 (860)

Double cross stitch in 962 (75)

Long-legged cross stitch in 522 (860)

Double cross stitch in 725 (305)

Backstitch in Madeira No. 22 gold

Satin stitch in 962 (75)

Algerian eye in 327 (101)

### Little Floral Garden
*(page 90)*

**DMC (Anchor)**

Four-sided stitch in 712 (926)

Long-legged cross stitch in 3805 (62)

Backstitch in Madeira No. 22 gold

Algerian eye in 712 (926)

Rice stitch in 722 (323) and Madeira No. 22 gold

Adapted cross stitch in 552 (99) and Madeira No. 22 gold

Satin stitch in 722 (323)

Satin stitch in 562 (210)

Satin stitch in 552 (99)

Satin stitch in 3805 (62)

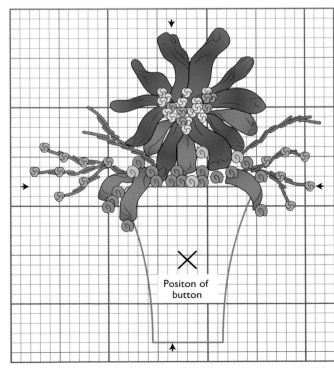

### Blue Ribbon Flower Card *(page 86)*

 Ribbon stitch in bright blue 7mm silk ribbon

 Ribbon stitch in pale olive 7mm silk ribbon

French knots in rose pink and pale pink 2mm silk ribbon

 French knots in DMC (Anchor) stranded cotton 745 (300) and 3821 (305)

 Stem stitch in DMC (Anchor) stranded cotton 3346 (267)

Positon of button

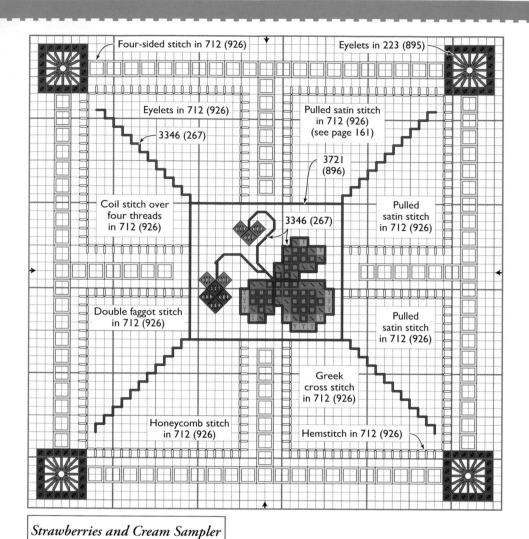

Four-sided stitch in 712 (926)

Eyelets in 223 (895)

Eyelets in 712 (926)

3346 (267)

Pulled satin stitch
in 712 (926)
(see page 161)

3721
(896)

Coil stitch over
four threads
in 712 (926)

3346 (267)

Pulled
satin stitch
in 712 (926)

Double faggot stitch
in 712 (926)

Pulled
satin stitch
in 712 (926)

Greek
cross stitch
in 712 (926)

Honeycomb stitch
in 712 (926)

Hemstitch in 712 (926)

### Strawberries and Cream Sampler
*(page 107)*

#### DMC (Anchor)

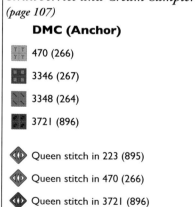

470 (266)

3346 (267)

3348 (264)

3721 (896)

Queen stitch in 223 (895)

Queen stitch in 470 (266)

Queen stitch in 3721 (896)

Use this alphabet to change
the initials on the key keeper
on page 41 (chart on page 174).

ABCDEFGHI
JKLMNOPQ
RSTUVWXYZ
abcdefgh
ijklmnopqr
stuvwxyz

## Mini Cream Sampler *(page 108)*

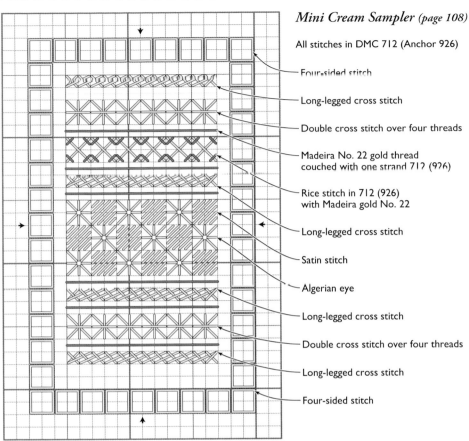

All stitches in DMC 712 (Anchor 926)

- Four-sided stitch
- Long-legged cross stitch
- Double cross stitch over four threads
- Madeira No. 22 gold thread couched with one strand 712 (926)
- Rice stitch in 712 (926) with Madeira gold No. 22
- Long-legged cross stitch
- Satin stitch
- Algerian eye
- Long-legged cross stitch
- Double cross stitch over four threads
- Long-legged cross stitch
- Four-sided stitch

## Lacy Flower Face *(page 109)*

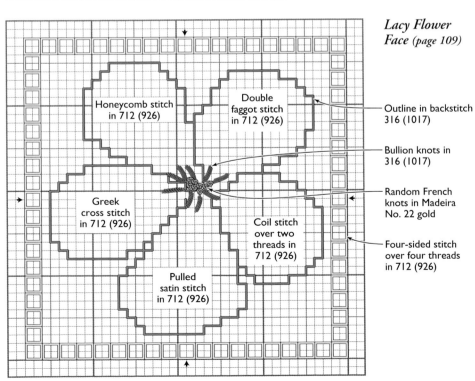

Honeycomb stitch in 712 (926)

Double faggot stitch in 712 (926)

Greek cross stitch in 712 (926)

Coil stitch over two threads in 712 (926)

Pulled satin stitch in 712 (926)

- Outline in backstitch 316 (1017)
- Bullion knots in 316 (1017)
- Random French knots in Madeira No. 22 gold
- Four-sided stitch over four threads in 712 (926)

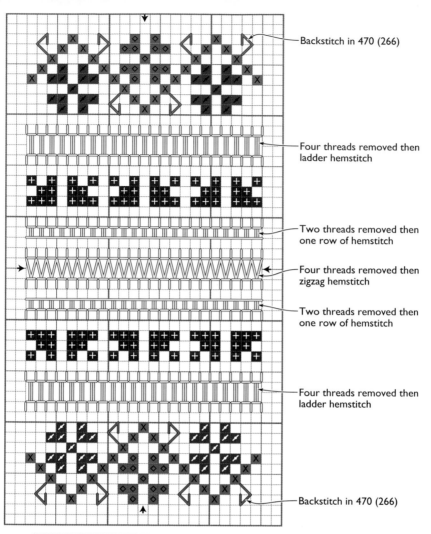

Backstitch in 470 (266)

Four threads removed then ladder hemstitch

Two threads removed then one row of hemstitch

Four threads removed then zigzag hemstitch

Two threads removed then one row of hemstitch

Four threads removed then ladder hemstitch

Backstitch in 470 (266)

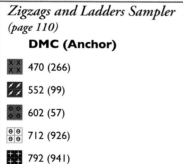

*Zigzags and Ladders Sampler*
*(page 110)*

**DMC (Anchor)**

470 (266)

552 (99)

602 (57)

712 (926)

792 (941)

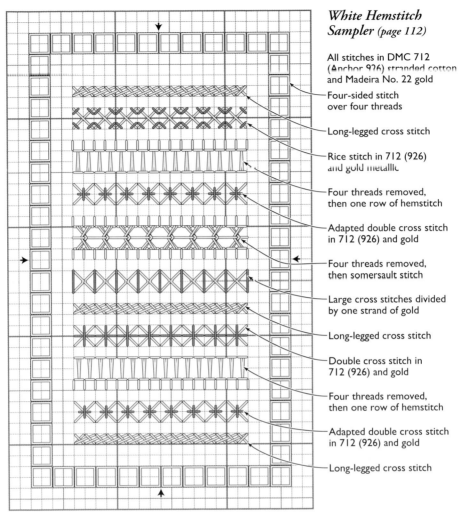

## White Hemstitch Sampler *(page 112)*

All stitches in DMC 712 (Anchor 926) stranded cotton and Madeira No. 22 gold

- Four-sided stitch over four threads
- Long-legged cross stitch
- Rice stitch in 712 (926) and gold metallic
- Four threads removed, then one row of hemstitch
- Adapted double cross stitch in 712 (926) and gold
- Four threads removed, then somersault stitch
- Large cross stitches divided by one strand of gold
- Long-legged cross stitch
- Double cross stitch in 712 (926) and gold
- Four threads removed, then one row of hemstitch
- Adapted double cross stitch in 712 (926) and gold
- Long-legged cross stitch

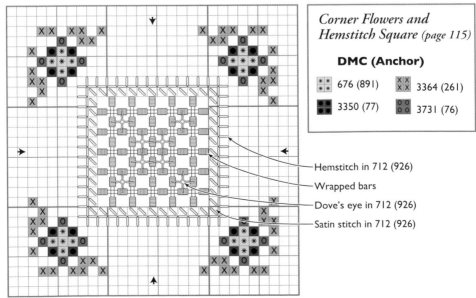

## Corner Flowers and Hemstitch Square *(page 115)*

### DMC (Anchor)

| | |
|---|---|
| 676 (891) | 3364 (261) |
| 3350 (77) | 3731 (76) |

- Hemstitch in 712 (926)
- Wrapped bars
- Dove's eye in 712 (926)
- Satin stitch in 712 (926)

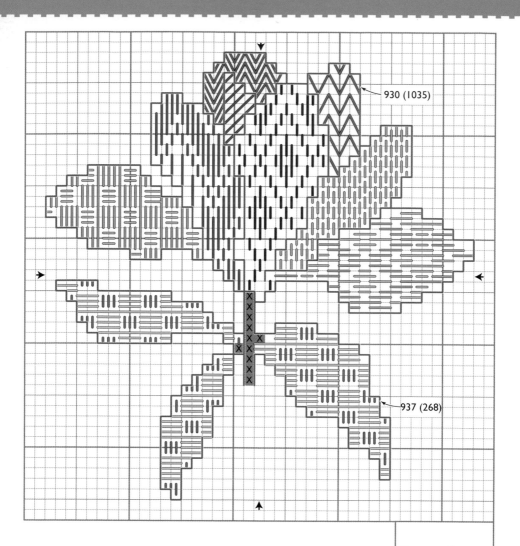

930 (1035)

937 (268)

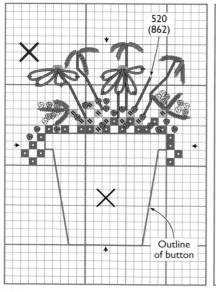

520
(862)

Outline
of button

✕ Position
of button

✕ Position
of charm

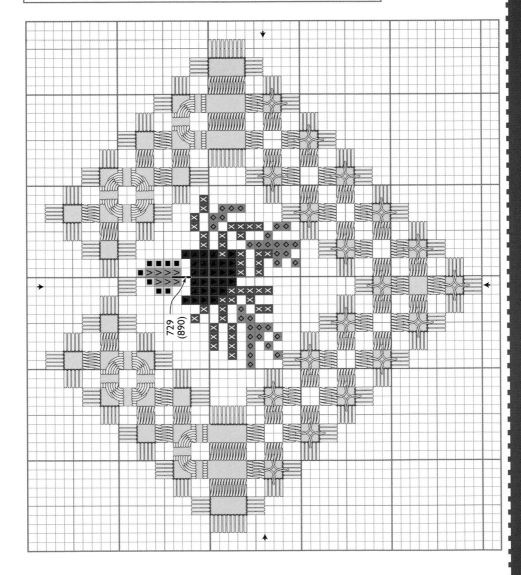

*Christmas Hardanger Heart (page 99)*

**DMC (Anchor)**

| | | | |
|---|---|---|---|
| ■ | 304 (19) | ▦ | 725 (305) |
| ✕ | 367 (216) | ⱽⱽ | 729 (890) |
| ▶ | 666 (46) | ◇ | 989 (242) |

Kloster blocks in
Anchor Perlé No.5
metallic silver

Needleweaving in
Anchor Perlé No.12 ecru

Corner needleweaving in
Anchor Perlé No.12 ecru

Wrapped bars in
Anchor Perlé No.12 ecru

Dove's eyes in
Anchor Perlé No.12 ecru

Red dotted line show
where to cut threads

729
(890)

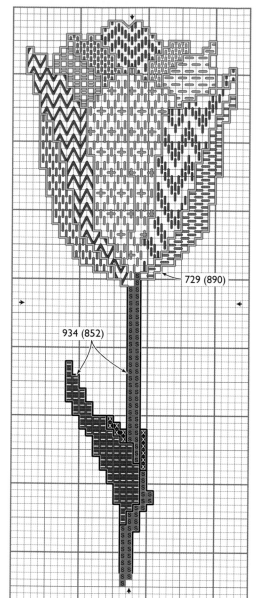

729 (890)

934 (852)

**Pattern Darned Tulip** *(page 84)*

## DMC (Anchor)

| | | |
|---|---|---|
| ⬛ 470 (266) | ▬ 221 (897) | ▬ 931 (1034) |
| ✕ 934 (852) | ▬ 327 (101) | ▬ 934 (852) |
| ▬ 937 (268) | ▬ 470 (266) | ▬ 3740 (872) |
| | ▬ 729 (890) | |

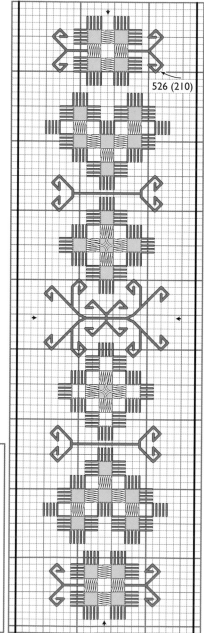

526 (210)

## *Multicoloured Hardanger Bookmark* *(page 96)*

▯▯▯▯▯ Kloster blocks Anchor Perlé No.8 multicolour 1375

✛ Dove's eyes Anchor Perlé No.12 ecru

〰 Needleweaving Anchor Perlé No.12 ecru

▬ Hemstitched edge Anchor Perlé No.12 ecru

┄┄ Red dotted lines show where to cut threads

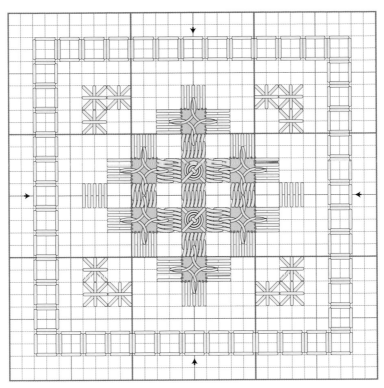

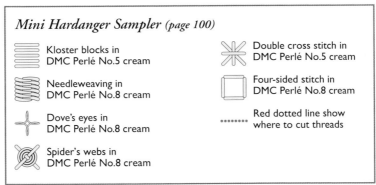

## Mini Hardanger Sampler *(page 100)*

Kloster blocks in
DMC Perlé No.5 cream

Needleweaving in
DMC Perlé No.8 cream

Dove's eyes in
DMC Perlé No.8 cream

Spider's webs in
DMC Perlé No.8 cream

Double cross stitch in
DMC Perlé No.5 cream

Four-sided stitch in
DMC Perlé No.8 cream

Red dotted line show
where to cut threads

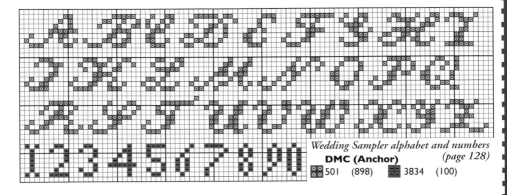

*Wedding Sampler alphabet and numbers*
*(page 128)*

**DMC (Anchor)**

501  (898)     3834  (100)

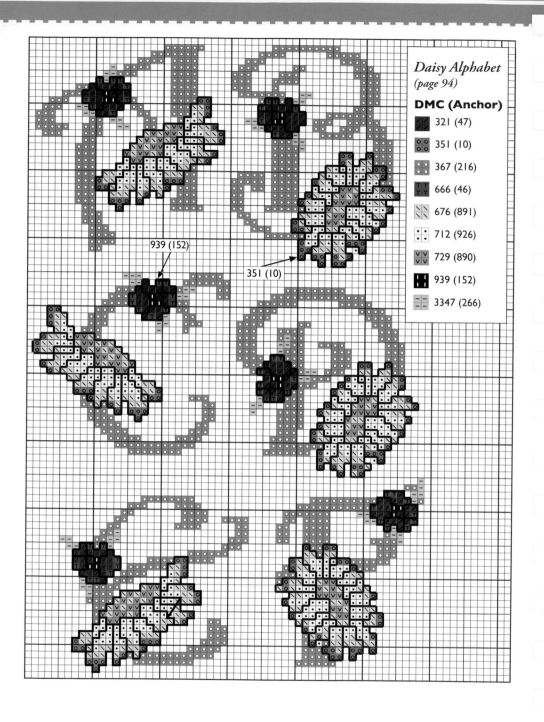

Daisy Alphabet
(page 94)

DMC (Anchor)

| | |
|---|---|
| ▨ | 321 (47) |
| ◦◦ | 351 (10) |
| ◦◦ | 367 (216) |
| T T | 666 (46) |
| \\ | 676 (891) |
| ∶∶ | 712 (926) |
| ∨∨ | 729 (890) |
| ▥ | 939 (152) |
| −− | 3347 (266) |

939 (152)

351 (10)

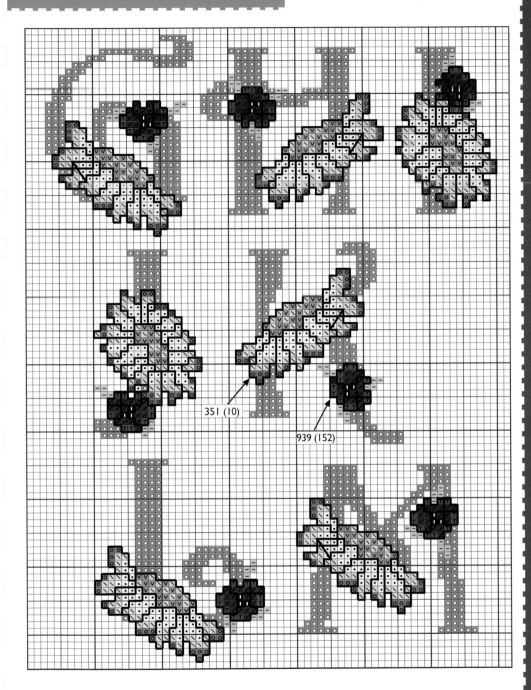

351 (10)

939 (152)

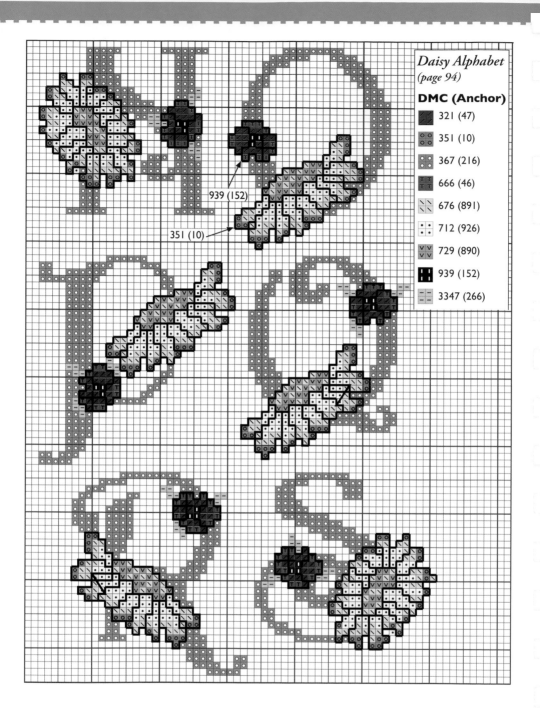

Daisy Alphabet
(page 94)

DMC (Anchor)

321 (47)
351 (10)
367 (216)
666 (46)
676 (891)
712 (926)
729 (890)
939 (152)
3347 (266)

939 (152)

351 (10)

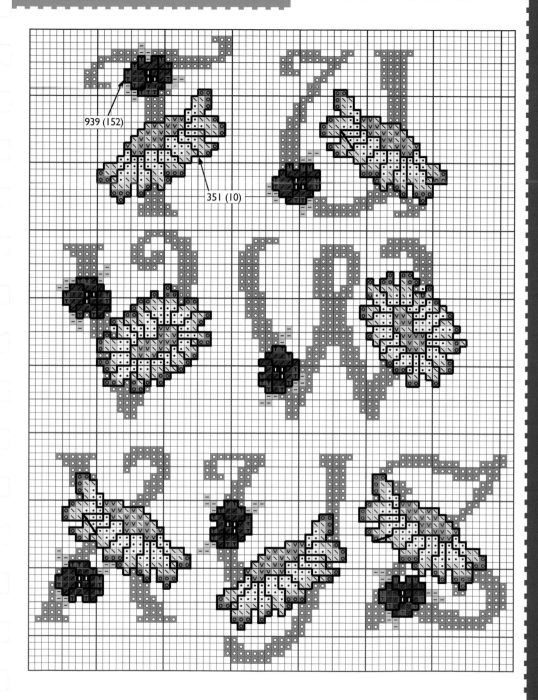

939 (152)

351 (10)

# FINISHING AND MAKING UP

Embroidery designs can be made up into a wonderful selection of objects, both practical and decorative and how they are made up or completed makes a great deal of difference to the look of the finished piece. This section describes some of the basic finishing techniques used in the book and suggests ways of displaying your embroidery. If you are unable to find any items mentioned – don't panic! – there are always alternatives on the market. Experiment!

## WASHING AND IRONING YOUR WORK

If it becomes necessary to wash your embroidery, hand wash the stitching in bleach-free soap, rinse well and remove excess water by squeezing gently in a soft, clean towel. Allow the piece to dry naturally.

    To iron a piece of embroidery, first cover the ironing board with four layers of thick white towel and press the work from the wrong side, using the steam setting if your iron has one. Take extra care when ironing work containing buttons and charms and avoid ironing metallic threads.

### JANE'S TIP
*If disaster strikes and you do get a difficult mark on the fabric there are now specialist bleaches for stain removal, which can save the situation – something to be kept for real emergencies. Apply with a cotton bud and a very good light.*

## STRETCHING AND MOUNTING

Professional framing can be very expensive, but we all feel that our larger projects deserve the professional touch. It is a great shame when, after spending hundreds of hours stitching a precious piece of cross stitch, the finished piece is just poked in an unsuitable frame without any further attention. By following the method explained below for padded mounting, you will be able to produce a very good result and have the pleasure of knowing that you completed the whole project on your own. The advantage of a padded mounting for embroidery is that any slightly 'lumpy bits' on the back of your work will be pushed into the padding rather than appear as raised areas on the front of the embroidery.

◆ Take time to make sure that you have centred the work carefully and that the edges are really straight, otherwise it will show when you put the completed piece in the frame.

◆ Pad all your completed pieces even cards as the padding raises the embroidery, which displays it to better effect.

◆ Use foamcore board, which consists of two layers of thin card with a layer of polystyrene between. This construction makes it easy to cut the board and to pin into the edge as the pins are actually inserted into the polystyrene. You will probably have to buy foamcore board at an artists' supply store rather than a needlework shop.

You will need: 3mm foamcore board, or acid-free mounting board; double-sided adhesive tape, or strong thread for lacing; polyester wadding (batting) for padding and glass- or plastic-headed pins.

**1** Using a sharp craft knife, cut a piece of foamcore to fit your frame (cut round the piece of glass that fits the frame).
**2** Attach a piece of wadding (batting) to the foamcore board using strips of double-sided adhesive tape, then trim the wadding to exactly the same size as the foamcore.
**3** Position your embroidery on top of the padding and centre it carefully in relation to the padded board. Fix the embroidery in position by pinning through the fabric into the edges of the board (see Fig 1). Start in

the middle of each side and pin towards the corners. Make sure your pins follow a line of Aida holes or a thread of linen so that your edges will be really straight. Adjust the fabric's position until you are completely confident that it is centred and straight.
**4** Turn the work over and, leaving the pins in place, trim the excess fabric to about 5cm (2in) all round and fold it to the back.
**5** Fix the edges of fabric in place using either double-sided tape or by lacing across the back using strong thread (see Fig 2). As the pins remain in place, it is still possible at this stage to adjust the position of the fabric and replace the tape or tighten the lacing. When you are completely satisfied with the result, remove the pins and assemble the work in its frame.

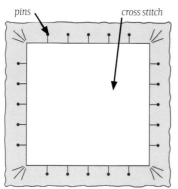

**Fig 1** *Pinning out your embroidery.*

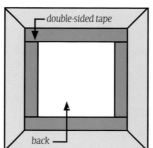
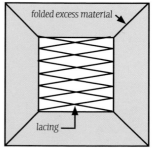

**Fig 2** *Fixing the fabric in place by taping or lacing.*

## FRAMING

Needlework generally looks better framed without glass. If you prefer to use glass with this method, you must ensure that the embroidery does not touch the underside of the glass. Insert very narrow strips of board (spacers) into the edges of the frame, between the glass and the mounted embroidery to hold them apart, before you assemble the frame. Always check that both sides of the glass are completely clean.
It is a good idea to line the back of the work with aluminium foil before adding the final backing board to the back of the picture, to discourage small insects from finding their way in. When the frame is assembled, seal the back using gummed paper tape, gently pushing the tape into the rebate. The tape will shrink slightly as it dries thus sealing the picture.

## Choosing a Frame

◆ When choosing a frame for a particular project, select the largest moulding you can afford and do not worry if the colour is not suitable. Ask the framer to make up the frame and a coloured or gold slip for you, but buy the frame, glass and so on in kit form (most framers do not mind!) and then decorate the frame yourself.

◆ You can use readily available products to decorate frames, for example car spray paint. There are dozens of colours but if you want more, try bicycle paints, which include even more colours!

◆ For subtle, matt shades, explore endless possibilities with emulsion paints from DIY shops, often available in tiny tester sizes, ideal for trial and error.

◆ Before you begin to paint a piece of moulding, take care to cover all nearby surfaces with paper or dust cloths, If the moulding is completely untreated, rub down gently with fine sand paper, clean with white spirit on a soft cloth and allow to dry completely before painting.

## Stretching and Starching Canvas Work

It is the nature of canvas to distort especially when worked in tent stitch, so it is necessary to stretch and starch the needlework to restore a regular shape. You will be able to use the board and squared paper many times and will soon master the technique.

You will need: a flat, clean board (e.g., chipboard); squared paper (e.g., dressmaker's graph paper); hammer and 2.5cm (1in) long nails; cold water starch (e.g., wallpaper paste without preservatives or anti-fungal agent); masking tape and kitchen palette knife.

**1** Cover the board with the squared paper and stick down with masking tape. Place the embroidery right side down on the paper. You should be able to see the squares on the paper through the unstitched canvas.

**2** Start at one corner and begin nailing down the canvas about 5cm (2in) from the embroidery, hammering in the nails far enough to hold the fabric firmly. Following the line in the canvas, align the canvas with the squared paper, placing nails about 2.5cm (1in) apart (any further apart and the needlework may acquire a scalloped edge).

**3** When you have completed the first side, go back to the corner and repeat for the side at right angles to it. Draw a pencil line on the canvas from the last nail on each

side to cross at the opposite corner to one you started from. Work out where this should come in relation to the lines on the graph paper and pull the embroidery and nail the corner and the last two sides. If your stitching is very distorted it may help to dampen the embroidery.

**4** When the last nail is in position the work should be completely square. Mix a small quantity of the starch to the consistency of soft butter and spread it evenly but sparingly with a knife over the canvas, avoiding the unstitched areas. Allow this to dry completely and then remove the nails to remove the work from the board. Not only will the work be completely square but the starch will have evened the tension so your stitches should look even better!

## MAKING UP A CUBE

The cube decorations on pages 45 and 61 are quite simple to make up and can be stuffed with polyester stuffing, perhaps with some crushed cinnamon sticks inside for a festive aroma. You will need to make a length of twisted cord (see page 41) and a tassel (see page 218).

1 Press the embroidery carefully on the wrong side with plenty of steam and on a towel and gently pull the squares back into shape. Trim the bare canvas edges to 1.25cm (½in) and clip corners.

2 Fold in all the canvas edges leaving one thread of canvas exposed. You will be able to fold up the squares to make a cube. Now work long-legged cross stitch on all the empty canvas threads between the squares and on the joins of your box shape. Tuck in the cord and tassel at opposite corners and fill with polyester wadding just before you complete the last seam.

## MAKING A BAG OR SACHET

A bag or sachet is easy to stitch, can be made in any size and has many different uses – holding small gifts, pot-pourri or wedding mementoes. A bag could be made entirely from Aida or an evenweave fabric, with the design embroidered directly on to the fabric, or it could be made from an ordinary dressmaking fabric with an embroidered panel sewn or fused on. The instructions that follow are for a sewn-on piece of embroidery – see page 216 for using fusible interfacing. You will need: sufficient fabric for the front and back of the bag; matching sewing thread and a length of cord or ribbon for a tie.

1 Cut out two rectangles of fabric according to the size you wish your bag to be, allowing for 6mm (¼in) seams. Stitch your piece of embroidery on to the front piece, perhaps fraying the edges of the fabric for a decorative effect.

2 With right sides of the bag rectangles together, pin and stitch both sides and the bottom of the bag, matching the edges for a neat finish. Press the side seams open.

3 To make the top of the bag, fold the top edge over to the wrong side by 6mm (¼in), press, then fold over again by another 4cm (1½in). Pin in place and sew two rows of stitching around the neck of the bag to form a casing for a tie. Turn the bag to the right side. Snip the side seam between the lines of parallel stitching, binding the cut edges with small

buttonhole stitches or over-stitching. (If preferred, you can make a bag like the one shown here, where the raw edge has been hemstitched and the ribbon is tied on the outside.)

4 To finish the bag with a tie, thread a piece of cord or ribbon through the channel and knot the ends to secure.

# MAKING A BELL PULL

A bell pull is another useful way of displaying cross stitch. You could use one of the designs charted in the Chart Library or design one of your own. A simple rectangular shape is the easiest to make up but you could make one with a pointed bottom end if you prefer. First, decide on the size of your bell pull – the length of the bell pull hanging rod determines the width of the fabric you need, so buy the bell pull ends and rods before you start stitching. You could use rustic twigs or cinnamon sticks instead of commercial rods.

You will need: bell pull hanging rods and ends; cotton backing fabric; decorative braid and matching sewing thread.

**1** Work your cross stitch design on to your stitching fabric.

**2** Turn under the edges of your fabric so that your design is central. Fold your backing fabric to the same size and press the turnings.

**3** Place the embroidered piece and the backing fabric wrong sides together (i.e., right sides outside) and pin. Slide the rods into position at the top and bottom, and add the bell pull ends, then slipstitch the fabric pieces together, adding decorative braid around the edges if desired.

# MAKING A BOOKMARK

Bookmarks make quick gifts. You could make your own as described here or mount your work in a commercial bookmark, or use a band as shown here.

**1** Decide on the size of your bookmark and stitch your design on to the fabric. Trim the fabric to within 1.25cm (½in) of the stitching all round.

**2** Hem all the sides. If you want to create a shaped point at the bottom, don't hem the bottom but turn it under by about 6mm (¼in), making sure that none of the embroidery is included, and tack (baste). Find the seam centre point and bring the two corners together so they meet at the back then slipstitch these two edges together. A tassel at the point would finish the bookmark off nicely.

## MOUNTING WORK IN CARDS AND TAGS

There are many card blanks available from needlecraft shops and mail-order companies or you can make your own using pretty papers, card and ribbon, as I have for the Vintage Viola Card shown below and the Lilac Boot Card on page 70.

### MOUNTING INTO A DOUBLE-FOLD CARD

**1** Open the folded card completely and check that the embroidered design fits in the opening.

**2** Apply a thin coat of adhesive or double-sided adhesive tape to the inside of the opening (see Fig 3). Position the design carefully, checking the position of the stitching before pressing down firmly.

**3** Fold the spare flap inside and stick in place with either double-sided adhesive tape or another thin application of adhesive. Leave to dry before closing and add ribbon trims as desired.

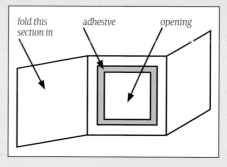

**Fig 3** *Open out the card and apply double-sided tape around the aperture.*

### MAKING HANDMADE CARDS

**1** In all cases, cut the finished embroidery to the required size (allowing for fraying the edges if appropriate).

**2** Select a coloured card to complement your embroidery threads and create a single-fold card and then embellish it with decorative paper.

**3** Attach the embroidery to the card with double-sided adhesive tape and add trims or other embellishments as desired.

### MAKING CARD PATCHES

One of the quickest methods of making a special card is to simply trim and fray the fabric around the project and stick the frayed patch on a piece of card using double-sided adhesive tape.

To make a tattered patch you need to use linen for the stitching as it frays more satisfactorily. Trim away the excess fabric and fray all four sides until you have the required size then gently tug at the corners to distort slightly.

## Using Commercial Products

There are many items available today that have been specially designed to display embroidery, such as trays, stools, fire screens, mugs, boxes, mirrors, trinket pots and coasters. To mount work in these products, you generally only need to follow the manufacturer's instructions, but it helps to back the embroidered work with iron-on interfacing.

### Using Iron-On Interfacing

Cross stitch embroidery can be stabilized with iron-on interfacing, which also helps prevent fraying when cutting the fabric. Double-sided interfacing can be used to fuse your embroidery to another fabric. Interfacing is available from needlework shops and good craft shops.

**1** Cut a piece of interfacing a little larger than the finished design size (including any unworked fabric needed to fill an aperture or ready-made item).

**2** Set the iron to the manufacturer's recommended heating (usually a medium setting). Do a test first on waste fabric and interfacing to make sure that they will bond without scorching the design.

**3** Place the stitching face down on a towel and iron on the interfacing, trimming off excess.

## Making Cushions, Pincushions and Scissors Keepers

Cross stitch embroidery can be made up into cushions, pincushions and scissors keepers following the same principles. Two pieces of fabric the same size and shape are joined together, with stuffing inserted into the centre. You could make a twisted cord (see page 41) and slipstitch this to the seam all round using matching thread. Tuck the raw edges inside the cover before slipstitching the gap closed or disguise the ends with a decorative button. Alternatively, use a ready-made cord for an edging. There are two main ways of joining the fabrics – using counted chain stitch or normal hand or machine sewing.

### Joining with Counted Chain Stitch

**1** Place the two fabric sections wrong sides together and sew together using counted chain stitch (or long-legged cross stitch).

**2** Insert the stuffing through an opening before the last side is completed. If a cord for scissors or to attach to a chatelaine is required, insert this immediately after stuffing and anchor it in place as the last side is stitched.

### Joining with Hand or Machine Sewing

**1** Pin the back and front pieces together, right sides facing.

**2** Stitch the pieces together, by hand or machine, leaving an opening for turning through.

**3** Turn right sides out, insert polyester filling and slipstitch the opening to close.

## MAKING A PURSE

There are many designs in the book that could be stitched and made up into a purse. You will need: fabric to make the purse, lining fabric, thin wadding (batting) and bias binding to edge the flap. Alternatively, buy ready-made binding.

**1** Decide what size the front flap is to be and stitch the flower design in the centre.
**2** Cut a piece of fabric as wide as the stitched piece and at least twice the length. With right sides together stitch the embroidered section to the patterned fabric and press the seam flat. Use this long narrow shape as a template to cut wadding and lining fabric.
**3** Sandwich the stitching, batting and lining together and tack in position. Trim the embroidered section to a gentle curve (draw around a plate). Using purchased or homemade bias binding, bind the short, straight edge of the purse (see page 219 for making and attaching binding).

**4** Fold the purse into three, checking that the flap falls in the correct position, and tack in position. Starting at the bottom fold, bind up one side of the pocket, around the curve and down the other side. Trim the binding at the bottom edge, slipping the raw edges inside and slipstitching in place.

## MAKING A PHOTOGRAPH CASE

A photograph case makes a lovely keepsake to hold some cute baby photos. You will need sufficient embroidery fabric to house the motifs and make up the case.

**1** Stitch the motifs in the positions in Fig 4. Trim the embroidery fabric to the size required: a piece of fabric 18 x 30.5cm (7 x 12in) once folded will hold a 10 x 15cm (4 x 6in) photo.
**2** Cut a piece of lining fabric 18 x 30.5cm (7 x 12in). Place the two pieces right sides together and sew together around each side, leaving a gap. Turn through to the right side, slipstitch the gap and press seams.
**3** Fold the bottom of the case up by about 11.5cm (4½in) and pin the side seams together. Fold the flap over to check that the position. Using tiny stitches and matching sewing thread, join the two side seams together.

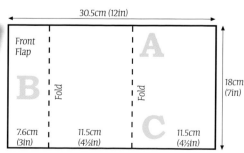

**Fig 4** Position of the motifs on the case. Fold the fabric at the dashed lines to create the case.

## Beaded Iris Chatelaine

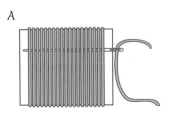

Making up this chatelaine is quite simple. You will need: linen for the back, felt for the lining and Vilene stiffening.

**1** Press your work on the wrong side, with at least two layers of towelling to cushion the beads.

**2** Using the solid lines on the chart, tack the shape of your chatelaine on your linen. Cut out this shape leaving 1.25cm (½in) seam allowance around it.

**3** Fold under this seam allowance and using the beaded shape as a pattern, cut Vilene to the same shape and then use the Vilene as a pattern to cut out the felt lining.

**4** Tuck the Vilene stiffening in under the folded-in edges on the linen and use herringbone to stitch down the seam allowance, making sure that your stitches do not come through to the right side.

**5** Make a twisted cord (see page 41).

**6** Make a beaded tassel for the bottom of the chatelaine with five or six beaded lengths as follows. Thread a beading needle with one strand of stranded cotton and thread on one bead. Now thread both ends of the cotton through the needle so that one bead is trapped at the bottom. Thread more beads on to the needle. When you have enough beaded lengths tie them together at the top with a firm knot.

**7** Place the felt lining over the turned-in edges including the knot of the tassel and the ends of the twisted cord and slipstitch in place.

**8** Fold the whole thing so that the two long straight edges meet (right sides out) and slipstitch the two edges together.

## Making a Tassel

Tassels are useful for adding a finishing touch to many projects, including cushions, cards and bookmarks. They can be made from various threads, usually from stranded cottons to match the cross stitch design, but you could also use metallic threads or tapestry wools.

**1** Decide on the tassel length and cut a piece of stiff card this size. Wrap the thread around the card (Fig 5) to form the body of the tassel, to the thickness required.

**2** Tie a thread around the top threads and then remove the tassel from the card. Cut across the threads at the bottom and tightly wrap a length of thread just below the loop at the top. Knot this and thread the ends through to join the other lengths. Trim the tassel ends if they are uneven.

**3** To attach the tassel, use matching thread through the loop at the top.

A
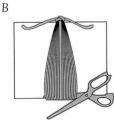

B

C

**Fig 5** *Making a tassel.*

## MAKING A MITRED CUSHION FRONT

A mitred front to a cushion or pillow gives it a professional touch and really sets off the embroidery. The Anemone Floral Cushion on page 53 uses pure silk fabric to great effect.

**1** Measure the embroidery and decide on the size the finished cushion is to be. Allow 1.25cm (½in) seam allowances throughout. Subtract the embroidery measurement from the two finished measurements, divide by two and add on the two seam allowances. This gives the total width of the border pieces. The length of the border pieces is the finished measurement of the cushion cover plus two seam allowances.

**2** Press the embroidery face down on several soft towels. Cut the linen to the required size plus two seam allowances.

**3** Find the mid-point of each edge by folding and mark with a pin. Fold each border panel in half to find the centre point and mark with a pin. Pin the border panels to the embroidery, matching centre points and leaving the edges free.

**4** Machine stitch these seams around each side of the square. The seams should meet at the corners exactly at right angles. Fold the embroidery in half diagonally, wrong sides together, and mitre the corners by stitching a line from the corner of the embroidery to the corner of the border panels (see Fig 6). Trim excess fabric and clip corners. Repeat for the remaining corners.

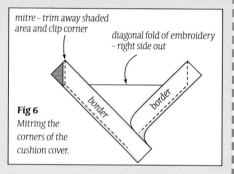

mitre – trim away shaded area and clip corner

diagonal fold of embroidery – right side out

border

border

**Fig 6** Mitring the corners of the cushion cover.

## MAKING BIAS BINDING

It is useful to be able to make your own bias binding as you will then be able to choose fabric that complements your project. Commercially made binding is available in various colours.

**1** To make bias binding, cut strips of fabric 4cm (1½in) wide across the grain of the fabric and machine sew them together at a 45-degree angle to make the length needed (Fig 7A).

**2** Attach the bias binding by hand or machine, first cutting the binding to the correct length. Pin the binding to the wrong side of the project, matching raw edges and then machine or hand stitch in place (Fig 7B). Now fold the binding to the right side and slipstitch neatly in position (Fig 7C). Press lightly to finish.

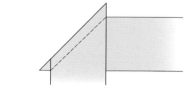

**Fig 7A** Joining bias strips at a 45-degree angle.

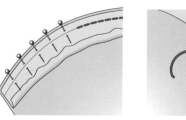

**Fig 7B and C** Pinning the binding to the front of the work, and then slipstitching the folded edge to the back of the work.

# BIBLIOGRAPHY

LOVE Janice, *Basics and Beyond* (Love 'n' Stitches, 1992)
O'STEEN Darlene, *The Proper Stitch* (Just Cross Stitch, 1994)
*The New Anchor Book of Hardanger Embroidery* (David & Charles, 2005)
*The Anchor Book of Ribbon Embroidery* (David & Charles, 1997)
*The Anchor Book of Counted Thread Embroidery Stitches* (David & Charles, 1987)
BISHOP, E. *A Collection of Beautiful Stitches* (Cross 'N' Patch, 2002)
DILLMONT, Therese  *DMC Library: The Encyclopaedia of Needlework* (Bracken, reprinted 1987)
The Embroiderer's Guild  *Making Samplers* (David & Charles, 1993)
McNEILL, Moyra  *Pulled Thread Embroidery* (Dover Publications, 1999)
O'STEEN, D.  *The Proper Stitch* (Symbol Of Excellence Publishers Inc, 1994)
SNOOK, Barbara  *Embroidery Stitches* (Batsford, 1972)

# ACKNOWLEDGMENTS

Without the support of my family and my team at The Cross Stitch Guild it would be simply impossible to continue writing cross stitch books. To all the following with love and thanks:

Bill, my special husband, who has continued to accept the many hours spent apart, my late nights and bad temper, the household muddle and late meals. Sue Hawkins (CSG Technical Director) who is always at the end of a phone day and night, and for her friendship, which has even survived working together. This book would not have happened without her.

Daphne Cording who works with me, keeping kit production on target and me in my place and Judy Reynolds, my housekeeper superstar who keeps me sane.

A special thanks to all my stitchers, pattern checkers and testers – they  have supported and encouraged me over the past twenty odd years and have made it possible for me to earn a living from my cross stitch passion: Susan Bridgens, Deborah Buglass, Elizabeth Burford, Lesley Clegg, Margaret Cornish, Neil Cuthbert, Jacqueline Davies, Elizabeth Edwards, Doreen Ely, Jean Fox, Ann Gerring, Kam Ghatoray, Joyce Halliday, Joan Hastewell, Jane Herbert, Janet Jarvis, Jane King, Margaret Locke, Margaret Pallant, Sue Smith, Suzanne Spencer, Jill Vaughan and Joan Winwood.

Vivienne Wells who is responsible for all things printed by the CSG and tries to keep me up to the task. To all the team at David & Charles for putting up with me, particularly Cheryl Brown who continues to have faith in me, and Linda Clements, who prevents me making silly mistakes and does not miss a thing! The design team who make such a lovely job of putting the pages together and Ethan Danielson who can read my writing and produces all the charts and excellent diagrams that make this book so special.

Thanks to all the generous suppliers of the materials and equipment required for this book, particularly Rainer Steimann of Zweigart for lovely fabrics, DMC Creative World and Coats Crafts UK for stranded cottons and metallic threads and Ian Lawson Smith for my wonderful cross stitch design programme.

## JANE GREENOFF AND THE CROSS STITCH GUILD

The Cross Stitch Guild was formed in March 1996 and quickly became a worldwide organization with a committed and enthusiastic body of members – over 2,000 in the first six months of operation. As word spreads it is clear that many cross stitch and counted thread addicts around the world are delighted to have a Guild of their own. The CSG has received an extraordinary level of support from designers, retailers, manufacturers and stitchers. Guild members receive a full-colour magazine *Stitch That* with Jane Greenoff  including free counted cross stitch designs and technical advice and information. The CSG also supplies cross stitch tours, weekends, cross stitch kits, gold-plated needles, stitchers' gifts, cross stitch design software and counted thread classes. Taster Membership and Full Membership is available all over the world and there is now a comprehensive website for members and non-members with discounted shopping.

www.thecrossstitchguild.com

For more information, to contact Jane or for the latest catalogue write to: CSG HQ, Pinks Barn, London Road, Fairford, Gloucestershire, GL7 4AR UK. Tel: from the UK 0800 328 9750; from overseas +44 1285 713799.

# SUPPLIERS

## UK

### Coats Crafts UK

PO Box 22, Lingfield House, McMullen Road,
Darlington, County Durham DL1 1YQ
tel: 01325 394237 (consumer helpline)
www.coatscrafts.co.uk
*For Anchor stranded cotton (floss) and other supplies.*

### Craft Creations Limited

1C Ingersoll House, Delamare Road, Cheshunt,
Herts EN8 9HD
tel: 01992 781900
www.craftcreations.com
*For greetings card blanks and card-making accessories*

### Crafty Ribbons

3 Beechwood, Clump Farm Industrial Estate,
Tin Pot Lane, Blandford, Dorset DT11 7TD
tel: 01258 455889
www.craftyribbons.com
*For ribbons, including YLI silk ribbons*

### DMC Creative World

Pullman Road, Wigston, Leicestershire
LE18 2DY
tel: 0116 281 1040
fax: 0116 281 3592
www.dmc/cw.com
*For a wide range of embroidery supplies and
DMC fabrics and threads*

### Framecraft Miniatures Ltd

Unit 3, Isis House, Lindon Road, Brownhills, West
Midlands WS8 7BW
tel/fax (UK): 01543 360842
tel (international): 44 1543 453154
email: sales@framecraft.com
www.framecraft.com
*For Mill Hill beads, buttons, charms, wooden and
ceramic trinket pots, notebook covers, key rings,
handbag mirrors and many other pre-finished items
with cross stitch inserts*

### Sue Hawkins

East Wing, Highfield House, Whitminster GL2 7PG
tel: 44 (0) 1452 740118
*For upholstered embroidery frames*

### Heritage Stitchcraft

Redbrook Lane, Brereton, Rugeley, Staffordshire
WS15 1QU
tel: +44 (0) 1889 575256
email: enquiries@heritagestitchcraft.com
www.heritagestitchcraft.com
*For Zweigart fabrics and other embroidery supplies*

### Willow Fabrics

95 Town Lane, Mobberley, Knutsford,
Cheshire WA16 7HH
tel freephone (UK): 0800 0567811
(elsewhere): #44 (0) 1565 87 2225
www.willowfabrics.com
*For embroidery fabrics, Madeira threads and
Kreinik metallics*

## USA

### Charles Craft Inc.

PO Box 1049, Laurenburg, NC 28353
tel: 910 844 3521
email: ccraft@carolina.net
www.charlescraft.com
*Coats Crafts UK supply Charles Craft products in the UK*

### Kreinik Manufacturing Company Inc

3106 Timanus Lane, Suite 101
Baltimore, MD 21244
tel: 1800 537 2166
email: kreinik@kreinik.com  www.kreinik.com
*For metallic threads and blending filaments*

### Mill Hill, a division of Wichelt Imports Inc.

N162 Hwy 35, Stoddard WI 54658
tel: 608 788 4600
www.millhill.com
*For Mill Hill beads and Framecraft products*

### Tokens & Trifles

Redefined Inc., PO Box 2243, Acton, MA 01720
tel: 001 (508) 428-9038
www.tokensandtrifles.com
*For Stitching Cards*

### Zweigart/Joan Toggit Ltd

262 Old Brunswick Road, Suite E,
Piscataway, NJ 08854-3756, USA
tel: 732 562 8888
email: info@zweigart.com
www.zweigart.com
*For cross stitch fabrics and pre-finished table linens*

# INDEX

**Bold pagination indicates instructions**

# GERMAN SHEPHERD DOG

KIM DOWNING

## German Shepherd Dog

Editor: Heather Russell-Revesz
Copy Editor: Ellen Bingham
Indexer: Elizabeth Walker
Designer: Mary Ann Kahn

TFH Publications
President/CEO: Glen S. Axelrod
Executive Vice President: Mark E. Johnson
Publisher: Christopher T. Reggio
Production Manager: Kathy Bontz

TFH Publications, Inc.
One TFH Plaza
Third and Union Avenues
Neptune City, NJ 07753

Discovery Communications, Inc. Book Development Team: Marjorie Kaplan, President and General Manager, Animal Planet Media / Kelly Day, EVP and General Manager, Discovery Commerce / Elizabeth Bakacs, Vice President, Licensing and Creative / JP Stoops, Director, Licensing / Bridget Stoyko, Associate Art Director

Copyright © 2011 by TFH Publications, Inc.

Printed and bound in China

11 12 13 14 15 16   1 3 5 7 9 8 6 4 2

Library of Congress Cataloging-in-Publication Data
Downing, Kim.
  German shepherd dog / Kim Downing.
    p. cm.
  Includes index.
  ISBN 978-0-7938-3717-5 (alk. paper)
  1. German shepherd dog. I. Title.
  SF429.G37D69 2011
  636.737'6--dc22

                         2010052260

This book has been published with the intent to provide accurate and authoritative information in regard to the subject matter within. While every reasonable precaution has been taken in preparation of this book, the author and publisher expressly disclaim responsibility for any errors, omissions, or adverse effects arising from the use or application of the information contained herein. The techniques and suggestions are used at the reader's discretion and are not to be considered a substitute for veterinary care. If you suspect a medical problem consult your veterinarian.

Note: In the interest of concise writing, "he" is used when referring to puppies and dogs unless the text is specifically referring to females or males. "She" is used when referring to people. However, the information contained herein is equally applicable to both sexes.

*The Leader In Responsible Animal Care for Over 50 Years!®*
www.tfh.com

# CONTENTS

# ORIGINS
# OF YOUR GERMAN
# SHEPHERD DOG

The German Shepherd's origins trace back to herding dogs who populated the German countryside.

As indicated by its name, the magnificent German Shepherd Dog's homeland is Germany. While the breed's history is not nearly as long as that of some others—only dating to the 1800s—its origin is one of purpose. Utility and intelligence were the goal established by the primary refiner (and noted father) of the breed, Max von Stephanitz.

## HERDING DOG BEGINNINGS

The beginnings of the breed started with an assortment of herding dogs who populated the country. In Germany, as in many other parts of Europe, herding dogs were necessary to move flocks. Those dogs were not of a specific type or of a named breed but were highly valued nonetheless. The best herding dogs were bred to other excellent herding dogs to continually improve on the skills of these dogs. What resulted was a shepherd-type dog whose background is unknown. However, the German Shepherd Dog is known to have closer ties to the wolf in his background than many other breeds, which can be seen in the early shepherd type ancestors of the breed.

## CREATING A GERMAN BREED

By the mid to late 1800s, there was a growing interest in Germany in creating a set breed type for various dogs and also creating a "German breed." A group called the Phylax Society was temporarily formed in 1891. Although it disbanded just a few years later, the early idea of creating a set breed type, maintaining records, and breeding for purpose was established.

## MAX VON STEPHANITZ

Max von Stephanitz, a former member of the Phylax Society, was a cavalry captain and longtime military man nearing the end of his career. He also had a fondness for farming and the dogs who had herding duties, and wanted to improve on what he saw and create a standard type for the best herding dog possible. He researched the herding dogs of other countries like England, visited shows, and envisioned what this ideal dog should be like.

By chance, he saw a herding dog who would become the foundation for the German Shepherd Dog breed. In 1899, while attending a show with a friend, he was taken aback by a dog named Hektor Linksrhein—whom he would later rename Horand v Grafeth—who possessed all the qualities that von Stephanitz believed were necessary for the ideal shepherd. He was so impressed with the dog's natural herding abilities that he purchased the dog on the spot.

Following the purchase of Horand, von Stephanitz created a new club, specifically for his fledgling breed, called Verein fur Deutsche Schaferhunde (loosely translated "the German Shepherd Dog Club of Germany"), or SV for short. Today, this is still the German club for the German Shepherd Dog.

As more people became familiar with Horand, more breeders requested to use him as a sire, and soon his progeny sprouted up everywhere. Von Stephanitz maintained tight control over the breeding of both Horand and all those who followed. He saw this as the only way to control the quality of the breedings and the breed. High levels of inbreeding are necessary to create a set-type, temperament, and other qualities, but inbreeding also begins to produce faults. Von Stephanitz controlled the breedings to limit these faults and to ensure that the health and temperament of the breed stayed at a high level.

## MILITARY AND POLICE WORK

With the onset of industrialization, even an exceptional herding breed soon found itself out of a job. While herding was still a necessary part of farm life, the sprouting of larger cities meant that these dogs needed to transform and show their versatility in new arenas. Luckily, von Stephanitz thought ahead to the future of the breed.

His lifelong military career meant that he had connections in all the right places, and he believed that the German Shepherd had the intelligence, workability, agility, loyalty, bravery, and versatility to prove useful in more arenas than just

The first German Shepherd Dogs probably arrived in the United States in the early 1900s.

herding. He was able to bring the German Shepherd Dog to other areas of service. Starting in World War I, the breed served many functions, from sentry and messenger dogs to personal protection dogs.

In the 1930s, the Germans established a full-scale war-dog training program that was the first of its kind. They recognized the great value of these dogs early on and built a large breeding and training facility for both military and police dogs near Frankfurt. These dogs were not only used by the German army but were provided to countries like Japan to use in World War II. By this time, Germany employed hundreds of thousands of working dogs.

## THE GERMAN SHEPHERD IN OTHER COUNTRIES

The bravery and intelligence of these dogs attracted the attention of military servicemen from other countries like the United States and England, and some of these servicemen brought dogs home with them. Because the United States was not using dogs in war, the German Shepherd Dogs' abilities seemed incredible.

### IN ENGLAND

The German Shepherd Dog was recognized by the English Kennel Club (KC) in 1919, but there were only 54 recognized dogs at that point. Within less than a decade, the numbers were over 8,000! This exponential increase in such a short time demonstrates the popularity of the breed at the time. Much of the English public, especially the older generations, will remember the German Shepherd Dog under another name—the Alsatian. With the end of World War I and the years leading into World War II, the KC worried that anything associated with Germany would lose favor. So until the late 1970s, the breed was actually known as the Alsatian to avoid any obvious connection to Germany. Before the 1980s began, the breed's name was officially returned to German Shepherd Dog.

## IN THE UNITED STATES

The German Shepherd Dog's journey to the United States followed a similar path as in England. It is believed that the first German Shepherd Dogs arrived in the early 1900s, with the first shepherd registered with the American Kennel Club (AKC) in 1908. By 1913, there was a national breed club, the German Shepherd Dog Club of America (GSDCA). The GSDCA is still the primary breed club that represents the breed both at home and abroad.

Just like in England, the "German" part of the breed name was dropped during war years. The AKC referred to the breed as the Shepherd Dog. The name returned to German Shepherd Dog by the 1970s.

## A NEW ROLE

The German Shepherd Dog had always enjoyed a rich herding history in its native country, but when the breed immigrated to other countries, new functions had to be designed. England had more than enough stellar herding breeds that were English in origin, and the United States didn't have a high need for herding dogs. Additionally, the exposure to the breed was during war times, so the versatility of the breed in functions other than herding is what was noted.

### MOVIE STAR

In America, the German Shepherd Dog immediately gained favor in a few different areas. In the early 1920s, the breed jumped onto the silver screen. Dogs like Strongheart and Rin Tin Tin represented a heroic breed that was capable of anything. This served to solidify the breed's popularity in America, and it was the AKC's number one registered breed from 1925 to 1928.

### SERVICE DOG

The German Shepherd is often considered the original service dog breed, and the very first seeing-eye guide dog for the blind was the German Shepherd Dog Buddy in 1928. For many years, the German Shepherd was the dog trained for

The first German Shepherd Dog registered with the AKC was in 1908.

this purpose. In recent years, the breed is used less frequently in service work, as Golden Retrievers and Labrador Retrievers have become more prominent, but the German Shepherd's work as a service dog breed is exemplary.

## MILITARY DOG

The United States began to employ the breed as the primary military working dog. Dogs had been used before, but Americans had not used them on a full-scale operation before and certainly hadn't done it like Germany. By the time the United States was thrust into World War II, our military still didn't possess true, trained working dogs. By 1942, a group called Dogs for Defense began to organize and started procuring dogs for the cause. They asked American citizens to support the war by donating pets who might be deemed suitable. There was no standard at the time—the main goal was to acquire dogs quickly!

The program had many ups and downs (such as no central location, inexperienced trainers, inconsistent quality in dogs), but the move was on to create a dog-training program as quickly as possible. By the summer of 1942, the military officially identified four areas of military dogs for training: messenger dogs, sentry dogs, mine-detection dogs, and patrol dogs.

The United States didn't know which breeds of dogs were best for training, but before long, the number of breeds had been whittled down to 30. Some breeds just weren't suitable for certain tasks. By the end of 1944, the U.S. government listed the German Shepherd Dog as one of seven dog breeds that would now be focused on for military training. The breed is still one of three primary breeds in use by the military today. German Shepherds work alongside Labrador Retrievers and Belgian Malinois in military activities.

Unfortunately, for many years, these brave dogs were considered nothing more than military equipment and were usually left behind in the warring country when the troops left. This didn't sit well with the American public, especially during the Vietnam War, and in 1967, the very first retired military sentry dog, a black-and-tan German Shepherd named Nemo, was officially sent home and retired from active duty.

## POLICE WORK

German Shepherds also play a prominent role (along with the previously noted two breeds) as police K-9 officers. Due to its versatility, the breed serves in multiple capacities. He makes an excellent patrol dog and is used extensively for apprehending individuals. Officers like to use the German Shepherd to control a fleeing suspect, because the dog is able to quickly control the situation and hold the person with a bite. Police also hold the German Shepherd in high regard for his high level of impulse control and attention to command. Once the dog bites and holds a suspect, the officer is able to call the dog off, even under high levels

German Shepherds play a prominent role in many countries as police K-9 officers.

of stimulation and excitement. His bite pressure and control are second only to the Rottweiler's.

## TRACKING, SCENT DETECTION, AND SEARCH AND RESCUE

This K-9 officer often has multiple roles and is not just assigned to one function. A police dog may be a patrol dog, a tracker, and a scent-detection dog. He makes an excellent tracking dog and can air scent and do ground-trailing work. He is often one of the first breeds brought in to follow a fresh track of a suspect.

Scent-detection dogs are trained to specifically detect one or more odors, commonly drugs, bombs, and arson materials. This scent-detection work allows them to work in schools as part of the Drug Abuse Resistance Education (DARE) program to search school lockers for drugs, and as part of U.S. Customs to search airplanes, boats, and other transportation vehicles for various contraband.

The German Shepherd's tracking abilities have allowed the breed to excel in search-and-rescue work as well, and the dogs and their handlers are routinely called upon to search for missing people. The breed played a role in the September 11 World Trade Center tragedy as part of the search-and-rescue mission in the rubble.

The German Shepherd's tracking abilities have allowed the breed to excel in search and rescue work.

## THE SOFTER SIDE

Although many people commonly associate this brave breed with police work, the German Shepherd Dog has a softer side too. He can make an excellent therapy dog, service dog, or valued companion.

## THE CLUBS

The German Shepherd Dog is a breed still heavily governed by the founding club of Germany—the SV. This club sanctions dog shows around the world and sets rules for what the dogs should look like and which dogs will be bred.

The SV uses various means to control the breed. There is a set standard, which is similar to the one used in America. Dogs are judged according to this standard, and those who fail to meet it are not allowed to be exhibited or bred. One example of their strict rules is the size of the dog; dogs are measured according to the standard, and those who are too large fall outside the guidelines. This is to maintain the working size of the breed—dogs who are too large are not good working candidates, because their size limits their agility.

The club also maintains control of the suitability of breeding dogs through the use of X-rays and examining the dog's joints. A dog's owner must submit X-rays that are reviewed by the SV and veterinary specialists. If a dog receives what is known as an "A stamp," he is okay to be bred. The dogs are continually assessed through breeding records and their progeny, as hip and elbow problems (dysplasia) are genetically passed on. As the progeny are X-rayed and recorded, a more viable picture of a sire or dam is produced, and breeders are able to assess how to properly breed their dog to limit the possibility of dysplasia.

The SV further judges dogs in large shows and Schutzhund events (which we will discuss further in Chapter 9). Dogs must be permanently identified by tattoo or microchip and must pass the Begleithund test, commonly referred to as the BH test, in order to compete at higher levels for any titles. The BH assesses the dog's obedience skills and temperament, and if a dog doesn't pass this test, he can't title or move forward.

The focus on health, temperament, and workability is the way that Germany has attempted to maintain control over the breed and its future. In some ways this has been successful, but in other ways it has not. Because kennel clubs like the AKC or KC are not as restrictive as the SV, dogs with a variety of problems may be bred, and the pups can still be registered. This is why we sometimes see health and temperament problems with dogs from unethical breeders.

## U.S. CLUBS
Other countries in the world have their own kennel clubs too, and some adhere to the SV standards set forth and some do not.

### German Shepherd Dog Club of America
The United States has one national parent club for the breed, the German Shepherd Dog Club of America (GSDCA). The GSDCA

The German Shepherd Dog Club of America is the United States' national parent club for the breed.

promotes all facets of the breed and is the number one recognized German Shepherd club both at home with the AKC and in the world with the World Union Organization of German Shepherd Dogs. The AKC guidelines do not have the same strict German standards.

What has occurred over the years in the United States is a difference in the appearance, style, temperament, and function of the German Shepherd. Some dogs are now solely bred for conformation shows; others specialize in performance areas like herding or obedience; and others are bred for Schutzhund or working careers. There's also been a rise in pet breeders and backyard breeders who know little about the breed or the standard. This results in oversized dogs, placid shepherds with little function, dogs who possess poor temperament, or dogs that are riddled with health problems. These breeding practices from unethical breeders are problematic for the breed and its perception.

Today, the focus has returned to a balanced German Shepherd Dog capable of doing anything. Responsible breeders breed for the total dog and perform routine health certifications to ensure the healthiest, soundest dogs possible.

### GSDCA-Working Dog Association
The German Shepherd Dog Club of America-Working Dog Association (WDA),

## German Shepherd Clubs

You can locate the clubs nearest you and learn more information through a quick Internet search:
- The American Kennel Club (AKC): www.akc.org
- The German Shepherd Dog Club of America (GSDCA): www.gsdca.org
- The German Shepherd Dog Club of America-Working Dog Association: www.gsdca-wda.org
- United Schutzhund Clubs of America: www.germanshepherddog.com
- Verein fur Deutsche Schaferhunde (SV) (site in German): www.schaeferhund.de

established in 1982, is the working component affiliated with the GSDCA. Its primary function is to adhere to the German standard of working tests through Schutzhund trials, and titling and breeding only those dogs who pass all SV requirements. All certifications and titles are run through and approved by the SV, even though the dogs live and compete in America. The WDA accepts and recognizes working titles obtained at other Schutzhund organizations' trials.

## The United Schutzhund Clubs of America

The United Schutzhund Clubs of America (USA) is another organization that titles dogs through Schutzhund trials. Currently, this club doesn't recognize any titles obtained in a WDA event. They require their members to choose between organizations.

## Regional Clubs

All clubs, the GSDCA, the GSDCA-WDA, and the USA, have a parent club but are represented regionally by smaller clubs. These regional clubs hold training classes, shows, and events and truly represent the breed and sports throughout the country.

# CHARACTERISTICS
# OF YOUR GERMAN
# SHEPHERD DOG

The German Shepherd Dog is known as one of the most versatile breeds of dogs in existence today. This is a large breed of dog who, on first impression, gives an air of elegance combined with strength. For those who know, love, and live with the breed, there is no equivalent.

## PHYSICAL CHARACTERISTICS

When producing German Shepherds, reputable breeders follow a written breed standard—which is a description of the "ideal" dog—and try to produce the highest quality dog who closely matches this standard. However, there are many variations in German Shepherds, and not all dogs are the ideal embodiment of the standard. The ideal Shepherd fits as many of these physical characteristics as possible.

This is a large breed of dog who, on first impression, gives an air of elegance combined with strength.

### SIZE

Because of his size, the German Shepherd Dog often appears threatening to strangers at first view. Don't be surprised if some people are excited to meet your dog while others are leery. I've even had people cross the street to avoid walking by one of my Shepherds!

#### Weight

The size of the dog varies by individual and also by gender. Males should be clearly masculine and larger. This is a breed where obvious secondary sex characteristics are important and creating effeminate looking males is undesirable. Males, at adult size, range anywhere from about 85 to just under 100 pounds (39 to 45 kg). Anything smaller than 85 pounds (39 kg) is a very small male; mid-80 pounds (39 kg) is a medium-sized male Shepherd. Anything larger than 100 pounds (39 kg) is very clearly oversized.

Females range on the smaller size, and a feminine look is desirable. The most desirable size for a female is 60 to 70 pounds (27 to 32 kg). A medium-sized girl weighs over 70 pounds (32 kg), and a large girl weighs up to 80 pounds (36 kg). Anything smaller than 60 pounds (27 kg) is very petite, and anything over 80 to 85 pounds (36 to 39 kg) is very oversized.

#### Height

In America, the average female Shepherd is about 20 to 22 inches (51 to 56 cm) tall, and the average male is about 24 to 26 inches (61 to 66 cm) tall, as measured at the wither (or shoulder) point. Even though there is a height standard for the breed, many of the pet German Shepherds bred in the United States are not produced according to height. This is unlike Germany, where a German Shepherd who does not fall with the height standards can't be shown or bred. These dogs are then placed in pet homes or exported to other countries.

## Oversized Dogs

It is important to note that there are divisions within German Shepherd Dog fanciers. American breeders do not have to meet the same standards as the countries that adhere only to Germany's breed rules. In Germany, if a dog doesn't meet the set rules and standards, that particular dog is not allowed to be bred. In America, there are no such rules, unless one exclusively shows within Schutzhund and adheres to the German rules standard. German Shepherds registered exclusively through the American Kennel Club (AKC) or alternative listings are not held to the same standards, especially in terms of size.

Because the standards are looser in the United States, some individuals have created greatly oversized German Shepherds and classified them as "Old World Style." These dogs are far removed from their original purposes. It is not normal or desirable for a German Shepherd Dog to weigh over 100 pounds (45 kg).

## COAT

The breed has a double coat, which means there is an undercoat held closely to the dog's body (this is the coat that sheds heavily seasonally) and an outercoat. The outercoat is different in texture to the softer undercoat. It lies on top and is longer and coarser yet smoother. It is also very shiny (if your dog is in good health and eating correctly). This outercoat helps to protect and keep the underlying coat dry. The undercoat is really an insulating layer. It is used primarily in cooler months to keep the dog warm, which is why when the weather begins to warm up, this underlayer sheds out. A tremendous amount of hair will be shed during this "blow out" time.

Puppies have very soft fur all over until the age of three to four months, when they begin to develop adult hair. The adult hair will first develop around the middle of his tail. It will be very shiny, longer in length, and of a very different texture. As a puppy approaches

Some German Shepherds have frilly hair along the ears—which can be attractive in a pet but is not desirable in the show ring.

four months of age, you will see a strip of adult hair begin to appear down his back, and the soft puppy fur will start to shed out.

### Length

Different lengths and styles of coats appear in the breed. Genetics helps to determine how much coat a particular dog will ultimately end up with. This is because the German Shepherd Dog carries a gene for long hair (which is not desirable in conformation). The more of this gene in the pedigree, the greater the quality and thickness of hair the adult dog will have.

The coat can range from very close coated to long coated. Close coated means less undercoat and a shorter outercoat than average. German Shepherds who are long coated have a much longer coat than average, although it can range from frilly hair along the ears and a bushy tail to as much coat as a Collie! These dogs make fine pets and are attractive, but it is not a desirable trait for showing. Because the long-hair factor is necessary in the genes to produce a nice, full coat on the average dog, longhaired dogs are routinely produced as a side effect.

## COLORS

The German Shepherd Dog comes in a variety of colors, including:

• **Black and Tan**: This is the most common color of Shepherd. The dog has a black saddle coat with any color shading of tan on the legs and face. The tan can range from a deep, reddish brown to a light, yellowish tan. How much tan an adult dog will have is all about genetics, but the lighter the puppy (or the more tan he already has at a young age), the lighter the adult dog will be. German Shepherds lighten as they age.

• **Black and Silver**: This is a variation of black and tan, except the tan is very, very light. It is almost an off-white color.

• **Bi-Color**: These dogs are almost all black in color save for just a few spots of dark tan. The tan normally appears just on the legs toward the bottom.

• **Black and Red**: This color is most commonly associated with West German pedigree lines. This is a beautiful coloration where the tan areas are dark orange-red.

• **Black**: These dogs are all black with no tan at all.

• **Sable**: The average dog owner may not be familiar with this unusual color. It is quite similar to the coat you would see on a coyote. The undercoat is lighter in

color, and the outercoat is tipped with a darker color. The sable can range from a black sable that is darker in color (a lighter undercoat with black over it) to a red sable that is lighter in color (a lighter undercoat with red tones over it).

- **White:** A white coat is not a desirable color for conformation. There are many people who love the white coat of a Shepherd, and although this is not a coat color desired in the German Shepherd Dog breed, attempts are being made to establish white dogs as a separate breed. In Europe, they are commonly known as the Berger Blanc Suisse, and a devoted club in America is establishing White Shepherds as a breed separate from the German Shepherd Dog. Currently, all white Shepherds registered with the AKC are registered as white German Shepherds, and these dogs can be shown in performance events but not in conformation.

There are variations that occur with all the coat colors. A few things you might see as variations of the coat colors:

- **White:** While a solid white dog is not desirable for conformation, some small spots of white often appear. The most common locations are the tip of the tail, the edge of the toes, or the chest. Very small spots often blend into tan as the puppy ages into adulthood. Larger chest spots do not fade. White never blends in on dark dogs, such as all-black dogs—it will always be very visible. Some small areas of white that are not distracting or too large are not disqualifying features in the show ring.
- **Ticking:** This occurs most frequently on females, but some males exhibit it as well. This is gray and/or white hairs that sprinkle throughout the back of the neck and down along the back, following the spine. It occurs in black-and-tan, silver, or red coat colors, and it is not normally apparent in the puppy coat. Ticking develops as the puppy gets his adult hair, and it becomes more prominent as the puppy reaches adulthood. How much ticking a dog may have is all about genetics, so a closer look at the parents will be a good indication.
- **Variations in the saddle:** Black-and-tan Shepherds have a saddle pattern for the black color. It covers their whole back, reminiscent of a saddle on a horse.

The German Shepherd is the only breed allowed to be presented with one rear leg forward and one back at AKC dog shows.

Ideally, this saddle area is a very solid, richly pigmented black color. Often you will find dogs with hairs of other colors that interrupt this black. It is similar to ticking along the back but can occur on the sides of the dog and is usually tan or red. Additionally, in some dogs the undercoat is more apparent and gives the black of the saddle a less saturated appearance.

## BODY

The German Shepherd's body style can range widely, depending on the pedigree and purpose of the individual dog.

### Show Style

Dogs who come from conformation or show lines usually have a prettier body outline and style but are more extreme in rear angulation than many of the working-line dogs. These show-line dogs also have more slope to their topline (the point of the back from the shoulders down to the tail). This is often referred to as the "show-style" German Shepherd. If the dog's hips are healthy, generally these dogs are physically fine. However, the stamina level and jumping ability of show-style dogs are affected. They don't make as good a working dog, herding dog, or agility dog as do working-style dogs.

### Working Style

Working-line dogs (and there is more than one style within this, too) are function over form—meaning that the way the dog looks is secondary to the way the dog works. Working dogs are more square in body shape (level backed) and have little rear angulation.

One body issue that can arise from some working lines is that the back, instead of sloping naturally from the shoulders to the tail, can rise in the middle. This means that the point at the shoulder and the point at the tail are both lower than the point at the middle of the back, creating a slight upside-down "U" shape. This is not as attractive, and there is also some concern as to long-term back health with this curved style.

### Stance

The way the German Shepherd stands is a very breed-specific trait. He tends to stand with one rear leg pulled slightly in from the other one. In fact, when the breed is shown in AKC shows, it is the only breed that is not squarely "stacked" (the proper show stance) but is instead presented with one rear leg forward and one back. You'll notice that Shepherds often choose to stand this way without anyone posing them.

## LIVING WITH THE GERMAN SHEPHERD DOG

The German Shepherd is a fabulous dog to live with. He is an excellent dog for an active person or family who wants an intelligent and loyal family member.

## PERSONALITY

I haven't yet met a German Shepherd I don't like! There is something magnificent about this breed, and those who have lived with one know they are truly special. However, that doesn't mean they are the right dog for every person.

### Loyalty

As a general rule, there is no dog more loyal to his person than this breed. He bonds extremely closely to his owner. It is not unusual for a German Shepherd to pick a favorite within a family, but he will still be close with everyone.

### Aloofness

He is a friendly dog but not a social butterfly, particularly as an adult dog. The standard says that a correct German Shepherd personality should include

**Protectiveness**

German Shepherds are natural guardians. If you're not prepared to live with a protective dog, this isn't the breed for you.

aloofness, and this is true for the breed. Being aloof doesn't mean the dog isn't friendly, but generally it means that whether he chooses to be petted or interact with new people is up to him. He will often say hello, perhaps solicit a pet, and then go about whatever he wants to. German Shepherds are not like Golden Retrievers or Labrador Retrievers, who love having affection from strangers lavished on them.

### Protective Instinct

German Shepherds are always watching. This is a key component of the breed as a guard dog. It is not something that is taught but is an intrinsic part of the dog. You will find that they will scan an area with their eyes, take note of new people or animals that enter an area and watch them move about, and become alert if something seems out of place. This is a perfectly natural part of the German Shepherd and is a desirable trait.

Many people who own this breed wonder whether their dog would ever protect them at all, because he is friendly with strangers and shouldn't be aggressive. But don't assume that because he treats invited guests in a friendly manner, they would be welcome without your presence! I've known many dogs who exhibit this classically. One such case was an adult male dog who allowed a guest in his home and spent the whole evening with her. The guest then retreated to a basement bedroom to spend the night. When she got up in the middle of the

Don't be surprised if your German Shepherd follows you from room to room— just to keep watch over his "flock."

## Dog Tale

Remember how large your adult German Shepherd will be! I've had more than one 90-pound (41 kg) boy who thought my lap still looked like a good spot, even as an adult. I've had to cut off the lap behavior before four months of age to avoid this.

night to use the upstairs bathroom, the dog quickly met her there and wouldn't allow her to leave the space until his owner woke up and approved of the guest. Anyone not prepared to live with and handle this protective nature should not own a German Shepherd Dog. Proper training and solid genetics make an exceptionally trustworthy dog, but the protective instinct is always present.

### Keeping Watch

Another thing that is second nature for the breed is keeping watch over you. He'll move from one area to another right along with you. If he is separated from you for too long, he will come and check on you. It's not that he is a "Velcro breed" who needs constant attention, but he wants to know where you are. This is partly what makes him an effective guard dog, but this is also a large component of the herding instinct—to always remain with the flock. Sometimes he will position himself at the entrance of a room to keep watch. Playing games of hide-and-seek with a new puppy intensifies this trait and makes training even easier.

### Noise

German Shepherds bark but usually not excessively. They will bark at people or animals that pass by your property. Some have a higher level of territorialness, which will increase the amount of barking. Left unsupervised in a yard, this issue can intensify and may create a problem behavior.

You will find that German Shepherds whine more than anything. Whining is used to express happiness, frustration, excitement, nervousness, and just about any other emotion!

## COMPANIONABILITY

The German Shepherd gets along with just about everyone, but individual dogs must be exposed to many different people and animals during the highest period of socialization (8–12 weeks) and continuing thereafter.

### Prey Drive

Most German Shepherds get along well with other animals, such as cats and other dogs, but there are some exceptions. Because the German Shepherd is a working breed, there are variations in individual dogs. All members of the breed have what is known as prey drive, or the desire to chase moving objects. The degree of prey drive is relative to the individual dog, but working lines usually have a higher level of prey drive. Dogs with low prey-drive levels chase moving objects very little or not at all. Medium-drive dogs will chase these objects but will stop short of hurting them. Very high-drive dogs are generally not suitable for homes with small animals, because the chasing game often ends with someone hurt or killed. These dogs can't handle running cats or small dogs without viewing them as potential prey. That's why it is important to select a puppy from a knowledgeable breeder. Be honest about what other animals the puppy will be living with and what your needs are to make sure that a puppy is properly matched to your family. A quality breeder will never allow you to have a puppy who is more than you can handle in terms of drive levels.

## With Cats

If your dog is good with your particular cats, never assume he will also be good with strange cats. Unfamiliar cats won't be viewed as "his cats," and he will chase and aggressively run them off the property. Always be careful when introducing new cats into your home.

## With Birds

It is much more difficult to pair a German Shepherd with birds than with cats. They have been known to kill chickens and other birds that move erratically. Once the dog has killed a bird, it is likely to continue the behavior. If you plan to try to keep a German Shepherd with a bird, it is advisable to have a very low-drive puppy or select an older dog from a rescue organization. You will have a far greater reliability with an established older dog who has demonstrated no interest in chasing birds.

German Shepherds who have been well socialized with other dogs will be dog-compatible canines.

## With Dogs

It is key for this breed to be socialized with other dogs from puppyhood on.

German Shepherds make wonderful babystitters and bond very tightly to children.

Take training classes, take your dog to lots of pet-friendly places, find suitable dog playmates for your dog, etc. German Shepherds may not be dog friendly if they have not had opportunities to meet other dogs and different types of breeds. He needs to view strange dogs as harmless and not potential threats. The occasional dog-aggressive German Shepherds are usually individuals who haven't had lots of positive exposures to other dogs. If you put the work in, your dog will be a friendly and dog-compatible canine, which allows you to have more than one canine housemate.

## With Children

The German Shepherd is generally excellent with children, if raised with proper exposure to them. They make wonderful babysitters and bond very tightly to children. My trusted babysitter when I was a child was an adult male German Shepherd. There are many stories of this breed protecting their child charges and keeping them out of trouble, but just as with any breed of dog, children should never be left unsupervised with them. Young children, in particular, don't have the capability to know the right way to interact with a dog or how to correctly read a dog's signals.

Some Shepherds will chase children who run and squeal. This is confusing for the dog, as running and squealing will activate their herding nature and prey drive. They will circle the children and attempt to control their running. Nipping can occur if the children don't stop running. For this reason, it is easier to have a German Shepherd with a child at least over the age of 6 or 7.

## ENVIRONMENT

The German Shepherd can fit in anywhere! He will live happily in any environment, from urban and suburban to country, so long as he is properly exercised each and every day through walking, playing, and other activities. He doesn't have to have a lot of indoor space or a large outdoor area, but the more space you have, the easier it will be to wear him out.

**BE AWARE!**
Exercising your dog every day helps prevents many unwanted behaviors like hyperactivity, destruction, and barking.

A fenced yard is a requirement if you plan to allow your dog off-leash outdoors. He has the potential to chase cars, bikers, and joggers, so he must be kept safe. The fence should be at least 4 feet (1 m) tall, as German Shepherds can jump and climb fences. But even 4 feet (1 m) may not be tall enough, because if he is left alone in the yard, is bored, and is unsupervised, he just might decide to jump the fence. A 6-foot-tall (2 m) privacy fence is best in order to avoid him climbing over or jumping out.

The German Shepherd Dog wants and needs to be with his family. This is not a breed of dog who should be left to languish outdoors alone. Don't consider purchasing a German Shepherd solely as an outdoor guard dog. Add a German Shepherd to your life only if you intend for him to be a valued member of the family.

## EXERCISE REQUIREMENTS

The German Shepherd cannot be left without exercise for long durations of time. It is essential that he is exercised every day or you run the risk of a hyperactive or destructive dog. If you don't enjoy taking a walk each day, playing with your dog, or spending time with him, this is not the breed for you. He is not for decoration; he is a working breed.

Walking is the most common and easiest way to exercise a German Shepherd. He can make a good jogging partner, but you should never, ever jog with your dog until he is at least one to one and a half years old, as his joints are still developing. A heavy regime of running or jumping prior to this time can permanently damage his elbows and hips.

You can incorporate other activities into your dog's life to fulfill the exercise requirements. Vigorous playtime of fetch or tug can be an added part of the exercise regime. German Shepherds just like to be part of what's going on, so consider how you can incorporate your dog into your life and you'll find lots of way to exercise him.

It is essential that the German Shepherd is exercised every day.

## TRAINABILITY

This is a wonderful dog to train. They are so versatile and want so much to work and please that not training your German Shepherd is a travesty. They excel at obedience work as well as additional activities, such as agility, tracking, herding, and Schutzhund. Many breed enthusiasts say that the breed might not be the best in every venue, but there is no other breed as capable of performing in so many capacities. This is why the German Shepherd Dog continues to be one of the most utilized working dogs.

There is one misconception about training this breed. Many people assume that because he is a large, strong breed with a guarding instinct, he must be trained with harsh methods or heavy hands. This is totally false! This is a sensitive breed that is very attuned to your body language and emotions—he is excellent at reading your moods. The best method for training your dog is positive reinforcement (which we'll discuss further in Chapter 7). German Shepherds respond very well to this method of rewarding good behavior with something the dog enjoys, like treats or play. They do require a strong, consistent leader, but this doesn't mean harsh methods, dominance rolls, or other "alpha" establishing behaviors. Instead, it simply means establishing rules, consistently enforcing them, and developing a manner of communication so the dog always knows what to expect. German Shepherds thrive on routine—they need it. If you are a clear communicator, your dog will thank you.

Training is very important with this breed, and it is best to begin training your puppy as soon as he comes home. Start with puppy kindergarten classes and continue training through adulthood. The Association of Pet Dog Trainers (APDT) is the best place to begin your search for training options. Their website (www.apdt.com) has a membership directory that will help you locate someone in your area.

The sky is the limit with a German Shepherd, so if you're looking for an all-around great dog to train, this dog more than meets the challenge.

**Budget Co n** [...]
Everything is b [...] i [...]
with a Germ an [...]
Shepherd! Ta k [...]
add up what it [...]
care for a lar g [...]
German She ph [...]
require a lot o [...]
food and su pp [...]
to properly ca [...]
them, so be su [...]
budget enou g [...]
to do the jo b.

# SUPPLIES
# FOR YOUR GERMAN
# SHEPHERD DOG

**B**ringing a German Shepherd into your life, whether a new puppy or an adult dog, is an exciting time. It is always best to obtain your supplies before you bring your new dog home so that you are ready. There are a lot of things you will want to have on hand along the journey with your new dog. Following are just a few of the items you will want to obtain.

## BABY GATES

Baby gates are a must-have item when housetraining your new puppy or dog. These are useful for blocking off doorways or open areas so that you can keep the puppy near you. It will be imperative that you fully supervise your new puppy or dog at all times until he is fully housetrained. Baby gates allow you to supervise more efficiently.

They are also effective to keep your puppy out of trouble! Many puppies will tear off around the house and try to disappear to where you won't find them. The gate will help keep the dog out of areas you don't want him in.

Additionally, if you are a mixed household that includes cats, I highly recommend using baby gates for your cats. Create a room or area that is dog-free for your cat by setting up a baby gate across the doorway. This room should have your cat's bedding, food and water, litter boxes, and toys inside of it.

German Shepherds can climb or jump over most baby gates (and fences too!), but if the boundary is taught early, it is generally respected. You can purchase baby gates that are taller or ones that have vertical bars instead of wire mesh squares. These are harder to climb or jump.

## BED

Where you want your dog to ultimately sleep and spend time is an individual choice. A German Shepherd is perfectly happy lounging on floors, a couch, or a bed. It is important to offer him a space that is not on hard flooring, so if your floors are hardwood or tile, a few beds throughout the house may be a good option for your dog, especially if you prefer that he not be on your furniture.

You will need a large bed! Try to find one with a removable, washable cover—and the more stuffing, the better. There are numerous therapeutic beds available that offer options for older, arthritic pets.

> **Budget Concerns**
>
> Everything is bigger with a German Shepherd! Take time to add up what it costs to care for a large breed. German Shepherds require a lot of food and supplies to properly care for them, so be sure you budget enough money to do the job.

Buy your puppy's supplies before you bring him home.

Additionally, German Shepherds, especially all black or very dark ones, get warm in the outdoor heat of summer. A pet bed made specifically for cooling is a welcome option.

## BITTER APPLE

Bitter apple spray is a necessity for any new puppy owner. This product will help you get through the period of teething, when your puppy thinks everything looks suitable to go inside his mouth. It doesn't normally stain or hurt items it is sprayed on, but the bitter taste will deter your puppy from chewing. It is most effective when wet, which means you will need to reapply to those areas your puppy wants to chew frequently.

## CAR SAFETY

Think ahead to car travel with your dog. Crates are best for long trips, but most people don't want to use a crate for errands around town and short trips to the park. However, you still want both your dog and you to be safe. It is not safe to have your dog freely moving around the car and potentially interrupting your driving. In the event of an accident, a loose dog could be gravely injured.

You have a couple of options for short drives: The first is to seatbelt your dog into a back seat. Most dog seatbelt systems consist of a harness that latches the dog right into your car seatbelt, locking him into place. The second option is to install a pressure-mounted car divider that can be placed behind the driver and passenger seat. This keeps your dog behind you at all times, allowing you to focus on driving.

A buckle collar is a good choice for everyday use.

## COLLAR

You should get two types of collars: a regular everyday collar and a collar for training. An adjustable, snap or buckle collar works best for your everyday collar. You might need to purchase more than one of these for your growing puppy.

You'll also need a collar for training and for taking your dog on walks. I recommend a martingale-style collar (also called limited-slip collar). This is the best all-purpose training collar and, unlike choke chains or pinch collars, is impossible to harm your dog with. Plus, because of the way it works, it is almost impossible for a dog to slip his collar off by backing out of it, which can happen with a buckle collar. As with any training collar, it should never be left on an unattended dog or used as an everyday collar.

## CRATE

Not everyone likes using a crate, but it is the most useful tool for housetraining a dog. It is also useful for a puppy or young adult dog who is not yet trustworthy in the house without chewing everything up! You will want to purchase a crate that is size appropriate. You want only enough room for the puppy to stand up, turn around, sit, and lie down in. This means you'll either need to purchase more than one crate or purchase one with a divider that makes it possible to expand the size as the dog grows. *Do not* create your own divider! For safety's sake, use only a divider that is professionally manufactured for your specific crate.

German Shepherds like to be able to see what is happening in their world. This means a wire crate is your best option. It allows your dog to see out of it easily, and it offers better ventilation to help keep your dog cooler while he's in it.

Keep in mind that crates are not to be used for long durations of time. This means that your puppy or dog shouldn't be crated for more than four to six hours at any stretch of time without being taken out. The general rule for the length of time a puppy should be crated is the age of the puppy in months plus one. My rule is asking a three-month-old puppy to go only about two to three hours at a time. By four months, the puppy should be able to wait four to five hours. If you're not able to do this, you may need to consider an alternative to the crate.

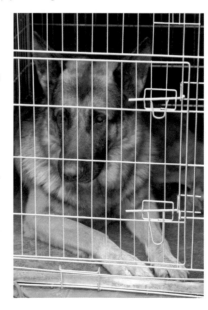

Keeping your dog crated in the car is the best option for long car rides.

## EXERCISE PEN

An exercise pen (or ex-pen) is an excellent option when a crate isn't. It is also a good

choice for those who don't really like the idea of the crate. An exercise pen is simply a puppy playpen.

They come in metal and plastic, are easy to set up, are temporary, and provide your dog with more space than a typical crate does. You need to be careful about what kind you purchase. If your dog is adept at jumping, you will want one that is a bit taller. Some ex-pens are sturdier than others, so check that out too. A German Shepherd puppy may be able to jump onto lighter types and tip them over.

You can set up the pen in an area without carpeting and place pee pads inside. This way, your puppy will have a place to go potty while you are away. Then, over the next few weeks, reduce the number of pads on the floor until you have only one down. This will be the one your puppy will use.

Using pee pads inside an exercise pen will not interfere with training your puppy to go outdoors for potty. You'll use them only inside the pen, and as your dog ages, they won't be necessary at all.

Exercise pens can also be used for puppy playtime in a confined area. If you're not able to adequately supervise him or would like to take him to an outside area that isn't fenced, an exercise pen can be quickly set up and used for this purpose.

## FOOD AND WATER BOWLS

German Shepherds are large dogs and require larger bowls than the average dog. It might be advisable to consider purchasing an elevated feeder for your dog's bowls. German Shepherds are susceptible to a condition known as bloat. Bloat is an emergency situation, and while researchers and veterinarians are not 100 percent sure what the causes of this life threatening problem are, some speculate that using a raised feeder may be beneficial for reducing air intake.

Additionally, if your puppy or dog inhales food very quickly at mealtime, you will want to slow him down. You can try using a special bowl or purchase a specially made obstacle that fits in any standard bowl to slow down the intake of food.

## IDENTIFICATION

Every dog's collar should have an ID tag on it that contains the current information of the owner. Make sure to always keep this information current! This ID tag is the first thing people will look for if your dog is lost. You can also purchase a specially made collar with your information printed directly on it.

In addition to an ID tag, you should opt for a more permanent form of identification. When he's old enough, your dog should get a microchip implanted in his body by your veterinarian. If you've adopted your dog, many shelters and rescue groups offer this service as part of the adoption fee or for a nominal fee.

If your dog's collar or tag becomes lost (or if someone should remove them), a microchip is permanent identification. The implanted chip can be scanned by a special machine, and the chip number is linked to an owner's information. All shelters will routinely scan a stray pet for a microchip before he is offered for adoption or euthanasia. Veterinarians also own the scanning equipment and check stray dogs that come into their office. However, just having the chip implanted isn't enough—don't forget to have the registration paperwork filed! The microchip is only good if the paperwork is filed with the registering company.

If your German Shepherd is lost, your best bet for getting him back is using an ID tag on a collar (because this is what the average person looks for) and a microchip (because this is what shelters and vets look for).

## GROOMING SUPPLIES

For the most part, the German Shepherd is a true "wash and wear" breed. They don't need frequent baths, and they don't need haircuts. However, they need their toenails trimmed regularly, and they shed a lot.

- The most important grooming tool you'll want to purchase is a deshedding tool that helps remove all the dead undercoat but doesn't damage the topcoat.
- For cutting toenails, you will want a good pair of large-breed toenail clippers. They come in two main varieties: scissor-style and guillotine style. I prefer the scissor-style as I find them easier to handle and use.
- You will also need a dog toothbrush (or a human soft-bristled toothbrush) as well as toothpaste made specifically for dogs. Never use human toothpaste for your dog. There are newer products on the market (including liquids and gels) that clean your dog's teeth without brushing, so this might be an option worth looking into.
- A quality shampoo and conditioner will be necessary for the few baths that you will give your dog. A product made for dogs is best, as the pH will be correct. Many people with German Shepherds like to select a brand that offers color enhancers, mainly black, to make their Shepherd's coat really shine.
- Waterless shampoo comes in sprays or foams and is beneficial for times in between baths. You can purchase bath wipes made for

You may find a scissors-style nail trimmer the easiest to use.

pets, but they are far more expensive than waterless shampoo.

- There are numerous scented sprays, many of them containing leave-in conditioners, which can be used to take away any doggy smell.

## LEASH

A standard 6-foot-long (2 m) leash is best for training and working with your dog. I also suggest this for your everyday walks in order to ensure a more controlled walk. This leash should be used for walks on sidewalks, in busy locations, and for taking your dog into stores and/or events. If you like to walk on trails or in the great outdoors, a retractable leash might be a good second leash to have on hand. You will also want to have a longer training leash (anywhere from 15 to 30 feet [5 to 9 m] in length) or a check cord. This will be a valuable tool for training *come* and *stay*.

## TOYS AND CHEWS

A variety of toys are good to have on hand if your particular German Shepherd likes to play, but not all of them do. I find that the fuzzy squeaky toys are the best option, and many non-toy-playing dogs like to play with these from time to time.

You need to supervise your dog with his toys. It is not uncommon to have a German Shepherd squeak a toy to death or begin to dismantle it and pull stuffing out! Too much ingested stuffing, fabric, or a squeaker could cause an intestinal blockage.

For dogs who absolutely love toys, a variety of rubber squeaky balls is necessary. These are excellent for outdoor play and long-distance throwing. Be very careful about the size of the balls. Many German Shepherds will hold the ball in their mouth, repeatedly squeaking it, and may do so while throwing their head back. If a ball is too small, it could lodge in his throat. Tennis balls and similar-sized balls are not good toys for this breed.

For those dogs who don't seem to like toys, you can often encourage play by creating a lure toy. Some German Shepherds may like a toy only when it is moving, because it simulates natural prey drive. Be aware that an adopted, older German Shepherd may come to you not knowing how to play at all.

Take a fuzzy toy and tie it to a piece of rope, then tie it to a dowel. You'll end up with a toy that is similar-looking to a cat toy on a pole. You can make the toy zip around erratically, which makes it far more interesting for many dogs. You can also tie the toy onto a fishing pole line. (If you do this, don't use any hooks!) It allows you to cast the line quite a distance away and quickly zip it about and reel it in.

It is a good idea to rotate all your dog's toys. Many German Shepherds will become bored with the same options, but if you rotate them and have only so many out at any given time, they seem fresher and more fun.

## ACTIVITY TOYS

Treat-dispenser toys are excellent for preoccupying your dog and working his brain. These toys can be filled with small treats or with your dog's kibble. In fact, you can feed your dog a whole meal this way. If you have a dog who inhales his food or is hard to slow down, you can feed him his dinner through a treat-dispenser toy, and he will get only a small amount at any given time.

## CHEWS

Plenty of chew toys will be necessary, especially when a German Shepherd is a puppy or is fairly young. Look for items that really allow him to express his urge to chew in an appropriate way. Avoid products that can cause a blockage, are hard to digest, or can cause an upset stomach. Instead, look for easily digestible items. Good options can be things like bully sticks and other meat-product chews. These are very digestible and easy to chew but are long lasting.

German Shepherds also like to chew on natural bones. The best options are knuckle bones and hollow shank bones, which hold up better to prolonged chewing compared with other options. Knuckle bones can be purchased raw and need to be refrigerated. You can also purchase raw knuckle bones from a local butcher. I like to fill the center of a hollow shank bone with some type of food item. Sometimes I spread peanut butter inside. I also like to use canned food mixed with a tiny bit of water. I freeze these bones to make a cold treat!

Edible manufactured dental bones can also be a good option. How long each one lasts varies, based on the treat item and how aggressive a chewer your dog is.

Always supervise your dog while he's enjoying a chew. While most items are safe for your dog to chew on, there is always the possibility of a dog trying to chew more than he can at one time. If the chew item becomes too small for chewing, be sure to take it away so the temptation to swallow it whole is removed.

## TRAINING SUPPLIES

The German Shepherd Dog must be trained—it makes him easier to live with and gives him rules to live by. Ideally, training should begin when you bring your new dog home.

Everyone should take their new dog to a training class taught with a positive trainer, but you can purchase a few supplies prior to the start of class.

- The standard 6-foot (2 m) leash will also be necessary for training. Many people prefer leather leashes to nylon. My favorite style of leash is made for working dogs. It is a cotton leash with rubber woven throughout. In my opinion, this is the best leash in the whole world for a large-breed dog and is the only leash I use.
- You will also want to have a longer training leash or line (as discussed previously).
- I would also suggest investing in a few books to learn a bit more about how to train a dog. Training books from Karen Pryor and Brenda Aloff are excellent starting points for learning about clicker training and positive reinforcement.

A longer training line can be a valuable tool for training *come* and *stay*.

# FEEDING YOUR GERMAN SHEPHERD DOG

Y**ou've probably heard the expression "You are what you eat" used about people, but it's just as true for our dogs. What your dog eats is directly related to his overall health. It shows in something as simple as the glossiness of his coat as well as in things we can't see, like bone development, organ health, and the effects of the aging process. It's essential to understand the best way to feed your German Shepherd to help keep him healthy.

## NUTRIENTS FOR A HEALTHY DIET

Just like our own food, it is important that a dog's diet be properly balanced to provide the correct level of nutrition for our dogs. Too much of any one particular vitamin or mineral can cause problems, and too much protein can be problematic, especially for puppies.

The safest way to know you are providing the right nutrients is to feed your dog a food that has been developed and tested to be nutritionally balanced and complete. These claims will always be identified on the container of food. A balanced food shouldn't require any supplementation with vitamins.

What should be in a balanced diet? All foods should contain proper amounts of carbohydrates, proteins, minerals, vitamins, fats, and moisture or water.

### PROTEIN

The protein content of a diet is particularly important. Protein supplies the dog with energy and is essential to his development. It provides him with over 20 essential amino acids that a dog's body doesn't naturally produce but must have in his diet.

While dogs are not obligate carnivores, meaning they don't have to eat meat to survive, meat is the best source of protein for them. Protein can also come in plant form, such as soybean meal. A food should have multiple sources of protein so that all nutritional needs are met and the proteins complement one another.

Another factor to consider with protein is its digestibility. Some proteins are more digestible and therefore more useful to

A healthy, glossy coat is a sign of a good diet.

the dog. Animal-based proteins are more digestible for the dog and have more value.

A good dog food should provide your dog with anywhere from between 24 to 29 percent protein. Grain-free foods have a much higher protein level, around 50 percent. This extra protein provides the essential amino acids, but then extra protein sources are broken down into energy.

When reading a food label, meat-based proteins should appear high in the ingredient list and should definitely be the first ingredient listed.

## PUPPY POINTER

German Shepherd puppies shouldn't be fed too much protein in their food. Feed only large-breed-formula puppy foods or begin changing to a quality adult food.

## CARBOHYDRATES

Carbohydrates are useful for a dog in two ways: energy and fiber. Carbohydrates are one of the primary sources of instant energy for a dog, but more complex carbohydrates also help provide fiber for proper gastrointestinal health. Brown rice or oats is a good source of carbohydrates, and it is best to avoid foods that rely on corn or simple wheat as the main sources.

## FATS

Too much fat definitely isn't a good thing, but every dog's diet needs fat. Fat provides flavoring, and it serves as an additional energy source for the dog. Fat also provides necessary essential fatty acids that help to maintain a dog's skin and coat health, among other things.

### Coat Check

A German Shepherd's coat becomes glossy and smooth when fed a nutritionally complete diet. If your dog's coat lacks shine, look to his diet for a cause.

## MINERALS

Minerals are an essential part of a dog's diet. They are responsible for many aspects of a dog's health, such as bone health, reactions in muscles and nerves, normal hormone production, oxygen levels, helping the body to retain proper levels of moisture, and more. A dog has to have correct levels of minerals, because not enough of one or too much of another can affect the whole system.

Minerals can be broken down into two types: those that are needed in higher amounts and those that require lower levels. Minerals like magnesium, calcium, potassium, sodium, phosphorus, and chloride are all minerals that are needed by a dog's body in higher levels. Additional minerals that are required in smaller amounts, although still important, are manganese, selenium, iron, copper, zinc, and iodine.

Each mineral is essential for the dog's growth, development, and proper health. A diet must be balanced in minerals, so food that has been carefully researched yields a proper balance and shouldn't require supplementation.

## VITAMINS

Vitamins work for our dogs just like they do for us. Research has shown they are complex, are needed in smaller amounts than other items in the diet, and are essential to a body's health. There are two types of vitamins: water soluble and fat soluble. Water-soluble vitamins are excreted from the body if not used; fat-soluble vitamins are stored in fatty tissue, which means an excess can lead to toxicity.

The necessary vitamins for a dog are exactly the same as the ones suggested for our intake. The fat-soluble kind include vitamins K, D, E, and A. The water-soluble vitamins essential for good health are vitamin C and the B-complex vitamins.

Make sure your dog has access to fresh, clean water.

There has even been research about adding extra vitamin C to a dog's diet to help curb pain from hip dysplasia.

## WATER

Water is absolutely essential to good health. Water is used in dry commercial foods, but the moisture content is always higher in canned foods. Your dog will need to drink more water if he eats only dry kibble. Whatever you choose to feed your dog, you need to make sure your dog has access to and is drinking fresh, clean water.

## COMMERCIAL FOODS

The best option for feeding your German Shepherd Dog is a diet primarily based in dry dog food, also called kibble. Kibble from a high-quality food manufacturer will be nutritionally complete and meet the most current requirements of appropriate levels of nutrients for your dog.

Kibble is a convenient way to feed your dog and is easily accessible. It doesn't require refrigeration and is easy to store. It helps to promote dental health by grinding away at the plaque on teeth while your dog eats. Kibble is also easy to use as a potential training reward item.

It is perfectly okay to add in other ingredients with your kibble. Some canned foods, which are moist, can be excellent options. They are higher in protein and meat value and provide a tasty addition to your dog's diet. It is advisable to add only one or two tablespoons of canned food to each of your German Shepherd's meals to avoid adding too many calories and risking weight gain.

I wouldn't advise a semi-moist food, as they are primarily comprised of filler grain binders and artificial colorants that your dog just doesn't need. They may be inexpensive to purchase, but they aren't worth the money.

Kibble (dry food) is a convenient way to feed your dog and is easily accessible.

I did a lot of research about nutrition and types of dog foods when deciding what to feed my German Shepherds. I settled on a high-quality kibble that my dogs enjoy, and I add whole, fresh-food items for added variety and nutrition. My dogs love cooked vegetables like green beans, broccoli, corn, peas, and sweet potatoes. Fish is also a nice, easy, and inexpensive addition. A frozen fish fillet can be quickly microwaved to flaky perfection, and my dogs love it.

## WHAT TO LOOK FOR

Consider the following when choosing the best kibble option for your German Shepherd Dog:

- Meat proteins should be listed as the very first ingredient and should appear more than once in the first five ingredients. They should be a clearly identified meat like chicken, lamb, fish meal, etc.
- Avoid by-products. These are the bits and pieces that aren't suitable for human consumption and can include a wide range of animal parts. The label never clearly identifies what the by-products actually are, so you'll have no way to know if it's hair, beaks, intestines, etc.
- Avoid fillers. Fillers like corn and wheat are inexpensive for a pet food manufacturer to use. If you look closely at the label of less expensive pet foods, you'll find that corn or wheat will rank highly on the list of ingredients and probably appear more than once. Dogs receive little nutrition or useable protein from these types of fillers, so feeding a dog food that is high in these ingredients doesn't provide him with enough of what he needs.
- Consider a product without wheat, corn, or soy. If your dog has itchy skin or allergies, one of these ingredients might be the culprit. There are several brands available that routinely produce food without these ingredients.
- Look for the use of natural preservatives like vitamin E. More foods are moving toward including natural preservatives, which is better for the dog's health. Natural preservatives keep a bag of food fresher for longer, but the food will still be perishable. Artificial preservatives, such as ethoxyquin, keep a food stable longer but have been linked to cancer in various studies.
- Avoid artificial colors. Our dogs don't care what color the food is! These

artificial colorants don't add to our dog's health, and there is much debate as to their suitability in our dog's food (and our own).

## READING THE LABEL

It's not a good idea to select a food based solely on which bag looks the most attractive or which commercial you like best on TV. The manufacturer can put anything on the front of the bag or show you anything in an advertisement, but it may have little to do with what is actually in the bag!

Pet food labels are regulated primarily by the Federal Department of Agriculture (FDA) and the Association of American Feed Control Officials (AAFCO), so all manufacturers must follow certain rules. According to the FDA, a manufacturer is required to list ingredients in the order of importance by weight. This means that the very first ingredient listed is the heaviest item by weight and is the most predominant item in the food.

Home-cooked diets incorporate various proteins, carbohydrates, and vegetables.

However, this can be slightly misleading, because a whole meat listed first also includes the approximately 75 percent of water that it is made of. When cooked, this water value dissipates, which means that the ingredient may not actually be the largest component. This is why it is important to note the order of the ingredients. If you see meat listed several times, this will help indicate a higher overall level of meat-based protein in the food.

Also keep in mind a manufacturer can say a lot of misleading things on a package that can be misinterpreted. For example, many pet foods tout the product as a "premium" diet or an "ultra" diet. However, there are no requirements that must be met to put this wording on a package, so a self-identified "premium" diet may have no more benefits to it than any other. The same goes for a food that is listed as "natural." There is no current definition of what is "natural," and organic foods aren't regulated in the pet food industry.

## NON-COMMERCIAL FOODS

Recently, with the many pet food recalls, more people are looking to feed their dog a diet that they prepare themselves. There's been a distinct rise in both home cooking and feeding raw diets for dogs.

### HOME-COOKED

Home-cooked diets are cooked meals that incorporate various proteins, carbohydrates, and vegetables. The recipes often have cutesy-sounding names in cookbooks, and they are easy to find on the Internet. But are they safe to feed your dog?

There are many holistic veterinarians who believe that home-cooked meals can be a beneficial part of a dog's diet. Since the food is not cooked at super-high heat levels, the enzymes aren't killed off. And you have quality control over the ingredients and know exactly what goes into your dog's food.

One problem that may arise is owners who simply put ingredients together and call it a dinner. That will yield a nutritional imbalance. Home-cooked meals require supplementation to ensure the proper levels of vitamins and minerals. Dogs also need to have variety, so it is advisable to rotate recipes and not feed the same meal each time.

**BE AWARE!**

A nutritionally incomplete diet can cause your German Shepherd a lot of problems, especially in young dogs. Always feed the best food you can afford that is nutritionally complete to maintain a healthy dog.

One of the challenges of preparing your own meals is getting your dog to eat everything. You might find times when your dog doesn't want to eat particular vegetables or grains, or that he doesn't like particular textures.

Any home-cooked recipes should be designed by a veterinarian or nutritionist. There are books available to help design a proper diet, but before embarking on this type of diet for your German Shepherd, consult with your veterinarian to determine the suitability.

## RAW

Raw diets, which are based on feeding dogs raw meat, have also grown in popularity. These diets require additional supplementation to ensure that there are proper vitamins and minerals available.

Some German Shepherds who suffer from pancreatic enzyme insufficiency are given a raw diet to help compensate for the dog's enzyme issues. However, this should not be a diet of choice for a growing German Shepherd puppy, as too much protein is a very bad thing for a large-breed puppy.

Supporters of a raw diet believe that it is a more natural diet for our dogs. Raw meat contains enzymes that stay intact because there is no heat applied, unlike commercial dog foods. Perhaps one of the best advantages of a raw diet is dental health. Raw bones contain a lot of tissue and ligaments that grind against a dog's teeth while chewing, helping to keep them clean.

Don't allow your dog to perform strenuous exercise right before or after he eats—it may help prevent bloat.

A dog fed solely raw meat runs the risk of not having enough variety. Also, if the owner doesn't do the proper research about what is nutritionally necessary, the dog may end up lacking a properly balanced diet. There is also some concern of bacterial contamination for the human caregiver, so care should be taken around the elderly, infants and children, pregnant women, and anyone with a compromised immunity.

A better alternative, if one is interested in feeding a raw diet, is to give a properly balanced meal as the primary source of food and provide the raw portion of the diet as a treat. (The raw portion should be less than 25 percent of the overall diet for a treat.) Do this by giving your dog safe raw bones, such as knuckle bones. German Shepherds love these as treats, and there is the added bonus of really clean teeth as a result of the chewing action.

## WHEN AND HOW MUCH TO FEED

The German Shepherd should always be fed on schedule and more than once a day. It is important that you feed your dog two smaller meals a day and avoid allowing him to run, play, or be too active prior to dinner. Your dog should remain relatively calm for at least an hour following dinner too.

The reason for these precautions is that too much food in the German Shepherd's stomach at one time and too much activity surrounding his mealtimes are possible culprits suspected in bloat (gastric dilatation volvulus). Bloat is a life-threatening situation where a dog's stomach fills with air and becomes twisted. With smaller meals, dogs are better able to process the amounts of food and move them through their system before the next feeding. This means that the stomach doesn't distend itself with too much food and the dog doesn't eat too quickly (ingesting a lot of air) due to excessive hunger at mealtime.

Free feeding, or leaving food available all day, is not recommended. Some German Shepherds can become picky eaters if allowed to free feed. It is best to offer the meals at set times and give him up to 30 minutes to complete eating it. After 30 minutes, take the bowl away.

As an alternative, you can offer some of your dog's kibble in either a treat dispenser toy for mental entertainment or use part of his daily kibble for training exercises. Dogs do very well when required to work for their food. This helps divide the food intake into small portions, gives the dog mental stimulation, and allows you to control how quickly he eats while still getting training exercises done.

## OBESITY

The German Shepherd isn't one of those breeds that retains weight by just looking at food! But that doesn't mean he can't become overweight like so many of our pet dogs are today.

Obesity simply means that a dog is eating more than he should and isn't exercising enough. It's easy to prevent the problem if you know what to look for and quickly change direction in how much you're feeding your dog.

When is a dog obese? An obese dog lacks a waistline after the end of the ribcage. These dogs look like a sausage link all the way from shoulder to rear without any tuck in the waist. Additionally, you can't easily feel the dog's ribs if you rub

Obesity simply means that a dog is eating more than he should and isn't exercising enough.

his side. You should always be able to feel at least the last couple of ribs without fighting through fat to do it! Last, obese dogs generally have excess skin or rolls. In the German Shepherd, these skin rolls are most prominent right behind the elbows and can be easily seen when he sits or moves his arm back to walk.

The German Shepherd dog shouldn't be allowed to carry extra weight. It's not good for his joints and body structure. He should always have a natural waistline. If you notice his waistline start to fade, a diet and lifestyle change is on the way! Gradually reduce the amount of kibble you provide each day at mealtimes. You can add in some vegetables like cooked green beans, carrots, sweet potatoes, and cooked brown rice if you think he is hungry with the reduced food intake. These items add fiber and make him feel full but lack the amount of calories and fat. Also be sure to step up his exercise routine (or start one if you've been lax in walking him regularly). Monitor his weight loss and consult with your vet if you're unsure about what the correct weight should be for your dog.

# GROOMING YOUR GERMAN SHEPHERD DOG

I f you're not okay with finding loose dog hair on your clothes, furniture, or carpeting, then the German Shepherd is not the breed for you! While it is an easy breed to groom and live with, hair will get everywhere—so be prepared to brush a lot.

## WHY IS GROOMING IMPORTANT?

Grooming functions in three very important ways:

**Shedding**

German Shepherds shed a lot! Be prepared to find hair on floors, furniture, and you. If keeping your home hair-free ranks highly on the priority list, this isn't the right breed for you.

1. **Hygiene:** Grooming keeps your dog clean and helps ward off skin conditions, parasites, and other issues that might arise from the accumulation of filth.
2. **Health:** Grooming involves looking at every part of your dog. Dogs who are handled and groomed every week are the ones whose lumps, skin issues, teeth problems, ear infections, and other problems are noticed. The sooner these health risks are noticed, the sooner they can be corrected. Regular grooming will also keep your dog's feet in shape (keeping toenails trimmed properly) and help you keep a check on your dog's weight. Sometimes a full coat will hide whether a dog needs to add weight. On the other hand, sometimes a full coat is blamed for a dog's obesity. When you regularly brush and touch your dog, you have a more accurate idea of whether he is in the target range on weight.
3. **Bonding:** Dogs love to be groomed if it is done regularly. Studies have shown that there are real health benefits—in the way of stress reduction—to both the owner and the dog from the simple act of brushing or petting.

## GROOMING SUPPLIES

Luckily, there aren't too many supplies you'll need for regular grooming of this breed. Here are the basics:

- **Brushing tools:** As your primary grooming tool, I highly recommend a deshedding tool that helps remove all the dead undercoat but doesn't damage the topcoat. A comb and a pin brush will round out your brushing tools.
- **Dental care:** You will need a dog toothbrush (or a soft-bristled human toothbrush) and toothpaste made specifically for dogs. You might also consider some of the newer products for oral hygiene that are applied to reduce plaque buildup.

- **Grooming sprays/products:** A waterless shampoo product (in spray or foam formula) is a good item for the colder winter months when a water bath is impractical. A grooming spray that adds shine or conditions is a nice addition to the brushing routine but not entirely necessary.
- **Ear care:** You will need an all-purpose ear cleaner. Liquid premade ear cleaners are available at pet stores and your veterinarian's office. Ones that aren't alcohol based are gentler on your dog's ears.
- **Toenail tools:** A good pair of large-breed toenail clippers is necessary. I prefer the scissor-style clipper. You'll also want to have styptic powder on hand in case you cut the quick inside the nail at any point.

## COAT AND SKIN CARE

Brushing and bathing your German Shepherd Dog just takes some fairly basic knowledge.

### BRUSHING

Brushing is essential to the German Shepherd. This breed has a double coat, which means that there are two layers to the dog's coat. There is a softer underlayer (or undercoat) that helps insulate the dog. The second layer of coat (or topcoat) is the one you see, and in and adult dog, it should be shiny and different in texture. The natural oils in this layer help to repel some water and keep the undercoat dry.

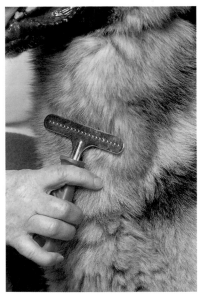

It's imperative to get all the dead coat out while your German Shepherd is blowing his coat.

The German Shepherd sheds year-round, but he has two times each year where he will "blow" his coat, which means the dead undercoat begins to tuft and come out by the handfuls. The worst time for blowing coat will be coming into the warmer months. You will find yourself brushing this dead coat out a few times a week, at least, for a couple of weeks. It is imperative to get *all of this coat out* because it helps the dog get cooler and the dead coat will mat into the remaining hair if it's not taken out. A deshedding tool is the very best tool you can use to get all the dead undercoat out.

For the rest of the year when your dog sheds normally, a pin brush works very well to pull out these loose hairs. How often you should brush your dog depends on how much hair you want to see around the house. A closer-coated German Shepherd has less topcoat and less undercoat, so he sheds less hair. The more fluffy in appearance your Shepherd is, the more coat will be shed regularly. A good brushing at least once a week is helpful to maintain the coat, but you might find the need to brush more frequently to catch the loose hairs.

A comb is the last tool you should need for brushing. This works well for the hairs on the neck and the feathering, or hairs on the dog's rear flanks/legs. This is sometimes the best tool for working through these areas where the hair gets thicker but the area is more sensitive.

### How to Brush

For regular maintenance:

- Take a pin brush and brush in the direction of the hair on your dog.
- Work down the back and sides.
- Lift your dog's head slightly and brush through his neck region. Take care, as this is a more sensitive area. A comb will help you if the area is thick and hard to brush through.
- Be careful when brushing around his stomach or down the backs of his rear legs. These are areas most German Shepherds are more sensitive about.
- Hold his tail while you brush it out. Don't brush hard, as the tail is sensitive down the middle where the bones are.
- When brushing your dog, use the same pressure you would if brushing your own head, and not any harder than that.
- Apply grooming spray or dog leave-in coat conditioner, if desired.

### BATHING

This breed doesn't need to be bathed as frequently as one might think. They are a very clean dog, and their hair stays clean easily. They also do not have a smelly nature to the coat, like some other breeds do.

Bathing shouldn't be done excessively or you will strip the hair of its natural oils and dry the dog's skin out. From spring through fall, I wouldn't bathe your dog more than one time a month, unless he is dirty from rolling in mud or playing in a pond. For dogs who are kept relatively clean and who live indoors, a monthly bath is more than adequate.

In between baths, you can use a quality waterless shampoo. This does an excellent job of removing any oil buildup or dust accumulation. Waterless

The German Shepherd is a clean breed that doesn't need to be bathed often.

shampoo is also recommended for the colder months of the year when bathing is harder to do. You can also use coat conditioners or sprays to give your dog a fresher smell in between baths.

Bathing a German Shepherd can be a bit trickier than smaller breeds. You can either bathe him indoors in your shower or bathtub (but you will need something to catch their hair or risk plugging up your drain), or you can bathe him outdoors in a portable tub or with the hose.

## How to Bathe

Outdoors is often the easiest way to go. To bathe your dog:

- Get your hose handy.
- Ideally, purchase a hookup for an indoor faucet where you can attach your hose to a laundry room or kitchen sink and run it outdoors. This allows you to use warmer water for the bath. You can also purchase a coiled hose, which makes for less of a headache with the hose getting in the way. Ones made for pets come with spray washers on the end and an on/off feature.
- Put your dog's leash and collar on. Either have a second person hold the dog, or tie him to a nearby post or something that he can't move.
- Once the water has been adjusted to the right temperature—lukewarm—begin to wet down the dog.
- Shampoo the dog all over, including down his legs, his stomach, his tail, and his bottom region. I like to use concentrated shampoos that can be diluted with water, which makes it easier to make sure all the soap is removed when rinsing.
- Rinse your dog. If desired, you can mix vinegar with water in a cup and pour it over your dog's coat. Rinse again. The vinegar helps cut the soap if you're not sure you got it all out.
- Apply conditioner evenly all over your dog, and work it in. Rinse.
- Allow your dog to shake excess water off. Towel off remaining moisture. It will take a few hours for your dog to dry, depending on the thickness of his coat and the air temperature. You can use a blow dryer to dry him faster if he is an older dog or if the temperature is cooler.

## DENTAL CARE

Regular care of your dog's teeth is one of the most commonly overlooked parts of grooming. Veterinarians report dental problems like tooth decay and gingivitis as some of the most common health problems they deal with each day. Dental problems don't just affect your dog's mouth or his breath. In fact, the bacteria that accumulate around the teeth can spread throughout his body and affect his organs, causing him system-wide health issues. This becomes an even greater issue in the older dog.

Additionally, a dog who is experiencing tooth decay and loose teeth must also contend with the discomfort that accompanies this problem. It is likely that his appetite will suffer or that he will not chew the food and simply swallow it to avoid chewing. This is also unhealthy for him and could cause other problems like choking, ingesting too much air while eating (which could lead to a very serious health emergency), and indigestion problems.

Ideally, you should brush your dog's teeth once a day, but at least a couple of times a week is necessary. If your dog already has tartar buildup, accumulation of debris around the gumline, or receding gums, a professional cleaning by your veterinarian should be scheduled before starting a routine dental care program.

There are newer products on the market that don't require brushing. Liquid or gel dental products can be applied in the evening so they help clean the teeth while your dog is sleeping. The combination of the natural ingredients in these products helps break up existing plaque and help reduce its formation. These products should be applied a couple of times a week for maintenance.

## HOW TO BRUSH TEETH

- Get your dog used to the taste of the toothpaste first by applying a small amount to the tip of your finger and just allowing him to lick it off.
- Also get him used to being touched around the mouth area. Lift his lips, lightly touch his canines with your finger, etc. Reward him.
- Once he is comfortable with the toothpaste and you touching him, apply a small strip of dog toothpaste to a wet soft-bristled brush.

You can use a finger brush if your dog isn't comfortable with a toothbrush.

- Gently lift his lip and lightly brush along his toothline. Apply no more pressure than you would if brushing your own teeth. You don't need to brush the inside of the teeth, only the surfaces you can see.
- Any sign of bleeding gums means you're either brushing too hard or he already has gum disease.
- If your dog isn't comfortable with the toothbrush, try using a finger toothbrush or even a small, damp washcloth.
- If choosing to use one of the gel products, follow the directions on the product. Generally, you apply a small amount along the gum line. His saliva will spread it throughout his mouth. You can use a brush to apply the product, but it is not necessary.

**BE AWARE!**

Creating a dental cleaning routine will help keep your German Shepherd's teeth white and clean. Use the opportunity to look for any changes in your dog's mouth like growths, spots, discoloration, and chipped or loose teeth.

## EAR CARE

German Shepherds are less prone to ear infections than many other breeds of dogs due to their upright ears, but they should still have their ears cleaned on a regular basis. In humid parts of the country, it is more likely for your dog to develop a possible infection.

A monthly cleaning of your German Shepherd's ears should suffice, unless your dog has a history of ear problems. I like to flush out the dog's ear as part of the cleaning routine to remove as much waxy buildup as possible.

When cleaning his ears, take note of what the ear looks like. If you notice any odors, excessive waxy buildup, dark brown wax, redness, or anything out of the ordinary, have your dog's ears examined by a veterinarian. Ear infections can not only be itchy and painful for your dog, but if left untreated, they can cause hearing loss.

### HOW TO CLEAN EARS

- Start with a good liquid ear cleaner and a clean paper towel or two.
- Gently hold your dog's ear in one hand (you might need a second person to hold your dog's head if he moves).

German Shepherds are less prone to ear infections than many other breeds of dogs due to their upright ears.

- Squeeze just a small amount of the cleaner into your dog's ear.
- Rub the ear at the base and up to the tip to work the cleaner throughout.
- Let go and step back! Allow him to shake his head, which will shake out any dirt or wax too.
- Once he has shaken several times, take your paper towel and lightly dry the inside of the ear, removing the oils and wax. You might want to apply some cleaner to your paper towel to help for oily buildup.
- DO NOT put your finger, the towel, or a Q-tip (or something similar) into the parts of the ear you can't see. This goes down into the ear canal. You can accidentally injure your dog or push any wax buildup further into the ear. Only clean the area you can see in the ear flap.
- Repeat this process for the second ear.

## EYE CARE

There really isn't anything you have to do for your German Shepherd's eyes unless your dog suffers from an eye condition. The only thing this breed deals with is a little eye accumulation (like sleep in the eye).

However, do routinely look at your dog's eyes. Look for possible scratches, debris in the eye, or excessive eye accumulation. Cats or sticks can easily scratch a dog's cornea, and if you notice any whiteness or marks on your dog's eye, have a vet look at this immediately.

Some level of accumulation in the corner of the eyes is normal (just like for people), but if your dog has excessive goo in the corners, if it's thick in nature, or if it's yellow colored, this needs to be looked at by a veterinarian. Your dog's eyes should be clear and relatively accumulation free.

### HOW TO CLEAN EYES
- Dampen a small towel with warm water.
- Gently rub downward and away from the eye with the towel.
- Repeat for the second eye.

Routinely look at your dog's eyes for possible scratches or excessive eye accumulation.

## NAIL CARE

Regular maintenance of your dog's toenails is imperative for foot health. Ideally, your German Shepherd's toenails shouldn't reach the floor at all. They should be trimmed short and be uniform. This helps prevent broken toenails and foot problems from long or curled nails. Long nails will affect your dog's gait and comfort level as well.

Cutting your dog's toenails once a week will keep them in the best condition, but they should be cut at least once every two to three weeks to keep them from getting too long. It is easy to cut your dog's toenails yourself. If you are concerned about how to do it at first, I suggest asking your veterinarian to show you how.

What makes the German Shepherd's toenails a little more difficult to cut is that most of them have solid black nails. This means that you can't see the quick (the vein that runs inside the nail) as easily as you can with white nails. The quick will bleed if you accidentally cut into with your clipper. It is uncomfortable for your dog, and you should try to avoid doing it. If it happens, use a little styptic powder and light applied pressure on the nail to quickly stop the bleeding.

Cutting your dog's toenails weekly reduces the chance of accidentally cutting the quick, because this way you will remove only the tip of the nail. When nails are allowed to grow longer than they should, the quick gets longer too. You'll need to cut more off a longer toenail, which means you are more likely to cut the quick, since it has grown longer too.

## HOW TO CUT TOENAILS

- As soon as you get your puppy or dog, get him used to having his feet touched a lot. Pick up a foot; give him a treat. This helps prepare him for the foot holding necessary in cutting toenails.
- Leave the nail-cutting tools out so that the sight of them is not upsetting.
- Pair up toenail cutting with something positive like food. Prepare enough treats (I use cheese or a meat treat) so that there is at least one treat for each toenail.
- If you have a puppy, you can hold him in your lap (at least for a few weeks). If you have an adult dog, you may need the help of a second person to hold the dog.
- If you find your dog to be a little antsy about the process, you can help take his mind off of it by spreading peanut butter inside a stuffable toy, applying it

to the outside of a chew, or simply getting a big spoonful and have the second person hold it and allow your dog to lick it while you work. This helps him think about something other than cutting toenails.

- Hold his foot in one hand and cut the toenail with the clippers in your other hand. Be careful to take off only a small amount!
- Give him a treat after each cut toenail. This reduces his stress and gives him something to look forward to.
- Make sure you cut the dewclaws. All German Shepherds have dewclaws on their front feet. A dewclaw is a toenail that appears higher on the foot than the others; it is a few inches (cm) up on the inside of each of the front legs. Rarely, some members of the breed have rear dewclaws too (although knowledgeable breeders remove these in young puppies if the trait runs in their line).

## FINDING A PROFESSIONAL GROOMER

This is not a breed that I would recommend using a professional groomer for, unless you are squeamish about cutting toenails. The German Shepherd is an easy breed to groom, especially if you begin a regular routine of grooming your puppy when he is very young and maintain it.

If you decide that you need assistance for cutting toenails, you will want to find a qualified person for grooming. Your veterinarian will offer toenail cutting as a service, and many vets also have professional groomers in their facility. There are also mobile groomers who will come to your home, and many own their own shops.

Ask around for recommendations. People who own small breeds like Toy Poodles, Miniature Schnauzers, or Yorkies must routinely use groomers, and they'll have a good feel for who does a good job. Your breed won't require the same level of grooming, but a good groomer is a good groomer. Do an Internet search to verify that no negative reports have been filed against the grooming shop or any of the groomers.

Make sure to inspect the facility before making an appointment. Some grooming shops allow smoking indoors, which means

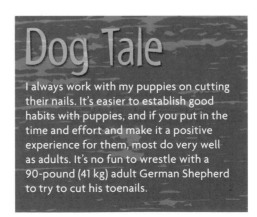

## Dog Tale

I always work with my puppies on cutting their nails. It's easier to establish good habits with puppies, and if you put in the time and effort and make it a positive experience for them, most do very well as adults. It's no fun to wrestle with a 90-pound (41 kg) adult German Shepherd to try to cut his toenails.

Regular maintenance of your dog's toenails is imperative for foot health.

your pet will come home smelling like smoke and flowers (from the pet spray). If you don't smoke, you might want to select a groomer where there is no smoking. Most important, follow your instinct. Is the place clean? Is the staff courteous? Is your dog comfortable going there? If you're concerned at all, don't use them.

Ask to meet the grooming staff. Larger grooming shops employ more than one groomer, so you want to make sure you are comfortable with the person who will work with your dog. You can ask for the same person each time.

If you're only having your dog's toenails cut, it might be advantageous to see if you can stay and wait while the procedure is done rather than leave him there all day long. German Shepherds are more sensitive to being left in small crates in strange places, and it can be stressful for them.

# HEALTH
# OF YOUR GERMAN
# SHEPHERD DOG

**P**urchasing a new puppy or adopting an adult German Shepherd is only the first step in caring for your new companion. This is a breed that needs an observant, knowledgeable owner as well as one who invests in proper healthcare. It is important to consider the costs of these healthcare needs when preparing to add a large dog like a German Shepherd to your household to make sure you can afford all that is necessary.

## FINDING A VETERINARIAN

The first step in taking care of your dog's healthcare needs is to find the right vet. This is much like finding a trusted family doctor for your family. Take the time to research all the vets in your local area, and visit the clinics to make sure you are really comfortable with the vet, her staff, and the facility.

### WHAT TO LOOK FOR

Here are some considerations when selecting a vet:
- First, is this veterinary clinic an American Animal Hospital Association (AAHA) certified clinic? An AAHA certification means that this clinic and vet are routinely inspected and must maintain certain levels of cleanliness and care.
- Does the veterinarian participate in ongoing educational opportunities? It's

The first step in taking care of your dog's health is to find the right vet.

important to know that your selected vet stays current with new technologies, new research studies, and new approaches in veterinary care.

- Are the staff members (receptionists and vet technicians) courteous, respectful, and knowledgeable? Are the technicians certified vet technicians?
- Is this veterinarian wary or fearful of large breed dogs, particularly German Shepherds? You'd be surprised to know how many vets have preconceived thoughts about the breed based on a possible bad experience or fear.
- How flexible is the veterinarian and clinic to your needs as a client? Do they offer varied hours? Are they available if you have an emergency?
- Do they offer any type of payment plan? Many clinics simply don't, but it's always best to ask if you think you might ever need assistance.
- Is the vet willing to answer questions and listen to you? There are some vets who don't like to be questioned, but there are other opinions and lots of research available on all types of behavioral and medical issues. You want a vet willing to listen if you need to ask about something, like new medication options, alternative therapies, etc.

If you don't currently have a veterinarian you trust, try to locate a good clinic prior to bringing home your new dog. Any newly purchased puppy or adopted dog should visit a veterinarian for a wellness check within one week of coming home. If you've purchased a puppy, be sure you know your breeder's health policy and your state's law about health standards that prevent a breeder from selling a sick puppy. There are time limits for when a vet visit must be scheduled, so know what they are from your breeder and state, and schedule a visit accordingly.

## ANNUAL VISIT

Dogs age at a much faster rate than people do, so problems that could take years to develop in people may progress in weeks or months in a dog. For example, the clinical signs of kidney disease are generally not apparent to the observer's eyes until most of the functionality of the kidneys is already gone. Only regularly scheduled blood tests can detect the slightest deficiencies early on.

What this means is that to keep your German Shepherd in tip-top shape, you need to schedule a wellness visit with your veterinarian each and every year. This not only helps to maintain the relationship with your vet, but it helps to make sure you prevent the onset of problems rather than just responding to them.

These yearly visits should include any necessary vaccination boosters, a fecal check for worms and parasites (if this is a concern), a heartworm

Ask your veterinarian about the most recent vaccination protocols.

check if you don't give your dog heartworm preventative during the winter (although I don't recommend taking this chance), and routine blood work to check vital levels. Your vet will also check your dog's weight, listen to his heart and lungs, and feel his body for unusual growths, lumps, lesions, or any other type of skin condition. When your vet inspects your dog's mouth and teeth, ask if it's time to schedule a dental cleaning as well.

In addition to the annual veterinary visit, keep an observant eye on your dog. Any unusual changes in his behavior, eating or drinking, activity level, or skin or body should warrant a vet visit in between annual visits.

## VACCINATIONS

The protocols surrounding vaccinations have changed drastically over the years. Sometimes it is hard to decide what vaccinations should be given and how often! The commonsense approach these days is to work closely with your vet to individualize vaccinations to your particular dog.

At one time, it was thought that dogs had to be routinely vaccinated every single year in order to be best protected. It has now been shown that dogs retain immunity much longer than anticipated, and many don't need an annual booster. Some vaccinations, like rabies, can provide immunity for three years.

Veterinarians can now do blood tests on an individual dog to determine how much immunity remains from a particular vaccination. When the blood titer levels show it is time for another vaccination, the appropriate one can be given.

There are core vaccinations that all dogs should have, such as parvo, distemper, and rabies, but there are also quite a few optional vaccinations that your dog may need depending on his lifestyle. If you groom, board, or want to train your dog, you will be required to vaccinate him with the bordetella vaccine to help prevent kennel cough. The vaccination for leptospirosis should be administered if your dog comes into contact with wildlife or visits trails, forests, or rivers. Dogs living rurally should be given the leptospirosis vaccination as well as possibly a vaccination for tick-borne Lyme disease.

When first visiting with your vet, you should inform her of your dog's lifestyle. Where does he frequent? Who is he around? Will you be traveling with him? These are all important factors that will affect which vaccinations to give him.

## SPAY/NEUTER

All pet German Shepherds should be spayed or neutered. Here's why:
- The health benefits are incredible. It is a myth that it is in the best interest of a dog to produce at least one litter. In fact, a female who is spayed before her first heat (meaning she never has a season at all) has the greatest health benefits of all.
- Both genders of dogs have drastically reduced chances of cancer like mammary and testicular cancers. Females also won't run the risk of pyometria, a serious reproductive organ infection. It infects only intact females, whether they are ever bred or not, and by the time most people realize the dog is sick, it is almost too late to save her. Emergency spay surgery and super-high dosing of medications are the only way to try and save the dog, but it's not always successful.

Breeding dogs is difficult and time-consuming and should be left to experts.

- Male dogs have improved prostate health and a reduced likelihood of roaming and aggression related to testosterone. Intact young adult male dogs are most often implicated in bites.
- A spayed female saves you from dealing with the annoyance of her coming into "season." An in-season dog must wear "pants" for the time period (which lasts for weeks) to avoid dripping blood in the house, and must be kept securely away from any male dogs. This means not leaving her unattended in the backyard either—even if the yard is fenced—as male dogs will climb, jump, or dig to get to her.
- You'll reduce the likelihood of your male dog feeling the urge to mark with urine on just about everything. If he is neutered before he ever starts marking, he may never even raise his leg. Once a dog begins marking, neutering won't stop him from doing it, but it will greatly reduce the frequency of when he does it.

Aside from all the health benefits to your individual dog, there are a few other reasons to spay and neuter. Ask yourself these questions if you're thinking about keeping your dog intact and/or potentially breeding:

- There are too many pet dogs produced each year. Unfortunately, we live in a society where people don't always view dogs as permanent family members. Would you be prepared to take back, at any age, a dog you had bred and placed? Would you give it a permanent home if you couldn't re-home it? If not, you'd only be contributing to the humungous number of dogs who are in animal shelters every year, many of whom are euthanized.
- Do you know the breed standard? Do you know the history of the breed? Its purpose? Its correct body style and temperament? Without this knowledge, you won't be producing a dog that meets the standard's ideals, and you certainly won't be able to strive to better the breed.
- Do you know the ins and outs of breed health? Do you know what genetic problems may occur? Do you know how to help prevent them and what tests should be done? If you are not dedicated to producing the healthiest dogs possible in a scientific manner, you are just adding to the health problems of the breed.
- Are you willing to guarantee any puppies you produce against temperament and health defects? This means you must be willing to take back a dog you bred at any age for any reason. You're then left with the tough decision as to whether you can keep the dog indefinitely or face euthanizing an unhealthy dog.
- Do you belong to a dog club, either all-breed or breed-specific? Do you do anything with your dogs like training, performance sports, therapy work, etc? Working with your dogs gives you a better appreciation for their function and puts you in touch with other reputable fanciers.

- Are you hoping to make money? It may come as a shock to you, but reputable breeders do not make money on their puppies. In fact, many often lose money in the pursuit of bettering the breed and producing the healthiest and soundest puppies they can.

Many individuals who end up breeding their dog know very little about the breed, its standard, its health, or what a good representative of the breed should be. Only people with the breed's best interest in mind should ever endeavor to reproduce it, and you should know what you're doing when you do.

## BREED-SPECIFIC ILLNESSES

Just as with any breed of dog, the German Shepherd Dog has some health concerns potential owners should know about. Some of them are minor, but there are a few major health issues or potential life-threatening emergencies. If you don't know what to look for or how to avoid them, you'll find yourself with a serious problem.

Always make sure to consult with your veterinarian if you notice any changes occurring with your dog. Don't wait for something to "fix itself," because there are many health issues that just won't fix themselves, and time may be of the essence.

### CARPAL SUBLUXATION SYNDROME

This is a condition that affects very young German Shepherds, with the typical onset occurring between three and four months of age. Carpal refers to the

Carpal subluxation syndrome affects very young German Shepherds.

pastern, which is similar to the wrist or ankle on a person. Most cases revolve around the front pasterns, but this syndrome can also affect the rear pasterns (or hock).

In carpal subluxation syndrome, the joint doesn't function 100 percent correctly and is too loose. A puppy with "downed pasterns," as it is commonly referred to, will over-flex from the pastern point to the end of his foot. This causes the puppy to walk on his whole foot/leg area instead of walking only on his pad.

Anyone purchasing a German Shepherd puppy should be aware of this problem, because many cases of carpal subluxation can be prevented. While there can be a genetic component in some pedigree lines, it can also be caused by a growing puppy's diet. German Shepherd puppies should be fed only a large-breed puppy formula with approved vitamin/nutrient ratios. They should *not* be supplemented with additional vitamins or minerals. Protein levels should be moderate, in the 24 to 28 percent range. Raw diets, grain-free kibble, and other high-protein foods are not appropriate for German Shepherd puppies. Additionally, in pedigree lines where carpal subluxation has been known to occur, switching a puppy to a high-quality adult food prior to his turning three to four months of age may be advisable.

While excess protein can contribute to the problem, especially if the dog is predisposed by genetics, it's not the only cause. Puppies exhibiting signs of downed pasterns should be examined by their vet to develop a course of action.

In mild cases of subluxation, it is possible to reverse the problem, but it can take months. Both diet changes and exercise changes, including less strenuous exercise and no exercising on hard surfaces, are necessary. Severe cases of subluxation may not be correctable, although a puppy can live a normal life with this syndrome.

Breeders can now test for dogs who carry the gene for degenerative myelopathy.

## DEGENERATIVE MYELOPATHY

Degenerative myelopathy (DM) is a tragic progressive disease that affects many German Shepherds. It is closely related to ALS (or Lou Gerhig's disease) found in people, and the effects are quite similar.

It is a nervous system–based disorder, where a dog's body slowly and progressively fails him, even though his brain and awareness remain consistent. In its early stages, the most prevalent symptom is dragging of rear feet. You'll hear just the tips of his nails dragging and notice an uneven pattern of wear on the nails. If you turn his rear toes under, you'll notice a delay in how long it takes him to notice and attempt to correct them.

There is no treatment for this disease, and it eventually leads to paralysis in the rear and possibly front legs, incontinence, breathing problems and pneumonia, and eventually death. While there is no treatment, there are steps to help manage your dog's situation, improve his quality of life, and lengthen the time he has left. Dog wheelchairs can be helpful for some dogs, and water-based physical therapy is particularly helpful to maintain a dog's strength and muscle memory.

There has been a lot of research into the causes of DM, which has shown that the disease is genetic and runs in families. Additionally, a genetic marker has been identified. Breeders can now test for dogs who carry the DM gene and should be able to tell you if a particular line is DM free or if a dog has a chance of being afflicted.

## EPILEPSY

Dogs who suffer from epilepsy experience chronic, recurrent seizures that are likely to be genetic in cause. It normally appears in younger dogs and may take an owner by surprise. There usually aren't any symptoms leading up to the first seizure, and the diagnosis is reached if the dog continues to be afflicted with seizures.

Seizures can range in their level of severity and frequency. Epilepsy is managed by medication to control the seizures. The efficacy of the medication is not as high in severe cases of epilepsy. The medication must be used for the life of the dog, and there is no cure.

**BE AWARE!**

If purchasing a puppy, go only to a breeder who does health scans and offers a health guarantee. This gives you the best chance for a healthy puppy.

## GASTRIC DILATATION VOLVULUS (GDV)

Gastric Dilatation Volvulus (also called bloat and torsion) is a life-threatening emergency that requires fast action and emergency surgery. Without surgery, an affected dog will die within hours, and the chances of survival are greatly improved the faster it is caught.

GDV affects many deep-chested breeds like the German Shepherd. Their deeper chest allows more air to be pumped into the stomach region. GDV starts with the stomach expanding with air. As it expands, or bloats, it begins to put dangerous pressure on nearby organs.

Bloating is only one aspect of GDV, although it is possible that air accumulation is all a dog will experience if the condition is caught in time. Otherwise, the flipping of the stomach, called torsion or volvulus, will follow. In this stage, nothing can enter or exit the stomach, so the dog is unable to relieve any gas buildup and pain. The longer that the stomach is twisted—possibly trapping other organs as well—the more tissue dies. A dog's chance of survival, even with surgery, lessens as the tissues and organs die. This is why GDV must be caught very early.

A dog in the early stages of GDV may appear restless and uncomfortable, or may attempt to drink more water. His stomach region will slowly grow in size and feel hard. He will try to throw up frequently, but it will either be unproductive or produce only foam. He may salivate a lot. The average pet owner not familiar with GDV and its symptoms might mistake these signs as the dog just not feeling well or having an upset stomach. Unfortunately, by the time the dog is fully distended or can't get up off the floor, it is almost always too late.

There may be a genetic component to Gastric Dilatation Volvulus.

Because there is much debate as to what causes GDV, it is very difficult to entirely prevent it. What is recommended is that a German Shepherd not be allowed to gulp down food quickly (as this ingests a lot of air) and not be active before or after mealtimes. The breed should also be fed two meals a day with smaller portions.

There may be a genetic component to GDV, with some pedigree lines more susceptible than others. In these cases, some owners take the preventative step of having the dog's stomach surgically tacked down, which permanently prevents it from flipping.

## HEMANGIOSARCOMA

While the German Shepherd Dog doesn't have a high rate of overall cancer incidence like other breeds do, the breed does have a higher rate of contracting hemangiosarcoma. This cancer originates in the blood system and is highly malignant. The spleen is one of the most common sites for these tumors.

Since the cancer originates in the blood vessels, the tumors are particularly bloody, and one of the largest worries is rupture. Many German Shepherd owners don't even know their dog is sick until the tumor in the spleen ruptures.

Unfortunately, the rupture and the dog's sudden collapse are often the first signs of this cancer. However, owners should also watch for exercise intolerance, lethargy, and any unusual bumps. While the occurrence in the spleen is high, it can occur anywhere there are blood vessels in the body.

## Dog Tale

Be open to new treatments when it comes to your dog's health. One of my dogs was unfortunately afflicted with Degenerative Myelopathy (DM) as he entered his senior years. For those who have experience with DM, it is one of the most terrible diseases your dog can experience. While I tried many treatments, water-based physical therapy on an underwater treadmill gave him over a year and a half of extra time. I wasn't sure he would be able to do it or that it would offer much help, but I trusted his physical therapist, and the results were amazing. He kept his muscle memory and was able to move his rear legs and walk for a long time. Without trusting a treatment that was new to me, he would never have had this extra time.

## HIP AND ELBOW DYSPLASIA

It's a myth that all German Shepherds have bad hips. In fact, all large breeds have to be careful about hip and elbow dysplasia, but the German Shepherd doesn't have a higher occurrence than any other large breed of dog.

Hip dysplasia is a condition where the ball joint doesn't fit correctly in the hip socket and slips in and out. There are grades of severity that can be assessed by a veterinarian by X-ray. Elbow dysplasia is similar in that the elbow joint often slips out of the socket. It, too, can be mild or severe. Both hip and elbow dysplasia can occur separately or together and can affect one limb or both.

In cases of mild dysplasia, a dog can often live a normal life with supplements, regular exercise to strengthen the muscles surrounding the joint, and special care as he ages. Severe cases of dysplasia generally require surgery to fully correct the problem and relieve the dog of pain.

When purchasing a puppy, there is no 100 percent guarantee that you will avoid dysplasia, but you can stack the cards in your favor. A quality and knowledgeable breeder will do all she can to certify that the parents and as many generations back as possible are free of dysplasia. When a dog turns two years of age, his X-rays are evaluated by professionals, and the results are registered with the Orthopedic Foundation for Animals (OFA), which is the standard used in America. The OFA's vets examine the X-rays, and if they determine them to be problem-free, the dog will be awarded a number for hips and/or elbows. Although this is not a guarantee that the dog won't produce puppies with dysplasia, the chances go down dramatically the more OFA dogs are in a pedigree. If you contact a breeder who doesn't use (or know about!) OFA, don't purchase a puppy from her.

Dogs imported from Germany and abroad should have what is known as an "A stamp," which is similar to the OFA X-ray evaluation process. Dogs can't be bred without an A stamp in Germany.

Make sure that you know the OFA certifications or A stamps in a particular puppy's or dog's pedigree. The more of these certifications that appear in a pedigree, the greater the likelihood your puppy won't be dysplastic.

**Regular Veterinary Care**
A healthy German Shepherd can be a valued companion for 8 to 13 years. Regular veterinary care is key to keeping your dog healthy.

## HYPOTHYROIDISM

Hypothyroidism is a condition where the thyroid glands don't produce enough of the hormone thyroxine, which helps control a dog's metabolism (among other things).

The problem often occurs in young adults, and symptoms include weight gain (even though the dog exercises and eats an appropriate amount of food); dry, flaky skin; coat problems (coarse, brittle hair that falls out easily); and lethargy.

Thyroid levels should also be checked if a seemingly normal dog begins to exhibit anxiety, aggression, or any other change in his behavior. Research done by institutions like Tufts University has shown that dogs with low-normal or

below-normal thyroid levels may show signs of aggression or nervousness, which can be helped with medication.

Luckily, hypothyroidism is easily managed by supplementing the thyroid with a daily dose of thyroxine. It is relatively inexpensive, but supplementation will last throughout the dog's life.

## MEGAESOPHAGUS

Megaesophagus is a life-threatening condition that occurs when a puppy's esophagus fails to function correctly. It stretches and expands, it works too slowly, and the food sits in the esophagus rather than working its way down into the stomach. Most puppy buyers won't encounter this problem, as the condition is apparent early on to a breeder. Puppies usually begin to exhibit the problem when first eating solid foods— around the age of weaning, four to five weeks of age.

Caring for these dogs is extremely difficult, and may or may not be successful depending on the severity of the condition. Aspiration pneumonia occurs frequently and is the largest risk for dogs with megaesophagus. Unfortunately, euthanasia is sometimes the only option.

In recent years, there have been more attempts to help dogs with megaesophagus live to adulthood or even have a normal life. Some manage well; others do not. Management involves feeding multiple soft meals per day to a dog who is standing and has his head elevated and neck extended. This encourages the food to work its way down to the stomach.

## PANCREATIC ENZYME INSUFFICIENCY

A dog's pancreas is responsible for producing enzymes that are used to help break down food. If a pancreas is not functioning correctly and doesn't produce the necessary enzymes, a dog is unable to properly process his food. The result is malabsorption.

Symptoms include constant diarrhea, weight loss (even with excellent appetite), and poor coat quality. The dog's stools are often discolored, excessively smelly, and oily or greasy looking.

Management includes daily supplementation with enzymatic replacers. Some people also use probiotic supplementation and feed a raw diet to improve the absorption of food and nutrients.

## PANOSTEITIS (PANO)

Pano is a temporary problem that affects the long bones of a dog, so it can occur in either the front or rear legs. The condition is generally related to the growth of the dog and seems to occur during growth spurts. It is most often seen in older puppies and young adults, and it generally resolves itself by about age two.

The first symptom most German Shepherds have is mild limping. The limping may affect just one limb, but it often appears to shift from one leg to another, especially as the limping becomes more pronounced or severe. A dog will appear lame, will not want to participate in much activity, and may have a loss in appetite. Each episode usually lasts a few weeks at a time.

The condition is uncomfortable for a growing dog, and most veterinarians will prescribe pain relief medication for two weeks at a time for each occurrence, if there is more than one. Keeping the dog quiet and allowing him to get enough

rest, along with pain medication, usually is enough to help him through each episode.

## PERIANAL FISTULAS

Perianal fistulas first appear as oozing holes surrounding a dog's anus. The holes are like ulcerated tunnels that go down into deeper tissue.

The problem is usually noticed when a dog has a problem defecating. He may appear constipated, straining, and able to produce only a small amount of stool each time. The stool may be soft, or he may have diarrhea. An afflicted dog will also constantly lick the area, because the problem is uncomfortable and painful. This is a progressive disease with no cure.

Treatment involves strong medications that often suppress the immune system. Surgery is sometimes used to try and correct some of the problems. Dogs are usually euthanized when quality of life is gravely impaired.

## VON WILLEBRAND'S DISEASE (VWD)

Von Willebrand's disease is a genetic blood disorder that is quite similar to hemophilia in people. The dog's blood simply doesn't clot like it should.

The instances of vWD have been greatly reduced in the past years, and it is likely that a puppy with this problem would never be sold. Most breeders are able to recognize the signs of a puppy afflicted with vWD, which include bleeding longer after injury. Minor cuts or abrasions would cause the puppy to bleed for long periods of time. The site of vaccination injections react poorly, and a surgery as simple as neutering can be very problematic. Some dogs experience internal bleeding, pass blood in their urine, or develop nosebleeds.

Dogs who show signs of active vWD disorder are usually euthanized due to the severity of the problem, and carriers of the gene shouldn't ever be bred.

## GENERAL ILLNESSES AND PROBLEMS

Aside from the breed-specific illnesses that might affect your German Shepherd, there are problems that any breed of dog may face. It is important to routinely schedule wellness exams with your veterinarian to find problems early on and help prevent the onset of serious diseases.

### ALLERGIES

Allergies affect other breeds, such as retrievers, at a much higher rate than that of German Shepherds, but there are times when a particular dog will be afflicted with itchy skin. The most common allergies are food allergies and contact allergies.

If allergies are worse in summer, then it's likely that the cause is pollen and other seasonal allergens.

Food allergies occur when a dog can't tolerate something in his diet. To find out exactly what's causing the problem requires strict food trials, but most dogs are sensitive to wheat, soy, or corn. Some dogs have reactions to certain proteins, which is why a fish- and sweet potato–based food is often a popular choice.

With contact allergies, where a dog is allergic to something he comes into contact with, the culprit can be harder to discover. If the problem is at its worst in summer, then it's likely that pollen and other seasonal allergens are at play.

Allergy testing can be done by a veterinarian to help determine exactly what causes the reaction in your particular dog. Medication and trying to avoid the allergen are the best ways to avoid an itchy-skin breakout.

## EYE PROBLEMS

Most eye problems in the German Shepherd occur as the dog ages. Occasionally, older German Shepherds are affected by pannus, which causes black pigmentation to cover the dog's cornea, resulting in blindness. Cataracts can also affect older dogs. And one of the more common issues is that an older dog's eye may not produce as many tears as it once did, which can lead to excessive debris accumulation in the corner of the eye.

## HEART PROBLEMS

A minority of German Shepherds can be affected with heart problems, ranging from mild to severe. A heart murmur is usually the first indicator of a problem, and your veterinarian can identify the cause. In a puppy or young dog, it is usually the congenital heart disorders, sub-aortic stenosis or patent ductus arteriosis (PDA), which can range from mild to severe and life threatening. Luckily, these conditions are not as common in the German Shepherd as in other breeds, and they should be spotted during a puppy's first wellness exam. Older dogs can develop cardiomyopathy or other age-related deterioration of the heart muscle.

## PARASITES

Fleas and ticks are common parasites that affect dogs. It is always best to try and prevent them from becoming part of your life, rather than to try to get rid of them after the fact. This is a harder challenge if your German Shepherd comes into contact with woods, tall grasses, and wildlife.

In these very flea- and tick-infested areas, a topical monthly treatment is often the best course of action for prevention, but always consult with your veterinarian for a recommended product. Used correctly, these products are generally safe for the average dog, but care must be taken with older dogs, very young dogs, very small dogs, underweight dogs, or dogs who are sick or immune compromised.

If you'd rather not apply a chemical-based preventative, invest in a flea comb. You can comb through your dog's coat each time he's been outdoors and catch adult fleas this way. A bath in a thick liquid dishwashing soap can kill those adult fleas, but this can be harsh on your dog's coat and skin so shouldn't be done frequently unless the flea infestation is heavy.

There are some supplements that purport to assist with flea problems. Some people believe heavily in Brewer's yeast or garlic, but this doesn't work for many dogs. Always talk to your veterinarian before giving any supplement, as large doses of garlic may be toxic to dogs.

Ticks are not killed by dishwashing soap, and you don't want to pull them off with a flea comb. They can also be easily concealed in a thick German Shepherd coat. They often like to attach on the face, around the neck, in the groin area, in the arm pits, or around the bottom under the tail, although they can attach anywhere! You will have to really feel every square inch (cm) of your dog to detect them, and

> ### Finding an Alternative Practitioner
>
> Always discuss the use of any alternative therapies with your veterinarian. You should also use the same commonsense approach to alternative therapies as you would with traditional medicine. Set the standards for any alternative practitioner at the same level as you would for your own veterinarian. The American Holistic Veterinary Medical Association (AHVMA) website (www.ahvma. org) is a good starting point for learning more about holistic and alternative medicine.

then the only way to get rid of them is to pull them off. Be very careful! You must remove the whole tick, so a tick-removal tool might be your best bet. If the tick breaks off or you leave its head in your dog's skin, it can cause a problem.

Most experts suggest taking the tick and dumping it into alcohol rather than squishing it. Also remember that ticks spread disease very quickly, within hours of attaching, so you don't want to leave any of them on your dog for any time length.

Flea and tick treatment drops are the best way to kill ticks once they attach, but not all products kill all ticks. Make sure they kill the ones that your dog is most likely to come into contact with.

## ALTERNATIVE THERAPIES

Recently, natural therapies that are an alternative to traditional western veterinary medicine have emerged with great success. These therapies closely match ones in the human sector, and their uses are largely the same. The following are a selection of therapies that might be of use for your German Shepherd at some point in his lifetime.

### ACUPUNCTURE

Acupuncture is the insertion of small needles at certain points on the body. This therapy is used primarily for pain relief, but it is also used for chronic or incurable conditions. Dogs don't mind the needles, and many actually seem to like it.

### MASSAGE

Pet massage is used primarily for stress relief. The Tellington touch (T-touch) is a method used on animals that is similar to massage. Proponents of massage and T-touch tout the stress-relieving benefits for all dogs.

### PHYSICAL THERAPY

While this isn't considered an "alternative" type of therapy in the human arena, it is still viewed as one for dogs. When a dog has a surgery or experiences limited mobility, physical therapy greatly improves recovery time and reduces pain.

### SUPPLEMENTS

Supplements range from vitamins and herbs to botanical essences and all kinds of things. Natural supplements aren't regulated and need to be closely monitored for safety. You should always speak with your veterinarian before giving your dog any kind of supplement, not just for overall safety but to make sure it doesn't interfere with any kind of treatment your pet is currently receiving.

## FIRST AID

When it comes to emergencies, the best policy is to always be prepared: Hope for the best; plan for the worst! In the case of our dogs, we should be prepared to administer first aid if necessary. While you won't be as qualified as a veterinarian, there are a few things you should have on hand in the case of an emergency. You can purchase a premade first-aid kit, or you can create one yourself. Your kit should include the following items:

- **Antibiotic ointment:** Keep a tube of antibiotic ointment in your kit for mild scratches and cuts to seal the wound and prevent early infections.

- **Gauze and bandages:** If your pet has a wound, you will need to wrap the area and protect it while waiting to see your vet. Use bandages like sterile gauze pads and stretchable vet wrap, not bandaids.
- **Hydrogen Peroxide (3 percent):** This can be used to induce early vomiting if a dog has ingested something dangerous, like chocolate. Peroxide should be given at a size-appropriate ratio, and you should speak with your vet prior to giving it. Remember—not all dangerous ingested items should be vomited. Poisons should be handled by a veterinarian.
- **Leash and collar:** You'll need these if your dog is sick or injured but can still walk. It's not safe to transport him or visit the emergency clinic without a way to secure him.
- **Muzzle:** Dogs don't always respond well when in pain, so having a muzzle in your kit can prevent your dog from biting anyone while he's in pain.
- **Pet thermometer:** In case you need to take your dog's temperature.
- **Saline solution:** A good sterile solution for cleaning wounds, eyes, or dirty areas on your dog.
- **Phone numbers:** Keep handy the phone numbers of the nearest emergency veterinary hospital and your veterinarian. Make sure you know how to locate the people you need beforehand, especially your veterinarian and the nearest emergency veterinary hospital. Phone the emergency hospital ahead of time to let them know what happened and that you are coming.
- **Stretcher:** This is invaluable if you own a German Shepherd! The larger the dog, the harder to safely move him to your car, especially if he is injured, older, or immobile.
- **Styptic powder:** For minor cuts and abrasions, styptic powder can help stop the bleeding when applied with mild pressure. This shouldn't be used for large wounds.

The German Shepherd starts to enter his senior years at about six years of age.

- **Syringe (without a needle):** For use in giving medications or for helping to flush out a wound.
- **Your dog's information and medical records:** Knowing where your dog's medical information is saves precious time in an emergency.

## SENIOR DOGS

The German Shepherd starts to enter his senior years at about six years of age. In many cases, you won't even notice, as the changes are quite subtle at first. But there are a few things that should be done to help maintain your shepherd's health as he enters this period:

- Add a joint supplement that contains glucosamine, chondroitin, and manganese to his diet. It helps with joint and connective tissue health and helps ward off the pain and discomfort of arthritis.
- Provide plenty of comfortable sleeping surfaces. Older dogs sleep more. To avoid building up large elbow calluses or pressure sores on hips, make sure to provide several orthopedic bed options.
- Maintain an exercise routine. A senior German Shepherd might seem like he wouldn't need as much exercise, but the truth is that exercise helps maintain crucial muscle mass. Elderly shepherds can suffer from muscle wasting, particularly in their rear legs, if they don't get up and move enough. Additionally, walks keep an older dog's mind fresh and active.
- Don't skip the yearly wellness exams with your veterinarian, which should include blood work to see how everything is working internally. Some vets recommend visiting twice a year for blood work when the dog is very advanced into senior years.

# TRAINING
# YOUR GERMAN
# SHEPHERD DOG

Training and working with a German Shepherd Dog should be a fun and fulfilling experience for both the owner and dog alike. While current theories on canine intelligence often list the Border Collie or Poodle higher on the I.Q. list, most German Shepherd Dog owners and trainers can tell you that this breed ranks higher than any other. Plus, their dedication is second to none!

**Be Consistent**
The German Shepherd is the most versatile and one of the most trainable breeds, but he requires consistent training to become a great companion.

## WHY TRAIN YOUR DOG?

Training is essential! Training is far more important than a lot of owners realize. It isn't just about the dog knowing how to sit or lie down. Instead, training does the following:

- **Develops a system of communication.** When you train your dog in basic commands, you help him learn how to communicate with you.
- **Develops a bond.** Training helps create a lasting and meaningful bond between a dog and his owner. This, in turn, helps make a reliable obedience connection and increases the likelihood of the dog listening to the owner.
- **Helps prevent behavior problems.** When you train a dog, you help ward off the onset of annoying or problematic behavioral problems, such as fear-based behaviors, aggression, and annoying issues like jumping on people, counter surfing, excessive barking, etc.

The vast majority of dogs who are relinquished to animal shelters in this country are dogs who lack basic training. Many of these dogs lost a home just because early and proper training was not undertaken.

## POSITIVE TRAINING

Positive training can be a bit confusing at first if you're not familiar with the concept. Every thinking animal (humans included) learns in pretty much the same way. While I could tell you exactly what I want because we share a common language, I'm not able to express that to my dog in the same way. Instead, I need to figure out another way to effectively communicate with my dog. One of the most effective ways to communicate with dogs is the same system used to communicate with performing animals in water shows.

Think about a sea lion show at a local zoo or a dolphin presentation at a marine park. These animals perform wonderful behaviors that are not commonly

It's essential to train your German Shepherd—not only will it increase your bond, but you'll be able to take your well-behaved dog just about anywhere!

presented in the wild. If you pay close attention, you'll notice that the trainer always has a whistle and bucket of fish. Each time the animal performs the task, the whistle is blown and a fish is thrown to a hungry animal. These performers "earn" their daily meals via these performances.

While working with dogs is a bit different, the concept behind the training is essentially the same. There is no physical force used to train the animal. Instead, you develop a consistent language for communicating with the animal. In the case of the marine animals, the whistle lets the dolphin know when he has done a correct behavior to earn the fish. This whistle "marks" the correct behavior.

## MARKING BEHAVIOR

Marking behavior is one of the easiest systems of communicating with your dog. It speeds up the training time frame and makes it easier for the dog to figure out how to earn what he wants (like a treat). In dog training, we don't really have a use for the whistle. Instead, most people rely on a clicker or a marker word.

A clicker is small box with a piece of metal attached. When depressed, the metal makes a distinctive metallic click sound. Clickers can be easily purchased at pet stores or online.

Instead of a clicker, I prefer to use a word ("YES!") as a marking tool, for several reasons:

1. Clickers can get lost, but I always have my voice available.
2. My dogs prefer to hear my voice.
3. I can add extra enthusiasm for work done well.

Some trainers prefer the consistent tinny sound of the clicker and dislike the variations in human voice that occur when using a marker word. However, I have seen too many dogs who love the human voice more! Plus, German Shepherds thrive on the bond with their person, and I find that the marker word has more significance and value for them.

## "Priming" the Marker

Your dog needs to equate the marker with food. You do this by "priming" (or adding value to) your clicker or marker word before you start training. All you need to do is have a dozen or so small treats ready, and just click or say "YES!" and give the treat to your dog. The dog isn't required to do anything, because you're simply building the association between the marker sound and the food. Now you're ready to use it!

## Using the Marker

This is how using a marker for training works: Click or use your marker word the moment the desired behavior happens, then treat. The marker always ends a dog's behavior. This makes it easier for the dog to figure out what to do. Here's an example:

Using rewards like treats can help teach many behaviors, such as Watch Me.

If I want to teach my dog the *watch-me* command, which means give me eye contact, I put a treat at his nose level and then move it up to my eyes, which lures his eyes up to mine. As soon as I get eye contact, I use my marker word—"YES!"—then treat him. He will learn in just a couple of repetitions that it is the eye contact that gets him the treat, as opposed to any number of other behaviors he might throw in.

Markers are primarily used to establish new behaviors. Once your dog knows the behavior, you can switch over to praise and treats ("Good Sit!") instead. However, you might keep a marker longer in certain situations:

**Training Theory**

Animals work their way through life evaluating information. If something good happens, we want to know how to increase the chances of it happening again. If something bad or scary happens, we want to know how to avoid it in the future. (Neutral occurrences are of less value for behavioral purposes.)

- **New locations:** Perhaps your dog knows a skill, but you're planning to try applying it in a new place. Sometimes, using the marker reaffirms that the dog is still correct, even in the new place.
- **Building confidence:** Some dogs are shy or lack a lot of confidence. These dogs might benefit from using the marker longer to help build up their confidence in their skills.
- **Progression-based learning:** Markers are always used longer when working on more-advanced and/or tougher skills, because it can be used to build the behavior in smaller steps and gradually increase the difficulty. For example, if you were to teach a service dog how to turn on a light switch, you don't start with the switch on the wall. You slowly teach the dog in small steps what you want and use the marker to increase the difficulty of the task, until one day the dog is turning on a wall light switch.

## The "No Reward" Mark

The "No Reward" mark is one of the best things about using a marker to train. A word like "Sorry," "Try Again," or "Nope" is used to let the dog know when he hasn't performed the task correctly and won't be getting a reward. It is used most effectively when the dog knows the skill and chooses not to do it (which will happen!).

I think of the No Reward mark as a way of catching my dog "red pawed." With just one word—"Nope"—I am basically telling my dog that we both know he can do it, and he'll have to try again if he wants something. This is super effective and helps avoid the constant repetition of the command ("Sit, sit, sit, sit . . ."), which is a problem many owners face.

Instead, if I ask a dog to sit, and he pretends not to hear me, I simply say "Nope." This identifies for the dog that he wasn't correct and will need to offer another behavior. Nine times out of ten, when I give the command a second time, the dog will do what was asked.

## TRAINING MISCONCEPTIONS

There are a few common misconceptions about positive-based training. The biggest one is that all you are doing is using treats and bribing the dog. Not true! Food is only

German Shepherds are sensitive in nature and should not be trained with harsh methods.

one part of the game and is used to reward the dog, not bribe him. If you use a system of marking the behavior, this is very clear to the dog.

Additionally, there are very few dogs who work entirely to please the owner. The German Shepherd Dog is one of the most owner-loyal breeds around, but there are variations in their personalities. Most of them still require and benefit from positive-based motivation. Motivation can come in the form of treats but also in toys, affections, privileges, etc.

The most reliably trained German Shepherds are trained using motivation. They are eager learners, and when an owner correctly uses motivation to train the dog, they are also eager workers.

Another training fallacy is that this breed requires a heavy hand. They don't need correction collars, physical punishment, harsh treatment, or other outdated training methods. I find that most German Shepherds thrive on positive reinforcement–based training principles. These dogs may look tough, but they are actually very sensitive in nature and easily pick up on an owner's directive, which is why heavy-handed training is totally unnecessary for the average German Shepherd.

So how do you correct a dog through a positive-based system? I like to call these corrections natural consequences of the situation. For example, if I ask my dog to sit at the door before going outside, and he chooses not to, the natural consequence is the door doesn't open. It takes only a couple of times for him to understand that he doesn't go out if he doesn't do what I ask.

## SOCIALIZATION

Socialization means positively exposing your puppy or dog to all sorts of new places, new sounds, new people (all ages and races), new animals (like cats and other dogs), different types of footing (tile, grass, concrete, pebble, etc.), and just about anything else you can think of.

While socialization is important for each and every dog breed, it is critical for the German Shepherd Dog. This breed is a protector and a natural guardian. It's instinctual—it is not something that's taught. This means that you must work hard to teach him how to live properly in the world.

Guard dog breeds make judgments each and every day about the people and things that come into their world. Is that visitor supposed to be in the house? Is that screaming child running down the street a threat? Is that person reaching out to pet me at the park trying to hit me? These are just a few of the questions that

Early and ongoing socialization will help your German Shepherd accept new things, including other dogs.

might go through your German Shepherd's head, and the decision about what to do takes him only a split second. A German Shepherd Dog who has not been thoroughly and properly socialized runs the risk of making a wrong decision when faced with something new. And the consequences for the owner include liability risks, lawsuits, loss of the dog, and terrible guilt.

## WHEN TO SOCIALIZE

Socialization should begin immediately after acquiring the dog, with the first critical period being from 8 to 12 weeks of age. This age is the most sponge-like and the most blank slate–like. Everything the puppy meets during this age helps to solidify how it will react in new situations as an older dog. This isn't the only socialization window; it is critical that it continue throughout your dog's life, with the first year of age receiving the most attention.

## HOW TO SOCIALIZE

When you expose your dog to new situations, always try to pair it up with something positive. Give him yummy treats that he really loves when he meets kids and new people. Play active games and use toys to encourage him to move across new types of footing. Be creative, but always keep it fun. A well-run puppy kindergarten class can not only be a great starting point for learning basic skills but is an excellent place for socialization with new puppies and people. Check the website for the Association of Pet Dog Trainers (APDT) for a class in your area.

You should never force your dog into any situation that makes him uncomfortable, as you then risk creating fear, but you should expose him at levels that are reasonable to his psyche. If he doesn't learn how to cope with new things at an early age, it will affect him forever. Lack of socialization is the number one cause of fear-based behaviors and aggression, so the easiest way to avoid them is to socialize heavily.

Socialization is what helps a guard-dog breed like the German Shepherd quickly decide in a new situation what is safe or threatening. If he has been positively exposed to young children and is accustomed to their quick movements and loud noises, he won't misinterpret them as a threat. If you fail to socialize your German Shepherd Dog, you run the risk of a dog who barks threateningly, growls, or even bites inappropriately.

## CRATE TRAINING

A crate can be a valuable tool when used properly. It can be used for a young German Shepherd not yet trustworthy in the home alone. It's an effective tool

Supervision is an important key to housetraining.

for housetraining and also helps safeguard a young puppy or dog from destructive chewing and consuming things that could be potentially harmful. A young, bored German Shepherd will chew, and chewing can remain an issue for up to two years of age. The crate is not, however, a tool for punishment or to be used excessively.

## CRATE RULES

There are a few rules for the proper use of crates:

- The crate should be size appropriate. This is especially important for housetraining. The crate should be just large enough so the puppy is comfortable standing up, sitting, lying down, or turning around. Too much space means possible accidents. You can either buy more than one crate as your puppy grows, or purchase one that uses a divider system.
- The crate should never be used for punishment! Don't use this as a tool to punish the dog for bad behavior like biting or jumping. This only confuses the dog, and it makes it more difficult for him to see it as a good place.
- Don't use the crate excessively. While crates are a good tool, they confine a dog's movement, so it is imperative that he isn't left in the crate for hours on end. Try not to leave any dog in a crate for more than four to six hours at one time without getting him out for exercise and playtime. For young puppies, the time in the crate might be even less. If your puppy is only two to three months

old, the puppy should be out every three hours, or you should use another system like an exercise pen.

- Teach your dog to enjoy the crate. Use a word like "Kennel." Show your dog a treat and toss it inside the crate. As he moves inside, say "Kennel." This way there is an easy command to the action. Additionally, consider giving him a safe chew item when he's inside the crate. One of my favorite things to do is to stuff a natural hollow shank bone with peanut butter or canned food and give this goodie during crate time.

German Shepherds adapt easily to the use of a crate—assuming it is not used excessively and has a positive connotation attached to it.

## HOUSETRAINING

The German Shepherd Dog is one of the easiest dogs to housetrain, provided you follow the rules.

### RULE #1: ALWAYS SUPERVISE!

Young puppies lack the ability to hold anything for more than a short amount of time. The minute you let them out of your sight, that's when the accident will happen. And with an older, untrained dog, it is still a good idea to supervise fully.

Supervision means knowing where the dog is at all times. This allows you to pay close attention to his body language, which will be an indication of when he has to go. Watch for sniffing, circling, pacing, acting restless, whining, barking at you, running to the door, or just plain running around quickly. Any of these actions can be a surefire indicator he has to go—now!

### RULE #2: WALK FREQUENTLY

Frequent potty walks to a backyard or other designated area are a given, as you want to avoid accidents. At first, young puppies need to be walked every 30 minutes to one hour, then can gradually be walked a bit more infrequently as they age.

Certain times are more important than others for taking him outside: first thing in

German Shepherds tend to be a very easy breed to housetrain.

the morning, immediately after he wakes up from a nap, after he has eaten dinner, after he has had a lot to drink, and after (or sometimes even during) a big play session. These are all times that your puppy will have to relieve himself.

When you walk your dog, always go outside with them, at least in the beginning. This is the only way to ensure that you know exactly what your dog has done outside. There are some puppies who won't "go" without a person nearby or who will simply play around and forget to go!

## Dog Tale

The best advice I can give for working with a German Shepherd is to learn to laugh. Training is supposed to be fun, and there will be times when your dog has something else on his mind. I've had one of my dogs make up a whole new course during a Rally trial. There was no point in being upset—she was doing all kinds of great skills . . . just not in any order I gave her!

## RULE #3: LIMIT FREEDOM IN THE HOUSE

This is especially key with a young puppy, but it's also a good idea with an untrained adult. Limiting freedom means you need to keep the dog with you at all times. Close open doors, or use baby gates to close off open areas. These are off-limit places. Restrict his area to near you. A crate or exercise pen is the best option for limiting your dog's freedom in the house when you can't be there to supervise him.

This restriction isn't mean and isn't forever. It keeps the puppy from disappearing into another room to have an accident and ensures that you know what he's doing at all times. It's simply easier to supervise a dog who is next to you. As he ages and there are no accidents in the house, freedom to other areas can be earned, and you can gradually open doors or open up gated areas.

## TROUBLESHOOTING

If you follow the three rules closely and consistently, you'll have a very well-trained German Shepherd. However, there are a few additional pointers that can assist you along the way:

- Put a word to the action. When you walk your puppy or dog and he is in the act of pottying, say "Good Potty" (or whatever word you choose). Always use a word when he relieves himself. This way, you can ask him if he needs to go potty or hurry up and go potty and he'll understand what you're talking about.

- You don't need to use treats for housetraining. German Shepherds do very well with just saying "Good Potty" in a happy voice and enthusiastic petting.
- Don't punish your dog for any indoor accidents. If you catch him in the act, quickly interrupt and take him outside immediately. Don't rub his nose in it or use any other outdated method. This does nothing but confuse the dog.
- Use a pet stain and odor remover that utilizes some type of enzymes to break down the odors fully. Just using a stain remover won't remove the odors, and any lingering odors could encourage your puppy to continue to have accidents.

## BASIC COMMANDS

Training your German Shepherd should be easy and fun and should begin early. There are a few behaviors that you can begin teaching right away, including *sit*, *down*, *stay*, *come*, and *heel* (walk nicely on a leash).

> ### Capturing a Behavior
>
> If these methods for *sit* and *down* don't work for your dog, you can use your marker and "capture" the behavior. Hold his dinner bowl or a favorite toy and wait for your dog to either sit or lie down all by himself. He won't know what you want him to do at first, and it may take five minutes for him to eventually sit or lie down; just wait. As soon as he does, mark (with a click or "YES!") and immediately reward with his dinner or toy.

For teaching these commands, you'll want to determine which food item your dog loves the most. Foods like cheese, hot dogs, and lunch meat often work best. Keep these treats very small—fingernail-sized.

With all new behaviors, don't worry about saying a command until you practice the skill a few times and make sure he understands what you are doing. Once you know he understands, then you can start using the command word as you begin working through the behavior.

## SIT

*Sit* is one of the first and easiest behaviors to train. *Sit* can become a dog's go-to behavior and has so many uses! You can ask your dog to sit before receiving dinner, to put the leash on, and for a visitor to pet him.

Here is how to do it:

- Take a treat and hold it directly in front of your dog's nose.
- Slowly move the treat over and across his head, allowing him to follow it with his nose.
- As he moves his nose backward, his body will automatically move into a sit, since it will become harder for him to stay balanced.
- As soon as his bottom hits the floor, mark it (with the clicker or by saying "YES!") and treat.

## DOWN

The *down* command works well for helping the dog to learn to settle and relax, or as part of a *stay*, or even in conjunction with cutting toenails. It is often easiest to begin this behavior with the dog already in the seated position. Then:

- Take a treat and hold it right in front of your dog's nose.
- Slowly move the treat straight down in front of him, parallel to his body line until you reach the floor. Move slowly enough that he follows it. This will cause him to lower his body toward the ground.
- Slowly move the treat along the ground in front of him a short distance so that he follows it with his nose. This will cause him to lie down. Mark (click or "YES!") and reward when he is fully lying down.

It sometimes takes a few tries before he will get it and lie down.

## STAY

*Stay* is all about a position and location. In other words, you are basically saying to the dog, "I want you to be in this exact position and location for the duration of *stay*." The most common positions used for *stay* are *sit* and *down*.

It is best to teach *stay* in baby steps so as to properly establish a solid foundation to build upon. This means thinking about *stay* in terms of time (how long the dog stays) and distance (how far away you are from him).

I like to train *stay* starting out with time, so I ask the dog to sit right in front of me and then ask him to stay. I don't move

"Sit" is one of the easiest behaviors to train.

away from him. He is no more than a foot or two (m) away, and because I don't move away from him, he is less likely to move. You always want to release him from the *stay* before he starts moving. You'll need a release word (like "Okay," "Break," "Free," etc.), which will consistently indicate to him when he is allowed to move. After you release him, you can give the reward. The order of training a *stay* is always: *Position (sit or down); Stay; Release (and dog moves); Reward.*

Build up to 10 to 20 seconds of your dog not moving out of a position until he is released by your release word. Then you can attempt to add distance. Slowly move away just a foot or two (m) at first. Make sure he can do that distance at the same time interval before you attempt to add more distance. Continue to add time in 5- to 10-second intervals as well.

Your dog needs to be correct at least 80 percent or more of the time before you increase the difficulty of his *stay* work. If he can't reliably hold one time, don't try to increase the time. The same goes for distance.

In the beginning, the *stays* should be easy enough so he gets them right the vast majority of the time. This means less frustration for him and lots of rewards. At some point, as you add in more time and distance, he will move before you have given him your release word. When this happens, you must immediately ask him to sit/stay again and get it right.

Your dog's age and maturity will affect how quickly he is able to progress with his *stay* skills, so tailor the difficulty of training to his age.

You can slowly add distance to your dog's stay command by moving back a few paces.

## COME

It is a good idea to begin working on your puppy's *come* command right away. It is easiest in the first few weeks when the puppy really wants to be with you. Luckily, German Shepherds are very owner oriented and generally want to follow their person and know where she is. This is something you will want to take advantage of when working on *come*.

The *come* command *always* needs to be very rewarding and positive. Never, ever work with your dog when you are frustrated or angry—otherwise, you will damage your dog's desire to come to you at all. Dogs do best with high-pitched voices, upbeat body language, and lots of praise and reward, especially in the beginning.

When you are inside your home, practicing *come* won't be that hard, but always use a leash when outdoors—you *must* be able to get your dog to come each and every time. Initially, a 6-foot (2 m) leash will work, and a longer line of 15 to 20 feet (5 to 6 m) can be used as your dog progresses.

Here is how to start your *come*:

- Position your dog in front of you. He doesn't need to sit or stay.
- Quickly move backward in a straight line away from your dog.
- While moving, call your dog ("Shaggy, come!"). A high-pitched voice works great for most German Shepherds, but a happy voice is the most important thing. Feel free to incorporate clapping, a bouncy step, etc. Whatever excites your dog to move to you!
- As you slow and stop your movement, make sure he comes right to you.
- Reward him only when he's right in front of you with yummy treats, a favorite toy, or a lot of happy praise from you.

You should always encourage your dog to come in nice and straight in front of you. This way, it will be a habit for him to come to you in the same place when he's off leash.

Here are a couple of additional tips:

- In the beginning, practice the *come* command at least three or four times a day, making sure it is always fun and enjoyable. You'll know what works—if your dog is excited to come to you, you've got it right! If not, go back to the drawing board and look at other rewards and changing your voice and body language.
- Don't be a killjoy! Don't use *come* just when you need your dog. This often ends whatever fun the dog was having. Instead, practice *come* when you don't actually need your dog, and then let him go play again.
- German Shepherds are very good at hide-and-seek games and enjoy them. Try sneaking away from your puppy and "hiding" in easy-to-find spots and

encourage him to come find you. Playing hide-and-seek will make him more sensitive to your movements, which can only enhance the overall *come* command.

## HEEL

Teaching the *heel*, also known as walking nicely on leash, means not allowing your dog to pull against you when walking. There are a few techniques that can assist you:

- Each time your dog pulls on the leash, stop moving entirely. Wait for him to notice that you aren't moving and look at you, then you can move forward again. This teaches the dog that the walk stops when he is pulling.
- You can also make turns. If your dog starts to pull or forge ahead, make a right, left, or about turn. This takes him away from where he really wants to go.
- Praise him with an enthusiastic "Yes!" or "Good Dog!" when he is right next to you. It will tell him that he's in the right place.
- Carry lots of rewards with you. Most German Shepherds seem to appreciate a slightly yummier treat, and I find that small bits of human food, like hot dogs, work best. Each time your dog is near you, give him a goody.

I always suggest that dog owners not allow their dog to have a whole lot of leash. Dogs walk at their best when trained to move alongside of you, not in front

Walks are much nicer when your dog doesn't pull on his leash!

of you. You can instill this good habit when your puppy is first learning how to walk on the leash.

Simply say "Let's Go" when you prepare to move forward, remember to reward your dog and give praise for when he's next to you, and stop moving (or try turning) when the dog tries to lunge or pull. Within a few weeks, most dogs will be walking nicely. If you find you need additional assistance, using a head halter or special harness can be helpful for some dogs (especially adult dogs learning how to walk correctly on lead for the first time).

**BE AWARE!**
The German Shepherd is a breed that needs a fair leader. Establish this early on with positive training. If you don't train this breed or become his respected leader, your dog will fill the void.

## FINDING A PROFESSIONAL TRAINER

If you've never trained a dog before, I would suggest joining a training class with a professional trainer. Someone experienced with large dogs and comfortable with German Shepherds would be best.

Look for a positive-based dog trainer. German Shepherds do not need a heavy hand! Try starting your search with the Association of Pet Dog Trainers (APDT). Their website (www.apdt.com) contains a membership listing and will allow you to search for someone in your area. You can also easily find out if the trainer is certified. Certified trainers have the initials CPDT-KA, which stands for "Certified Pet Dog Trainer-Knowledge Assessed."

Evaluate the trainer before attending a class. What kind of experience do they have? Is there positive feedback in the area from local vets or other pet owners? Does the trainer mind you watching a class before attending? These are all factors to consider.

If there are no APDT trainers in your area, look to see if there is a local kennel club. Many kennel clubs also conduct pet-owner training classes and have experienced trainers, although most are not certified or trained in specialized services or behavior issues.

Even if you've trained a dog before, a training class is a good way for your puppy or dog to practice his skills, and it will give you a refresher as well.

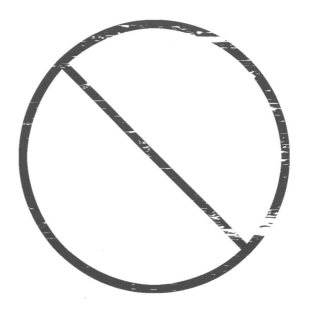

# SOLVING PROBLEMS WITH YOUR GERMAN SHEPHERD DOG

The best way to solve problem behaviors is to prevent them in the first place. For most dogs, proper socialization and early training will help you avoid the majority of problems. Every once in a while, problems can occur due to genetics. Also, an older German Shepherd who's been adopted might have lacked early training and socialization. The good news is that any problem can be worked on and solved!

## WHAT IS A PROBLEM BEHAVIOR?

A problem behavior is relative to each owner. For example, German Shepherds love to chase moving objects, which is what makes them fantastic herding dogs. But this very instinct can become a problem behavior in a farm setting with chickens! So one person's desired behavior might be another one's problem.

The best way to define a problem behavior is any behavior that impedes a dog's or owner's life or happiness. For example, if your dog is barking constantly, this is definitely going to affect you and the dog.

Through training and management, you can modify a dog's behavior to make it less problematic. I will note that there are times when a behavior is problematic because the dog is not a good fit for an owner. This is why it is essential to make sure that the German Shepherd Dog and his personality fit you well before you get one.

## BARKING

Barking is often cited as a nuisance by many dog owners, but there are various reasons that a dog will bark and more than one solution. Part of the solution relates to the type of barking the dog is doing, so identifying the cause of the barking is the first step.

### CAUSES OF NUISANCE BARKING

- **Territorial barking:** German Shepherds are excellent guard dogs and will bark at anything that comes near the property. Dogs who are left unsupervised in a backyard are often the worst offenders of this type of nuisance barking. This is the kind that gets the most neighbor complaints!
- **Demand barking:** This is the dog who barks in order to get you to do

**Problem or Breed Trait?**
Problem behaviors are subjective to an owner. Make sure the behavior you have a problem with isn't really just a breed trait.

Daily exercise can help prevent may problem behaviors caused by boredom.

something— pet him, let him outside, play with him, etc. This often starts accidentally but quickly becomes annoying.

- **Loneliness:** German Shepherds don't like to be alone, and many will express this vocally. They are more likely to howl or whine than bark, but it can still be quite audible.
- **Frustration:** Some German Shepherds will bark out of frustration. For example, if the dog is held back from getting to something (like a fence separates him from something), he might develop a barking habit out of frustration.
- **Jealously:** German Shepherds are all individuals, but because they bond so tightly to an owner, they tend to view themselves as "the dog." This means that they can develop jealously with canine housemates and bark or growl at them.

## SOLUTIONS

Once you know the cause of barking, you can start working on the solution.

### Reward/Ignore

Remember to reward him when he's quiet. Oftentimes, people are quick to correct the barking ("No!") but forget all about rewarding the silence and good behavior. As a general rule, reward and acknowledge the behavior you want and try to ignore the behavior you don't want.

This is especially true of demand barking. Once you do something for your dog because he barked at you, the dog will use this "barking card" over and over and over again. You must ignore the barking dog 100 percent of the time and reward him only when there is silence—even if it is for just a moment or two. For example, if your dog barks at you for play, ignore him by turning your back, pretending you can't hear him, or leaving the room. Engage him in a game only when he has ceased to bark.

## Ask for an Alternate Behavior

You can also ask for an alternate behavior instead of barking. For example, if your German Shepherd is chasing and barking at your cat (which will happen if you have cats!), try asking him to come to you instead. He can't chase and bark at the cat if he is coming to you.

## Proper Management

Some of the other kinds of barking can be corrected through proper management. Don't leave your German Shepherd in a situation where he will be lonely. He will be much happier if he is allowed to be part of the family at all times. This also helps with territorial barking. Most German Shepherds begin this habit because they have been left alone, unattended in the yard instead of with the family.

Your German Shepherd should be part of the family—too much unsupervised time outside can lead to problem barking.

Don't develop the bad habit in the first place—limit unsupervised time outdoors. Additionally, when you are outside and the dog barks, simply stop the behavior by asking the dog to come to you.

Don't forget how key socialization is for your puppy, and you can prevent a lot of territorial barking by making sure your German Shepherd has met a lot of new people throughout his life. The under-socialized dogs often have a harder time with strangers just walking by.

## Redirect

We've already discussed asking your dog for an alternate behavior, such as the *come*. Similar to this is the *redirect*, where you redirect your dog's attention onto something else. This might be a game of tug, playing with toys, a chew bone, or some other activity. This moves their mind from one activity to another, leaving the barking behind. It works especially well for puppies and younger dogs.

### Teach the *Quiet* Command

Another solution is to teach your dog a *quiet* command:

- Have treats ready during a time you know your puppy is likely to bark (or you can encourage him).
- Position yourself in front of your puppy.
- When he barks, place your finger in front of your mouth and say "Shhhh." Most puppies will stop barking to look at you quizzically.
- As soon as he stops, say "Quiet" and reward him with a treat. You're going to reward only the silence, not any barking.

If you work on this command and also randomly reward and acknowledge your dog when he's quiet all on his own, he is likely to convert his noisy behavior to being more silent.

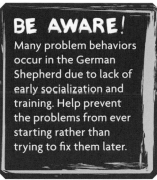

**BE AWARE!**

Many problem behaviors occur in the German Shepherd due to lack of early socialization and training. Help prevent the problems from ever starting rather than trying to fix them later.

## CHEWING

German Shepherds are typically prone to chewing during only two phases of their lives: teething/puppyhood and early adolescence. The solution to the problem varies based on the phase.

### PUPPYHOOD

For the teething puppy, it is just about impossible for him not to chew. German Shepherds have pin-prick teeth at this point and use them all the time! They love to chew on anything they can get their mouths on, so you should have a lot of safe, age-appropriate items for him to chew.

Ask your veterinarian what would be appropriate for your puppy to chew based on his size and age. Always check the warning labels on any manufactured treats, as they are all different, and many treats are too hard for baby teeth. You have a lot of options for a teething puppy:

- Bully sticks, springers, and other meat chews are not overly hard, and puppies can gnaw on them. They last a long time for younger puppies.
- Frozen veggies, like green beans or sweet potato sticks, can be a good option. You can use fresh veggies too, but many puppies love frozen items for their teeth.
- Ice cubes work well as a play toy and chew item.
- Toys that freeze. Many manufacturers now make toys that can be wet down and frozen for puppies to play with.

- Dehydrated meats, like natural jerky, are usually not too tough for puppies. I also like to give my puppies a product that is made of dried fish skin from Iceland.

This phase generally lasts until later puppyhood, about seven months of age. As the puppy ages, you can use harder chew toys. Just be careful and watch the puppy while he chews any items to ensure that they are safe.

In addition to chew toys, you'll want to purchase bitter-apple spray to help prevent your puppy from chewing on inappropriate things. This spray works well on things your puppy likes to frequently chew, but you'll need to reapply it often, as it works best when wet.

Last, prevention is key. Try to put away any items lying around the house that your German Shepherd puppy may chew on. That means clothes and shoes need to go into closets, toys should be in toy boxes, and papers should be organized or in the recycling bin. Don't leave anything lying around that you don't want chewed on. A little bit of management and prevention go a long way!

## ADOLESCENCE

The most destructive chewing phase occurs in adolescence because the dog is just bigger at this time. This is when the chewing becomes a larger problem for

Teething puppies need to chew, so make sure to provide them with appropriate chew toys.

most owners. The cause of this type of chewing is generally boredom and lack of exercise.

The best way to solve this type of chewing is through lots of exercise and stimulation. Dogs get bored. Sitting in the backyard or in the house isn't interesting enough for your dog each and every day—especially when it comes to a young dog.

Every single day, you need to make sure your German Shepherd is getting enough exercise. They love to go on walks, so a good long walk should be a part of your daily routine. If you're not doing this already, you need to start now!

**BE AWARE!**

Don't go jogging with your dog prior to one to one and a half years of age. Your dog's bones and joints are still developing, and heavy exercise prior to adulthood can cause permanent damage and early arthritis.

Look for ways to give your dog something to do to stimulate his brain. Training exercises are one avenue. You can also use treat-dispenser toys for his kibble, which help him work his brain. If he's your only dog, you can also hide small piles of food for him to search out and find in the house (or just in one room).

Set your puppy up for success—don't leave anything lying around that you don't want him to get into.

Food-stuffed toys work well for many dogs. I like to use natural bones, and if you use a hollow shank bone, you can stuff these with peanut butter, canned food, squeeze cheese, or whatever you'd like to. You can also use other bones, like raw knuckle bones or shank bones. These really work a dog's jaws and help prevent nuisance chewing. Make sure you stick with knuckle bones or shank bones for safety, but you should supervise your dog while it chews for the best safety policy.

Last, much as in puppyhood, management and prevention go a long way to stopping this problem. I can't stress this enough—*don't leave things lying around that you don't want chewed!*

## DIGGING

Digging is far less of an issue with German Shepherds than other breeds of dogs. The only times I've ever seen it in this breed is occasionally in puppyhood (digging up grass) or in the adult dog who is hunting (digging up moles) or trying to escape an enclosure.

If a dog is left with nothing to do or is unsupervised in the backyard, he will sometimes dig. Digging might also occur if he's left alone in a hot area. German Shepherds will create a depression in soil to make a cooler spot to lie down in. Always provide your dog with a cool area to rest in. It's best to keep your dog indoors during very hot weather, but if he's going to be outside for a little while be sure to provide a small water pool (although not all German Shepherds like a pool) or a cooling mat to lie on.

If your German Shepherd is digging in the yard, he may be looking for a spot to cool down. Provide him with an area to cool off outside.

Just like chewing, prevention can help stop this problem. Give your dog plenty of daily exercise outside of your yard and activities to do while at home. If your dog is hunting for an animal underground, like a mole, the digging will continue unless you find a way to remove the underground animal. Try to prevent wild animals from nesting or burrowing in the yard, or you run the risk of the dog digging it out and killing it.

If your dog has frequent digging spots, try to discourage him from digging in those spots by filling them most of the way up with dirt, then placing a sheet of wire (like chicken wire) down on top, and covering it with a layer of rocks before fully covering it with dirt. This makes it less desirable for the dog to dig in again.

## HOUSESOILING

If your German Shepherd is having accidents in the house, there are really only two reasons: It's medical or it's your fault. While this might seem harsh, this breed is one of the absolutely easiest to housetrain and one of the most reliable.

## MEDICAL ISSUES

Medical issues are usually easy to identify—a normally housetrained dog begins to have frequent accidents within the home. The most common medical issues are urinary related and can range from a simple infection to incontinence/bladder weakness. Both of these are easy to take care of with medications and some management.

Bowel accidents are often temporary and related to stomach sensitivity or stress, but there are some more serious medical conditions that can cause diarrhea, ranging from parasites to food absorption issues. If your dog has chronic diarrhea, it is important to determine the health issue behind it.

## HOME ISSUES

If your dog is declared healthy by his veterinarian, then it's time to look in the mirror. The most common reason for housesoiling relates entirely to the owner. German Shepherds are so reliable with housetraining that accidents are almost always the fault of the owner. If your dog begins to have accidents in the house, ask yourself, "Do I walk him enough?" While the adult German Shepherd can go many hours without being walked, he really should be walked at least once or twice in a six- to eight-hour period. If you're repeatedly asking the dog to go for longer time frames than this, you need to re-evaluate the situation. You may need to hire a dog walker or have a family friend come walk your dog at least once during the day.

Has anything changed within your home? This can cause a normally reliable dog to suddenly begin having accidents, particularly with

If your housetrained German Shepherd suddenly begins having accidents in the house, he may be experiencing a medical issue.

male dogs who aren't neutered. If your dog is still intact and marking in your house, neutering him will greatly reduce his urgency to urinate everywhere.

Try to reduce any stress surrounding a new change to the home. Visitors can be wonderful, but they disrupt a dog's routine. Accidents that begin occurring around new people, new animals, or any stress-inducing change need to be managed for the best effect. This means trying to stay as close to your pet's routine as possible and limiting his stress by giving him "away from the action" time.

While accidents are happening, it is important to fully supervise your dog. This usually means limiting his freedom within the home by closing open doors or using baby gates to block open areas. This way, the dog is near to you at all times, and you can see what he is doing. As the accidents begin to diminish, he can again have house freedom.

Really and truly, accidents should not occur with a housetrained German Shepherd.

## JUMPING UP

Many German Shepherds like to jump on their owner as an excited hello. Luckily, this problem is generally easy to fix in this breed.

## PREVENTION

The best course of action is to prevent the problem in the first place. The habit of jumping on people is often established when they are puppies. The German Shepherd is cute, fuzzy, and irresistible as a puppy, and since it can be hard to visualize at that small size how truly large the adult dog will be, many people don't see the harm in allowing the puppy to do it. Unfortunately, a 20-pound (9 kg) puppy is much different than a 90-pound (41 kg) adult!

If you don't ever want your German Shepherd to jump on anyone, the easiest thing to do is to teach your puppy from day one that jumping is not the way to get anything he wants. Puppies come prewired to jump on people because they instinctually jump up at adult dogs and lick their faces, out of submission and for food solicitation. When the puppy is removed from his mother and littermates and brought into a human family, he simply tries to apply this instinctual behavior to people. Jumping will become a solidified habit if his new human family reciprocates his jumping with affection, petting, and overall happiness.

The best way to prevent your puppy from jumping is to *always* ignore all attempts at jumping. No touching, talking, or getting him excited. Instead, turn away or sidestep him so he doesn't make contact. When he calms down, that's the time to pet him. Pretty soon, he will realize that nothing he wants seems to happen when he jumps.

## OLDER DOGS

Training an older dog not to jump is similar. The main difference is that older dogs have an established habit, so it can take longer to reverse it. Here are a few tips for stopping jumping in an adult dog:

- When you're out, try to make your homecoming less important by ignoring your dog for 15 minutes. This reduces the dog's urgency to jump as part of the greeting.
- Turn your back and ignore him, or preferably sidestep him, so he doesn't make contact at all.
- As he falls off or by you, you can say "Off" to put a command to the action.
- When he calms down, offer to pet him. Use a calmer voice and calmer body language to avoid increasing his excitement level again.
- Alternatively, ask him to sit once he calms down a bit. You can then pet and reward him for sitting. Sitting is an oppositional behavior to jumping—your dog can't sit and jump at the same time.

It is important to note that sometimes jumping will get worse before it gets better, especially if the habit is well established. This is because your dog might get frustrated that the jumping no longer works, so he might try a bit harder. Luckily, this phase doesn't last long, and not all dogs do it.

Be careful not to reward your dog even once in a while for jumping up. A dog who occasionally gets petted when he jumps will jump much more frequently and on more people because at least once in a while it works. This could be very problematic with children or elderly individuals, so it's best to not reward jumping at all.

## NIPPING

The German Shepherd is a herding breed, and by nature, herding breeds have the potential to nip. Nipping is a form of biting, but it is usually not as hard. It's more like a pinch, with the dog grabbing something with the front part of its mouth. Nipping is highly effective for controlling movement and instinctively comes out when German Shepherds are herding. It can also appear in day-to-day situations, usually when something is moving quickly.

Herding breed, by nature, have the potential to nip.

While most German Shepherds will go their whole lives without nipping of any kind, there can be some situations where nipping can arise:

- Chasing other animals (like cats)
- People or children who are running
- Strangers in the house

## CHASING OTHER ANIMALS

Chasing small animals (especially cats) is very natural to the majority of German Shepherds. It can range from mild interest to over-the-top obsession, depending on the individual and his prey drive. Nipping will usually follow a chase sequence, as cats almost always run!

There are a few things you can do to work through this problem. First, make sure you've given your cat a lot of options for getting away. Cat towers at least 6 feet (2 m) tall or other high-up places are preferable. You can also use a baby gate or cat door to give your cat his own room where the dog can't enter. This allows you to place your cat's food, water, litter box, and favorite toys and bedding in a safe place.

Next, you'll want to make sure that the dog is walked every day and is receiving plenty of exercise. The younger the German Shepherd, the more exercise he'll need.

Third, you'll want to interrupt the dog anytime he gets into chasing the cat. You can use the *come* command to bring the dog back to you, then redirect his attention onto some other activity.

German Shepherds really love to chase and bite at cats, so you'll need to be creative about preventing the chasing in the first place, and then interrupting him if he does give chase.

## PEOPLE OR CHILDREN WHO ARE RUNNING

Most of the time, German Shepherds don't actually end up nipping when they're running next to someone. Some herding breeds, like Corgis, are very quick to nip ankles or legs when people run, whereas German Shepherds are more likely to become aroused, whine, or closely follow those people who are moving.

The greatest likelihood for nipping occurs with small toddlers or young children who run quickly here, there, and everywhere and make lots of noises and squeals while doing it. Even then, the German Shepherd won't immediately nip; he will likely follow the youngster and whine for a while. Nipping would be used only to control the movement of the person—to stop or redirect the child.

The easiest management option is to ask the child not to run or be as noisy around the dog. You can use a *come* to bring the dog back to you, or if the action is very lively, leash the dog. This allows you to more directly supervise the dog's

Small animals or running children can excite your Shepherd's prey drive.

behavior and make sure the dog follows through with a *come* command.

## STRANGERS IN THE HOUSE

Nipping can sometimes happen if your dog is territorial about his property and/or is not used to strangers visiting your house. Sometimes the dog will

**PUPPY POINTER**

Puppies are very moldable little beings. Any problem behavior can be worked through with training, so never give up!

follow new people around quite closely while they move within the house, and nip if the person tries to move from one area to another. As with running people, the nipping is used to control movement.

This issue arises most often with dogs who are more genetically predisposed to territorial aggression or with dogs who haven't been socialized to new people.

The best way to work through this situation is to leash the dog for all guests. This prevents any nipping accidents. Then, it's all about helping the dog to see that new people to the home, when allowed in by you, can be a good thing. Lots of socialization really helps the dog accept visitors to the home, but you can also increase the positive association by having guests provide your dog with a nice treat as well.

Anytime your dog develops an issue you don't know how to fix, seek professional help.

## WHEN TO SEEK PROFESSIONAL HELP

It is not a failure to seek professional help. Any time your dog develops an issue that you don't know how to fix, you should look for someone to help you. There is always a way to work through problems, but you shouldn't expect that you'll have the answer for everything. Even trainers are continually learning new ideas about ways to deal with behavioral issues!

The best time to seek help is before a small issue becomes a large one. It is always easier to correct something before it has become a huge problem. For example, if your German Shepherd puppy is growling at new people, don't wait to ask for help until he grows into an adult and bites someone.

You should always seek professional help if your dog is demonstrating aggression, at any level. It is imperative to correctly identify what is happening and develop a plan to work through it. If done improperly, the situation can be made much worse.

Start your search with the Association of Pet Dog Trainers (APDT). Look for a positive-based trainer who really has knowledge about dogs and experience working with them. Don't be afraid to ask for references or to find out how comfortable they are working with German Shepherds. Not everyone is comfortable with this breed.

A knowledgeable trainer will know if she can help you with your problem or if she should refer you to someone with more experience. She can also provide suggestions as to whether a visit with a veterinary behaviorist would be warranted.

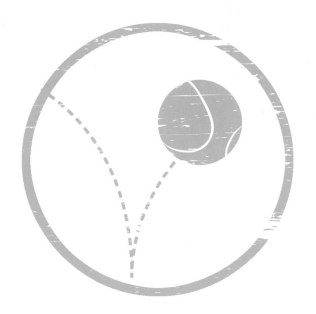

# ACTIVITIES WITH YOUR GERMAN SHEPHERD DOG

There are so many fun activities and performance sports that you and your German Shepherd can participate in. Some dogs do best in one or two sports, and other dogs enjoy competing in everything! Visiting the American Kennel Club (AKC) Web site will allow you to search for events in your area. Go and watch some different shows and events to give you a full idea of what's involved and whether it would be something you might like to participate in.

## SPORTS AND ACTIVITIES

In the United States, the most common venue for competitive sports is the American Kennel Club (AKC). They offer titles at various levels of abilities in all the following performance sports, except Schutzhund.

### AGILITY

Agility is by far the most popular performance sport. It's an exciting competition that consists of a timed obstacle course. You and your dog will be required to work with things like tunnels (both open and closed), weave poles, jumps, and contact obstacle equipment like the dog walk, A-frame, and seesaw.

German Shepherds aren't the number one breed for this sport, due to their size. The fastest dogs are smaller, but German Shepherds are very competent at this sport. They are more reliable than some of the faster breeds, like Border Collies,

Agility is a fun, fast-paced sport.

because they are a tad slower so generally don't make as many speed-related mistakes. They're also a bit more cautious.

In addition to the AKC, the other two popular competitive venues are the North American Dog Agility Council (NADAC) and the United States Dog Agility Association (USDAA). You can compete in all the venues, but there are different rules and sometimes different equipment that you will need to familiarize yourself with.

Agility has a lot of titles available, and they become progressively more difficult to attain. The biggest factor in titling is a dog's speed and reliability. The best dogs really, really enjoy the sport. They are both fast and confident and are not worried about the equipment. The dogs who are more cautious or worried don't do as well in all formats. As a side note, agility is used for many dogs to build confidence, especially in dogs who are shy or are rescued dogs. While many may never compete, often, with extra time and work, some surprise everyone and do compete successfully.

## CONFORMATION (SHOWING)

With televised dog shows growing in popularity, like the Westminster Kennel Club Dog Show, more people are becoming familiar with conformation showing. Conformation is all about a dog's body structure and gait. Dogs who are exhibited in dog shows must meet the breed standard requirements. Every breed has its own written breed standard. This standard specifies the adopted ideals that breeders work toward when producing dogs, and it includes things like proper temperament, size, color, head and eye shape, body outline, movement, etc. In a conformation show, while it looks like dogs are being judged against each other, they are really being judged against the written standard. The winning dogs are the ones who most represent the standard. A show dog should be a physical embodiment of the written standard with as little deviation as possible.

The average pet dog is not a conformation show dog. If you are interested in showing, the best way to become involved is to purchase a show puppy from a reputable, well-respected show breeder. Showing is difficult, and you'll need to become familiar with what exactly is required in the show ring, because it is no fun to show a pet-quality dog—it will be disappointing and expensive!

A show dog needs to be a physical embodiment of the written standard with as little deviation as possible.

There are two types of shows: specialty and all-breed. Only German Shepherds are shown at specialty shows, and all the registerable breeds participate in all-breed shows. Sometimes there are two types of German Shepherds: the specialty one and the all-breed one. The quality is generally higher at a specialty show, and it is harder to compete and win at this level.

Although you can show your own dog, the majority of owners hire a professional handler to showcase their dog, especially at larger shows where the competition is harder.

The point of conformation shows is to complete a dog's championship title. The requirement for a championship title is earning 15 points. Points are determined by the number of dogs entered in the show in each gender and, subsequently, how many dogs a dog beats to win the show. You have no control over whether you win or not. It is up to the judge of the day and her interpretation of what the breed standard should look like.

Conformation shows can be fun, but they can also be expensive and frustrating. Many newcomers wear out quickly, as you won't (and shouldn't expect to) win every show you enter your dog in.

The best way to learn about conformation shows and whether you would enjoy them is to attend a few different all-breed and specialty shows. Sit ringside and watch. Speak with different breeders/exhibitors ringside or before or after the show. Really try to absorb what it's all about and whether it would be a good fit for you.

## HERDING

The German Shepherd Dog has herding origins, and many members of the breed have a natural instinct that can be cultivated into herding. These dogs can be used on working farms for moving sheep and for guardian work, but the vast majority of herding titling dogs don't live anywhere near a farm.

This is the challenge of obtaining a herding title. You have to have sheep to do this sport, so if you don't presently live with your own sheep, you need to locate an instructor who can assist you with working with livestock. You'll likely find you wish you had more opportunities to work with the stock, because practice is what makes the best herding dog. Those people who are bit by the herding bug often change their lifestyle and purchase their own sheep!

Herding is a real exercise in control, as the dog needs to listen to the handler even though there are animals moving all around him. This is exceptionally hard and takes a lot of work. In herding trials, the dogs are not allowed to bite the stock! You must be able to call your dog off the sheep or other animals if

*Many German Shepherds have a natural instinct for herding.*

necessary. Additionally, the dog works at a distance from you and will make his own decisions at times, but he also needs to be skilled at working with you and taking direction. He needs to hear you tell him which way to go or when to stop altogether. Titles are obtained through herding trials, and there are many levels as well as different livestock courses. The handler and dog team are given a set course time, and the team obtains points based on how well the dog completes the challenges within the course and moves the stock.

Not all dogs work well for herding, but luckily you can easily find out if your German Shepherd still has the instinct. A knowledgeable herding trainer can very quickly assess your dog's herding instinct and tell you where to go from there.

## OBEDIENCE AND RALLY

Obedience and rally are the most readily available performance sports, so opportunities to participate in these sports are easier to come by.

### Obedience

Obedience is a test of both dog and handler on training skills that get progressively more difficult. There are three levels of titles. The novice title is attainable to just about every dog and handler. The other higher-level titles are more difficult, and not every dog will be able to complete the necessary skills.

At the novice level, your dog will be required to perform skills like *sit, down, come, stay* (done in a group stay in a line), stand for exam (where the judge will approach and touch the dog and it shouldn't move), and walk on leash (both on and off leash).

The successive levels include more difficult off-leash walking sequences and other elements, including a drop into a *down* position during a recall, retrieving a dumbbell thrown over a jump, maintaining longer *stays* with the handler out of sight, and even scent-distinction work. The best dogs are truly a sight to see as they navigate these upper levels.

A lot of training is necessary to compete in obedience, as your dog should be at a level where he will work with minimal commands from you, with absolutely no food rewards, and with no touching during the exercises. During obedience tests, you are allowed to talk to your dog (other than a command) or praise him only after the completion of an exercise.

## Rally

Rally is a fun and newer sport that is really taking off in popularity. It is based on obedience, but while obedience is always conducted the same way, and the handler always knows what to expect during a trial, rally is totally the opposite!

Rally is made up of lots of learned behaviors, including weaving around cones, jumping over a jump, heeling quickly, asking the dog to stop and stay while moving, staying in one spot with the handler walking a circle around the dog, multiple turns and about turns, backing the dog up three paces, and much more!

A rally course is determined by the judge of the day, which means that no course will ever be the same. The judge sets up a course of "stations," which are usually cones with numbered signs. You follow the numbers and complete the course in order while doing the skills.

The best part of rally is that you are able to talk to your dog if you want, unlike obedience, which must be silent except for the commands. It is a lot of fun, because the pressure isn't as heavy as obedience and the course always changes.

Rally has multiple titles in varying levels of difficulty, and it becomes progressively harder. The first level of rally is done entirely on leash. The upper levels are entirely off leash.

## SCHUTZHUND

Schutzhund is the original German Shepherd Dog sport. While other breeds can compete, the German Shepherd participates extensively in this sport. It was created to determine the working suitability of a dog. Those deemed not fit or

## Dog Tale

Training for and participating in performance sports is one of the best ways to build a bond with your dog and to increase his abilities. I have used training and competing to increase both the trust and the confidence of more than one dog. It's amazing how a dog changes when he trusts you, and how excited and proud he is of his accomplishments.

Agility is considered one of the best sports for confidence building. In fact, many service dog groups utilize agility equipment in their programs to encourage both trust and confidence in young future service dogs!

Protection work is
one component of
Schutzhund.

able to compete at all levels were dropped from the breeding gene pool and not used as working dogs.

This sport is still governed by the German club Verein für Deutsche Schäferhunde (SV), and all paperwork is run through them, even if the dog competes in the United States. All participants must adhere to German rules, including hip and elbow verifications, permanent identification, and the passing of a basic temperament and obedience evaluation called the BH. A dog must pass the BH test in order to further compete in any Schutzhund events.

There is a misconception among the general public that this is a sport of biting or that the dogs are dangerous. In fact, a well-bred Schutzhund dog is incredibly trustworthy and highly trained and controlled. For many years, the AKC didn't endorse the sport, as it, too, viewed it as a promotion of biting. Now the AKC will recognize and add Schutzhund titles obtained in trials to a dog's official record for a small fee.

Those who love and engage in the sport know that it is really intense and time-consuming. There are three components to earning a title: obedience, tracking, and bite work (protection). A dog can't compete in just one event and must pass all three in order to title. As with other performance events, the work becomes progressively more difficult in order to title at the upper levels.

If you think you might be interested in competing, it's a good idea to see what it's all about firsthand. There are tons of local Schutzhund clubs sprinkled all across the United States. Attend a few trials, visit a local club, and talk to a few sport enthusiasts. This is the best way to determine if your dog is right for the sport (because not all are) and if you will have the time necessary to train and compete.

There are two major national clubs that offer titling events: the German Shepherd Dog Club of America's Working Dog Association (GSDCA-WDA) and the United Schutzhund Clubs of America.

## THERAPY WORK

Therapy work is a valued activity for both dog and handler, but not all dogs are destined for it. A therapy dog must have an excellent temperament and strong nerves, and enjoy visiting with lots of new people.

If you intend to do therapy work, your dog needs to be highly socialized to lots of situations and people early on. Most therapy opportunities involve visiting nursing homes, schools, hospices, or medical facilities. Your dog should be comfortable with older people, children, wheelchairs, walkers, medical odors, uniforms, strange and/or quick movements, and loud noises like squealing. He should be tolerant to accidentally being stepped on, having his tail or ears tugged, or being petted roughly. If your dog is not comfortable in all settings, therapy

work will be very stressful for him.

A therapy dog must also be trained. He has to know how to walk correctly on leash, how to leave things alone on command, how to stay when asked, etc. This isn't just about manners—it's about safety. He can't think that jumping on people is appropriate or he could easily hurt someone. He must also be used to working away from you so that he doesn't experience stress if someone else is petting him or holding his leash at a distance from you.

A therapy dog must have an excellent temperament and strong nerves, and enjoy visiting with lots of new people.

There are many therapy opportunities available to you and your dog. Independent groups all across the country have their own requirements in order to participate.

You should ask your veterinarian or dog trainer if there are any local organizations that offer organized therapy opportunities. These groups usually work with several places (like a particular nursing home or school), and they schedule regular visits. You can participate as frequently as you desire.

You can also organize visits on your own. Visit the Delta Society website (www.deltasociety. org) to learn what it takes to become a Delta-certified therapy dog. Then, decide whom you most would like to visit. Would your dog make a good "listener" for children to read to? Would your dog be a candidate for helping someone with their physical therapy? Or would your dog love to simply hang out near someone and offer comfort in that person's final days? Approach facilities that match your interests and your dog's abilities, and ask about scheduling visits for therapy work.

There are few things more rewarding than watching your dog help someone in ways that possibly no person can. You will find a child embarrassed to read to an adult easily reading to a dog. I know someone whose German Shepherd encouraged a woman to speak for the first time in years. If you pursue therapy, be prepared to become emotionally invested in your work.

## TRACKING

Tracking is the one sport where you must allow your dog to lead you. We can't teach the dog how to do scent work; we just show him what trail to follow.

In tracking, dogs work 35 feet (11 m) in front of their handler following scent tracks that vary in length and degree of difficulty. There are multiple titles to be earned in tracking. A dog earns a title with just one successful track completion in a trial—but that's not as easy as it sounds!

Tracking requires a dog who has a good nose for scenting, is focused and can follow the track without much deviation (while ignoring outside stimuli), and is confident. German Shepherds do very well at tracking work.

Beginning tracking work focuses on a heavily laid food track. The dog moves from one food drop to the next, while at the same time following along a person's foot trail. This way, the dog begins to learn to follow the scent. This becomes important as less food is laid on a trail. Once a dog can handle working a track with no food drops, several turns, and crossing a few surfaces, he just might be ready to work toward a title.

**BE AWARE!**
Not properly preparing your dog prior to working out could lead to stress injuries. Use stretching exercises and massage to lessen the chance for damage.

The main difference between the titles is the difficulty of the track. Tracks for upper titles are longer and more difficult, as a dog must be able to comfortably work at longer distances, potentially over obstacles, through all kinds of grass lengths and surfaces. At the highest level, a dog will be asked to complete a track in a more populated setting in the city.

## TRAVELING WITH YOUR DOG

Traveling with your dog can be an enjoyable experience, and German Shepherds love to go wherever you do. You'll need to make sure that the ride is both enjoyable and safe.

Traveling with a larger dog takes some preparation on your part.

### BY CAR

Safety has to be the very first consideration with taking your dog in the car. A German Shepherd is a large dog, and it's not appropriate to ever place him in the front seat, allow him to jump from back to front, or climb onto you. This isn't safe for you, the dog, or fellow drivers on the road. Instead, you will want to use one of the following options:

- **Crate:** For long travels, especially over highways, a crate is usually your best choice. Your dog is safely confined in case he becomes tired or restless because of the long duration of travel. More important, if you're involved in a vehicular accident, your dog has less chance of a severe injury. A crate prevents the dog from being thrown loose onto a highway and hit by a car, and in the event of a rollover, he is protected better in a crate. It also prevents him from flying forward into the windshield, especially if you take the precaution of strapping the crate securely in the car.
- **Seatbelts:** There are several different seatbelt systems that can properly secure your dog into a car seat. Some utilize a harness, but all of them secure the dog to a car seatbelt. This way the dog can't roam in the car, and it won't be airborne in an accident.
- **Divider:** This is used primarily for SUVs and similar vehicles, but there are a number of different types of dividers to separate the front seats from the rear area. The dog can still move about in the back area, but he can't come forward

at all. This helps keep the dog out of the way, allowing you to drive. It also will stop the dog from flying forward in the event of an accident.

Remember to always take comfort and safety supplies with you when you take your dog on the road, especially for longer journeys. Include items like water, food, bowls, leash, collar, and identification information. Consider adding a temporary tag to your dog's collar that identifies a cell phone number or a local number in case your dog is lost in a new location. You might also carry a current photograph of your dog and a copy of his medical records in case he is lost or injured.

Last, remember to stop every couple of hours and walk your dog. Dogs get stiff in the car and need regular exercise to stretch their limbs and go potty. Try to select quieter areas like rest areas. Always walk him on leash.

## BY AIR

Because of his size, the German Shepherd is a bit more difficult to transport by air. He can't ride anywhere in the passenger section and must be shipped via cargo instead.

You need to know the airline's shipping regulations, so check with your individual carrier. Dogs must be shipped in approved crates (usually plastic airline crates) of the appropriate size. Too large of a crate and the dog could be jostled about during the flight or in transport to and from the plane. Your dog will not be allowed on the plane if he is not in an airline-approved, correctly sized crate.

Regulations for shipping dogs have become much more stringent in recent years. This is to attempt to make air flight safer for the dogs. One of the biggest areas of restriction is over air temperature. The outdoor air temperature at departure and arrival locations must be above or below a certain degree. Know the degree threshold in your area, as the airlines will not ship your dog if the temperature is not right. This usually means shipping dogs early in the morning before the temperature gets too hot, or no air travel if the weather is very cold.

If you are concerned about flying your dog, you might consider one of the newer pet-only airlines that are starting up. Or you can transport your dog by vehicle, either your own or through a pet transport service.

## PET-FRIENDLY LODGING

Not all hotels are dog friendly, which may be due to bad experiences with previous canine guests. If you know where you are traveling, it is advisable to contact the hotels in advance and inquire about their pet policies.

Most hotels that allow pets require you to pay a pet deposit, in case your dog causes any problems, or stains or destroys something. It is important to ask if

Your German Shepherd can make a wonderful traveling companion, since he's happy to be anywhere you are!

there is a size restriction for dogs, as sometimes a large dog won't be allowed. You need to know in advance what is and isn't allowed.

When you speak with the hotel personnel, ask what the surroundings are like, or if you know someone in the area, ask them to check it out in advance for you. You'll want to know how much grass is available around the hotel for walking your dog. The more grass there is, the better.

Ask for a ground floor room when making reservations. This is the easiest place to quickly get a dog outside for a walk. Also, unless your dog is good with stairs or the elevator, it will be less stressful on both you and him to stay on the ground floor.

When you do find a hotel that openly welcomes you and your dog, make sure you bring a crate with you. There may be times, like when you are eating out, when your dog will be left in the room without you. Using a crate is far safer in case someone opens the door, and can also prevent any destruction. Hang the "Do Not Disturb" sign, but don't count on someone to notice it. Accidents happen. Additionally, bring appropriate chew items like stuffable toys or bones to keep your dog preoccupied while you are out and to avoid howling or barking.

Remember to be a good guest so that the hotel continues to allow dogs, and particularly German Shepherds, into their hotel in the future. Bad experiences in one or two hotels may cause a whole hotel chain to stop allowing dogs.

# RESOURCES

## ASSOCIATIONS AND ORGANIZATIONS

### BREED CLUBS

**American Kennel Club (AKC)**
5580 Centerview Drive
Raleigh, NC 27606
Telephone: (919) 233-9767
Fax: (919) 233-3627
E-Mail: info@akc.org
www.akc.org

**Canadian Kennel Club (CKC)**
89 Skyway Avenue, Suite 100
Etobicoke, Ontario M9W 6R4
Telephone: (416) 675-5511
Fax: (416) 675-6506
E-Mail: information@ckc.ca
www.ckc.ca

**Federation Cynologique Internationale (FCI)**
Secretariat General de la FCI
Place Albert 1er, 13
B – 6530 Thuin
Belqique
www.fci.be

**German Shepherd Dog Club of America (GSDCA)**
E-Mail: info@gsdca.org
www.gsdca.org

**The German Shepherd Dog Club of America-Working Dog Association (GSDCA-WDA)**
732 Lindley Blvd.
DeLand FL 32724
Telephone: (386) 736-2486
Fax: (386) 738-4741
E-Mail: wdaoffice@cfl.rr.com
www.gsdca-wda.org

**The Kennel Club**
1 Clarges Street
London
W1J 8AB
Telephone: 0870 606 6750
Fax: 0207 518 1058
www.the-kennel-club.org.uk

**United Kennel Club (UKC)**
100 E. Kilgore Road
Kalamazoo, MI 49002-5584
Telephone: (269) 343-9020
Fax: (269) 343-7037
E-Mail: pbickell@ukcdogs.com
www.ukcdogs.com

**United Schutzhund Clubs of America**
3810 Paule Ave.
St. Louis, MO 63125-1718
Telephone: (314) 638-9686
Fax: (314) 638-0609
E-Mail: USAoffice@
GermanShepherdDog.com
http://germanshepherddog.com/index.html

**Verein für Deutsche Schäferhunde (SV)**
www.schaeferhunde.de

## PET SITTERS

**National Association of Professional Pet Sitters**
15000 Commerce Parkway, Suite C
Mt. Laurel, New Jersey 08054
Telephone: (856) 439-0324
Fax: (856) 439-0525
E-Mail: napps@ahint.com
www.petsitters.org

**Pet Sitters International**
201 East King Street
King, NC 27021-9161
Telephone: (336) 983-9222
Fax: (336) 983-5266
E-Mail: info@petsit.com
www.petsit.com

## RESCUE ORGANIZATIONS AND ANIMAL WELFARE GROUPS

**American Humane Association (AHA)**
63 Inverness Drive East
Englewood, CO 80112
Telephone: (303) 792-9900
Fax: 792-5333
www.americanhumane.org

**American Society for the Prevention of Cruelty to Animals (ASPCA)**
424 E. 92nd Street
New York, NY 10128-6804
Telephone: (212) 876-7700
www.aspca.org

**The Humane Society of the United States (HSUS)**
2100 L Street, NW
Washington DC 20037
Telephone: (202) 452-1100
www.hsus.org

**Royal Society for the Prevention of Cruelty to Animals (RSPCA)**
RSPCA Enquiries Service
Wilberforce Way, Southwater,
Horsham, West Sussex RH13 9RS
United Kingdom
Telephone: 0870 3335 999
Fax: 0870 7530 284
www.rspca.org.uk

## SPORTS

**International Agility Link (IAL)**
Global Administrator: Steve
Drinkwater
E-Mail: yunde@powerup.au
www.agilityclick.com/~ial

**The World Canine Freestyle Organization, Inc.**
P.O. Box 350122
Brooklyn, NY 11235
Telephone: (718) 332-8336
Fax: (718) 646-2686
E-Mail: WCFODOGS@aol.com
www.worldcaninefreestyle.org

## THERAPY

**Delta Society**
875 124th Ave, NE, Suite 101
Bellevue, WA 98005
Telephone: (425) 679-5500
Fax: (425) 679-5539
E-Mail: info@DeltaSociety.org
www.deltasociety.org

**Therapy Dogs Inc.**
P.O. Box 20227
Cheyenne WY 82003
Telephone: (877) 843-7364
Fax: (307) 638-2079
E-Mail: therapydogsinc@
qwestoffice.net
www.therapydogs.com

**Therapy Dogs International (TDI)**
88 Bartley Road
Flanders, NJ 07836
Telephone: (973) 252-9800
Fax: (973) 252-7171
E-Mail: tdi@gti.net
www.tdi-dog.org

## TRAINING

**Association of Pet Dog Trainers (APDT)**
150 Executive Center Drive Box 35
Greenville, SC 29615
Telephone: (800) PFT-DOGS
Fax: (864) 331-0767
E-Mail: information@apdt.com
www.apdt.com

**International Association of Animal Behavior Consultants (IAABC)**
565 Callery Road
Cranberry Township, PA 16066
E-Mail: info@iaabc.org
www.iaabc.org

**National Association of Dog Obedience Instructors (NADOI)**
PMB 369
729 Grapevine Hwy.
Hurst, TX 76054-2085
www.nadoi.org

## VETERINARY AND HEALTH RESOURCES

**Academy of Veterinary Homeopathy (AVH)**
P.O. Box 9280
Wilmington, DE 19809
Telephone: (866) 652-1590
Fax: (866) 652-1590
www.theavh.org

**American Academy of Veterinary Acupuncture (AAVA)**
P.O. Box 1058
Glastonbury, CT 06033
Telephone: (860) 632-9911
Fax: (860) 659-8772
www.aava.org

**American Animal Hospital Association (AAHA)**
12575 W. Bayaud Ave.
Lakewood, CO 80228
Telephone: (303) 986-2800
Fax: (303) 986-1700
E-Mail: info@aahanet.org
www.aahanet.org/index.cfm

**American College of Veterinary Internal Medicine (ACVIM)**
1997 Wadsworth Blvd., Suite A
Lakewood, CO 80214-5293
Telephone: (800) 245-9081
Fax: (303) 231-0880
Email: ACVIM@ACVIM.org
www.acvim.org

**American College of Veterinary Ophthalmologists (ACVO)**
P.O. Box 1311
Meridian, ID 83860
Telephone: (208) 466-7624
Fax: (208) 466-7693
E-Mail: office09@acvo.com
www.acvo.com

**American Holistic Veterinary Medical Association (AHVMA)**
2218 Old Emmorton Road
Bel Air, MD 21015
Telephone: (410) 569-0795
Fax: (410) 569-2346
E-Mail: office@ahvma.org
www.ahvma.org

**American Veterinary Medical Association (AVMA)**
1931 North Meacham Road, Suite 100
Schaumburg, IL 60173-4360
Telephone: (847) 925-8070
Fax: (847) 925-1329
E-Mail: avmainfo@avma.org
www.avma.org

ASPCA Animal Poison Control
Center
Telephone: (888) 426-4435
www.aspca.org

British Veterinary Association
(BVA)
7 Mansfield Street
London
W1G 9NQ
Telephone: 0207 636 6541
Fax: 0207 908 6349
E-Mail: bvahq@bva.co.uk
www.bva.co.uk

Canine Eye Registration
Foundation (CERF)
VMDB/CERF
1717 Philo Rd
P O Box 3007
Urbana, IL 61803-3007
Telephone: (217) 693-4800
Fax: (217) 693-4801
E-Mail: CERF@vmbd.org
www.vmdb.org

Orthopedic Foundation for
Animals (OFA)
2300 NE Nifong Blvd
Columbus, Missouri 65201-3856
Telephone: (573) 442-0418
Fax: (573) 875-5073
Email: ofa@offa.org
www.offa.org

US Food and Drug Administration
Center for Veterinary Medicine
(CVM)
7519 Standish Place
HFV-12
Rockville, MD 20855-0001
Telephone: (240) 276-9300 or (888)
INFO-FDA
http://www.fda.gov/cvm

## PUBLICATIONS
### BOOKS
Aloff, Brenda. *Canine Body Language A Photographic Guide: Interpreting the Native Language of the Domestic Dog.* Dogwise Publishing, 2005.

Aloff, Brenda. *Positive Reinforcement: Training Dogs in the Real World.* Neptune City: TFH Publications, Inc., 2001.

Dunbar, Ian. *Before and After Getting Your Puppy: The Positive Approach to Raising a Happy, Healthy, and Well Behaved Dog.* New World Library, 2004.

McConnell, Patricia. *The Other End of the Leash: Why We Do What We Do Around Dogs.* New York: Ballantine Books, 2003.

Pryor, Karen. *Don't Shoot the Dog: The New Art of Teaching and Training.* New York: Bantam, 1999.

Pryor, Karen. Getting Started: Clicker Training for Dogs. Waltham: Sunshine Books, 2005.

## MAGAZINES
### AKC Family Dog
American Kennel Club
260 Madison Avenue
New York, NY 10016
Telephone: (800) 490-5675
E-Mail: familydog@akc.org
www.akc.org/pubs/familydog

### AKC Gazette
American Kennel Club
260 Madison Avenue
New York, NY 10016
Telephone: (800) 533-7323
E-Mail: gazette@akc.org
www.akc.org/pubs/gazette

### Dog & Kennel
Pet Publishing, Inc.
7-L Dundas Circle
Greensboro, NC 27407
Telephone: (336) 292-4272
Fax: (336) 292-4272
E-Mail: info@petpublishing.com
www.dogandkennel.com

### Dogs Monthly
Ascot House
High Street, Ascot,
Berkshire SL5 7JG
United Kingdom
Telephone: 0870 730 8433
Fax: 0870 730 8431
E-Mail: admin@rtc-associates.
freeserve.co.uk
www.corsini.co.uk/dogsmonthly

## WEBSITES
Nylabone
www.nylabone.com

TFH Publications, Inc.
www.tfh.com

# INDEX

Note: Boldfaced numbers indicate
illustrations.

GERMAN SHEPHERD DOG

## PHOTO CREDITS

## DEDICATION

Thank you to my parents for instilling a love for the breed, and thank you to those individual shepherds that have entered my life, having either already exited or that still remain. They have made it worthwhile!

## ABOUT THE AUTHOR

Kim Downing, CPDT-KA, is a certified professional trainer, a member of the Association of Pet Dog Trainers and the German Shepherd Dog Club of America, and a former service dog trainer. Since 2005, she has been offering group dog training classes as well as private instruction. She is also a freelance writer specializing in topics about dogs and training. Kim has lived with German Shepherds her whole life and currently trains her dogs in obedience, rally, and agility. She lives in Kansas with several German Shepherds. Visit her on the web at www.yourbestdog.com.

## ABOUT ANIMAL PLANET™

Animal Planet™ is the only television network dedicated exclusively to the connection between humans and animals. The network brings people of all ages together by tapping into our fundamental fascination with animals through an array of fresh programming that includes humor, competition, drama, and spectacle from the animal kingdom.

## ABOUT *DOGS 101*

The most comprehensive—and most endearing—dog encyclopedia on television, *DOGS 101* spotlights the adorable, the feisty and the unexpected. A wide-ranging rundown of everyone's favorite dog breeds—from the Dalmatian to Xoloitzcuintli—this series surveys a variety of breeds for their behavioral quirks, genetic history, most famous examples and wildest trivia. Learn which dogs are best for urban living and which would be the best fit for your family. Using a mix of animal experts, pop-culture footage and stylized dog photography, *DOGS 101* is an unprecedented look at man's best friend.